New Trends in Data Warehousing
and Data Analysis

Annals of Information Systems

Volume 1:
Managing in the Information Economy: *Current Research Issues*
Uday Apte, Uday Karmarkar, *eds.*

Volume 2:
Decision Support for Global Enterprises
Uday Kulkarni, Daniel J. Power, Ramesh Sharda, *eds.*

New Trends in Data Warehousing and Data Analysis

Editors

Stanisław Kozielski
Robert Wrembel

 Springer

Editors
Stanisław Kozielski
Silesian University of Technology
Gliwice, Poland
Stanislaw.Kozielski@polsl.pl

Robert Wrembel
Poznań University of Technology
Poznań, Poland
Robert.Wrembel@cs.put.poznan.pl

ISSN: 1934-3221
ISBN-13: 978-0-387-87430-2   e-ISBN-13: 978-0-387-87431-9
DOI: 10.1007/978-0-387-87430-2

Library of Congress Control Number: 2008934456

Printed on acid-free paper

springer.com

Preface

A modern way of managing enterprises, institutions, and organizations is based on knowledge, that in turn, is gained from data analysis. In practice, business decisions are taken based on the analysis of past and current data, continuously collected during the lifetime of an enterprise. A data analysis technology, widely accepted by research and industry, is based on data warehouse architecture. In this architecture, data coming from multiple distributed and heterogeneous storage systems are integrated in a central repository, called a data warehouse (DW). Such integrated data are analyzed by the so-called On-Line Analytical Processing (OLAP) queries and data mining applications for the purpose of: analyzing business performance measures, discovering and analyzing trends, discovering anomalies and patterns of behavior, finding hidden dependencies between data as well as predicting business trends and simulating business solutions. The DW and OLAP technologies are applied in multiple areas including among others: sales business, stock market, banking, insurance, energy management, telecommunication, medicine, and science.

From a technical point of view, a data warehouse is a large database, whose size ranges from several hundreds of GB to several dozens of TB or even several PB. The size of a DW, high complexity of OLAP queries and data mining algorithms as well as the heterogeneous nature of data being integrated in a DW cause serious research and technological challenges. Intensive research has been conducted in multiple fields including among others: (1) conceptual modeling of DWs and logical data models, (2) DW loading (refreshing), (3) assuring efficient execution of OLAP queries and data mining algorithms, (4) managing materialized views, (5) data analysis techniques, (6) metadata management, (7) managing the evolution of DWs, (7) stream, real-time, and active data warehouses, and (8) warehousing complex data (e.g, XML, multimedia, object, spatial).

Typically, a DW applies the so-called multidimensional data model. In this model, analyzed data, called facts, are referenced by multiple dimensions that set up the context of an analysis. Such multi-dimensional spaces are called data cubes. In practice, a data cube can be implemented either in relational OLAP (ROLAP) servers or in multidimensional OLAP (MOLAP) servers.

A DW is filled with data by means of the so-called Extraction-Transformation-Loading (ETL) processes. They are responsible among others for: extracting and filtering data from data sources, transforming data into a common data model, cleansing data in order to remove inconsistencies, duplicates, and null values, integrating cleansed data into one common data set, computing summaries, and loading data into a DW.

OLAP queries typically join multiple tables, filter and sort data, compute aggregates and use complex groupings. Since these queries are very complex and they often read terabytes of data, their execution may take dozens of minutes, hours, or even days. Therefore, one of the most important research and technological problems concerns assuring an acceptable performance of OLAP queries. Well developed solutions to this problem are based on materialized views and query rewriting, advanced index structures as well as on parallel processing and data partitioning techniques.

Materialized views applied to storing precomputed results of OLAP queries are one of basic DW objects. Multiple solutions have been proposed for selecting optimal sets of materialized views for a given query workload, for efficient refreshing of materialized views as well as for assuring materialized view consistency during a DW refreshing.

In order to support OLAP processing, a standard SQL has been extended with multiple clauses as well as with predefined specialized analytical and forecasting functions. Moreover, multiple data mining algorithms have been integrated into DW management systems.

In order to work properly and efficiently, all of the above mentioned techniques need to use metadata. Managing various types of metadata in DWs has also received a lot of attention, resulting in widely accepted industry standard CWM, supported by major DW software vendors.

An inherent feature of data sources is their evolution in time that concerns not only their content but also their structures. The evolution of structures of data sources has an impact on deployed ETL processes as well as on the structure of a DW. The most advanced approaches to handling the evolution of data sources are based on temporal extensions and versioning mechanisms.

Traditional DWs are refreshed periodically overnight and users execute their analytical applications after a DW refreshing. For some DW applications, however, such a DW usage is inappropriate. For example, monitoring the intensity of traffic, controlling physical parameters of technological processes, monitoring patients' vital signs by means of various kinds of sensors require an on-the-fly analysis. Monitoring credit card usage in order to detect unauthorized usage requires frequent DW refreshing and mechanisms of automatic data analysis. Such requirements led to the development of stream data analysis systems, active and real-time data warehouses.

Modern information systems often store huge amounts of data in various Web systems. Typically, data are represented in these systems as XML and HTML documents, images, maps, and data of other complex structures. These data are as important as traditional text and numerical data, and therefore, there is a need to analyze them in a similar way as in traditional DWs. This requirement motivates researchers to design and build data warehouses from Web data sources and to provide OLAP functionality for XML documents, multimedia data, and spatial data.

Despite substantial achievements in the DW and OLAP technologies that have been made for the past 30 years, DW and OLAP technologies still are and will be very active areas of research and technological development.

The aim of this special issue of the Annals of Information Systems is to present current advances in the data warehouse and OLAP technologies as well as to point to the areas for further research. The issue is composed of 15 chapters that in general address the following research and technological areas: advanced technologies for building XML, spatial, temporal, and real-time data warehouses, novel approaches to DW modeling, data storage and data access structures, as well as advanced data analysis techniques.

Chapter 1 overviews open research problems concerning building data warehouses for integrating and analyzing various complex types of data, dealing with temporal aspects of data, handling imprecise data, and ensuring privacy in DWs.

Chapter 2 discusses challenges in designing ETL processes for real-time (or near real-time) data warehouses and proposes an architecture of a real-time DW system.

Chapter 3 discusses data warehouse modeling techniques, based on multidimensional modeling. In particular, the chapter covers conceptual, logical, and physical modeling.

Chapter 4 proposes an approach to personalizing a multidimensional database. The authors present a model and a language that allow to define user preferences on schema elements. User preferences are expressed by means of weights associated with schema elements and they express user interest in data.

Chapter 5 covers designing spatial (geographical) data warehouses. It proposes a metamodel for the support of the design of spatial dimensional schemas.

Chapter 6 presents a technique for approximate answering range-sum queries on data cubes. To this end, the authors propose tree-based data structures for separately storing sampled data and outliers data. The proposed technique assures a good quality of approximate answers.

Chapter 7 addresses a problem of summarizing multidimensional search spaces, called data cubes. The authors propose the concept of the so-called closed cube, which is a cover for a data cube. The authors show that the closed cube is smaller than its competitor, i.e. a quotient cube, and it can be used for deriving a quotient cube.

Chapter 8 analyzes multiple index structures for multiversion data warehouses. In particular, the paper describes how to extend index structures designed for data with linear evolution in order to handle data with branched evolution and it provides an analytical model for comparing various index structures for multiversion DWs.

Chapter 9 discusses the application of WAH compressed bitmap indexes to indexing text data for full-text search. The chapter also presents performance characteristics of the proposed indexing technique in three systems, namely MySQL, FastBit, and MonetDB.

Chapter 10 proposes the optimization of OLAP queries by means of applying horizontal partitioning of tables and bitmap join indexes. The partitioning schema and the set of bitmap indexes are selected by means of genetic and greedy algorithms. The proposed optimization techniques are validated experimentally.

Chapter 11 discusses the application of the x-BR-tree index to spatial data. The chapter provides an analytical cost model of spatial queries with the support of the x-BR-tree index, followed by its experimental evaluation.

Chapter 12 proposes a formal model for representing spatio-temporal and non-spatial data about moving objects. Based on the model, the authors propose a query language allowing to query such data. The main idea is based on replacing object trajectories by sequences of object stops and moves.

Chapter 13 addresses the problem of data mining in a multidimensional space in a data warehouse. The authors propose a compact representation of sequential patterns, called closed multidimensional sequential patterns, which allows to reduce the search space. The proposed representation and mining algorithms are followed by experimental evaluation.

Chapter 14 presents issues on modeling and querying temporal semistructured data warehouses. Such a DW is modeled as a graph with labeled nodes and edges. The temporal aspect is added to the graph by means of labels denoting validity times. The model is supported with a query language based on path expressions.

Chapter 15 contributes a multidimensional data model of a data warehouse, called "galaxy", that supports the analysis of XML documents. The authors also propose a technique and a tool for integrating XML documents and loading them into a DW.

Acknowledgements

The editors would like to acknowledge the help of all involved in the review process of this special issue of the Annals of Information Systems. The reviewers provided comprehensive, critical, and constructive comments. Without their support the project could not have been satisfactorily completed.

The alfabetically ordered list of reviewers includes:

- Carlo Combi, University of Verona, Italy
- Karen Davis, University of Cincinnati, USA
- Pedro Furtado, University of Coimbra, Portugal
- Marcin Gorawski, Silesian University of Technology, Poland
- Carlos Hurtado, Universidad de Chile, Chile
- Krzysztof Jankiewicz, Poznań Unviersity of Technology, Poland
- Rokia Missaoui, Universite du Quebec en Outaouais, Canada
- Tadeusz Morzy, Poznań Unviersity of Technology, Poland
- Mikolaj Morzy, Poznań Unviersity of Technology, Poland
- Stefano Rizzi, University of Bologna, Italy
- Alkis Simitsis, IBM Almaden Research Center, USA

- Jerzy Stefanowski, Poznań Unviersity of Technology, Poland
- Alejandro Vaisman, University of Buenos Aires, Argentina
- Kesheng Wu, University of California, USA

The editors would also like to thank Professor Ramesh Sharda for his invitation to guest edit this special issue.

Gliwice and Poznań, Poland   *Stanisław Kozielski*
June 2008   *Robert Wrembel*

Contents

1 Warehousing The World: A Vision for Data Warehouse Research ... 1
Torben Bach Pedersen
1.1 Introduction 1
1.2 Background 3
    1.2.1 Data Analysis Problems 3
    1.2.2 Point-To-Point Integration 4
    1.2.3 Integration Using Data Warehouses 5
    1.2.4 Business Intelligence 7
1.3 Challenges From New Types Of Data 8
1.4 Current Approaches To Integrating Different Types Of Data...... 9
    1.4.1 Overview 10
    1.4.2 An Example: Multidimensional + Text Integration 11
    1.4.3 Taking A Step Back 11
1.5 Warehousing The World..................................... 12
    1.5.1 The World Warehouse............................. 12
    1.5.2 World Warehouse Challenges 14
1.6 Conclusion and Future Work 16
References 16

2 Near Real Time ETL 19
Panos Vassiliadis and Alkis Simitsis
2.1 Introduction 19
2.2 Traditional ETL 21
    2.2.1 Operational issues and challenges 22
    2.2.2 Variations of the traditional ETL architecture 24
2.3 The case for Near Real Time ETL 25
    2.3.1 Motivation 25
    2.3.2 General architecture 26
    2.3.3 Industrial approaches 28
    2.3.4 The infrastructure of near real time ETL 31
    2.3.5 Research and engineering issues for near real time ETL . 33

          2.3.6   Summing up 43
  2.4   Related Work 43
  2.5   Conclusions 48
  References 48

3   Data Warehousing Meets MDA 51
Jose-Norberto Mazón and Juan Trujillo
  3.1   Introduction 51
  3.2   Related Work 53
  3.3   Multidimensional Modeling of Data Warehouses with MDA 53
          3.3.1   A Multidimensional Computation Independent Model ... 55
          3.3.2   A Multidimensional Platform Independent Model 58
          3.3.3   Reconciling a Multidimensional Model with Data Sources 60
          3.3.4   Multidimensional Platform Specific Models 63
          3.3.5   From PIM to PSM 64
  3.4   Implementation 66
  3.5   Conclusions and Ongoing Work 67
  References 69

4   Personalization and OLAP Databases 71
Franck Ravat and Olivier Teste
  4.1   Introduction 71
          4.1.1   Paper Issue and Related Works 72
          4.1.2   Contributions and Paper Outline 73
  4.2   Personalized Multidimensional Modelling 74
          4.2.1   Concepts and formalisms 74
          4.2.2   Personalization Rules 78
  4.3   Personalized OLAP Manipulations 79
          4.3.1   Multidimensional Table 79
          4.3.2   Extended OLAP Algebra 81
          4.3.3   Discussion 85
  4.4   A Personalized Multidimensional Database System 85
          4.4.1   Database System Architecture 85
          4.4.2   R-OLAP storage 86
          4.4.3   A Rule Definition Language 87
          4.4.4   Personalization Process 88
  4.5   Concluding Remarks 90
  References 91

5   A Metamodel for the Specification of Geographical Data
Warehouses 93
Valéria Cesário Times, Robson do Nascimento Fidalgo, Rafael Leão da
Fonseca, Joel da Silva, and Anjolina Grisi de Oliveira
  5.1   Introduction 93
  5.2   Formal Definitions for a Geographical Data Warehouse Metamodel 95
  5.3   A Metamodel for GDW 100

        5.4   A CASE Tool for Modelling Geographical Data Warehouses 103
        5.5   Design Issues. 107
        5.6   Related Work. 110
        5.7   Conclusions and Future Work 112
        References 113

6   **Pushing Theoretically-Founded Probabilistic Guarantees in
     Highly-Efficient OLAP Engines** 115
     Alfredo Cuzzocrea and Wei Wang
        6.1   Introduction 116
        6.2   Related Work. 118
        6.3   TP-Tree Overview 120
        6.4   Efficiently Detecting, Indexing, and Querying Outliers of
               Multidimensional Data Cubes 122
        6.5   TP-Tree: A Tree-Like, "Self-Adjusting" Synopsis Data Structure
               for Approximate Query Answering in OLAP 125
               6.5.1   Tunable Partitions of Data Cubes 125
               6.5.2   TP-Tree Data Organization 126
               6.5.3   Updating the TP-Tree 127
               6.5.4   Deriving the Theoretical Bound. 129
        6.6   Querying the TP-Tree. 130
        6.7   Experimental Assessment 132
               6.7.1   Experiment Setup 133
               6.7.2   Synthetic Query-Workloads against Synthetic Data Cubes 137
               6.7.3   Synthetic Query-Workloads against Real Data Cubes. . . . 139
               6.7.4   Benchmark Queries against Real Data Cubes 140
               6.7.5   Sensitivity Analysis. 141
               6.7.6   Construction Cost with Synthetic Query-Workloads
                        against Synthetic Data Cubes. 141
        6.8   Conclusions and Future Research Efforts 142
        References 142

7   **Closed Cube Lattices** 145
     Alain Casali, Sebastien Nedjar, Rosine Cicchetti, and Lotfi Lakhal
        7.1   Introduction 145
        7.2   Cube Lattice Framework 148
        7.3   Closed Cube Lattices 151
        7.4   Lattice Isomorphism and Algorithmic Aspects 153
        7.5   Relationships between Closed Cubes and Quotient Cubes. 154
        7.6   Experimental results 156
        7.7   Conclusion. 158
        References 159

8   Design and Analysis of Index Structures in MultiVersion Data
Warehouses 165
Khaled Jouini and Geneviève Jomier
8.1   Introduction 165
8.2   Basic Concepts 167
       8.2.1   DW Versions and Entity Versions 167
       8.2.2   DW Version Range 169
8.3   Indexing Data in MultiVersion Data Warehouses 169
       8.3.1   Primary Indexes.................................. 169
       8.3.2   Secondary Indexes................................ 173
8.4   Analysis and Comparison 174
       8.4.1   Previous Work 174
       8.4.2   Steady State Analysis 174
       8.4.3   The B+V-tree as primary index 176
       8.4.4   The OB+tree as primary index...................... 177
       8.4.5   The BT-Tree as primary index 178
       8.4.6   Secondary indexes................................ 179
8.5   Simulation 180
       8.5.1   Storage Cost of Primary Indexes 181
       8.5.2   Query Cost of Primary Indexes 182
       8.5.3   Query Cost of Secondary Indexes 182
8.6   Conclusion.. 183
8.7   Acknowledgments 184
References 184

9   Using Bitmap Index for Joint Queries on Structured and Text Data . 187
Kurt Stockinger, John Cieslewicz, Kesheng Wu, Doron Rotem, and
Arie Shoshani
9.1   Introduction 188
9.2   Related Work.. 189
       9.2.1   Indexing techniques for structured data 189
       9.2.2   Database Systems for Full-Text Searching 191
       9.2.3   Compressing Inverted Files 192
9.3   Case Study: The Enron Data Set 193
9.4   Extending Bitmap Indexes to Support Full Text Search 195
9.5   Integrating FastBit into MonetDB........................... 196
       9.5.1   Why MonetDB? 196
       9.5.2   Integrating MonetDB and FastBit 198
9.6   Experiments... 198
       9.6.1   Data Statistics 199
       9.6.2   Size of Bitmap Indexes 200
       9.6.3   Query performance on structured data 201
       9.6.4   Query Performance for Text Searching................ 203
       9.6.5   Query Performance for both Numerical and Text Data ... 204
9.7   Conclusions and Future Work 205

References 207

10   HP&BJI: A Combined Selection of Data Partitioning and Join
Indexes for Improving OLAP Performance 211
Kamel Boukhalfa, Ladjel Bellatreche, and Zaia Alimazighi
10.1   Introduction 212
10.2   Data Partitioning 214
        10.2.1   Methodology to Horizontal Partition Relational Data
                  Warehouse 215
        10.2.2   Horizontal Partitioning Selection Process 216
        10.2.3   Coding Fragmentation Schema 217
        10.2.4   Limitation of the Proposed Coding 218
        10.2.5   Effect of Horizontal Partitioning on Queries 219
10.3   Bitmap Join Indexes 219
        10.3.1   Complexity Study of Selecting BJIs 220
        10.3.2   Formulation of BJI Selection Problem 221
10.4   Identification of Similarity between Horizontal Partitioning and
        BJIs 221
10.5   Description of HP&BJI 223
        10.5.1   Formalization of the Combined Selection 224
        10.5.2   Genetic Algorithm for Selecting Horizontal Schema 225
        10.5.3   Greedy Algorithm for Generating BJIs 225
10.6   Experimental Studies 226
        10.6.1   Evaluation of four Optimization Approaches 227
        10.6.2   Validation on ORACLE10g 229
10.7   Conclusion 231
References 232

11   Cost Model for X-BR-tree 235
Marcin Gorawski and Marcin Bugdol
11.1   Introduction 235
11.2   X-BR-tree 236
        11.2.1   X-BR-tree structure 236
        11.2.2   Cost Model 238
11.3   Tests 242
        11.3.1   The Number of Leaves of X-BR-tree 242
        11.3.2   Estimation of Cost Model 243
11.4   Conclusion 247
References 247

12   Querying and Mining Trajectory Databases Using Places of Interest . 249
Leticia Gómez, Bart Kuijpers and Alejandro Vaisman
12.1   Introduction 250
        12.1.1   Contributions and Paper Organization 251
        12.1.2   Related Work 252
12.2   Preliminaries and Background 253

12.3   Querying Moving Object Data 257
12.4   The Stops and Moves Fact Table 259
12.5   A Query Language for Stops and Moves 261
12.6   Implementation and Case Study 264
        12.6.1   Computing the SM-MOFT 265
        12.6.2   Implementing the smRE Language 266
        12.6.3   Using smRE for Data Mining 270
12.7   Future Work 273
12.8   Acknowledgments 273
References 274

13 **OLAP-Sequential Mining: Summarizing Trends from Historical Multidimensional Data using Closed Multidimensional Sequential Patterns** 275
Marc Plantevit, Anne Laurent, and Maguelonne Teisseire
13.1   Introduction 275
13.2   Related Work 277
        13.2.1   Multidimensional Sequential Patterns 277
        13.2.2   Closed Patterns 278
        13.2.3   Particularity of the Multidimensional Framework 280
13.3   CMSP - Closed Multidimensional Sequential Patterns 281
13.4   *CMSP*: Mining Closed Multidimensional Sequential Patterns 282
        13.4.1   Order Within The Itemset of a Sequence 283
        13.4.2   *CMSP_Cand* 285
        13.4.3   *CMSP_Free*: Mining Closed Multidimensional Sequential Patterns Without Candidate Set Maintenance . 288
13.5   Experiments 292
        13.5.1   Synthetic Data 293
        13.5.2   Real Data Cube 295
13.6   Conclusion 295
References 296

14 **Modeling and Querying Temporal Semistructured Data Warehouses** 299
Carlo Combi, Barbara Oliboni, and Giuseppe Pozzi
14.1   Introduction 299
14.2   Related work 300
        14.2.1   Temporal Semistructured Data Models and Languages .. 300
        14.2.2   XML Warehouses 302
14.3   A Data Warehouse for Temporal Semistructured Data - GEMDW . 303
        14.3.1   Hierarchy of Dimensions 306
        14.3.2   Multi-Fact Schema 307
        14.3.3   Attributes with Multiple Cardinality 307
        14.3.4   Atemporal Aggregations 308
        14.3.5   Temporal Aspects 310
        14.3.6   Views 316

    14.4   DW-QL: a Query Language for GEMDW 318
         14.4.1   Roll-Up in DW-QL 318
         14.4.2   Drill-Down in DW-QL 319
         14.4.3   Slicing in DW-QL 319
         14.4.4   Selection in DW-QL 320
    14.5   Conclusions 321
    References 322

15 Designing and Implementing OLAP Systems from XML Documents 325
Franck Ravat, Olivier Teste, Ronan Tournier, and Gilles Zurfluh
    15.1   Introduction 325
         15.1.1   Related works 326
         15.1.2   Objectives and contributions 328
    15.2   Multidimensional Model for XML Document Data Analysis 329
         15.2.1   Conceptual Model 329
         15.2.2   Case Study 330
         15.2.3   OLAP analysis with a galaxy 331
    15.3   Design Process 332
         15.3.1   Analysis Phase 333
         15.3.2   Confrontation Phase 336
         15.3.3   Implementation: Creation of Multidimensional
                  Structures and Loading 339
    15.4   Data Integration Tool 340
         15.4.1   Tool Architecture 340
         15.4.2   Tool Interfaces 341
    15.5   Conclusion and Future Works 342
    References 343

Chapter 1
Warehousing The World: A Vision for Data Warehouse Research

Torben Bach Pedersen

Abstract Data warehouses (DWs) have become very successful in many enterprises, but only for relatively simple and traditional types of data. It is now time to extend the benefits of DWs to a much wider range of data, making it feasible to literally "warehouse the world". To do this, five unique challenges must be addressed: warehousing data about the physical world, integrating structured, semi-structured, and unstructured data in DWs, integrating the past, the present, and the future, warehousing imperfect data, and ensuring privacy in DWs.

1.1 Introduction

Data warehouses (DWs) have become very successful in many enterprises, by allowing the storage and analysis of large amounts of structured business data. DWs are mostly based on a so-called "multidimensional" data model, where important business events, e.g., sales, are modeled as so-called facts, characterized by a number of hierarchical dimensions, e.g., time and products, with associated numerical measures, e.g., sales price.

The multidimensional model is unique in providing a framework that is both intuitive and efficient, allowing data to be viewed and analyzed at the desired level of detail with excellent performance. Traditional data warehouses have worked very well for traditional, so-called structured data, but recently enterprises have become aware that DWs are in fact only solving a small part of their real integration and analysis needs.

There is a multitude of different types of data found in most enterprises even today, including structured, relational data, multidimensional data in DWs, text data in documents, emails, and web pages, and semi-structured/XML data such as elec-

Torben Bach Pedersen
Aalborg University, Selma Lagerløfs Vej 300, 9220 Aalborg Ø, Denmark,
e-mail: tbp@cs.aau.dk

tronic catalogs. With the current developments within mobile, pervasive and ubiquitous computing, most enterprises will also have to manage large quantities of geo-
related data, as well as data from a large amount of sensors. Finally, many analytical
models of data have been developed through data mining.

The problem with current technologies is that all these types of data/models cannot be integrated and analyzed in a coherent fashion. Instead, applications must
develop ad-hoc solutions for integration and analysis, typically for each pair of data
types, e.g., relational and text. This obviously is both expensive and error-prone.
Privacy protection is, although important, often ignored or given low priority, given
the problems with doing the integration and analysis in the first place.

The vision is to develop a breakthrough set of technologies that extend the benefits of DWs to a much wider range of data, making it feasible to literally "warehouse
the world". To do this, five unique challenges must be addressed. The challenges are:

1. Warehousing data about the physical world
2. Integrating structured, semi-structured, and unstructured data in DWs
3. Integrating the past, the present, and the future
4. Warehousing imperfect data
5. Ensuring privacy in DWs

The common base for addressing these challenges could be a new kind of data
model, inspired by multidimensional and semi-structured data models, but capable
of supporting a much wider range of data. Specifically, support will be added for
handling geo-related data (geo models, etc), sensor data (high speed data streams,
missing or incorrect values, etc), semi-structured and unstructured data (enabling
analysis across structured, semi-structured, and unstructured data), and imperfect
(imprecise, uncertain, etc.) data. Support for privacy management will also be built
into the framework.

In this context, the research can explore query languages, query processing and
optimization techniques, data integration techniques, and techniques for integrating
databases, sensors, and analytical/predictive models of data [1]. Ideally, the contributions would all be integrated into a common prototype system, so that the solutions can be evaluated experimentally using large volumes of real-world data.

This will enable the creation of a World Warehouse that provides the same benefits to all the described data types as is currently available in traditional DWs for
structured data only. The World Warehouse enables the integration and analysis of
all types of data using the developed data model and query language. As a distinguishing feature, the World Warehouse is protected by an all-encompassing "shield"
that provides integrated privacy management. All queries to the DW must pass
through, and be approved by, the shield, thus ensuring that privacy is not violated.

A large amount of previous work has already been done within the areas of the
five challenges, by a large number of researchers. Work has been done on aspects of
geo-warehousing [6, 16, 17, 18] and data streams/sensor data [20], and integrating
"pairs" of data types such as (relational, semi-structured) [4], (multidimensional,
semi-structured) [9, 10, 11, 19], (multi-dimensional, text) [14, 15], etc.

Privacy management is currently a hot topic [2, 3], but the special issues related to data warehousing have not been considered in depth yet. Overall, the contributions have not addressed the main issue of integrating and analyzing such diverse types of data coherently and efficiently. It is novel to look at these challenges in combination. Other novel challenges are as follows.

First, the traditional distinction between "real" data values and functions or models that describe data should be broken down. Instead, these two aspects will be seen as a duality of the same thing, much like the duality of particles and waves in nuclear physics. The conversion between the two aspects is achieved by folding data into models and unfolding models into data. The unfolding mechanism means that models/functions can be used in queries just as "real" data values. This unified view will enable much easier integration of past data in databases, present data from sensors, and predicted future data from models.

Second, all data values have an attached uncertainty and imprecision, no matter whether they are "real" historical data or "fake", future, predicted data. Always having a notion of the "imperfection" of the data [12, 13, 17] also makes it much more natural to compress/aggregate data into patterns/models, e.g., wavelets or Bayesian networks, which can then be unfolded to re-provide the original data.

Third, the idea of folding/unfolding can aid in privacy protection. Privacy can be protected by folding (aggregating/compressing/) actual data values into patterns which is just one kind of function/model describing the data. This of course comes at the cost of some imprecision, but this is also captured natively in the framework. Current approaches to privacy protection such as generalization, condensation, randomization, cloaking, etc., are all special cases of this mechanism, and it is expected that the benefits of a more general approach can be significant.

Fourth, the integrated privacy management "shield" can be enforced by a mechanism based on certification. The idea is that the privacy requirements for a particular data item are built into the data item itself using a special privacy dimension. Any query accessing the data item (typically using some kind of aggregation function) will then have to provide a certificate that states how the query preserves privacy. The certificate will then be matched against the privacy requirements. If the requirements are met, the data item releases the desired value, otherwise it will refuse to release the value or provide a properly anonymized value instead.

1.2 Background

1.2.1 Data Analysis Problems

We will start by recapturing what the rationale for data warehouses was in the first place. Data is born in so-called "operational systems," (On-Line Transaction Processing (OLTP) systems) that handle various specific tasks such as accounting, billing, direct mail, etc. When trying to do data analysis on such data, the following problems are encountered:

- *The same data is found in many different systems.* For a company that the author has collaborated with, the number of different systems holding customer data grew from 14 to 23 in just a couple of years, both due to mergers and to buying new software!
- *The same concept is defined differently.* A similar concept, e.g., Customer, may be defined very differently in different systems, and it may literally take years to agree on a common definition.
- *Data is suited for operational systems (OLTP).* The data models and structures are aimed at specific applications like accounting, billing, etc., and do not support analysis across business functions, which is what is really needed.
- *Data quality is bad.* Most often, operational data will contain issues like missing data, imprecise data, or varying data quality due to different use of the OLTP systems.
- *Data is volatile.* In the operational systems, data may be deleted when they are no longer needed for the particular business functions, e.g., billing data could be deleted 6 months after the bill was paid. However, data may be needed much longer for analysis purposes.
- *Data change over time.* In typical OLTP systems, no historical information is kept, since it is not needed. For example, the billing system just needs to know the current address of a customer. However, for analysis purposes, the complete address history is necessary.

1.2.2 Point-To-Point Integration

These problems can be solved by performing some kind of *integration* of data, e.g., combining customer data from several OLTP systems to provide a more comprehensive view of the customer. The aim here is to create a new database for data analysis purposes where the above problems are addressed. If is often advantageous not to create just one, huge analysis database, as such a database might be too large and complex for most purposes, but instead create several analysis databases, each specific to a certain group of analysts. These specialized databases are called *data marts* (DMs).

In the pre-DW era, the typical way of building such systems was one-at-a-time, and without coordination. Data sources were integrated as needed, in an ad-hoc fashion. Data integration was thus performed directly from "source point" to "target point" (DM) which is why this type of integration is often called "point to point integration." This type of system is illustrated in Figure 1.1.

Let us consider a line in Figure 1.1, referred to as a *connection* between a source and a mart. Each connection has to deal with a number of hard problems, specifically handling heterogeneous systems written in different programming languages,

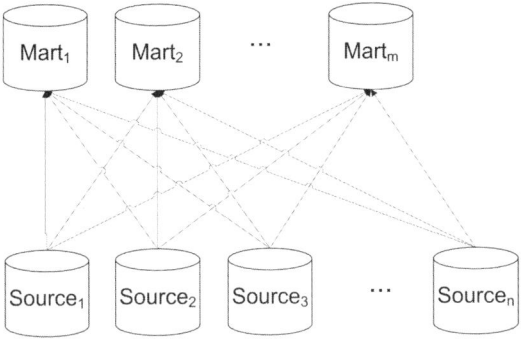

Fig. 1.1 Point-to-Point Integration

different operating systems, different DBMSes, different types of data, different data models, different data definitions, etc. When doing point-to-point data integration, as in Figure 1.1, it is clear that the number of *connections* between sources and targets (DMs) grow quadratically, with n sources and m marts, the number of required connections is $n \times m$. Adding a new source requires the development of up to m new connections Adding a new mart requires the development of up to n new connections. This obviously does not scale to high numbers of sources and marts. Perhaps even worse, this type of integration most often leads to the development of "incompatible" data model concepts, i.e., the different marts can be seen as isolated "data islands", where key concepts are defined differently and numbers cannot be compared across marts.

1.2.3 Integration Using Data Warehouses

The solution to the problems of point-to-point data integration was the creation of a new, consolidated analysis database, called a *data warehouse* (DW). Inmon [5] defines a DW as an "analysis environment" where data items are:

- *Subject oriented.* This is in contrast to the function orientation of OLTP systems.
- *Integrated.* Data is integrated both logically (same definitions) and physically (in the same database).
- *Stable.* Data is not deleted after a short period of time, and can be kept as long as it is needed for analysis purposes.
- *Time variant.* Data can always be related to the time when it was valid, and the DW maintains several versions of data items.
- *Supporting management decisions.* This refers to that the data is organized in a *multidimensional data model.*

To build the data warehouse, data from the operational systems are:

- *Extracted* from the source systems.
- *Cleansed*, to correct missing or imprecise values.
- *Transformed* to a multidimensional format.
- *Aggregated* to the needed granularity. Sometimes, the atomic detail in the operational systems is not needed for analysis purposes.
- *Loaded into DW and DMs*. The data is loaded into the DW, and subsequently into the marts.

When using a data warehouse for data integration, the picture is as in Figure 1.2.

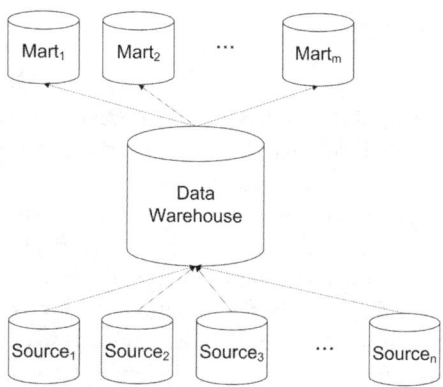

Fig. 1.2 Integration using a Data Warehouse

Here, data is extracted from a source, transformed, and put into the DW. Data is then taken from the DW and put into the marts. For this type of solution, the total number of connections for n sources and m marts is $n + m$, i.e., linear (rather than quadratic) scale-up. It is worth noticing that no transformation takes place when going from DW to marts, only the simple selection of a subset of the data. The connections from DW to marts are thus quite simple and straightforward, and may in some cases be achieved in a purely virtual way using constructs like DBMS views. The connections from sources to DW are similar in complexity to the point-to-point connections, but the difference is that there are a lot less of them. This means that adding a new source requires only 1 new connection, as does adding a new mart. This integration approach is thus scalable to very high numbers of sources and marts. The main challenge in the integration is to make the data definitions conform to each other. Now, the basic concepts of multidimensional modeling and its use for data conformance will be recaptured.

Multidimensional modeling is the process of modeling the data in a universe of discourse using the modeling constructs provided by a multidimensional data model. Briefly, multidimensional models categorize data as being either *facts* with associated numerical *measures*, or as being *dimensions* that characterize the facts and are mostly textual. For example, in a retail business, *products* are sold to *customers* at certain *times* in certain *amounts* and at certain *prices*. A typical fact would be a *purchase*. Typical measures would be the amount and price of the purchase. Typical dimensions would be the location of the purchase, the type of product being purchased, and the time of the purchase. Queries then aggregate measure values over ranges of dimension values to produce results such as the total sales per month and product type.

When doing "large scale" integration in data warehouses using multidimensional modeling, for many types of data (many cubes) and several user groups, the most important task is to ensure that analysis results are comparable across cubes, i.e., that the cubes are somehow "compatible." This is ensured by (as far as possible) picking dimensions and measures from a set of common so-called *conformed* dimensions and measures [7, 8] rather than "re-defining" the same concept, e.g., product, each time it occurs in a new context. New cubes can then be put onto the common "DW bus" [8] and used together. This sounds easier than it is, since it often requires quite a struggle with different parts of an organization to define for example a common Product dimension that can be used by everyone.

1.2.4 Business Intelligence

The ultimate goal for the DW is to use it to for so-called *business intelligence* (BI) purposes. Briefly stated, BI is the process of using the data in an enterprise to make the enterprise act "more intelligently." This is achieved by analyzing the available data, finding trends and patterns, and acting upon these. A typical BI application shows analysis results using "cross tab" tables or graphical constructs such as bar charts, pie charts, or maps. An example screenshot of the BI tool sold by the Danish company TARGIT is seen in Figure 1.3. Such BI applications are typically very easy to use, and can be used by non-technical business people like business analysts or managers.

We have now surveyed the motivation for data warehouses and the main advantages, including high ease-of-use, that DWs enable in BI systems. However, we must remember that it is (with current DW technology) only possible to achieve this for *structured* data (numbers, categorical data, etc.), typically stored in relational databases. In the next section, we will see that the current development within IT requires that such BI-like solutions become available for a much wider range of data types.

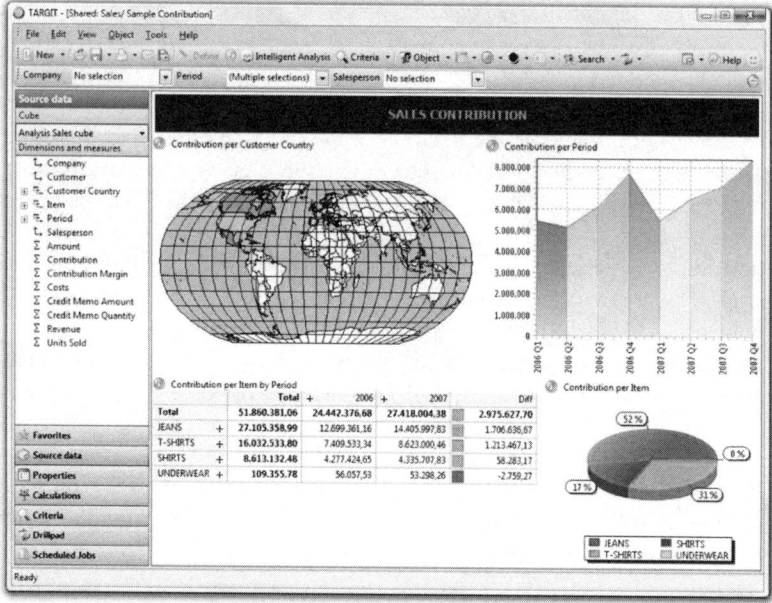

Fig. 1.3 Example BI Application

1.3 Challenges From New Types Of Data

In recent years, we have witnessed a significant change in both the volume of data and the types of data available for analysis purposes. There is now a multitude of different types of data found in most enterprises. This data of course includes "old-fashioned" structured, relational data, supplemented with multidimensional data in data warehouses. It has been complemented with a huge amount of text data in documents, emails, and web pages, as well as semi-structured/XML data such as electronic catalogs. Given current developments within mobile, pervasive and ubiquitous computing, e.g., the increasing use of GPS and other geo-positioning devices, most enterprises will also have to manage large quantities of geo-related data, as well as data from a large amount of sensors (temperature, humidity, RFID, etc.). Finally, "derived data/information" in the form of analytical models of data developed through data mining also needs to be managed. The challenges created by this situation are illustrated in Figure 1.4.

At the bottom of the figure, we see the different types of data that must be managed, namely:

- *Relational (structured) data.*
- *Multidimensional data*
- *Text data*
- *Semi-structured data*

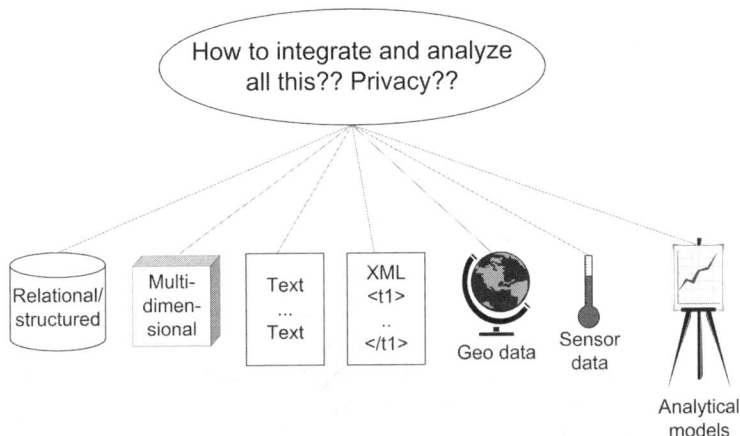

Fig. 1.4 Challenges

- *Geo-related data*
- *Sensor data*
- *Analytical Models*

The big question then becomes: "how do we integrate and analyze this multitude of data?" A related issue is that the availability of all this data implies potential threats to the privacy of individuals. For example, GPS data about an individual's movement may be coupled with "gossip" from web blogs about this person and spending information from the structured sources. Another, equally important questions is thus "how do we protect the privacy of individuals in this mountain of data?"

The next section will look at some existing approaches to integration and analysis of these different types of data.

1.4 Current Approaches To Integrating Different Types Of Data

This section presents an overview over different approaches to integration and analysis of different types of data, followed by a more detailed look at one such approach, for integration of multidimensional and text data. Most of the cited examples come from the author's own work, but many other systems exist. This is not meant to be an exhaustive survey, but rather to provide examples that illustrate the point made at the end of the section.

1.4.1 Overview

It is safe to say that a large amount of related previous work has already been done, both within integration of different types of data, and specifically within the areas of the five challenges. For example, work has been done on integration of multidimensional and geo-related data (geo-warehousing) [6, 16, 17, 18]. Another line of work considers integration of multidimensional and sensor data in the form of data streams [20]. A good example of integrating relational and semi-structured data is the WSQ/DSQ system [4]. The integration of multidimensional and semi-structured (XML) data for analysis purposes has been explored in the OLAP-XML federation system [9, 10, 11, 19]. Finally, the integrated analysis of multi-dimensional and text data has been explored in the R-cube system [14, 15]. Many more examples of systems integrating other combinations of the types of data in Figure 1.4 also exist. This situation is illustrated in Figure 1.5, where each such combination of types, e.g., (multidimensional,text) represent one line.

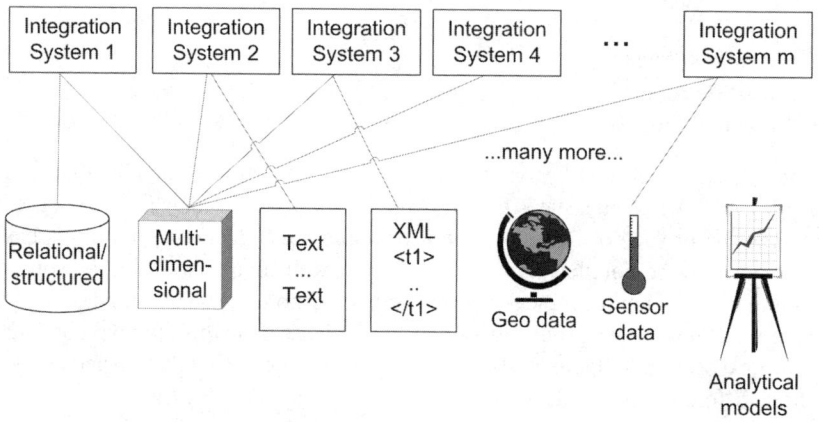

Fig. 1.5 Pair-wise integration of different types of data

Privacy management is already a hot topic in the database community [2, 3]. However, it seems that the special issues related to data warehousing have not been considered in depth yet, especially the problems emerging when combining different types of data, as outlined above.

1.4.2 An Example: Multidimensional + Text Integration

Let us now look in more detail at one particular system, the *R-Cube* system for integrating multidimensional and text data [14, 15]. The motivation for the system is as follows. Business intelligence tools are currently efficiently applied to analyze the huge amounts of structured data that companies produce. These organizations also produce lots of text documents and use the WWW as their largest source of external information. Although such documents include highly valuable information that should also be exploited by the organizations, they cannot be analyzed by current OLAP technologies as they are unstructured and mainly contain text. Most often, such documents are available in XML-like formats.

The R-cube system employs XML document warehouses that can be used by organizations to store unstructured information coming from their internal and external sources. The proposed architecture for the integration of multidimensional warehouse data with a warehouse of text-rich XML documents is called a *contextualized warehouse*. In order to cope with the many different topics addressed in the documents in the XML document warehouse, the system applies well-known Information Retrieval (IR) techniques to select the context of analysis from the document warehouse. First, the user specifies an *analysis context* by supplying a sequence of keywords (e.g., an IR condition like "financial crisis"). Then, the analysis is performed on a so-called R-cube (Relevance cube), which is materialized by retrieving the documents and facts *related to the selected context*. Each fact in the R-cube will be linked to the set of documents that describe its *context*, and will have assigned a numerical score that represents the *relevance* for the given fact with respect to the specified context, e.g., how important the fact is when the context is "financial crisis"). The papers [14, 15] provides R-cubes with a formal data model and query algebra and presents a prototype R-cube system.

The R-cube system is very powerful and allows qualitatively new types of analyses to be performed, thus empowering the analysts considerably.

1.4.3 Taking A Step Back

Systems such as the R-cube system are all very fine, but we can observe that it required a large, dedicated research and implementation effort, i.e., a whole line of research, just to enable the integrated analysis of ONE combination of the types of data in Figure 1.4. The total number of such combinations is 42(!) even with the current types of data, and it is certain that new types of data, e.g., multimedia, will have to be integrated soon. Thus, the total number of lines in Figure 1.5 will grow *quadratically* with the number of types of data. The question now is "doesn't this look familiar?" or more concretely "doesn't Figure 1.5 look familiar?" The answer is of course "Yes", as the pairwise integration of types of data in Figure 1.5 structurally resembles the pre-DW point-to-point integration in Figure 1.1. Since this is the case, a truly scalable solution should try to repeat "the DW success story" and perform the integration using a common "hub", meaning that the "complexity" once again will drop from quadratic to linear in the number of types of data.

In summary, it can be said that the "pairwise" integration contributions so far have not addressed the main issue of integrating and analyzing such diverse types of data coherently and efficiently and that it is novel to look at the total integration problem rather than the pairwise components of it.

1.5 Warehousing The World

Now, a vision of another, more scalable, approach to the integration of different types of data for analysis purposes will be presented.

1.5.1 The World Warehouse

The overall idea in the vision is to repeat the "data warehouse success" when integrating different types of data for analysis purposes. Basically, this means that data of a particular type should only need to be "integrated" once, and the results of the integration should be put into a common, "harmonized" data store that can accommodate all these types of data (OR their derivations) and still support data analysis tasks very well.

The concept of the World Warehouse (WW) is illustrated in Figure 1.6. Starting from the center of the figure, we see that the WW has the form of the cube, meaning that it is based on multidimensional modeling principles. Inside the WW, we see that the content has different "shades." Intuitively, this means that data in the WW is "not just black and white." More concretely, this refers to the fact that all data in the WW has a built-in notion of "perfection," i.e., precision and certainty of the data. Thus, data may be very precise and totally certain (like ordinary DW data) or quite imprecise and rather uncertain, e.g., due to sampling errors or due to the fact that the data comes from an analytical model rather than a traditional data sources.

At the bottom of the figure, sources with different types of data is connected to the WW through only ONE "connection" per data type, e.g., one for text, one for geo-data, etc. This means that the difficult task of integrating a particular type of data can (mostly) be handled once-and-for-all, by figuring out how this particular type of data should be mapped into the WW data model and developing algorithms and tools for doing this.

Similarly, the analysis systems only has one "connection" each to the WW. This means that they can take advantage of all the functionality and types of data available in the WW, and they are also relieved of the very difficult tasks of performing the integration of different types of data themselves (as the systems in the previous section had to do).

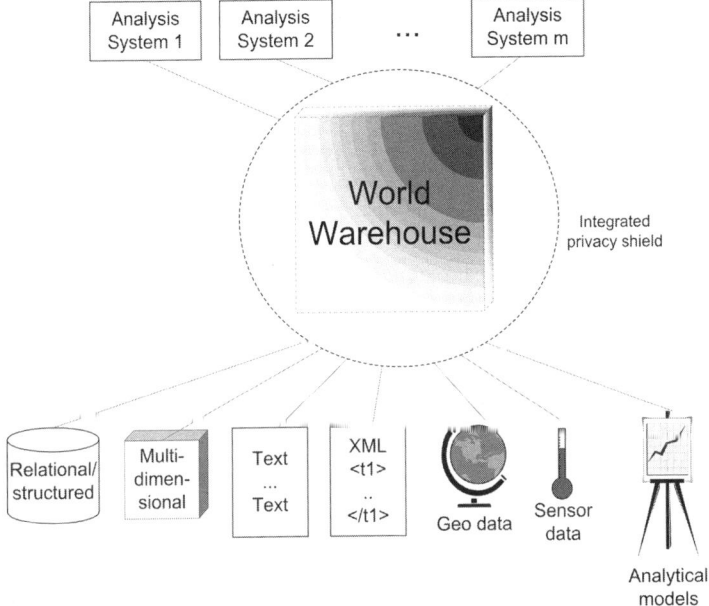

Fig. 1.6 The World Warehouse

Finally, the WW is surrounded by an "integrated privacy shield." This shield makes sure that data privacy is not violated in the WW. This can be done in two situations. First, when data from the sources is coming in, the shield may analyze the data and find that certain modifications (aggregation, swapping, randomization,...) needs to be performed on the data *before* it is placed in the WW. Second, when data is requested from an analysis system, the WW may decide to perform modifications to the query or the query result in order to protect privacy.

In summary, the WW approach means that the "complexity" of the integration of all the different types of data for n types of data and m analysis systems drops to $n + m$ (from $n * m$). The "hard" tasks such as integrating a new type of data or protecting privacy are generally handled only once, by the WW rather than in the analysis systems, meaning great relief for the development of the analysis systems.

The basis for the WW will be a novel kind of data model. This model should encompass the best of several worlds. First, it should support multidimensional modeling concepts, as these have proven superior for analysis purposes. Second, it should support the flexibility and generality found in semi-structured data models. At the same time, the model should be capable of supporting a much wider range of data. Specifically, support will be added for handling geo-related data (geo models, etc), sensor data (high speed data streams, missing or incorrect values, etc), semi-structured and unstructured data (enabling analysis across structured, semi-structured, and unstructured data), and imperfect (imprecise, uncertain, etc.) data.

As mentioned above, support for privacy management will also be built into the model.

In this context, there are almost endless possibilities for research. It is relevant to explore query languages, query processing/optimization techniques, data integration techniques, and techniques for integrating databases, sensors, and analytical/predictive models of data [1]. The contributions have to be concrete enough to enable integration of them into a common prototype system. This system should be set up as an open source project. The integrated system will enable the solutions to be evaluated experimentally using large volumes of real-world data.

The creation of the World Warehouse will provide the same benefits to all the described data types as is currently available in traditional DWs for *structured data only*. The WW enables the integration and analysis of all types of data using the developed data model and query language. A distinguishing feature of the WW is the protection by an all-encompassing "shield" that provides integrated privacy management. All queries to the DW must pass through, and be approved by, the shield, thus ensuring that privacy is not violated.

We will now look at the challenges related to realizing the WW.

1.5.2 World Warehouse Challenges

Warehousing Data About The Physical World

First, the WW needs to be able to handle data stemming from the physical world such as geo-related data (GPS readings, maps, transportation networks,...) and data from sensors in the environment (temperature, humidity, ...). Issues include the handling of various geo models as well as issues related to sensor data, such as managing high speed data streams, missing or incorrect values, etc.

Integrating Structured, Semi-structured, and Unstructured Data in DWs

Second, the WW needs to be able to effectively integrate semi-structured and unstructured data for analysis purposes. This is necessary for enabling analysis across structured, semi-structured, and unstructured data. One particular challenge in this respect is how to overcome the issue that multidimensional data are usually very homogeneous and structured, while semi-structured and unstructured data is, by nature, very heterogeneous (and obviously not very structured). An idea for achieving this is to store *derivations* of the data in the WW, rather than the data themselves, e.g., to store the fact that a particular sentence in a particular document is related to the sale of vegetable oil in the Japanese market, in the WW, rather than storing the sentence itself.

Integrating The Past, The Present, And The Future

Third, the WW has to support the seamless and integrated querying of *past* data (as current DW data), *current* data (continuously streaming in from sensors), and *future* data (predicted using analytical models). It should be possible to say "SELECT sales FROM cube WHERE month=<next month>" just as easily as selecting data from the last month. One way of doing this is to break down the traditional distinction between *"real" data values* and *functions/models* that describe data. Instead, these two aspects should be seen as a duality of the same thing, much like the duality of particles and waves in nuclear physics. The conversion between the two aspects can be achieved by *"folding"* data into models and *"unfolding"* models into data. The unfolding mechanism means that models/functions can be used in queries just as "real" data values. This unified view will enable much easier integration of past data in databases, present data from sensors, and predicted future data from models.

Warehousing Imperfect Data

Fourth, in the WW all data values have an attached uncertainty and imprecision, no matter whether they are "real" historical data or "fake", future (predicted) data. Always having a notion of the "imperfection" of the data [12, 13, 17] also makes it much more natural to compress/aggregate data into patterns/models, e.g., wavelets or Bayesian networks, which can then be unfolded to re-provide the original data. One particular challenge is how to balance the added complexity of managing the data imperfection with the requirements for high performance in the analysis.

Ensuring Privacy in DWs

Fifth, just as important the protection of privacy is, just as hard it is to realize effectively. However, we note that the idea of folding/unfolding can actually also aid in privacy protection. Privacy can be protected by folding (aggregating/ compressing/ ...) actual data values into patterns (which is just one kind of function/model describing the data). This naturally comes at the cost of some imprecision, but this is also captured natively in the WW. Current approaches to privacy protection such as generalization, condensation, randomization, cloaking, etc., are actually all special cases of this general mechanism. Thus, it is expected that the benefits of a more general approach can be significant.

   Another idea for the integrated privacy management "shield" is enforcement by a mechanism based on certification. Here, the idea is that the privacy requirements for a particular data item are *built into the data item itself* using a special *privacy dimension*. Any query accessing the data item (typically using some kind of aggregation function) will then have to provide a *certificate* that states how the query preserves privacy. This certificate will be issued by a trusted external party, just like present-day certificates, e.g., for browser plug-ins. The certificate will then be matched against the privacy requirements. If the requirements are met, the data item releases the desired value, otherwise it will refuse to release the value or provide a properly anonymized value instead.

1.6 Conclusion and Future Work

Data warehouses have become very successful in many enterprises, as they help data integration and analysis significantly. However, DW work only for relatively simple and traditional types of data. This paper presented the original ideas and advantages of data warehouses and showed that today's data integration efforts that aim to integrate different kinds of data, e.g., structured and text data, in some ways correspond to the pre-DW era of point-to-point integration, with all the associated problems. This paper thus presented the idea that it is now time to extend the benefits of DWs to a much wider range of data, making it feasible to literally "warehouse the world".

In order to do this, five unique challenges have to be addressed. 1) warehousing data about the physical world; 2) integrating structured, semi-structured, and unstructured data in DWs; 3) integrating the past, the present, and the future; 4) warehousing imperfect data; and 5) ensuring privacy in DWs. The paper provided ideas about how to address these challenges.

References

1. D. Gawlick. Querying The Past, The Present, and the Future. In *Proceedings Of The Twentieth International Conference on Data Engineering*, p. 867, 2004.
2. J. Gehrke. Models and Methods for Privacy-Preserving Data Publishing and Analysis. In em Proceedings Of The Twentysecond International Conference on Data Engineering, p. 105, 2006.
3. G. Gidofalvi, X. Huang, and T. B. Pedersen. Privacy-Preserving Data Mining on Moving Object Trajectories. In *Proceedings of The Eighth International Conference on Mobile Data Management*, pp. 60–68, 2007.
4. R. Goldman and J. Widom. WSQ/DSQ: A practical approach for combined querying of databases and the web. In *Proceeding of the 2000 ACM International Conference on Management of Data*, pp. 285–296.
5. W. Inmon. *Building The Data Warehouse, 4th Ed.* Wiley Computer Publishing, 2005.
6. C. S. Jensen, A. Kligys, T. B. Pedersen, and I. Timko. Multidimensional Data Modeling For Location-Based Services. *VLDB Journal*, 13(1):1-21, 2004.
7. R. Kimball and M. Ross. *The Data Warehouse Toolkit, 2nd Ed.*. Wiley Computer Publishing, 2002.
8. R. Kimball, L. Reeves, M. Ross, and W. Thornthwaite. *The Data Warehouse Lifecycle Toolkit*. Wiley Computer Publishing, 1998.
9. D. Pedersen, J. Pedersen, and T. B. Pedersen. Integrating XML Data in the TARGIT OLAP System. In *Proceedings Of The Twentieth International Conference on Data Engineering*, pp. 778-781, 2004.

10. D. Pedersen, K. Riis, and T. B. Pedersen. XML-Extended OLAP Querying. In *Proceedings of The Fourteenth International Conference on Scientific and Statistical Database Management*, pp. 195–206, 2002.

11. D. Pedersen, K. Riis, and T. B. Pedersen. Query optimization for OLAP-XML federations. In *Proceedings of The ACM Fifth International Workshop on Data Warehousing and OLAP*, pp. 57–64, 2002.

12. T. B. Pedersen, C. S. Jensen, and C. E. Dyreson. Supporting Imprecision in Multidimensional Databases Using Granularities. In *Proceedings of The Eleventh International Conference on Scientific and Statistical Database Management*, pp.90-101, 1999.

13. T. B. Pedersen. Aspects of Data Modeling and Query Processing for Complex Multidimensional Data. Ph.D. thesis, Faculty of Engineering and Science, Aalborg University, 2000.

14. J. M. Pcrcz, R. Berlanga, M. J. Aramburu, and T. B. Pedersen. R-Cubes: OLAP Cubes Contextualized With Documents. In *Proceedings of The Twentythird International Conference on Data Engineering*, pp. 1477–1478, 2007.

15. J. M. Perez, R. Berlanga, M. J. Aramburu, and T. B. Pedersen. Contextualizing Data Warehouses with Documents. *Decision Support Systems (Special Issue: Best Papers of DOLAP'05)*: 45(1):77–94.

16. I. Timko and T. B. Pedersen. Capturing Complex Multidimensional Data in Location-Based DWs. In *Proceedings of The Twelfth ACM International Workshop on Geographic Information Systems*, pp. 147-156, 2004.

17. I. Timko, C. E. Dyreson, and T. B. Pedersen. Probabilistic Data Modeling and Querying for Location-Based Data Warehouses. In *Proceedings of The Seventeenth International Conference on Scientific and Statistical Database Management*, pp. 273–282, 2005.

18. I. Timko, C. E. Dyreson, and T. B. Pedersen. Pre-Aggregation with Probability Distributions. In *Proceedings of The Ninth ACM International Workshop on Data Warehousing and OLAP*, pp. 35–42, 2006.

19. X. Yin and T. B. Pedersen. Evaluating XML-Extended OLAP Queries Based on a Physical Algebra. *Journal of Database Management*:17(2):84–114, 2006.

20. X. Yin and T. B. Pedersen. What Can Hierarchies Do for Data Streams? In *Proceedings of The First International Workshop on Business Intelligence for the Real-Time Enterprises*, pp. 4–19, 2007.

Chapter 2
Near Real Time ETL

Panos Vassiliadis and Alkis Simitsis

Abstract Near real time ETL deviates from the traditional conception of data warehouse refreshment, which is performed off-line in a batch mode, and adopts the strategy of propagating changes that take place in the sources towards the data warehouse to the extent that both the sources and the warehouse can sustain the incurred workload. In this article, we review the state of the art for both conventional and near real time ETL, we discuss the background, the architecture, and the technical issues that arise in the area of near real time ETL, and we pinpoint interesting research challenges for future work.

2.1 Introduction

The demand for fresh data in data warehouses has always been a strong desideratum from the part of the users. Traditionally, the refreshment of data warehouses has been performed in an off-line fashion. In such a data warehouse setting, data are extracted from the sources, transformed, cleaned, and eventually loaded to the warehouse. This set of activities takes place during a loading window, usually during the night, to avoid overloading the source production systems with the extra workload of this workflow. Interestingly, the workload incurred by this process has been one of the fundamental reasons for the establishment of data warehouses, since the immediate propagation of the changes that take place at the sources was technically impossible, either due to the legacy nature of the sources involved or simply due to the overhead incurred, mainly for the operational source systems but also for the warehouse. In most cases, a data warehouse is typically updated every 24 hours.

Panos Vassiliadis
University of Ioannina, Ioannina, 45110, Hellas, e-mail: pvassil@cs.uoi.gr

Alkis Simitsis
Stanford University, Palo Alto, California, USA, e-mail: alkis@db.stanford.edu

Still, during the last five years business users are pushing for higher levels of freshness. To give an example, we mention a case study for mobile network traffic data, involving around 30 data flows, 10 sources, and around 2TB of data, with 3 billion rows [1]. In that case study, it is reported that user requests indicated a need for data with freshness at most 2 hours. However, business user requirements are getting more pressing as the time passes.

Nowadays, new types of sources enter into the scene. In several applications, the Web is considered as a source. In such a case, the notion of transaction at source side becomes more flexible, as the data that appear at a source web site are not always available later; therefore, if instant reaction to a change is not taken, it is possible that important information will not be gathered later, by the off-line refreshment of the warehouse. At the same time, business necessities - e.g., increasing competition, need for bigger sales, better monitoring of a customer or a goal, precise monitoring of the stock market, and so on - result in a demand for accurate reports and results based on current data and not on their status as of yesterday. Another crucial issue that questions the conventional way of thinking about ETL is the globalization of the economy and the commodity trading business. The usual process of ETL-ing the data during the night in order to have updated reports in the morning is getting more complicated if we consider that an organization's branches may be spread in places with totally different time-zones. Based on such facts, data warehouses are evolving to "active" or "live" data producers for their users, as they are starting to resemble, operate, and react as independent operational systems. In this setting, different and advanced functionality that was previously unavailable (for example, on-demand requests for information) can be accessible to the end users. For now on, the freshness is determined on a scale of minutes of delay and not of hours or a whole day. As a result, the traditional ETL processes are changing and the notion of "real-time" or "near real-time" is getting into the game. Less data are moving from the source towards the data warehouse, more frequently, and at a faster rate.

The ETL market has already made efforts to react to those new requirements (a relevant discussion can be found in subsection 3.3.) The major ETL vendors have already shipped "real time" ETL solutions with their traditional platforms. In practice, such solutions involve software packages that allow the application of light-weight transformations on-the-fly in order to minimize the time needed for the creation of specific reports. Frequently, the delay between the moment a transaction occurs at the operational site and the time the change is propagated to the target site is a few minutes, usually, five to fifteen. Such a response should be characterized more as "near real time" reaction, rather than "real time", despite how appealing and promising can the latter be in business terms.

Technically, it is not straightforward how to engineer this kind of systems, neither with respect to the overall setting and architecture, nor with respect to the algorithms and techniques employed for the ETL tasks. Similar to the case of conventional ETL processes, the commercial solutions proposed so far for near real time ETL are rather ad hoc without following a standard or a unified approach. At the same time, despite efforts targeting individual problems of this topic [29, 33, 17, 34, 25] the research community has not provided a complete approach for the design and management of near real time ETL processes, so far. In this article, we delve into the details of the near real time ETL process and we highlight its special characteristics, with a particular point of view towards a Quality of Service (QoS) oriented architecture.

Contributions. Specifically, the main contributions of this article are as follows.

- We provide a high level discussion on the issues related to the traditional ETL processes and we denote their problems and constraints.
- We elaborate on the motives that boost the need for near real time ETL and we discuss appropriate architectures that can enable the desired functionality.
- We detail the infrastructure of near real time ETL. We present alternative topologies, issues related to parallelism and partitioning techniques, and issues concerning the communication of the different parts of the architecture.
- We provide a thorough analysis on research and engineering issues for all the phases of near real time ETL. Specifically, we discuss technical issues concerning the sources, the data processing area (the counterpart of data staging area in a near real time environment), and the warehouse, along with issues related to the flow regulators between both the source and the data processing area and the data processing area and the data warehouse.
- Finally, we discuss the state of the art in both research and industry, and we elaborate on the different industrial approaches already existing in the market.

Outline. The structure of the rest of this article is as follows. In Section 2, we give a brief overview of the techniques used and the problems of traditional ETL processes. In Section 3, we discuss the case of near real time ETL processes, we present the motivation for their use, we delve into more technical details such as their architecture and infrastructure, and also, we discuss interesting challenges and research issues for this area. In Section 4, we present the related work, and in Section 5, we conclude with a summary of the important points that have been raised.

2.2 Traditional ETL

A traditional data warehouse architecture consists of four layers: the data sources, the back-end, the global data warehouse, and the front-end. Typically, the data sources can be any of the following: On-Line Transaction Processing (OLTP) systems, legacy systems, flat files or files under any format. Modern applications have started to use other types of sources, as well, such as web pages and various kinds of documents like spreadsheets and documents in proprietary word processor formats.

The set of operations taking place in the back stage of data warehouse architecture is generally known as the *Extraction, Transformation, and Loading* (ETL) processes. ETL processes are responsible for the extraction of data from different, distributed, and often, heterogeneous data sources, their cleansing and customization in order to fit business needs and rules, their transformation in order to fit the data warehouse schema, and finally, their loading into a data warehouse.

The global data warehouse keeps a historical record of data that result from the transformation, integration, and aggregation of detailed data found in the data sources. Moreover, this layer involves datastores that contain highly aggregated data, directly derived from the global warehouse (e.g., data marts and views.) The front-end level of the data warehouse architecture consists of applications and techniques that business users use to interact with data stored in the data warehouse.

2.2.1 Operational issues and challenges

Traditionally, ETL processes deal with the following generic categories of problems:

- *Large volumes of data.* The volumes of operational data are extremely large, and incur significant data management problems in all three phases of an ETL process.
- *Data quality.* The data are not always clean and have to be cleansed.
- *Evolution of data stores.* The evolution of the sources and the data warehouse can eventually lead even to daily maintenance operations.
- *Performance issues.* The whole process has to take place within a specific time window and it is necessary to optimize its execution time. In practice, the ETL process periodically refreshes the data warehouse during idle or low-load, periods of its operation; e.g., every night. Any failures of the process must also be compensated within the specified time windows.

Additionally, in each individual phase of an ETL process several issues should be taken into consideration.

Extraction. The extraction conceptually is the simplest step, aiming at the identification of the subset of source data that should be submitted to the ETL workflow for further processing. In practice, this task is not easy, basically, due to the fact that there must be minimum interference with the software configuration at the source side. This requirement is imposed by two factors: (a) the source must suffer minimum overhead during the extraction, since other administrative activities also take place during that period, and, (b) both for technical and political reasons, administrators are quite reluctant to accept major interventions to their system's configuration.

There are four policies for the extraction of data from a data source. The naïve one suggests the processing of the whole data source in each execution of the ETL process; however, this policy is usually not practical due to the volumes of data that have to be processed. Another idea is the use of triggers at the source side; typically, though, this method is not practical due to abovementioned requirement regarding the minimum overhead at the source site, the intervention to the source's configuration and possibly, the non-applicability of this solution in case the source is of legacy technology. In practice, the two realistic policies suggest either the consideration of only the newly changed - inserted, deleted or updated - operational records (e.g., by using appropriate timestamps at the source sites) or the parsing of the log files of the system in order to find the modified source records. In any case, this phase is quite heavy, thus, it is executed periodically when the system is idle.

Transformation & Cleaning. After their extraction from the sources, the data are transported into an intermediate storage area, where they are transformed and cleansed. That area is frequently called Data Staging Area, DSA, and physically, it can be either in a separate machine or the one used for the data warehouse.

The transformation and cleaning tasks constitute the core functionality of an ETL process. Depending on the application, different problems may exist and different kinds of transformations may be needed. The problems can be categorized as follows: (a) schema-level problems: naming and structural conflicts, including granularity differences, (b) record-level problems: duplicated or contradicting records, and consistency problems, and (c) value-level problems: several low-level technical problems such as different value representations or different interpretation of the values. To deal with such issues, the integration and transformation tasks involve a wide variety of functions, such as normalizing, denormalizing, reformatting, recalculating, summarizing, merging data from multiple sources, modifying key structures, adding an element of time, identifying default values, supplying decision commands to choose between multiple sources, and so forth.

Usually the transformation and cleaning operations are executed in a pipelining order. However, it is not always feasible to pipeline the data from one process to another without intermediate stops. On the contrary, several blocking operations may exist and the presence of temporary data stores is frequent. At the same time, it is possible that some records may not pass through some operations for several reasons, either for data quality problems or possible system failures. In such cases, these data are temporary quarantined and processed via special purpose workflows, often involving human intervention.

Loading. After the application of the appropriate transformations and cleaning operations, the data are loaded to the respective fact or dimension table of the data warehouse. There are two broad categories of solutions for the loading of data: bulk loading through a DBMS-specific utility or inserting data as a sequence of rows.

Clear performance reasons strongly suggest the former solution, due to the overheads of the parsing of the insert statements, the maintenance of logs and rollback-segments (or, the risks of their deactivation in the case of failures.) A second issue has to do with the possibility of efficiently discriminating records that are to be inserted for the first time, from records that act as updates to previously loaded data. DBMS's typically support some declarative way to deal with this problem (e.g., the MERGE command.) In addition, simple SQL commands are not sufficient since the 'open-loop-fetch' technique, where records are inserted one by one, is extremely slow for the vast volume of data to be loaded in the warehouse. A third performance issue that has to be taken into consideration by the administration team has to do with the existence of indexes, materialized views or both, defined over the warehouse relations. Every update to these relations automatically incurs the overhead of maintaining the indexes and the materialized views.

2.2.2 Variations of the traditional ETL architecture

In the majority of cases, a conventional ETL process is designed and executed, as previously described, in three major phases: Extract, Transform, and Load. However, for several business or technical reasons, other approaches are considered too. We will not elaborate on cases that involve only a subset of the ETL phases (e.g., extract and load), but we will briefly discuss a specific alternative that nowadays, gains some business interest: the case of Extract, Load, and Transform, ELT.

The crux behind the introduction of ELT solutions is twofold and based on both the feasibility of acquiring increasingly better hardware, often more powerful than needed for data warehousing purposes, and the increasing amounts of data to be handled. Hence, in the context of ELT, instead of first creating a snapshot of the operational data in the DSA and then performing the appropriate transformations, the goal is to create a snapshot of the operational data directly in the data warehouse environment, using quick batch-loading methods. Then, depending on the business needs, the administrator can decide what types of transformations to execute either on the way of data into the data marts for OLAP analysis or on a transaction-by-transaction basis in a data-mining algorithm.

The ELT approach seems beneficial in the presence of several conditions. It seems as a good solution when the operational database machines do not have enough power - while, at the same time, the data warehouse server is a more powerful machine - or when there is a slow network connection among the sources and the target warehouse. Moreover, when the population of the data warehouse is based on a single integrated version of the operational data, then having the transformation occur within the database might prove more effective, since it can take advantage of the sophisticated mechanisms that a standard RDBMS provide; e.g., the capability of issuing inserts, updates and deletes in parallel, as well as the execution of several algorithms for data mining, profiling, cleansing, and so on, from a SQL command line. Additionally, as it is stressed in a recent article [19], ELT may be more beneficial than other conventional architectures due to the following reasons: (a) it leverages RDBMS engine hardware for scalability and basically, it scales as long as the hardware and RDBMS engine can continue to scale; (b) it keeps all data in the RDBMS all the time; (c) it is parallelized according to the data set; and finally, (d) disk I/O is usually optimized at the engine level for faster throughput. Currently, most major players in the market provide ELT solutions as well; e.g., Informatica Pushdown ELT, Sunopsis ELT, Oracle Warehouse Builder, and Microsoft DTS.

Finally, an even newer trend suggests the use of ETLT systems. ETLT represents an intermediate solution between ETL and ELT, allowing the designer to use the best solution for the current need. In that case, we can classify transformations in two groups. A first group of fast, highly selective, non-blocking transformations may be executed in advance, even in streaming data, before the fast loading of the data to the warehouse area. Then, part of the incoming data can be used for fast, near real-time reporting, while the rest can be manipulated later on in a subsequent phase. Such a vision guides us to the case of near real-time ETL, which will be the focus of the rest of this article.

2.3 The case for Near Real Time ETL

2.3.1 Motivation

Traditionally, ETL processes have been responsible for populating the data ware-house both for the bulk load at the initiation of the warehouse and incrementally, throughout the operation of the warehouse in an off-line mode. Still, it appears that data warehouses have fallen victims of their success: users are no more satisfied with data that are one day old and press for fresh data -if possible, with instant re-porting. This kind of request is technically challenging for various reasons. First, the source systems cannot be overloaded with the extra task of propagating data to-wards the warehouse. Second, it is not obvious how the active propagation of data can be implemented, especially in the presence of legacy production systems. The problem becomes worse since it is rather improbable that the software configuration of the source systems can be significantly modified to cope with the new task, due to (a) the down-time for deployment and testing, and, (b) the cost to administrate, maintain, and monitor the execution of the new environment.

The *long term vision for near real time warehousing* is to have a self-tuning archi-tecture, where user requirements for freshness are met to the highest possible degree without disturbing the administrators' requirements for throughput and availability of their systems. Clearly, since this vision is founded over completely controversial goals, a reconciliation has to be made:

A more pragmatic approach involves a semi-automated environment, where user requests for freshness and completeness are balanced against the workload of all the involved sub-systems of the warehouse (sources, data staging area, warehouse, data marts) and a tunable, regulated flow of data is enabled to meet resource and workload thresholds set by the administrators of the involved systems.

In the rest, we will translate this vision into a list of more concrete technical goals. First, we start with the goals that concern the implementation of a near real time warehouse with a view to Quality-of-Service (QoS) characteristics:

1. *Maximum freshness of data.* We envision a near real time data warehousing en-vironment able to serve the users with as fresh data as possible in the warehouse.
2. *Minimal overhead of the source systems.* For near real time warehousing to work, it is imperative to impose the minimum possible additional workload to the sources, which -at the same time-is sustainable by the sources.
3. *Guaranteed QoS for the warehouse operation.* The near real time warehouse administrator should be equipped with tools that allow him to guarantee service levels concerning the response time to queries posed, the throughput of all the systems involved and the freshness of data offered to the users.
4. *Controlled environment.* Since unexpected events occur throughout the daily operation of the near real time warehouse, its administrator should be equipped with the potential to respond to these events and tune the flow of data from the sources towards the warehouse with minimal effort. Any kind of optimization, prediction and automatic support of the administrator in this task is highly

valuable.

Practical considerations involve the following goals, too:

5. *Scalability in terms of sources involved, queries posed by the end users and volumes of data to be processed.* Naturally, it is expected that over time, requests for more fresh data from new sources, more available data, and a more energetic user community will have to be serviced by the warehouse. In this case, before other measures are taken (e.g., exploiting Moore's law with new hardware), the degradation of performance should be smooth.
6. *Stable interface at the warehouse side.* Apart from the smooth performance degradation due to new sources, development costs should be bounded, too. It would be convenient for developers and administrators if the warehouse would export a stable interface for its refreshment to all its source sites.
7. *Smooth upgrade of the software at the sources.* We envision a transition to a system configuration where the modification of the software configuration at the source side is minimal.

2.3.2 General architecture

We envision the general architecture of a near real time data warehouse consisting of the following elements: (a) Data Sources hosting the data production systems that populate the data warehouse, (b) an intermediate Data Processing Area (DPA) where the cleaning and transformation of the data takes place and (c) the Data Warehouse (DW). The architecture is illustrated in Figure 2.1.

Each source can be assumed to comprise a data store (legacy or conventional) and an operational data management system (e.g., an application or a DBMS, respectively.) Changes that take place at the source side have first to be identified as relevant to the ETL process and subsequently propagated towards the warehouse, which typically resides in a different host computer. For reasons that pertain to the QoS characteristics of the near real time warehouse and will be explained later, we envision that each source hosts a *Source Flow Regulator* (SFlowR) module that is responsible for the identification of relevant changes and propagates them towards the warehouse at periodic or convenient intervals, depending on the policy chosen by the administrators. As already mentioned, this period is significantly higher that the one used in the current state-of-practice and has to be carefully calculated on the basis of the source system's characteristics and the user requests for freshness.

A *Data Processing Flow Regulator* (DPFlowR) module is responsible of deciding which source is ready to transmit data. Once the records have left a certain source, an ETL workflow receives them at the intermediate data processing area. The primary role of the ETL workflow is to cleanse and transform the data in the format of the data warehouse. In principle, though, apart from these necessary cleansings and transformations, the role of the data processing area is versatile: (a)

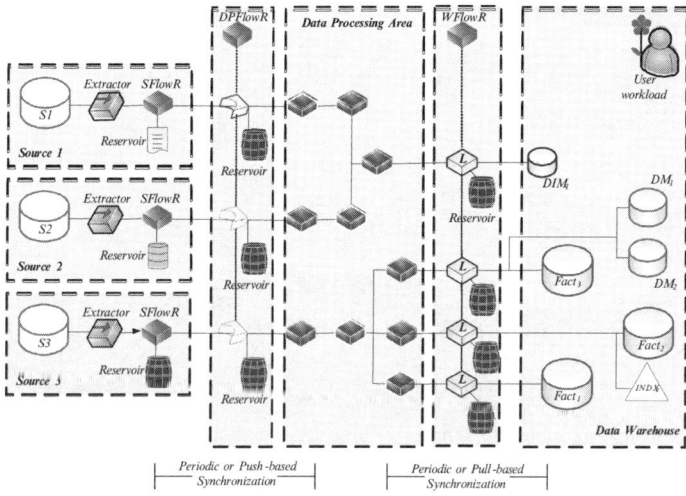

Fig. 2.1 Architecture of near real time data warehouse

it relieves the source from having to perform these tasks, (b) it acts as the regulator for the data warehouse, too (in case the warehouse cannot handle the online traffic generated by the source) and (c) it can perform various tasks such as checkpointing, summary preparation, and quality of service management. However, it is expected that a certain amount of incoming records may temporarily resort to appropriate *Reservoir* modules, so that the DPA can meet the throughput for all the workflows that are hosted there.

Once all ETL processing is over, data are ready to be loaded at the warehouse. A Warehouse Flow Regulator (WFlowR) orchestrates the propagation of data from the DPA to the warehouse based on the current workload from the part of the end-users posing queries and the QoS "contracts" for data freshness, ETL throughput and query response time. Clearly, this is a load-balancing task, which we envision to be implemented over a tunable QoS software architecture.

The Data Warehouse per se, is a quite complicated data repository. There are different categories of constructs in the warehouse, which we broadly classify as follows: (a) fact tables, containing the records of real-world events or facts, that the users are mainly interested in, (b) dimension tables, which contain reference records with information that explains the different aspects of the facts, (c) indexes of various kinds (mainly, B+-trees and bitmap indexes) which are used to speed-up query processing and (d) materialized views, which contain aggregated information that is eventually presented to the users. In the rest of our deliberations, the term 'materialized view' will be used as a useful abstraction that allows us to abstract al kinds of summaries that are computed once, stored for the users to retrieve and query and regularly updated to reflect the current status of a one or more fact tables (e.g., data marts, reports, web pages, and any possible materialized views per se.)

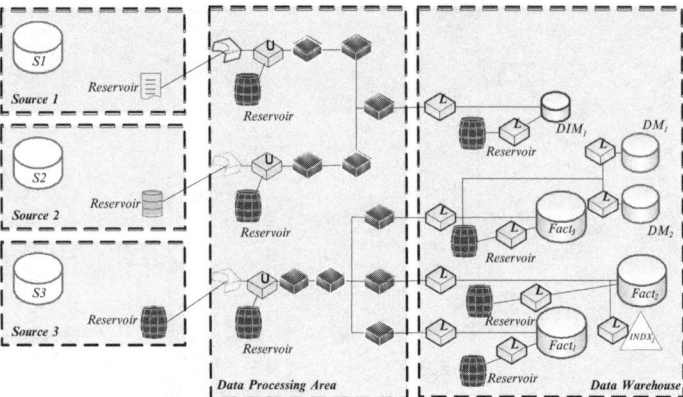

Fig. 2.2 Compensating actions for a near real time data warehouse

Each of these constructs has a clear role in a traditional ETL setting; in the case of near real time ETL, these constructs are possibly accompanied by auxiliary structures that alleviate the burden of refreshing them very frequently.

In an ideal world, all the involved systems (sources, data processing area and warehouse) would be able to process all the data within the given time windows. Clearly, this cannot be the case in practical situation, due to many possible reasons, like the high rate of user queries, the high rate of updates, the high cost of certain parts of the transformation and cleaning stage, or even the failure of a part of the overall architecture at runtime. Practically this results to the necessity of reserving parts of the propagated data for later processing. In other words, a simple selection mechanism in the flow regulators needs to decide which data will be processed by the ETL workflow in near real time and which parts will be reserved in main memory, staged at the hard disk or simply shed in order to be processed later, during an idle period of the warehouse. Similarly, a failure in the near real time processing area or the warehouse can lead to data not propagated to the warehouse on time.

These practical considerations lead to the necessity of a compensation scheme that operates in an off-line mode (much like the traditional ETL mechanisms) and completes the missing parts of data in the warehouse and the materialized views (Figure 2.2.)

2.3.3 Industrial approaches

Alternative architectures for near real time ETL has been suggested in the industrial literature. In this section, we briefly describe the alternative approaches and we pinpoint their advantages and disadvantages. For further details, we refer to [18] for an excellent review of such approaches.

2.3.3.1 (Near) Real time partition

The case of near real time ETL is discussed in an industrial book [18]. Although the description is informal and very abstract, the notion of real time partitions (RTP) seems that offer a solution to the problem of near real time ETL; however, for getting better performance several assumptions are considered too.

The key idea is to maintain two versions of the star schema representing a data warehouse. (One can imagine a virtual star schema defined by appropriate union view(-s) on top of the two star schemas.) One version should be static and the other real time, in terms of their population. Hence, using that approach, for each fact table of the data warehouse, a separate real time fact table is considered with the same characteristics as the static one - e.g., same grain and dimensionality. The real time fact table should contain only today's data that are not yet loaded to the static fact table. The static fact table is populated using conventional nightly batch loads. The main difference from the conventional method is that the real time fact table periodically populates (in short periods of time) the static fact table before being emptied.

The real time fact table should have significant performance gains, thus, the indexing in that table is minimized. In doing so, both the loading effort and the query response times are greatly benefited. However, the main advantages of this idea stem from the assumption that the whole real time fact table should fit in main memory for further fast processing. Although it may be possible to cache the fact table in memory in some cases, given that it contains data of only one day, still, this is a very ambitious assumption.

2.3.3.2 (Near) Real time ETL approaches

As usual, different alternative approaches have been proposed in the market to handle the need for freshness in a data warehouse. In what follows, we briefly mention the most prominent approaches using terminology adapted from [18] and identify their limitations.

Enterprise Application Integration, EAI. These approaches have the ability to link transactions across multiple systems through existing applications by using software and computer systems architectural principles to integrate a set of enterprise computer applications. An EAI system is a push system, not appropriate for batch transformations, whose functionality entails a set of adapter and broker components that move business transactions - in the form of messages - across the various systems in the integration network. An adapter creates and executes the messages, while a broker routes messages, based on publications and subscription rules.

The main benefit from an EAI system is fast extraction of relevant data that must be pushed towards the data warehouse. In general, an EAI solution offers great real time information access among systems, streamlines business processes, helps raise organizational efficiency, and maintains information integrity across multiple systems. Usually, it is considered as a good solution for applications demanding low latency reporting and bidirectional synchronization of dimensional data between the operational sources and the data warehouse. However, as nothing comes without a cost, they constitute extremely complex software tools, with prohibitively high development costs, especially for small and mid-sized businesses. Also, EAI implementations are time consuming, and need a lot of resources. Often, many EAI projects usually start off as point-to-point efforts, but very soon they become unmanageable as the number of applications increase.

Fast transformations via Capture - Transform - Flow (CTF) processes. This solution resembles a traditional ETL process too. CTF approaches simplify the real time transportation of data across different heterogeneous databases. CTF solutions move operational data from the sources, apply light-weight transformations, and then, stage the data in a staging area. After that, more complex transformations are applied (triggered by the insertions of data in the staging area) by microbatch ETL and the data are moved to a real time partition and from there, to static data stores in the data warehouse. CTF is a good choice for near real time reporting, with light integration needs and for those cases where core operations may share periods of low activity and due to that, they allow the realization of data synchronization with a minimal impact to the system.

Fast loading via microbatch ETL. This approach uses the idea of real time partitioning (described in section 2.3.3.1) and resembles traditional ETL processes, as the whole process is executed in batches. The substantial difference is that the frequency of batches is increased, and sometimes it gets as frequent as hourly. Several methods can be used for the extraction of data - e.g., timestamps, ETL log tables, DBMS scrapers, network sniffers, and so on. After their extraction the data are propagated to the real time partition in small batches and this process continuously runs. When the system is idle or once a day, the real time partitions populate the static parts of the data warehouse. The microbatch ETL approach is a simple approach for real-time ETL and it is appropriate for moderate volumes of data and for data warehouse systems tolerant of hourly latency. The main message it conveys, though, is mainly that dealing with new data on a record-by-record basis is not too practical and the realistic solution resolves to finding the right granule for the batch of records that must be processed each time.

On-demand reporting via Enterprise Information Integration (EII). EII is a technique for on-demand reporting. The user collects the data he needs on-demand via a virtual integration system that dispatches the appropriate queries to the underlying data provider systems and integrates the results. EII approaches use data abstraction methods to provide a single interface for viewing all the data within an organization, and a single set of structures and naming conventions to represent this data. In other words, EII applications represent a large set of heterogenous data sources as a single homogenous data source. Specifically, they offer a virtual real time data warehouse as a logical view of the current status in the OLTP systems. This virtual warehouse is delivered on-the-fly through inline transformations and it is appropriate for analysis purposes. It generates a series of (SQL) queries at the time requested, and then it applies all specified transformations to the resulting data and presents the result to the end user. EII applications are useful for near-zero latency in real time reporting, but mostly for systems and databases containing little or no historical data.

2.3.4 The infrastructure of near real time ETL

The software architecture described in section 2.3.2 is constructed in such a way that the goals of section 2.3.1 are achieved with QoS guarantees. In this subsection, we discuss possible alternatives for the infrastructure that hosts this software architecture and facilitates the near real time refreshment of the data warehouse.

A traditional approach towards the topology of the near real time warehouse would structure it as a linear combination of tiers - in fact, as a 2-tier or 3-tier configuration. Apart from the traditional architectural configurations, it is quite natural for an endeavor of the magnitude of a near real time warehouse to opt for configurations where the architecture exploits some forms of parallelism. In this subsection, we discuss how different parallelism techniques affect the execution of ETL processes and suggest improvements in the presence of certain requirements. In general, there exist two broad categories of parallel processing with respect to the flow and volume of data: *pipelining* and *partitioning*.

In Figure 2.3, the execution of an abstract ETL process is pictorially depicted. In Figure 2.3(a), the execution is performed sequentially. In this case, only one instance of the ETL process exists. Figures 2.3(b) and 2.3(c) show the parallel execution of the process in a pipelining and a partitioning fashion, respectively. In the latter case, larger volumes of data may be handled efficiently by more than one instance of the ETL process; in fact, there are as many instances as the partitions used.

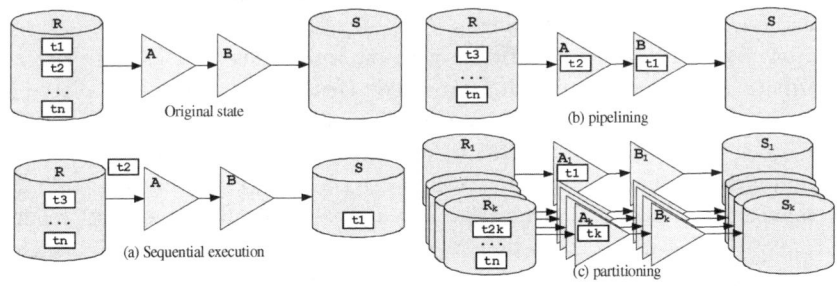

Fig. 2.3 (a) Sequential, (b) pipelining, and (c) partitioning execution of ETL processes [37]

Pipelining methods. The execution of an ETL process can be coarsely divided in three sub-processes: extraction, transformation, and loading. In pipeline parallelism, the various activities of these three sub-processes are operating simultaneously in a system with more than one processor. While the ETL process lasts, the extraction module reads data from the sources and keeps feeding a pipeline with the data it had already read. In the meantime, the transformation module runs in another processor and it is continuously sending data to another pipeline. Similarly, the loading module, which runs in a third processor, is writing data to the target recordset. This scenario performs well for ETL processes that handle a relative small volume of data.

Partitioning methods. For large volumes of data, a different parallelism policy should be devised: the partitioning of the dataset into smaller sets. The idea is to use different instances of the ETL process for handling each partition of data. In other words, the same activity of an ETL process would run simultaneously by several processors, each processing a different partition of data. At the end of the process, the data partitions should be merged and loaded to the target recordset(s). For partitioning, many implementations have been proposed with the common goal to provide equal size partitions to facilitate the load of data to a single target. The most frequently used methods are the following. (Here, we use a terminology adopted from the DataStage tool [2], but the categorization is typical of a broader group of commercial ETL tools.)

- *Round robin partitioning*. The records are distributed among the different processing nodes in a round robin fashion: the first record goes to the first node, the second record to the second node, and so forth. This method is appropriate for resizing uneven partitions of an input data set and it is often used as the default method for the initial partitioning.
- *Random partitioning*. The records are randomly distributed across all processing nodes. This method can be used for resizing partitions, as well, and it can guarantee that each processing unit handles (near) equal-sized partitions. Moreover, this method produces results that are similar to the ones of the round robin method, but with a higher overhead than the latter due to extra processing required for the estimation of a random value for each record; this value is used as a criterion for the partitioning.
- *Hash by field partitioning*. Tuples with the same values for all hash key attributes are assigned to the same processor. Hence, related tuples are placed in the same partition. This property may be a prerequisite for a certain activity (e.g., duplicate elimination.) A similar method that requires simpler computation is the modulus partitioning, which is based on a key column modulo the number of partitions. Range partitioning is another method that places related tuples (having their keys within a specified range) in the same partition. This can be useful for preparing a dataset for a total sort.
- *Follow-the-database partitioning*. This method suggests to partition data in the same way a DBMS would partition it. Therefore, the tuples processed by the ETL process and the respective tuples of a database table would be handled by the same parallel operator (this may significantly reduce the I/O cost.) Such a method is useful for update operations, and works very well when the warehouse is partitioned too.

Two additional methods are frequently used in ETL processes to facilitate the partitioning. Although they do not intend the direct partitioning of the input data, still they are useful in an environment consisting of subsequent activities. The goal of both methods is to efficiently pass partitioned data through a sequence of ETL activities.

- *Same partitioning.* This method does not perform a repartitioning, but it takes as inputs the partition outputs of the preceding stage. Essentially, it does not allow redistribution of data, which remains in the same processor, but, it is useful for passing partitioned data between activities.
- *Entire partitioning.* This method is appropriate when a parallel execution is desired and at the same time, all instances of an activity in all the processors should have access to the complete dataset if needed. Example application is the creation of lookup tables.

The reverse of the partitioning operation is to gather all the data together again. Typical approaches include: round robin, ordered, and sorted merge gathering. In general, this procedure is non-deterministic. Nevertheless, if order matters, a sorted merge should be favored.

Combination. In practice, a combination of pipelining and partitioning can be used to achieve maximum performance. Hence, while an activity is processing partitions of data and feeding pipelines, a subsequent activity may start operating on a certain partition before the previous activity had finished.

Several commercial ETL tools (e.g., DataStage) provide the functionality of repartitioning data between the activities of the process. This can be useful in many cases, such as when alteration of data groups is needed; e.g., in the case where data are grouped by month and a new grouping per state is needed.

2.3.5 Research and engineering issues for near real time ETL

Having discussed the alternatives for the infrastructure of a near real time data warehouse, we can now proceed to discuss the main research challenges raised for each of the main components and their overall setup. We organize this discussion on terms of the individual stages of data in the warehouse and summarize the discussion with regards to the overall setting of a near real time warehouse at the end of this section.

2.3.5.1 Technical issues concerning the Sources

There are several critical technical issues concerning the sources. Both due to political reasons [7] and due to the sensitivity of source systems, interventions to the source systems can only be minimal for the following causes.

- Sources are the production systems of the organizations, which implies that their main purpose is to facilitate the everyday transactions of the organization with external entities; e.g., customers, providers, and so on. Overloading the source systems with ETL responsibilities might slow down the tasks that these systems are primarily intended to support to an extent that might jeopardize their primary functionality.

- Quite often, sources are legacy systems, and dealing with this fact from a software point of view means that it is practically impossible to intervene in their configuration at a significant extent. It is noteworthy that this is not a minor issue; in fact, the reason for the existence of these legacy systems is the cost and risk of their replacement with modern substitutes.

The main technical challenge at the source side is the identification of the data that must be propagated towards the data processing area at every transmission. This task has typically been referred at as *Extraction* (the 'E' in the E-T-L triplet.) We will refer to the data that are identified as changes as the *extracted delta* of the source. The important parameters of the data extraction problem are:

- *Minimal intervention to the configuration of the source system.* As already mentioned, this might not even be an option in legacy systems, but in any case, it is reasonable to anticipate that the list of available technical solutions is small.
- *Lightweight footprint of the extraction mechanism.* Due to the importance of the primary functionality of data sources, the resources spent (e.g., main memory or CPU cycles) and the overhead incurred to the source system (e.g., extra operations, locking of data) for the identification of the data that belong to the extracted delta have to be minimal.
- *Effectiveness Constraints.* A certain level of completeness might be desirable, e.g., all relevant data must be identified and included in the extracted delta. Correctness is also necessary here: no uncommitted data should be pushed towards the data processing area.
- *Efficiency Constraints.* Efficiency constraints might hold, too. For example, it is reasonable to require that the throughput of the extraction is above a certain threshold (or, in a similar problem formulation, that the task is performed within a relatively small time window, each time.) Also, it is possible that insertions and updates are identified as different as they occur and thus, separately kept at the sources, so that it is easier for the subsequent data processing to handle them appropriately.

Technically, the available solutions towards the identification of the changes that must be propagated to the warehouse are not satisfactory. The technical means we already possess for the extraction step are oriented towards the traditional data warehouse refreshment mode, where the extraction is performed off-line in rare frequency and with a relatively large time window. Specifically, inapplicable solutions involve (a) the reprocessing of the whole source as a naïve solution and (b) the comparison of the current snapshot of the source with its previous version for the extraction of deltas. On the other hand, we can also comment on some techniques that seem to be fit for the near real time ETL process, although each comes with problems:

- *Enterprise Application Integration (EAI) middleware.* In this case, the data production applications are enriched via EAI middleware and communicate with the data processing area by sending any changes that occur.
- *Log sniffing.* Log sniffing - also called log parsing or log scrapping - involves parsing the contents of a log between two timestamps and "replaying" the changes at the data processing area. Although inapplicable to sources without logging facilities, the solution sounds appealing, since the log file is an append-only file and the contention for the usage of different parts of it can be reasonably handled.
- *Triggers.* Another possibility, involves the usage of triggers in the source that are activated whenever a modification takes place in the source database. The triggers can write the modifications in a special purpose table, file or main memory construct that is processed whenever the extraction phase is activated. Still, triggers are only applicable to relational DBMSs, interfere with the setup of the source database and impose a considerable operational overhead at the source system.
- *Timestamping.* A final possibility involves adding timestamps with transaction time to all the tables of the source and extract only the ones with timestamps with greater value than the one of the last extraction. Still, this solution misses deletions (at least in its simple version) and significantly interferes with the source DBMS and possibly the source applications.

Summarizing, the problems of data extraction at the sources can be formulated as (a) an effectiveness problem and (b) an efficiency problem. The effectiveness problem calls for the construction of a mechanism that identifies changes with minimal intervention to the source's configuration and with light footprint in terms of main memory and CPU usages. The efficiency problem is an optimization problem that relates the volume of data to be propagated with a certain frequency from a data source towards the data processing area, the necessary mechanism for the task, and tries to minimize the necessary resources such that the efficiency and effectiveness constraints are respected.

A variant of the problem has to with the compensating operation of the warehouse refreshment process, which practically reverts back to the traditional problem of data extraction: in this case, the important constraint is to complete the extraction and transportation of the data within a much larger time window, in a batch mode.

2.3.5.2 Flow regulators between the source and the Data Processing Area

As already mentioned, it is imperative that the overall flow of data from the sources towards the warehouse is adapted in such a way that the source systems are not overloaded. The mechanism that we envision for the near real time extraction of data from the sources employs a global scheduler that directs the order with which sources are triggered to start the transmission of the extracted data they have collected as well as local regulators at the sources that adapt the flow of data to the processing capacity of the source system, whenever this particular source is activated for transmission.

Simply put, the main idea involves (a) a *Data Processing Flow Regulator* (DPFlowR) module, which is responsible of deciding which source is ready to transmit data and (b) a *Source Flow Regulator* (SFlowR) module for each source, which compiles changes in blocks and propagates them towards the warehouse.

The Data Processing Flow Regulator has to decide the order of the activation of sources, the time window for the activation of each source and notify the server of the Data Processing Area for this activation (since, there is an ETL flow that will receive the newly arrived source data for further processing.) This decision possibly depends upon the availability of the source systems, their workload (that can be reported to the DPFlowR by the corresponding SFlowR for each source) and the workload of the server of the Data Processing Area.

Whenever activated, the Source Flow Regulator knows that there is a time window for the transmission of collected data. If the collected data are more than the volume that can be transmitted during the time window (due to server load, network connection or any other reasons), then there is a part of the data that will not be propagated to the warehouse during this particular transmission. If the source server is not so loaded, it is possible to perform some form of sampling for the choice of the data to be reserved. These data can be buffered either for the next transmissions over the regular operation of the near real time warehouse or for the compensation period. Also, these data can be completely discarded (if the source server is too busy to perform this kind of extra staging) and re-extracted at the compensation period.

A communication part takes place between the data processing area and the source. Several issues arise concerning, concerning the protocol of transmission (e.g., is TCP or UDP) and the completeness of transmitted data. In other words, unless other considerations arise, it is important to achieve a packet-lossless transmission. It is also noteworthy that any compression and encryption operations (that are typically encountered whenever a source communicates with the warehouse) should also be part of the decisions made by the Source Flow Regulator.

In our understanding, the sensitive part of the architecture lies in the sources, thus, the fundamental criteria for scheduling decisions concern their availability and load; nevertheless, in case the Data Processing Area server is continuously too loaded it is possible that the sensitivity of the decision must be shifted towards the DPA. Due to these possible sensitivities, we can only emphasize the importance of a Quality-of-Service approach to the system architecture. As it has probably been made obvious so far, the frequency of communication between a source and the Data Processing Area, the time window for the transmission, the volume of data to be transmitted and the scheduling protocol constitute a highly controlled mechanism (a plan or a "contract", if you like) for orchestrating the population of the Data Processing Area from the sources. The mechanism for handling any possible deviations from this plan is also part of the QoS-oriented nature of the architecture.

A second point we would like to emphasize here is the role of the flow regulation mechanism as a buffer between the data warehouse and the sources. In our opinion, it is practically improbable to ever achieve a modus operandi where committed changes are directly propagated from the sources to the warehouse. As already explained this is due to the deep nature, architecture and technical characteristics of the sources as production systems for their organizations. Therefore, a compromise must be achieved and such a compromise requires a regulation policy that allows the sources to be relieved from the burden of feeding the warehouse with data when they are too loaded. The flow regulation mechanism implements this compromise.

From a technical viewpoint, there are three implications that result from this observation:

- There is a technical choice for the modus operandi of the propagation process which can be (a) periodic (with significantly higher frequency than the current ETL processes), (b) pull-based, with the data processing area requiring data from the sources or (c) push-based, with the sources sending extraction deltas to the data processing areas at their earliest possible convenience. Due to the sensitivity of the sources, we believe that the pull-based option is rather hard to implement; nevertheless, in all cases, precautions have to be taken to allow a source to be relieved from extra processing if it is unable to perform it at a given time point.
- A rather simple implication concerns the control of the flow regulation. We anticipate that the overhead of scheduling the whole process will be assigned to the DPA server; still, this requires some coordination with the source systems. Still, a clear research issue concerns the scheduling protocol itself (i.e., the order by which the DPA receives data from the sources along with the time window that each connection is activated.) Obviously, the scheduling problem is more complicated in the case of parallel and partitioned DPA, where multiple activation can -and have to- take place each time.
- A final implication concerns the granularity of the propagated data. There are two ways to deal with this issue: either to deal with each modification in isolation or to compile blocks of records at the source side. In the first case, whenever a data manipulation command is committed, the transportation mechanism is notified and deals with it in isolation. In the second case, nothing is ready for transportation, until a number of records is completed. Then, all records together are sent to the data processing area. Clearly, a near real time data warehouse practically has no other option than the latter (see also [17] for an experimental evaluation of the overhead incurred at the sources.)

Summarizing, the main problem for the control mechanism that facilitates the near real time propagation of extracted changes from the sources to the warehouse requires to relate (a) a scheduling protocol that regulates the order of source activations and the time window for each such activation, (b) the characteristics of the propagation (data volumes, frequency), (c) the necessary CPU and main memory resources of the DPA server, and (d) the communication protocol between sources and the DPA, in order to transfer as many data as possible to the Data Processing Area (and, ultimately, increase the data warehouse freshness) with quality of service guarantees, such as bounded latency per record packet, bounded packet losses during transmission, no starvation problems for any source, and so on.

2.3.5.3 Technical issues concerning the Data Processing Area

The Data Processing Area involves one or more servers that host workflows of transformation and cleaning activities (along with any temporary data stores) that take
extracted source deltas as input and produce records ready to be stored at the warehouse fact and dimension tables.

The Data Processing Area is the equivalent of the Data Staging Area of the traditional ETL processes, where all the cleaning and transformations take place. The
main technical differences of a traditional warehouse with a near real time setting
are also reflected in the difference between DPA and DSA and are summarized as
follows:

- In the case of near real time ETL, the frequency of execution is significantly
  higher, and both the data volumes to be processed as well as the time windows
  for the completion of the task are much smaller.
- Due to small time allowance and the pressing demands for high throughput, data
  staging is not always available or desirable. The same applies for costly operations, such as external sorting, that allow faster algorithms (sort-merge join or
  sort-based aggregations) to be employed at the DSA, in the case of traditional
  ETL.
- On the other hand, due to the smaller volume of data that are processed each
  time, many operations can be performed in main memory. This makes the memory allocation problem much more important in the case of near real time ETL.
- In the case of traditional ETL, the retention of data for further processing is
  performed only for data that are detected as problematic ("dirty") as well as
  in the case of failures. In the case of near real time ETL, data are reserved
  also for performance reasons, when data completeness is traded for processing
  throughput.

As an overall desideratum, it is also interesting to point out that a near real time
ETL process is focused towards achieving high throughput at its end points, whereas
a traditional ETL process is focused towards meeting the deadline of its time window for completing the processing of all the incoming tuples.

Note also that the DPA acts as a flexible buffering area: the input rate of
records is not controlled by the DPA administrator, but rather, depends on the
characteristics and the workload of the sources, each time; at the same time, the
DPA has to guarantee a certain rate of processed records that are ready to be
loaded at the warehouse whenever appropriate, necessary, or dictated by the user
needs. Therefore, CPU, main memory and storage capabilities along with adaptive
processing mechanism must be at hand, for handling either an overload of incoming records or a high demand for output records that can be loaded to the warehouse.

From a server configuration point of view, the DPA is a clear candidate for parallelism and partitioning. The technical options have been explained in a previous
subsection, so here we would only like to point out that due to the nature of DPA as

a flexible buffer, extra processing and storage resources can frequently prove to be very helpful.

From a software architecture point of view, we can identify several interesting technical challenges. First, the question arises on how to architect the ETL activities and their communication. Clearly, intermediate staging temporary tables are not an option. A possible solution for the communication of ETL activities is to use input/output queues at the end points of each activity. Still, this solution is not without problems: for example, "a proper emptying rate for the ETL queues has to be determined. A high arrival rate compared to the configured service rate will result in instability and queue length explosion. On the contrary, a very high service rate potentially results in too many locks of the queue (resulting again in delay, contrary to what would normally be expected). It is obvious that the service rate should be close to the arrival rate in order to have both efficient service times, and as less locks as possible." [17]. Moreover, a certain degree of checkpointing might also be desirable; plugging such functionality to the above architecture while retaining throughput guarantees is not obvious. Although this solution gives a first possibility for structuring the interconnection of ETL activities in a multi-threaded environment, extending it to parallel, partitioned or both parallel and partitioned environments is not straightforward. Other options should be explored too.

The overall research problem that pertains to the DPA involves a negotiation of conflicting goals as well as some hard constraints that cannot be neglected. Specifically, one has to find a workable solution that takes into consideration: (a) the requests (or possibly "contracts" in a QoS setting) for data freshness and completeness by the end users at the warehouse, (b) the incoming rates of data that the sources can offer or sustain, (c) the ETL process that the data must go though, parts of which are simply non-replaceable (even if some cleaning is temporarily omitted, there are several transformation that simply have to be respected for schema and reference value compatibility of the produced data and the warehouse), and (d) the software and hardware configuration of the DPA. The overall goal is to satisfy as much as possible the end users, concerning the volume and freshness of the produced data (in other words: the DPA must maximize the throughput of produced data), without sacrificing any strong constraints on these values and to minimize the resources spent for this purpose. The technical decisions that must be taken, concern the following aspects:

- It is possible that the DPA must resort to the reservation of a certain amount of incoming records, so that the DPA can meet the abovementioned throughput for all the workflows that are hosted there. In this case, a first decision must be made on whether the server needs or can perform tuple reservation and a second decision must be made on how many and which tuples will be reserved. A very important architectural decision involves whether the reservation of tuples will be performed once, at the reception of data from the sources, or many times, within several activities in the ETL workflows.

- A second important problem concerns the scheduling of the ETL workflows in the DPA server. This is a classical scheduling problem at a first sight; nevertheless, complicated workflows, each with several activities are involved, requiring scheduling policies that are both simple (and thus, quick to decide) and reasonably accurate.

- Apart from the assignment of CPU cycles to workflows and activities, a third problem concerns the allocation of main memory to workflows and activities. This is a very important decision, possibly more important than the scheduling protocol, since the problem faced in near real time ETL workflows is a main memory processing problem, to a large extent.
- Finally, given the above particularities, there is always the problem of deciding the optimal configuration of the involved ETL workflows, both at the physical and the logical level. The problem is more intense since very few results already exist for the traditional case of ETL.

Variants of the above problems do exist, too. For example, instead of a global scheduling policy, one could think of eddie-like self-adaptive activities that take local decisions. This can be generalized to the overall architecture of the near real data warehouse. Micro- and macro-economic models can also be employed [34]. Another clear variant of the overall problem, with significant importance for the design of the DPA, involves fixing some of the desired measures (source rates, throughput) and trying to determine the best possible configuration for the DPA server. Finally, it should be stressed that the research community is not equipped with appropriate benchmarks to experiment with; this creates problems both for the validity of experimental results and for the repeatability of the experiments.

2.3.5.4 Flow regulation between the Data Processing Area and the data warehouse

Once data pass through the transformation and cleaning process in the data processing area they have to be loaded at the data warehouse. In the traditional ETL setting, this problem had a straightforward solution: all data would pass through the appropriate data loader, which is a vendor specific tool that takes care of the loading of data in a manner that is more efficient than any other alternative. Apart from the dimension and fact tables of the warehouse, special care is taken for any indexes or materialized views, too. In the case of near real time ETL, the luxury of the off-line idle warehouse that is loaded with data is no longer available and a new architecture must be investigated mainly due to the fact that the warehouse server is used by the end users for querying purposes at the same time that data are loaded to the queried tables or materialized views.

We envision an architecture where the flow of data from the DPA to the warehouse is regulated by a *data Warehouse Flow Regulator* (WFlowR) so that (a) the warehouse receives data according to the demands of users for freshness and completeness, (b) the querying processes that are initiated by the users are not significantly delayed and (c) no data are lost at the DPA side due to the overflow of produced tuples as compared to the availability of loading at the warehouse side. The ultimate desideratum is to maximize the satisfaction of the above antagonizing goals while spending as few system resources as possible in terms of main memory, hard disk and CPU cycles.

The technical issues that arise are similar to the case of flow regulation between sources and the DPA and can be listed as follows:

- Once again, we need to take care of communication protocols, compression and encryption as well as a decision on the granularity of transmitted data.
- A scheduling policy concerning the order of data transmission is important. More important than that, though, is the issue of modus operandi, which offers the following options: (a) periodic, (b) push-based, propagating blocks of produced records to the warehouse as they come and (c) pull-based, where the scheduler decides to push data towards the warehouse given a request by the users or a predicted decrease of the warehouse load. As already mentioned, we anticipate the DPA to be the means to alleviate the possible overload of the sources and the warehouse and therefore, we find the second alternative less likely to be of practical use in warehouses with high load. On the contrary, this is a really useful solution for underused warehouses.
- Again, since the warehouse load, the user requests, and the tuple production are antagonizing goals, it is possible to perform a certain amount of tuple reservation in an attempt to produce a solution that respects all the possible constraints and maximizes a satisfaction function that combines the above goals.

2.3.5.5 Technical issues concerning the Warehouse

The data warehouse side of the ETL process is responsible for refreshing the contents of the warehouse with newly produced data that come all the way from the sources. This task is called *Loading* (the 'L' in the E-T-L triplet) and comprises the following sub-tasks, in the following order:

- Loading of the dimension tables with lookup, reference values
- Loading of the fact tables with factual data
- Maintenance of indexes and materialized views

In a traditional ETL environment, this task is performed via vendor specific tools called loaders, when the data warehouse is idle -or even off-line. To this day, vendor-specific loaders are the fastest way to implement the loading of data to a relational database. Also, dropping and recreating the indexes is sometimes of comparable time and efficiency with respect to storage and querying than incrementally maintaining them. Unfortunately, the luxury of an idle warehouse is not present in a near real time warehouse, where the loading has to take place concurrently with the answering of queries posed by the end users. Therefore, the near real time warehouse has to find an equilibrium between two antagonizing goals, the near real time refreshment of its contents and the on-line answering of queries posed by the end users. This antagonism has at least two facets:

- A contention for server resources, such as main memory and CPU cycles, that has a clear impact on the performance (at least as far as the end users perceive it.)
- A contention for database resources, such as transaction locks, in the case of strict isolation levels (although, we anticipate that the user requests for consistency of the data they receive is low - and in any case, contradicting the requirement for as fresh data as possible.)

The technical topics that result from this problem concern the hardware configuration of the warehouse, the design of the data warehouse, and the implementation of a loading mechanism that maximizes data freshness without delaying user queries above a certain tolerance level. Specifically, these topics can be detailed as follows.

A first concern involves the hardware configuration of a data warehouse. Although warehouses are not as rigid hardware environments as sources are, still, it is not straightforward how to migrate an existing warehouse to a highly parallel and partitioned architecture that is probably needed for a near real time warehouse. Moreover, the scientific community is not in possession of a cost model that can relate the extent of parallelism and partitioning required to sustain a near real time ETL process along with on-line querying.

A second concern, with a clear research challenge involves the design of the data warehouse. For the moment, a warehouse is built on the basis of a star or snowflake schema, combined with bitmap of B+ tree indexes for performance reasons. On top of these constructs, data marts, reports, web pages and materialized views are also maintained by the refreshment process, once data have been loaded to the fact tables. Remember that so far, in the context of our deliberations, we have abstracted all these constructs as materialized views. The research question that arises asks whether new kind of schema structures, along with novel kinds of indexes and even, novel kinds of materialized views are necessary for the implementation of near real time data warehousing.

A third topic involves a scheduling problem: in what order do we schedule the loading of the data warehouse tables, and what time windows are allowed for each table, every time we activate a loading process? Naturally, this problem spans both traditional relations and data structures as well as the aforementioned novel structures that might prove useful for near real time warehousing. A parameter of the problem that might possibly complicate the solution has to do with the refreshment strategy: different choices have to be made in the case where the strategy is periodic as opposed to the case where the strategy is pull-based. Obviously, in the case of partitioning and parallelism, the problem is complicated (although the available computing power is much more) since we need to schedule the simultaneous loading of different constructs or parts of them.

A final topic of research concerns both the warehouse and the flow regulation towards it and has to do with the monitoring of the current workload and the forecast of the forthcoming workload in the very near future. Monitoring is a problem per se, since it has to trade off accuracy with simplicity and a small footprint. Predicting the near future in terms of user load is even harder, to a large extent due to the irregular nature of the behavior of the users. Still, any form of scheduling for the

ETL process requires some estimation for the forthcoming user load and thus, a reasonable accurate such estimation is valuable.

2.3.6 Summing up

Coming back to the big picture, the main idea is that the data processing area has to be regulated so that the user request for fresh and complete data is balanced against the computational needs of (a) the source systems (due to their regular workload and the non-negotiable nature of their configuration and performance), (b) the data processing area (due to the rigid necessity for transforming, and sometimes, cleaning source data to a schema and value set that is acceptable for the warehouse), and (c) the warehouse (due to the on-line support of user queries.) Both the user requests and the computational needs of the involved systems can be formulated in part as non-negotiable hard constraints and in part as negotiable soft constraints, accompanied by a satisfaction function that has to be maximized. This formulation can lead to a quality of service problem, provided that we have the means to relate the involved parameters and measures via a realistic cost model.

The overall problem for near real time data warehousing is reduced to the design and regulation of such an environment in terms of (a) hardware configuration, (b) software architecture and, given the above, (c) resource allocation so that an acceptable compromise can be found for all these antagonizing goals.

2.4 Related Work

Terminological issues

We believe it is worthwhile to spend some lines to discuss terminological issues. We have chosen to use the term near real time warehousing, despite the fact that different variants already exist for this name.

Why not *active* ETL or data warehousing? In [17], the term *active data warehousing* is used in the sense of what we now call near real time data warehousing -i.e., it refers to an environment "where data warehouses are updated as frequently as possible, due to the high demands of users for fresh data". Some years before, the term *active data warehouse* has also been used in [29, 33] to refer to a warehouse that is enriched with ECA rules that provide automatic reporting facilities whenever specific events occur and conditions are met.

We have decided not to use the term, both due to its relevance with active databases and due to its previous usage in a different context. The relevance to active databases is particularly important, since it carries the connotations of ECA rules and triggers as well as a tuple-level execution model for the triggering of the ETL process (as opposed to our understanding for a block-based execution model.)

Why not *real time* ETL or data warehousing? For obvious reasons, industry favors the term *real time* warehousing as it comes with the connotation of instant propagation of source changes to the warehouse [4, 28, 40]. As already mentioned, in this article, we take a more pragmatic approach, where there is a specified frequency for the propagation of changes to the warehouse in blocks of tuples. A second, important reason is that the term *real time* comes with hidden semantics in computer science: scheduling with "real time" constraints for successful completion before a specified deadline. Databases have also been related to such deadline constraints during the '90s, overloading the term even more [16]. Therefore, we decided to avoid this term, too.

Why *near real time* ETL? We believe that the term is the closest possible to the abovementioned industrial terminology and reflects quite accurately the meaning of the discussed concept. The term has also been used by a large industrial vendor (Oracle) in the past.

At the same time, we would also like to point out that other terms are available. Thiele et al [34] use the term *living data warehouse* environments. Oracle also uses the term *on-time data warehousing*. We find both these terms excellent candidates, too.

Traditional ETL

Despite the fact that the importance of this problem has already been recognized by industrial needs for more than two decades, only recently, with the turning of the century, research dealt with the challenging problem of ETL processes. Initial research efforts regarding traditional ETL processes have mainly focused on modeling and design issues. Several alternatives have been proposed for the conceptual design of ETL processes that use different formalisms and design methods as, for example, UML [35, 20], Semantic Web [31, 32], whilst some other efforts follows their own approach [39]. However, so far there is not a clear winner, since the admission of a standard unified method is not yet a fact. Additionally, logical models for ETL processes have been proposed too, e.g., [38].

Later on, during the last five years, research has dealt with challenges beyond the modeling of ETL processes. Some efforts towards the optimization of ETL processes have been proposed [30, 36], along with efforts related to individual operators, such as the DataMapper [5]. Although, we find research work on data cleaning [12, 11, 27], data fusion [3, 22], and schema mappings [13, 26] related to ETL processes, the work proposed on that fields originally was not directly connected to the ETL technology.

Apart from research efforts, currently, there is a plethora of ETL tools available in the market. All major database vendors provide ETL solutions and in fact, they practically ship ETL tools with their database software 'at no extra charge' [14, 21, 24]. Of course, there are plenty of other ETL tools by independent vendors, such as Informatica [15]. The former three tools have the benefit of the minimum cost, because they are shipped with the database, while ETL tools from the latter category have the benefit to aim at complex and deep solutions not envisioned by the generic products.

Efforts related to near real time ETL

Real time reporting. In [29, 33] the authors, discuss an architecture for near-real time reporting, which they call *active warehousing*. The active warehouse includes a rule-based engine at the warehouse side that is responsible of detecting whether any Event-Condition-Action (ECA) rule, registered by the user needs to be fired. The ECA rules that are registered by the user serve as the mechanism via which reports are generated to the user whenever certain events occur and specific conditions are met. The events are mostly temporal events or executions of methods at the OLTP systems. The action part of the rules can be either the local analysis of data at the warehouse or the combined analysis of warehouse with source data (obtained via a request to the OLTP system.)

The core of the approach lies in the fact that the warehouse is enriched with a rule-based engine that triggers the appropriate rules whenever certain phenomena take place at the data. Coarsely speaking, the user registers a sequence of (cube-based) reports that he/she wants to be generated whenever the data fulfill specific conditions; e.g., a certain trend is detected in the most current data.

There are significant differences with the near-real time architecture we discuss in this article. In [29, 33], the extraction is assumed to take place periodically and the loading is performed in an off-line fashion. In other words, the ETL part of warehousing is downplayed and the architecture mostly resembles an Enterprise Information Integration environment for real time reporting. Also, to the best of our knowledge, the presented papers are not accompanied by any published experimental results on the actual behavior of an active warehouse with respect to its effectiveness or efficiency.

Data Warehouse Partitioning and Replication. Node partitioned data warehouses have been investigated to a large extent by Furtado [9, 8, 10]. The main idea of node-partitioned warehousing is to employ a cluster of low cost interconnected computers as the hardware platform over which the warehouse is deployed. The cluster is a shared-nothing architecture of computers, each with its own storage devices and data are distributed to the nodes so as to parallelize the processing of user queries. The system configuration involves neither too expensive specialized mainframe servers, nor a parallel configuration with specialized connections among the nodes.

The main problems of node-partitioned warehousing are the placement of data to nodes, and the processing of queries given that placement. Since data warehouses comprise dimension tables that come both in small and large sizes, as well as facts of high volume, Furtado proposes a scheme where small dimensions are replicated in several nodes, large dimensions are partitioned on the basis of their primary keys and facts are partitioned on the basis of their workload, with the overall goal to balance query processing and data transfer in the cluster of nodes. Furtado has extensively experimented with alternative configurations for the placement of data in nodes.

Also, replication issues have been considered, to increase the fault-tolerance of the partitioned data warehouse.

Load Balancing. The paper [34] by Thiele et al, deals with the problem of managing the workload of the warehouse in a near real time warehouse (called real time warehouse by the authors.) The problem at the warehouse side is that data modifications arrive simultaneously with user queries, resulting in an antagonism for computational resources.

The authors discuss a load-balancing mechanism that schedules the execution of query and update transactions according to the preferences of the users. Since the antagonism between user queries and updates practically reflects the inherent conflict between the user requirement for data freshness and the user requirement for low response times, for each query the users pose, they have to specify the extent to which they are willing to trade off these two measures (which are also called Quality of Data and Quality of Service by the authors.) The scheduling algorithm, called WINE (Workload Balancing by Election), proposes a two-level scheduling scheme. The algorithm takes as input two queues, one for the queries and one for the updates and starts by deciding whether a query or an update will be processed. Since each query is annotated by a score for freshness and a score for fast processing, for each of these two categories, all the scores in the query queue are summed; the largest score decides whether a query or an update will take place. Then, once this decision has been made, a second decision must be made with respect to which transaction in the appropriate queue will be scheduled for processing.

Concerning the query queue, the system tries to prioritize queries with a preference towards low response time; at the same time, this also helps queries with higher preference for completeness to take advantage of any updates that concern them in the meantime. Actions against starvation are also taken by appropriately adjusting the QoS values for delayed query transactions. Concerning the update queue, updates that are related to queries that are close to the head of the query queue (thus, are close to been executed) are also prioritized. This is achieved by appropriately adjusting an importance weight for each update, according to their relevance to upcoming queries. Specific measures are taken to hold the consistency of the warehouse with respect to the order in which they arrive at the warehouse.

To the best of our knowledge, the paper is the only effort towards the load balancing of a near real time warehouse. Of course, the focus of the paper is clearly on the loading side, without any care for the extraction, transformation or cleaning part of the process. From our point of view this is a benefit of a layering and the near-real time nature of the architecture that we propose. We believe that the organization of updates in blocks and the isolation of the different concerns (Extract - Transform - Load) in different systems allow the derivation of useful algorithms for each task.

System choices. In [17], the authors propose a framework for the implementation of near real time warehouse (called "active" data warehousing by the authors), with the goals of: (a) minimal changes in the software configuration of the source, (b) minimal overhead for the source due to the "active" nature of data propagation, (c) the possibility of smoothly regulating the overall configuration of the environment in a principled way.

The paper was built upon the idea of separating the extraction, the transformation and cleaning and the loading tasks. In terms of system architecture, the ETL workflow is structured as a network of ETL activities, also called *ETL queues*, each pipelining blocks of tuples to its subsequent activities, once its filtering or transformation processing is completed. In order to perform this task, each ETL activity checks its queue (e.g., in a periodic fashion) to see whether data wait to be processed. Then, it picks a block of records, performs the processing and forwards them to the next stage. Queue theory is employed for the prediction of the performance and the tuning of the operation of the overall refreshment process. The extraction part in the paper involved ISAM sources and a simple method for extracting changes in legacy source systems, without much intervention to the system configuration was also demonstrated. The loading at the warehousing was performed via web services that received incoming blocks for the target tables and performed the loading.

The experiments proved that this architectural approach provides both minimum performance overhead at the source and the possibility of regulating the flow towards the warehouse. The experiments also proved that organizing the changes in blocks results in significant improvement in the throughput of the system and the avoidance of overloading of the sources.

The paper lacks a deep study of different activities involved in ETL scenarios (i.e., the activities employed were filters and aggregators, without a wider experimentation in terms of activity complexity.) Also, although the usage of queue theory seemed to be successful for the estimation of the processing rates of the ETL workflow, it has not been tested in workflows of arbitrary complexity (which hides the possibility of bringing queue theory to its limits.) Finally, web services are quite heavy, although they present a reliable (syntactically and operationally) and thus promising middleware, for the interoperability of the different parts of the system. Despite these shortcomings, the experimental setup and the architectural choices give a good insight to the internals of a near real time data warehouse and justify, to a broad extent, our previous discussion on the architecture of a near real time data warehouse.

Related areas

Another area related to our approach is the one of **active databases**. In particular, if conventional systems (rather than legacy ones) are employed, one might argue that the usage of triggers [6] could facilitate the on-line population of the warehouse. Still, related material suggests that triggers are not quite suitable for our purpose, since they can (a) slow down the source system and (b) require changes to the database configuration [4]. In [23] it is also stated that capture mechanisms at the data layer such as triggers have either a prohibitively large performance impact on the operational system.

2.5 Conclusions

The topic of this article has been near real time ETL. Our intention has been to sketch the big picture of providing end users with data that are clean, reconciled (and therefore, useful) while being as fresh as possible, at the same time, without compromising the availability or throughput of the source systems or the data warehouse. We have discussed how such a configuration is different from the setting of an ETL process in a traditional warehouse. We have sketched the high level architecture of such an environment and emphasized the QoS based characteristics we believe it should have. Moreover, we have discussed research topics that pertain to each of the components of the near real time warehouse, specifically, the sources, the data processing area, and the warehouse, along with issues related to the flow regulators that regulate the flow of data under data quality and system overhead "contracts".

Clearly, the importance, complexity and criticality of such an environment make near real time warehousing a significant topic of research and practice; therefore, we conclude with the hope that the abovementioned issues will be addressed in a principled manner in the future by both the industry and the academia.

References

1. J. Adzic and V. Fiore. Data Warehouse Population Platform. In *DMDW*, 2003.
2. Ascential Software Corporation. DataStage Enterprise Edition: Parallel Job Developer's Guide. In *Version 7.5, Part No. 00D-023DS75*, 2004.
3. J. Bleiholder, K. Draba, and F. Naumann. FuSem - Exploring Different Semantics of Data Fusion. In *VLDB*, pages 1350–1353, 2007.
4. D. Burleson. New Developments in Oracle Data Warehousing. In *the Web, available at: http://dba-oracle.com/oracle_news/2004_4_22_burleson.htm*, 2004.
5. P. J. F. Carreira, H. Galhardas, J. Pereira, and A. Lopes. Data Mapper: An Operator for Expressing One-to-Many Data Transformations. In *DaWaK*, pages 136–145, 2005.
6. S. Ceri and J. Widom. Deriving Production Rules for Incremental View Maintenance. In *VLDB*, pages 577–589, 1991.
7. M. Demarest. The Politics of Data Warehousing. In *the Web, available at: http://www.noumenal.com/marc/dwpoly.html*, June 1997.
8. P. Furtado. Experimental Evidence on Partitioning in Parallel Data Warehouses. In *DOLAP*, pages 23–30, 2004.
9. P. Furtado. Workload-Based Placement and Join Processing in Node-Partitioned Data Warehouses. In *DaWaK*, pages 38–47, 2004.
10. P. Furtado. *Data Warehouses and OLAP: Concepts, Architectures and Solutions*, chapter Efficient and Robust Node-Partitioned Data Warehouses. IRM Press (Idea Group), January 2007.
11. H. Galhardas, D. Florescu, D. Shasha, and E. Simon. AJAX: An Extensible Data Cleaning Tool. In *SIGMOD Conference*, page 590, 2000.
12. H. Galhardas, D. Florescu, D. Shasha, E. Simon, and C.-A. Saita. Declarative Data Cleaning: Language, Model, and Algorithms. In *VLDB*, pages 371–380, 2001.
13. L. M. Haas, M. A. Hernández, H. Ho, L. Popa, and M. Roth. Clio Grows Up: from Research Prototype to Industrial Tool. In *SIGMOD Conference*, pages 805–810, 2005.
14. IBM. IBM Data Warehouse Manager. In *the Web, available at: http://www-3.ibm.com/software/data/db2/datawarehouse/*, 2005.

15. Informatica.   PowerCenter.   In *the   Web,   available   at: http://www.informatica.com/products/powercenter/*, 2005.
16. B. Kao and H. Garcia-Molina. An Overview of Real-Time Database Systems. In Springer-Verlag, editor, *Proceedings of NATO Advanced Study Institute on Real-Time Computing. Available at: http://dbpubs.stanford.edu/pub/1993-6*, October 9 1992.
17. A. Karakasidis, P. Vassiliadis, and E. Pitoura. ETL queues for active data warehousing. In *IQIS*, pages 28–39, 2005.
18. R. Kimball and J. Caserta. *The Data Warehouse ETL Toolkit (chapter 11)*. Wiley Publishing, Inc., 2004.
19. D. E. Linstedt. ETL, ELT - Challenges and Metadata. In *the Web, available at: http://www.b-eye-network.com/blogs/linstedt/archives/2006/12/etl_elt_challen.php*, December 2006.
20. S. Luján-Mora, P. Vassiliadis, and J. Trujillo. Data Mapping Diagrams for Data Warehouse Design with UML. In *ER*, pages 191–204, 2004.
21. Microsoft.   Data   Transformation   Services.   In *the   Web,   available   at: http://www.microsoft.com/sql/prodinfo/features/*, 2005.
22. F. Naumann, A. Bilke, J. Bleiholder, and M. Weis. Data Fusion in Three Steps: Resolving Schema, Tuple, and Value Inconsistencies. *IEEE Data Eng. Bull.*, 29(2):21–31, 2006.
23. Oracle. On-Time Data Warehousing with Oracle 10g - Information at the Speed of your Business. In *the Web, available at: http://www.oracle.com/technology/products/bi/pdf/10gr1_-twp_bi_ontime_etl.pd*, August 2003.
24. Oracle. Oracle Database Data Warehousing Guide 11g Release 1 (11.1). In *the Web, available at: http://www.oracle.com/pls/db111/portal.portal_db?selected=6*, September 2007.
25. N. Polyzotis, S. Skiadopoulos, P. Vassiliadis, A. Simitsis, and N. Frantzell. Meshing Streaming Updates with Persistent Data in an Active Data Warehouse. *IEEE Trans. Knowl. Data Eng.*, 20(7), 2008.
26. E. Rahm and P. A. Bernstein. A Survey of Approaches to Automatic Schema Matching. *VLDB J.*, 10(4):334–350, 2001.
27. V. Raman and J. M. Hellerstein. Potter's Wheel: An Interactive Data Cleaning System. In *VLDB*, pages 381–390, 2001.
28. M. Rittman. Implementing Real-Time Data Warehousing Using Oracle 10g. In *the Web, available at: http://www.dbazine.com/datawarehouse/dw-articles/rittman5*, 2006.
29. M. Schrefl and T. Thalhammer. On Making Data Warehouses Active. In *DaWaK*, pages 34–46, 2000.
30. A. Simitsis, P. Vassiliadis, and T. K. Sellis. State-Space Optimization of ETL Workflows. *IEEE Trans. Knowl. Data Eng.*, 17(10):1404–1419, 2005.
31. D. Skoutas and A. Simitsis. Designing ETL Processes Using Semantic Web Technologies. In *DOLAP*, pages 67–74, 2006.
32. D. Skoutas and A. Simitsis. Ontology-Based Conceptual Design of ETL Processes for Both Structured and Semi-Structured Data. *Int. J. Semantic Web Inf. Syst.*, 3(4):1–24, 2007.
33. T. Thalhammer, M. Schrefl, and M. K. Mohania. Active Data Warehouses: Complementing OLAP with Analysis Rules. *Data Knowl. Eng.*, 39(3):241–269, 2001.
34. M. Thiele, U. Fischer, and W. Lehner. Partition-based Workload Scheduling in Living Data Warehouse Environments. In *DOLAP*, pages 57–64, 2007.
35. J. Trujillo and S. Luján-Mora. A UML Based Approach for Modeling ETL Processes in Data Warehouses. In *ER*, pages 307–320, 2003.
36. V. Tziovara, P. Vassiliadis, and A. Simitsis. Deciding the Physical Implementation of ETL Workflows. In *DOLAP*, pages 49–56, 2007.
37. P. Vassiliadis, A. Karagiannis, V. Tziovara, and A. Simitsis. Towards a Benchmark for ETL Workflows. In *QDB*, pages 49–60, 2007.
38. P. Vassiliadis, A. Simitsis, P. Georgantas, M. Terrovitis, and S. Skiadopoulos. A generic and customizable framework for the design of ETL scenarios. *Inf. Syst.*, 30(7):492–525, 2005.
39. P. Vassiliadis, A. Simitsis, and S. Skiadopoulos. Conceptual modeling for ETL processes. In *DOLAP*, pages 14–21, 2002.
40. C. White. Intelligent Business Strategies: Real-Time Data Warehousing Heats Up. In *DM Review. Available at: http://www.dmreview.com/article_sub.cfm?articleId=5570*, August 2002.

Chapter 3
Data Warehousing Meets MDA
A Case Study for Multidimensional Modeling

Jose-Norberto Mazón and Juan Trujillo

Abstract Multidimensional (MD) models are the cornerstone of data warehouse (DW) systems since they allow users to better understand data for decision support, while the performance is improved. MD modeling consists of several phases in the same way as traditional database design: conceptual, logical and physical. In this paper, we argue that designing a conceptual MD model of a DW and deriving its logical representation are very complex, prone to fail, and time consuming tasks. Specifically, two main issues must be considered: (i) the joint analysis of both, information needs of decision makers, and the available operational data sources that will populate the DW, in order to obtain a conceptual MD model, and (ii) the development of formal and automatic transformations between the conceptual and logical design phases. However, no significant effort has been done to take into account these issues in a systematic, well structured and comprehensive development process. To overcome the lack of such process, in this paper, the MD modeling of the DW is aligned with the Model Driven Architecture (MDA) by specifying how to design the different kind of models (CIM, PIM, and PSM), and the required Query/View/Transformation (QVT) transformations between them. To exemplify every part of our approach, a case study is provided throughout the paper.

3.1 Introduction

Data warehouse (DW) systems integrate huge amounts of historical data from operational sources, thus providing useful information for decision makers in an organization. Both practitioners and researchers agree that the development of these systems must be based on the multidimensional (MD) modeling [7, 9], which structures information into facts and dimensions. A fact contains interesting measures (fact attributes) of a business process (sales, deliveries, etc.), whereas a dimen-

Dept. of Software and Computing Systems, University of Alicante, e-mail: {jnmazon, jtrujillo}@dlsi.ua.es

sion represents the context for analyzing a fact (product, customer, time, etc.) by means of dimension attributes hierarchically organized[1]. Specialized design approaches for MD modeling have been come up to reduce its inherent complexity [8, 29]. Most approaches start defining a conceptual MD model and then, deriving its logical representation. Conceptual design provides mechanisms to specify an implementation-independent MD model either from operational data sources (bottom-up approaches [5, 6, 11, 34]) or from user requirements (top-down approaches[3, 28, 30, 36]), while the logical design aims at deriving a logical model tailored to one specific database technology on the basis of the conceptual model. The implementation of a DW is then based on a set of guidelines and heuristics to derive a logical representation of the conceptual model, thus trying to reduce the semantic gap between them [29]. However, no significant effort has been done to develop an overall approach which

1. combines both a top-down and a bottom-up strategies in an integrated fashion (i.e. considering data sources and information needs of decision makers in early stages of the development), and
2. bridges the semantic gap between conceptual and logical representations, by means of formal and easy-to-use mechanisms, that allow designers to preserve all information captured by advanced conceptual MD models in logical representations, thus avoiding the very tedious, repetitive and prone to fail task of manually applying guidelines.

Considering the above-mentioned drawbacks, in this paper, we describe how to align the MD modeling for DWs with the Model Driven Architecture (MDA) [22] by means of a case study. In concrete, within our MDA-based approach, a conceptual MD model of the DW is developed from user requirements. This initial MD model must be then reconciled with the data sources. The following step is to apply model transformations to automatically obtain several logical models as a basis of the implementation of the DW. In this paper, we describe each element of this approach. First, there is a Computation Independent Model (CIM) for DWs based on the i* framework [37] which contains the main user requirements of the DW. There is also a Platform Independent Model (PIM) based on our UML (Unified Modeling Language) profile [25] for conceptual MD modeling [11]. A set of Query/View/Transformation (QVT) [23] relations for reconciling the PIM with the available operational data sources is also defined. Then, different Platform Specific Models (PSMs) can be developed as logical models depending on the underlying database technology. Different packages of the Common Warehouse Metamodel (CWM) [20, 21] are used to define each PSM. Finally, we have also defined a set of QVT transformation rules in order to obtain the final implementation of the MD model of the DW.

The remainder of this paper is structured as follows. Section 3.2 presents how MDA has been used until now in DW development. Section 3.3 describes our MDA-based approach for MD modeling of DWs. Throughout this section, a case study is

---

[1] We refer reader to [33] for a further explanation of the different characteristics of MD modeling.

used to clarify every theoretical concept. The implementation of our approach by using a well-known CASE tool is briefly described in Section 3.4. Finally, we point out our conclusions in Section 3.5.

3.2 Related Work

MDA has been successfully used in several application domains, such as web services [1], web applications [18], development of user interfaces [35], and so on. However, to the best of our knowledge, only one effort has been developed for aligning the design of DWs with the general MDA framework, the Model Driven Data Warehousing (MDDW) [27]. This approach is based on CWM [20], which is a metamodel definition for interchanging DW specifications between different platforms and tools. Basically, CWM provides a set of metamodels that are comprehensive enough to model an entire DW including data sources, ETL processes, DW repository, and so on. These metamodels are intended to be generic, external representations of shared metadata. The proposed MDDW is based on modeling a complete DW by using elements from various CWM packages. However, as stated in [17], CWM metamodels are (i) too generic to represent all peculiarities of MD modeling in a conceptual model (i.e. PIM), and (ii) too complex to be handled by both final users and designers. Furthermore, a requirement analysis phase is not taken into account in the MDDW approach. Therefore, we deeply believe that it is more reliable to design a CIM by using a well-proven requirement analysis technique in order to assure that the information needs will be addressed, and then deriving a conceptual model of this CIM as a PIM based on a rich conceptual modeling approach easy to be handled. Then, this PIM should be checked against data sources and transformed into a CWM-compliant PSM in order to assure the interchange of DW metadata between different platforms and tools.

3.3 Multidimensional Modeling of Data Warehouses with MDA

A DW is an integrated collection of historical data in support of management's decisions. According to this definition, in the MD modeling for the DW, it is not only important to take into account the information needs of decision makers, but also the existing data sources that will populate the DW. On the other hand, the MD modeling of the DW resembles the traditional database design methods because it is widely accepted [6] that the design of such repository must be structured into a variety of steps during which a conceptual design phase is performed, whose results are transformed into a logical data model as the basis of schema implementation. This way of proceeding claims for the automation of these transformations. In this section, we define an MDA approach for the MD modeling of DWs in a systematic, well structured and comprehensive way. Our aim is to improve the MD modeling by facing two key issues: (i) user requirement and data sources must be considered together in early stages of the development (i.e. by combining both bottom-up and top down approaches), and (ii) formal transformations must be established to obtain the final implementation of the MD model in an automatic way, thus bridging the semantic gap between conceptual and logical models. In Fig. 3.1, we show a symbolic diagram that will help to understand our approach:

- The requirements are modeled in a CIM.
- An initial PIM is derived from a CIM. This PIM specifies every MD property without taking into account any database technology.
- The initial PIM is directly obtained from user requirements and it must be checked that this PIM agrees with the available operational data sources in a reconciling process. This process is done by using several QVT relations based on a set of multidimensional normal forms.
- Several PSMs are derived from a PIM, thus taking into account the different platforms in which the DW could be deployed (relational, multidimensional, etc.). The transformations between PIM and PSM are formally defined by using QVT.
- From every PSM the necessary code is derived. However, the PSM is close to the corresponding database technology, and then it is quite straightforward to derive this code. Thus, we do not develop this issue in this paper, and we focus on the other above-presented models and transformations.

In this section, a case study is introduced in order to better show how to apply our approach. It is based on a case study from [4] and relates to a company that comprises different dealerships that sell automobiles across several countries. This case study will be referenced throughout this section.

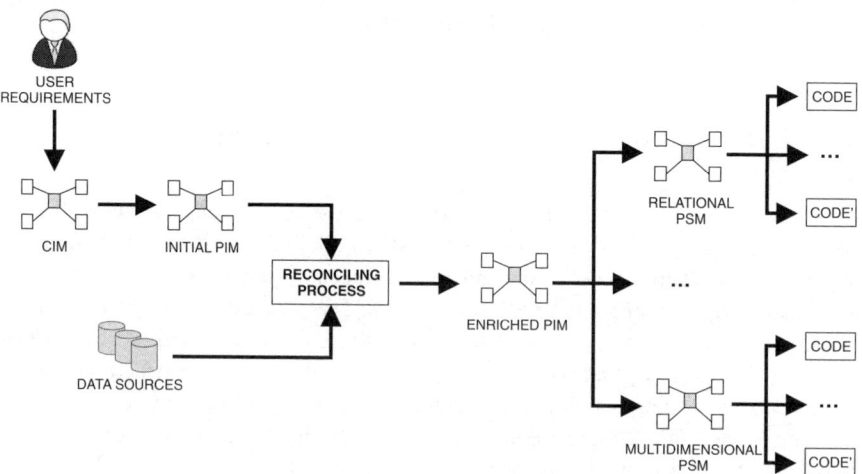

Fig. 3.1 Overview of our MDA-based approach for the MD modeling of DWs.

3.3.1 A Multidimensional Computation Independent Model

Specifying requirements allows designers to develop a DW which meets the real needs of organizations, thus increasing the success of a DW project [30]. Importantly, this task is not trivial, since it is related to understand and specify decision processes, so there is a major gap between those that are experts in the domain and their requirements on the one hand (i.e., decision makers) and those that are experts in the design and construction of the DW which satisfies the requirements (i.e., DW developers), on the other hand. Following an MDA approach allows to overcome this problem, since the requirements for the DW are modeled in a Computation Independent Model (CIM) and they will be traceable to the following design phases. A CIM shows the system in the environment in which it will operate, thus helping to present exactly what the system is expected to do. Therefore, our CIM describes the DW requirements within its business environment, so it plays an important role in bridging the above-mentioned gap. Our CIM is defined according to the approach presented in [13]. In this approach, for each decision maker we define the goals that a DW helps to achieve and their corresponding information requirements (i.e. data provided by the DW to achieve goals) as follows. First, *strategic goals* must be specified. They are main objectives of the business process. They are thought as changes from a current situation into a better one. For example: "increase sales", "increase number of customers", "decrease cost", etc. Their fulfillment causes an immediate benefit for the organization. Once strategic goals are defined, *decision goals* must be specified. They aim to take the appropriate actions to fulfill a strategic goal (i.e. how can a strategic goal be achieved?). For example, "determine some kind of promotion" or "open new stores". Their fulfillment only causes a benefit for the organization if they help to reach strategic goals. Finally, *information goals* must be specified from decision goals. They are related to the information required by a decision goal to be achieved. For example, "analyze customer purchases" or "examine stocks". Their fulfillment helps to achieve decision goals. *Information requirements* can be directly obtained from the information goals above-described. These requirements are related to interesting measures of business processes (contained in facts) and the context for analyzing these measures (dimensions and their hierarchies). Then, the MD elements needed for achieving the defined goals can be obtained from these information requirements.

In order to model strategic, decision and information goals, as well as information requirements in a CIM, we have adapted the i* framework [37] for the DW domain by means of a UML profile. The different elements of i* are shown in Table 3.1. On the basis of these i* elements, we have extended this profile by including new stereotypes for modeling strategic goals, decision, goals, information goals (goals stereotyped as STRATEGIC, DECISION or INFORMATION), and information requirements (tasks stereotyped as REQUIREMENT) [13]. Furthermore, the requirement analysis for DWs needs some MD concepts to be added (in the sense of [3]). Therefore, the following concepts are added as resources in the CIM: business processes related to strategic goals of decision makers (BUSINESSPROCESS stereotype), relevant measures related to information requirements of decision makers (MEASURE), and contexts needed for analyzing these measures (CONTEXT). Additionally, foreseen relations between contexts of analysis can be modeled. For instance, the *city* and the *country* contexts are related because cities can be aggregated in countries. For modeling these relationships, we use the (shared) aggregation relationship of UML (ASSOCIATION UML metaclass).

Table 3.1 Main stereotypes of the UML profile for i*.

Stereotype	Extends	Description	Icon
ACTOR	Class	It is an entity that carries out actions to perform goals. It is related to several intentional elements (goal, task or resource).	
GOAL	Class	It is a condition or state that the stakeholder would like to achieve. In the DW context, strategic, decision and information goals can be represented by using it.	
TASK	Class	It represents a particular way of doing something. In the DW context a task is related to the way that the data is required (information requirement).	
RESOURCE	Class	It is an entity which must be available to be used. In the DW context a resource is related to a piece of data, e.g. a measure.	
MEANS-ENDS	Association	It describes how goals are achieved by representing which are the necessary elements for achieving the goal.	
DECOMPOSITION	Association	It defines what other elements need to be available in order to perform a task.	

In summary, several steps must be followed to properly define a CIM: (i) discovering the actors (i.e. decision makers), (ii) discovering their goals according to the classification previously described, (iii) deriving information requirements from information goals, and (iv) obtaining the MD concepts related to the information requirements. Furthermore, how to obtain an initial PIM from the CIM must be also specified (as we state in the next section).

Our case study relates to a company that comprises different dealerships that sell automobiles across several countries. In this case study, we focus on the "sales manager" actor (as it is shown in Fig. 3.2). The strategic goal of the sales manager is "increase automobile sales". From this strategic goal three different decision goals are derived: "decrease sale price", "determine promotion according to a country", and "give incentive to salespersons". From each of these decision goals the following information goals have been obtained: "analyze automobile price", "analyze automobile sales", and "study salesperson sales". The information requirements obtained are as follows: "analyze the automobile sale price", "analyze the amount of automobile sold by customer age", "analyze total amount by customer, city and country", and "analyze total amount by salesperson and date". In Fig. 3.2, each of these elements are defined as goals (strategic, decision, and information goals) or tasks (information requirements) according to our UML profile for using the i* framework in the DW domain.

Finally, the information requirements allow us to consider some MD elements. Specifically, the measures are *quantity*, *price*, and *total*, and the elements that represent the context of analysis are *salesperson*, *date*, and *automobile*. *Customer*, *age*, *city*, and *country* also represent the context of analysis, and they are related each other, since they are useful for aggregating the customer data.

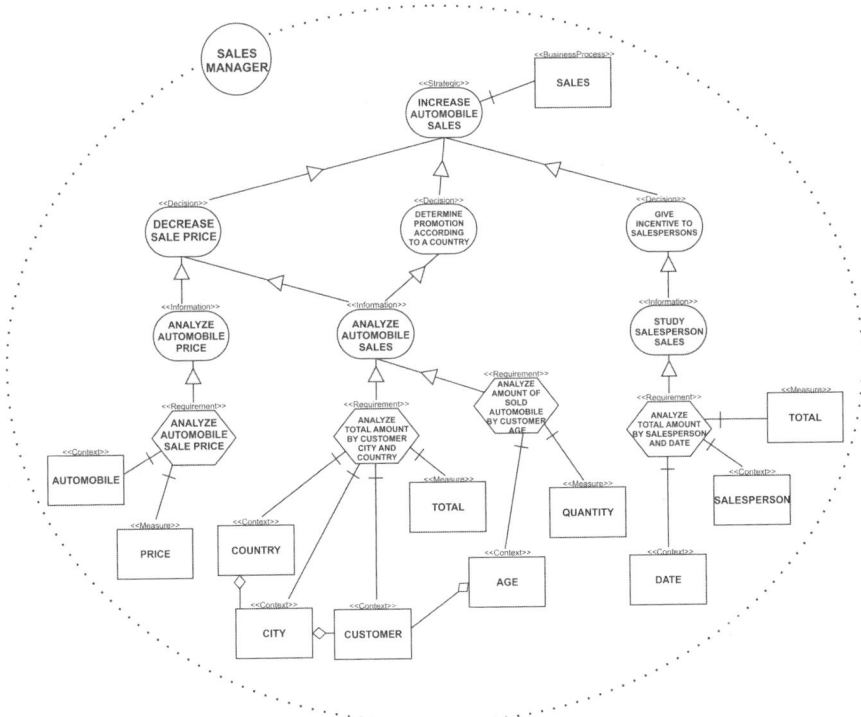

Fig. 3.2 i* model for sales manager actor.

3.3.2 A Multidimensional Platform Independent Model

A PIM is a view of a system from the platform independent viewpoint [22]. This means that this model describes the system hiding the necessary details related to a particular platform. This point of view corresponds to the representation of the MD elements at a conceptual level. The major aim at this level is to specify the main MD properties without taking into account any specific technology detail, therefore the specification of the MD model is independent from the platform in which it will be implemented. This PIM is developed following our UML profile for MD modeling presented in [11]. This profile contains the necessary stereotypes in order to elegantly represent MD properties at the conceptual level (see Table 3.2), via a UML class diagram.

Our profile is formally defined and uses the Object Constraint Language (OCL) [24] for expressing well-formed rules of the new defined elements, thereby avoiding its arbitrary use. We refer the reader to [11] for a further explanation of this profile and its corresponding OCL constraints.

We have developed a set of QVT relations for obtaining an initial PIM from the CIM. In this paper we describe one of these relations: OBTAINFACT (see Fig. 3.3). In this relation, the source domain is a set of elements of the CIM that represents the hierarchy of strategic, decision, and information goals of decision makers. This hierarchy is built on PROPERTY and CLASS (stereotyped as STRATEGIC, DECISION, or INFORMATION) UML metaclasses. An information requirement is also

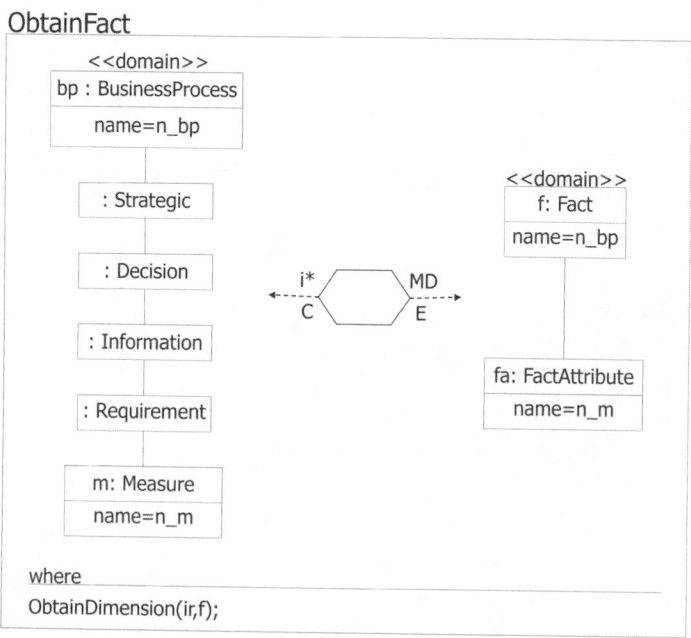

Fig. 3.3 Obtaining *fact* classes and their attributes via a QVT relation.

Table 3.2 Main stereotypes of our UML profile for MD modeling of DWs.

Stereotype	Extends	Description	Icon
FACT	Class	Classes of this stereotype represent facts in an MD model, consisting of measures (the values being analyzed).	
DIMENSION	Class	They represent dimensions in an MD model, consisting on hierarchy levels.	
BASE	Class	Classes of this stereotype represent dimension hierarchy levels consisting of dimension attributes.	**B**
FACTATTRIBUTE	Property	These properties represent attributes of a fact (i.e. measures) in an MD model. It can represent a derived measure, thus including a derivation rule.	**FA**
DIMENSIONATTRIBUTE	Property	They represent descriptive information of a dimension hierarchy level in an MD model.	**DA**
DESCRIPTOR	Property	They represent descriptor attributes of a dimension hierarchy level in an MD model.	**D**
ROLLS-UPTO	Association	They represent relationships between two BASE classes. Role R represents the direction in which the hierarchy rolls-up, and role D represents the direction in which the hierarchy drills-down.	—

represented by using the REQUIREMENT stereotype. Finally, a strategic goal is related to a business process (BUSINESSPROCESS), while the information requirement is related to a measure (MEASURE). The OBTAINFACT relation enforces the following set of elements in the PIM: a fact (FACT stereotype) containing one fact attribute (FACTATTRIBUTE). Once this relation holds, the OBTAINDIMENSION relation must be carried out (according to the *where* clause) in order to derive every required dimension and their hierarchies in the initial PIM. For instance, when the OBTAINFACT relation is executed in our case study, it takes the previously defined CIM (Fig. 3.2) as an input to create certain MD elements in the PIM. This relation creates a *sales* fact related with the *sales* business process, and, following the hierarchy of goals "increase automobile sales"→"determine promotion according to a country"→"analyze automobile sales"→"analyze total amount by customer city and country", when the relation finds the *total* measure, the corresponding fact attribute associated with the *sales* fact is created. The OBTAINFACT relation is executed as many times as the pattern of the source domain of the QVT relation is found in the CIM. Therefore, the *price* and *quantity* fact attributes are also created. Additionally, the *where* clause of the relation is executed, then dimensions and their hierarchies are also created from the related contexts and aggregations modeled in the CIM. After applying every QVT relation to the defined CIM, an initial PIM is obtained (i.e. the conceptual MD model of Fig. 3.4). This PIM delivers enough information in a suitable way to accomplish the information requirements and goals of decision makers. From now on, we describe our approach by focusing on the *customer* dimension of this initial PIM.

3.3.3 Reconciling a Multidimensional Model with Data Sources

Since the DW integrates the information provided by data sources, it is crucial not only taking into account the requirements, but also the data sources in early stage of the development process. Therefore, once a first initial PIM has been derived from the CIM, it must be reconciled with the available data sources in order to assure,

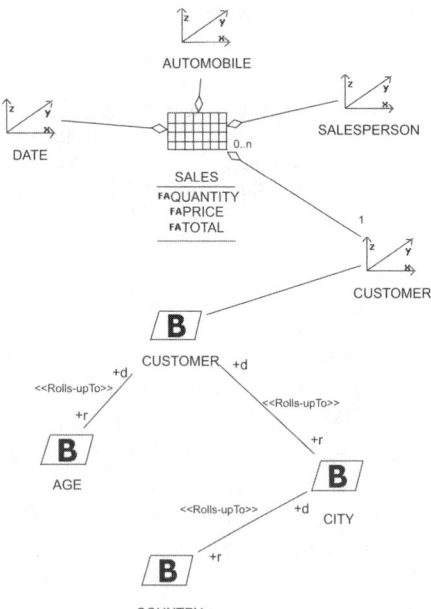

Fig. 3.4 Initial PIM derived from information requirements.

among others properties [10], that analysis potential provided by the data sources is captured by the PIM, and that the PIM represents a MD model that will be properly populated from the available data sources. To this aim, several QVT relations have been developed [15, 16] based on multidimensional normal forms [10]. These QVT relations enforce the above commented properties in the PIM by creating, deleting or modifying the necessary MD elements. We assume that the data source model is the relational representation of the data sources in third normal form. In concrete, we model the data sources with the CWM relational metamodel, since it is a standard to represent the structure of data resources according to a relational database. On the other hand, this data source model must be marked before the QVT relations can be applied. Marking models is a technique that provides mechanisms to extend elements of the models in order to capture additional information [19, 22]. Marks are used in MDA to prepare the models in order to guide the matching between them. A mark represents a concept from one model, which can be applied to an element of other different model. These marks indicate how every element of the source model must be matched. In our approach, the data source model is marked by appending a suffix to the name of each element according to the MD conceptual model. In particular, we assume that the data source tables which correspond to FACT, DIMENSION, and BASE are marked with the suffixes *FACT*, *DIM*, and *BASE*, respectively; while data source columns which correspond to FACTAT-TRIBUTE, DIMENSIONATTRIBUTE, and DESCRIPTOR are marked with *MEASURE*, *DA*, and *D*. Finally, a foreign key representing a ROLLS-UPTO association is marked with *ROLLS*.

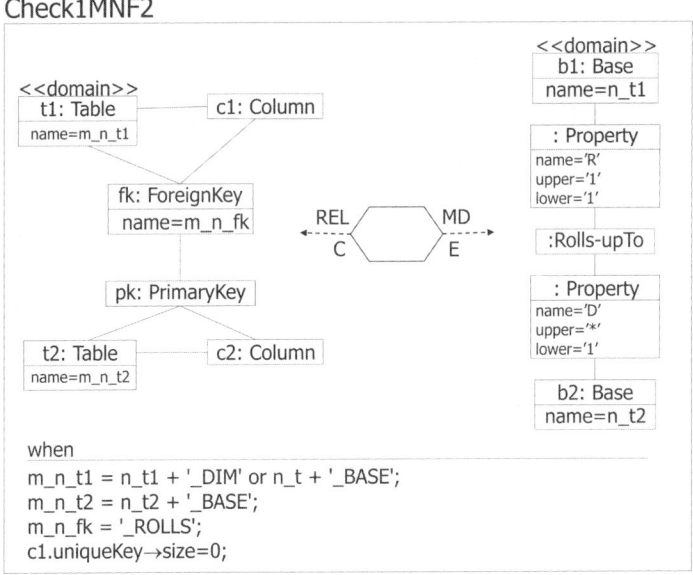

Fig. 3.5 Check1MNF2 checks if the analysis potential provided by the data sources is captured.

To gain an insight into this reconciling process between MD model and data sources, the CHECK1MNF2 relation is shown in Fig. 3.5 (see [16] for a comprehensive description of other QVT relations). This relation checks that the analysis potential provided by the data sources is captured by the PIM, according to the first multidimensional normal form [10] (i.e. the functional dependencies among dimension levels contained in the source databases must be represented as roll-up associations in the PIM). Therefore, when this relation holds, then there exists a ROLLS-UPTO association between BASES in the PIM if there is a functional dependency between columns of different tables in the data source model.

After applying every QVT relation to the initial PIM (see Fig. 3.4) and the available data sources for our case study (Fig. 3.6), the new enriched PIM can be seen in Fig. 3.7. This enriched PIM includes the following changes regarding the initial PIM: (i) the derivation rule for the derived fact attribute *total*, (ii) the deletion of the BASE class *age*, converting it into a dimension attribute that belongs to the *customer* hierarchy level, and (iii) the inclusion of each attribute (and its type) in the BASE classes. In this way, the enriched PIM of our case study captures the analysis poten-

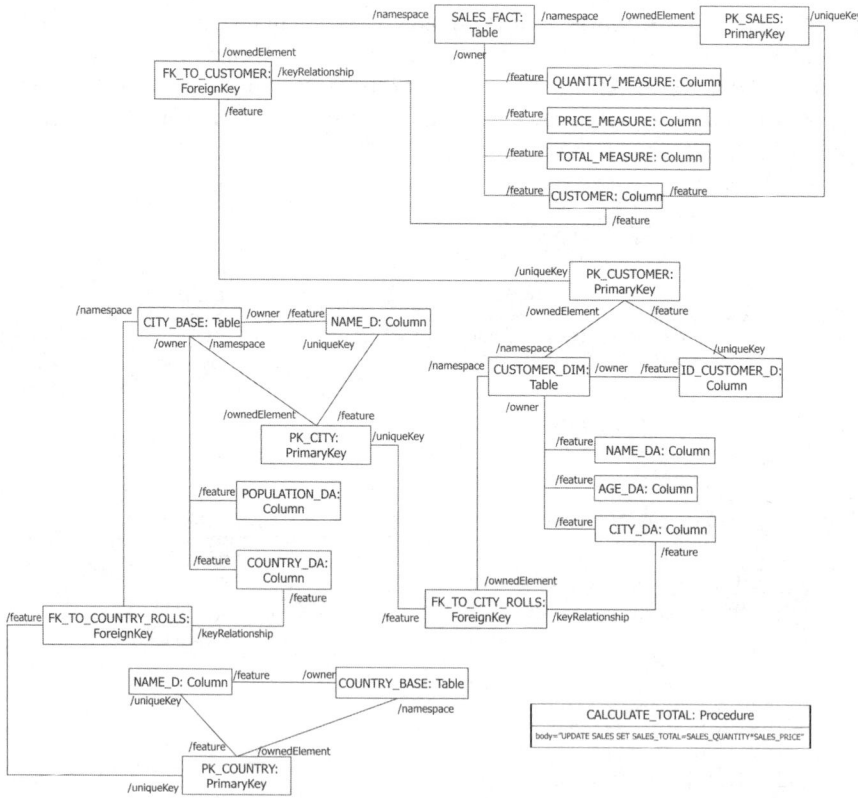

Fig. 3.6 Relational model (already marked) of the data sources of our case study based on CWM.

tial provided by the data sources and it represents a MD model that will be properly populated from the available data sources.

3.3.4 Multidimensional Platform Specific Models

A PSM is a view of a system from the platform specific viewpoint [22]. It represents the model of the same system specified by the PIM but it also specifies how that system makes use of the chosen platform or technology. In MD modeling, platform specific means that the PSM is specially designed for a kind of a specific database technology, thus considering a PSM as a logical model of the DW. These systems can use relational technology (relational database to store multidimensional data) or multidimensional technology (structures the data directly in multidimensional structures). In our approach, each PSM is modeled by using the resource layer from CWM. Specifically, we use the relational and the multidimensional metamodels:

- Relational metamodel. It contains classes and associations that represent every aspect of relational databases. With this metamodel we can represent tables, columns, primary keys, foreign keys and so on. This metamodel can be seen in Fig. 3.8.
- Multidimensional metamodel. It contains common data structures that represent every MD property. However, multidimensional databases are not as standardized as relational ones, since the former generally defines proprietary data structures. Therefore, this multidimensional metamodel only defines commonly

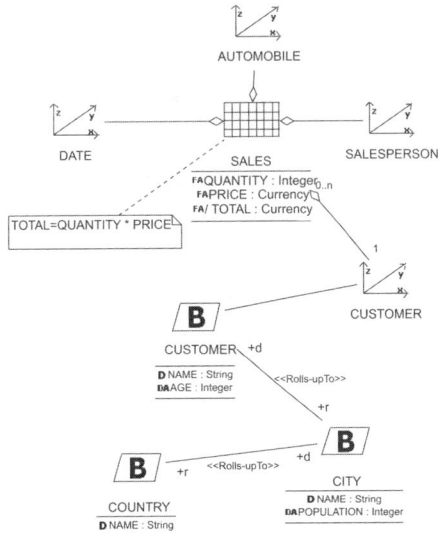

Fig. 3.7 Improved PIM by means of data sources.

used data structures in order to be generic enough to support a vendor specific extension. In this paper, we use the part of the multidimensional metamodel shown in Fig. 3.9 that corresponds to an *Oracle Express* extension defined in Volume 2, Extensions, of the CWM Specification [21].

3.3.5 From PIM to PSM

According to the QVT relations language, we have developed every relation to obtain both a transformation between our PIM and a PSM for a relational platform, and a transformation between our PIM and a PSM for a multidimensional platform. Due to space constraints, we focus on describing two of the developed QVT transformation rules. We refer the reader to [14, 12] for further explanation.

In Fig. 3.10, we show the DIMENSION2TABLE relation, a QVT transformation rule for dealing with dimensions and obtaining a PSM tailored to relational technol-

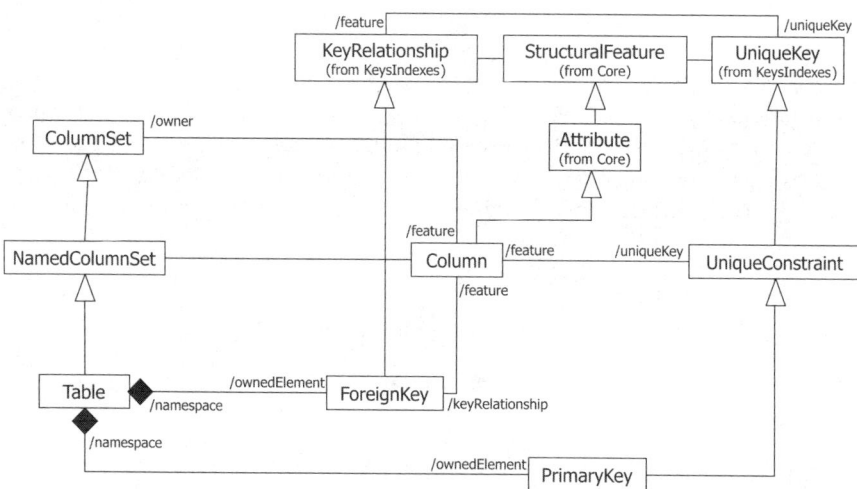

Fig. 3.8 Excerpt from the CWM Relational metamodel.

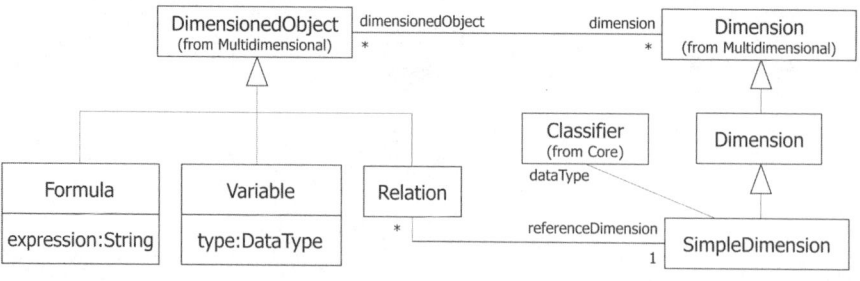

Fig. 3.9 Excerpt from the CWM Multidimensional metamodel.

ogy based on a star schema [9] (i.e. every DIMENSIONATTRIBUTE of every BASE class belonging to one DIMENSION class is stored in the same table, named *dimension table*). The source model of this relation is a set of elements that represents a DIMENSION associated with a BASE. This set of elements must be matched against a unique TABLE. This TABLE must own a PRIMARYKEY. In order to store every DIMENSIONATTRIBUTE (and DESCRIPTOR) in this TABLE, several QVT relations are called in the *where* clause: DIMENSIONATTRIBUTE2COLUMN, DESCRIPTOR2COLUMN, and BASE2TABLE.

Furthermore, we focus on describing one of the QVT relations which deal with the derivation of a PSM tailored to multidimensional technology based on *Oracle Express*: DIMENSION2SIMPLEDIMENSION (see Fig. 3.11). The source model of this transformation is a set of elements that represents a DIMENSION class and a BASE class with a DESCRIPTOR property. This set of elements must be matched against a SIMPLEDIMENSION (according to the *Oracle Express* metamodel). The type of the SIMPLEDIMENSION is the corresponding type of the DESCRIPTOR according with a conversion function UML2OETYPE, which turns a UML data type into an *Oracle Express* data type. Once this transformation rule is carried out, the following relations must be done according to the *where* clause: DIMENSIONATTRIBUTE2VARIABLE, BASE2SIMPLEDIMENSION, and FACT2SIMPLEDIMENSION.

Within our case study, we can apply the QVT transformations on the enriched PIM (recall Fig. 3.7) to obtain both a PSM for relational technology and a PSM for multidimensional technology. The resulting PSMs can be viewed in Fig. 3.12 and 3.13, respectively.

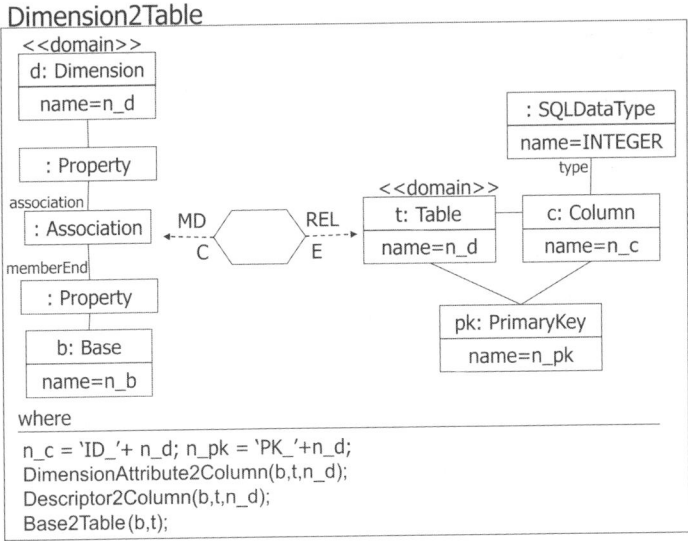

Fig. 3.10 Transforming dimensions into tables.

3.4 Implementation

The defined profiles and QVT relations have been implemented in an MDA-compliant CASE tool (*Borland Together Architect*). This tool supports developers in the design of software applications by using several MDA features. One of the most valuable features of *Borland Together Architect* is the QVT language in order to implement transformations and relations between models. *Borland Together Architect* is based on the *Eclipse* development platform, so it can be extended by means of plugins in order to add more features and new functionality. In order to implement this approach, several new plugins have been developed: (i) a plugin based on our UML profile for i* in DW domain, (ii) a plugin based on our UML profile for MD modeling, and (iii) a plugin that comprises the relational and multidimensional metamodels of CWM. Once these plugins have been developed and integrated into the *Eclipse* platform, the facilities provided by *Borland Together Architect* can be used to define and execute every QVT transformation rule. In this section one snapshot is provided (see Fig. 3.14) to illustrate the implementation of one of the QVT relations (DIMENSION2SIMPLEDIMENSION) within BORLAND TOGETHER ARCHITECT.

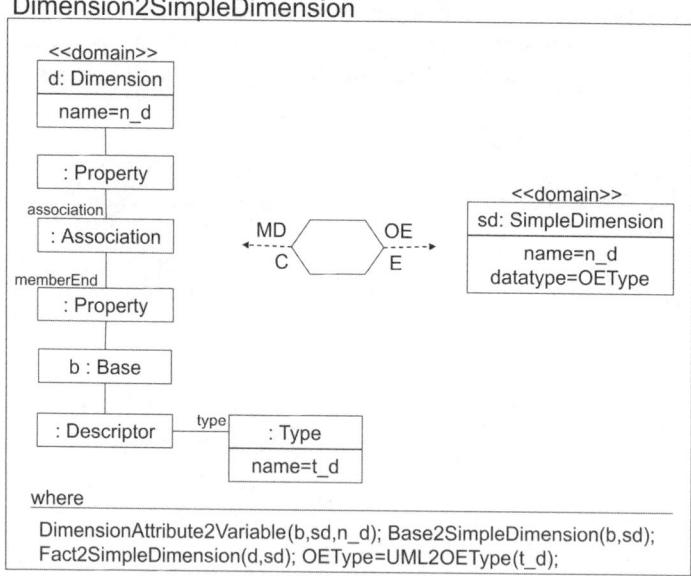

Fig. 3.11 Transforming dimensions into simple dimensions.

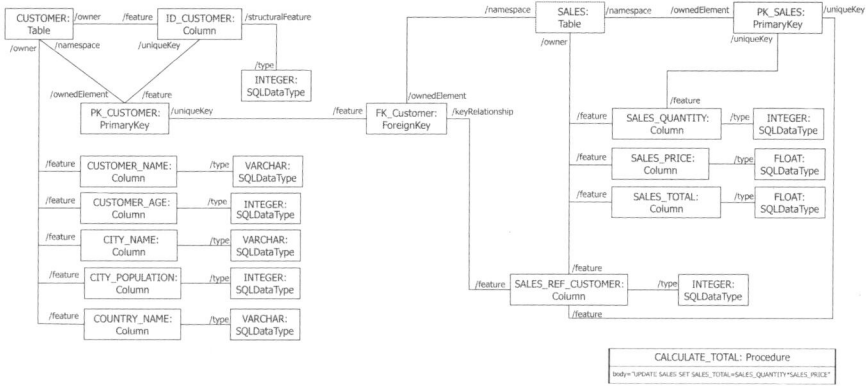

Fig. 3.12 Relational-based PSM of our case study (star schema).

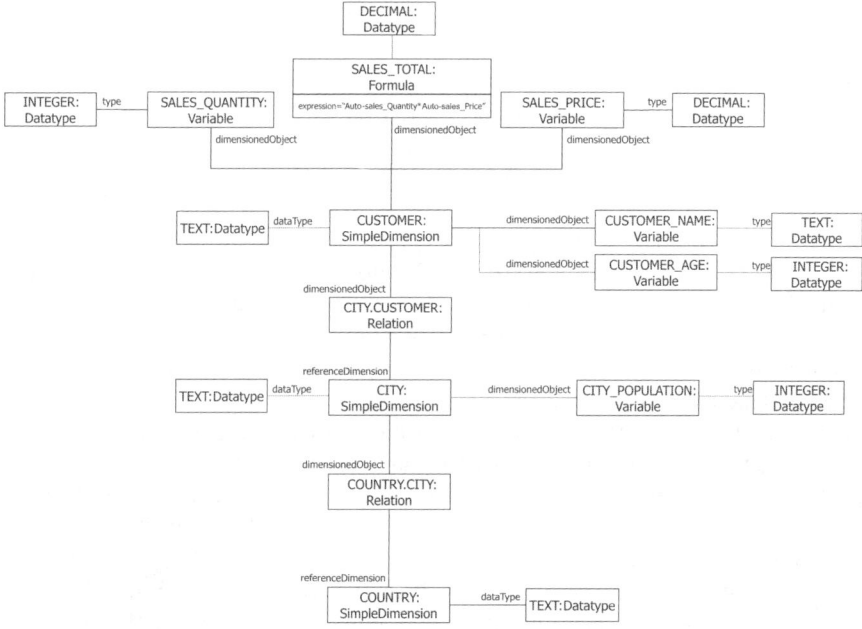

Fig. 3.13 Multidimensional-based PSM of our case study (Oracle Express).

3.5 Conclusions and Ongoing Work

In this paper we have introduced our MDA approach, by means of a case study, in order to face two key issues in MD modeling: (i) the reconciliation, in early stages of the development, of information needs of decision makers, and the available operational data sources that will populate the DW, and (ii) the development of formal and automatic transformations between the conceptual and logical design phases.

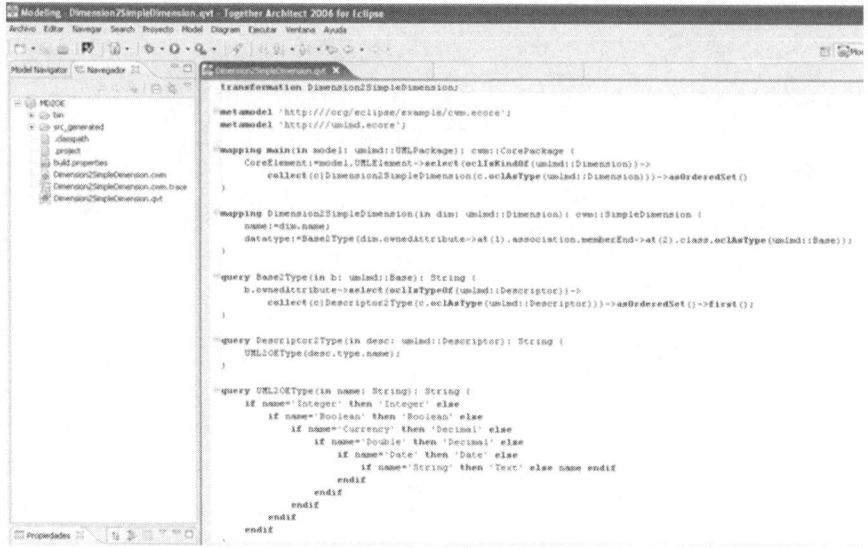

Fig. 3.14 Implementation of the QVT relation Dimension2SimpleDimension.

In our approach, we have aligned every stage in the DW development with MDA as follows: (i) specifying the requirements in a CIM, based on a UML profile of the i* framework; (ii) describing how to use UML to build a PIM for the MD modeling of the DW repository; (iii) reconciling this PIM with the information provided by the available data sources which will populate the DW; (iv) using CWM to build PSMs tailored to several database technologies; and (v) formally establishing QVT transformations between these models.

A case study has been used throughout the paper in order to better show how every model is defined and every transformation is applied. The great benefit of our MDA approach is that MD modeling is carried out within a systematic, well structured and comprehensive development process, thus decreasing its inherent complexity, saving time and effort.

Our ongoing research work consists of the integration of our proposal into a comprehensive MDA framework for the development of the whole DW system described in [14]. In this framework every part of a DW (data sources, ETL processes, DW repository, etc.) is designed by following an MDA approach in order to increase productivity, portability, interoperability, reusability and adaptability of DW systems. Actually, we have already covered some areas, e.g. data mining [38, 39], security [2, 32, 31], or data analysis [26].

Acknowledgements This work has been partially supported by the ESPIA project (TIN2007-67078) from the Spanish Ministry of Education and Science, and by the QUASIMODO project (PAC08-0157-0668) from the Castilla-La Mancha Ministry of Education and Science (Spain). Jose-Norberto Mazón is funded by the Spanish Ministry of Education and Science under a FPU grant (AP2005-1360).

References

1. J. Bézivin, S. Hammoudi, D. Lopes, and F. Jouault. Applying MDA approach for web service platform. In *EDOC*, pages 58–70. IEEE Computer Society, 2004.
2. E. Fernández-Medina, J. Trujillo, R. Villarroel, and M. Piattini. Developing secure data warehouses with a UML extension. *Inf. Syst.*, 32(6):826–856, 2007.
3. P. Giorgini, S. Rizzi, and M. Garzetti. GRAnD: A goal-oriented approach to requirement analysis in data warehouses. *Decis. Support Syst.*, 45(1):4–21, 2008.
4. W. Giovinazzo. *Object-Oriented Data Warehouse Design. Building a Star Schema*. Prentice-Hall, 2000.
5. M. Golfarelli, D. Maio, and S. Rizzi. The Dimensional Fact Model: A conceptual model for data warehouses. *Int. J. Cooperative Inf. Syst.*, 7(2-3):215–247, 1998.
6. B. Hüsemann, J. Lechtenbörger, and G. Vossen. Conceptual data warehouse modeling. In M. A. Jeusfeld, H. Shu, M Standt, and G. Vossen, editors, *DMDW*, volume 28 of *CEUR Workshop Proceedings*, page 6. CEUR-WS.org, 2000.
7. W. Inmon. *Building the Data Warehouse (3rd Edition)*. Wiley & Sons, New York, 2002.
8. M. Jarke, M. Lenzerini, Y. Vassiliou, and P. Vassiliadis. *Fundamentals of Data Warehouses*. Springer, 2000.
9. R. Kimball and M. Ross. *The Data Warehouse Toolkit*. Wiley & Sons, 2002.
10. J. Lechtenbörger and G. Vossen. Multidimensional normal forms for data warehouse design. *Inf. Syst.*, 28(5):415–434, 2003.
11. S. Luján-Mora, J. Trujillo, and I.-Y. Song. A UML profile for multidimensional modeling in data warehouses. *Data Knowl. Eng.*, 59(3):725–769, 2006.
12. J.-N. Mazón, J. Pardillo, and J. Trujillo. Applying transformations to model driven data warehouses. In A. M. Tjoa and J. Trujillo, editors, *DaWaK*, volume 4081 of *Lecture Notes in Computer Science*, pages 13–22. Springer, 2006.
13. J.-N. Mazón, J. Pardillo, and J. Trujillo. A model-driven goal-oriented requirement engineering approach for data warehouses. In J.-L. Hainaut, E. A. Rundensteiner, M. Kirchberg, M. Bertolotto, M. Brochhausen, Y.-P. P. Chen, S. S.-S. Cherfi, M. Doerr, H. Han, S. Hartmann, J. Parsons, G. Poels, C. Rolland, J. Trujillo, E. S. K. Yu, and E. Zimányi, editors, *ER Workshops*, volume 4802 of *Lecture Notes in Computer Science*, pages 255–264. Springer, 2007.
14. J.-N. Mazón and J. Trujillo. An MDA approach for the development of data warehouses. *Decis. Support Syst.*, 45(1):41–58, 2008.
15. J.-N. Mazón, J. Trujillo, and J. Lechtenbörger. A set of qvt relations to assure the correctness of data warehouses by using multidimensional normal forms. In D. W. Embley, A. Olivé, and S. Ram, editors, *ER*, volume 4215 of *Lecture Notes in Computer Science*, pages 385–398. Springer, 2006.
16. J.-N. Mazón, J. Trujillo, and J. Lechtenbörger. Reconciling requirement-driven data warehouses with data sources via multidimensional normal forms. *Data Knowl. Eng.*, 63(3):725–751, 2007.
17. E. Medina and J. Trujillo. A standard for representing multidimensional properties: The Common Warehouse Metamodel (CWM). In Y. Manolopoulos and P. Návrat, editors, *ADBIS*, volume 2435 of *Lecture Notes in Computer Science*, pages 232–247. Springer, 2002.
18. S. Meliá, J. Gómez, and N. Koch. Improving web design methods with architecture modeling. In K. Bauknecht, B. Pröll, and H. Werthner, editors, *EC-Web*, volume 3590 of *Lecture Notes in Computer Science*, pages 53–64. Springer, 2005.
19. S. Mellor, K. Scott, A. Uhl, and D. Weise. *MDA distilled: principles of Model-Driven Architecture*. Addison Wesley, 2004.
20. Object Management Group (OMG). Common Warehouse Metamodel (CWM) Specification 1.1. http://www.omg.org/cgi-bin/doc?formal/03-03-02.
21. Object Management Group (OMG). Common Warehouse Metamodel (CWM) Specification 1.1. Volume 2. Extensions. http://www.omg.org/cgi-bin/doc?ad/2001-02-02.

22. Object Management Group (OMG). MDA Guide 1.0.1. http://www.omg.org/cgi-bin/doc?omg/03-06-01.
23. Object Management Group (OMG). MOF 2.0 Query/View/Transformation. http://www.omg.org/cgi-bin/doc?ptc/2005-11-01.
24. Object Management Group (OMG). Object Constraint Language (OCL) Specification 2.0. http://www.omg.org/cgi-bin/doc?ptc/03-10-14.
25. Object Management Group (OMG). Unified Modeling Language Specification 2.0. http://www.omg.org/cgi-bin/doc?formal/05-07-04.
26. J. Pardillo, J.-N. Mazón, and J. Trujillo. Model-driven OLAP Metadata for Data Warehouses. In *BNCOD*, page In Press, 2008.
27. J. Poole. Model Driven Data Warehousing (MDDW). http://www.cwmforum.org/POOLEIntegrate2003.pdf.
28. N. Prakash, Y. Singh, and A. Gosain. Informational scenarios for data warehouse requirements elicitation. In P. Atzeni, W. W. Chu, H. Lu, S. Zhou, and T. W. Ling, editors, *ER*, volume 3288 of *Lecture Notes in Computer Science*, pages 205–216. Springer, 2004.
29. S. Rizzi, A. Abelló, J. Lechtenbörger, and J. Trujillo. Research in data warehouse modeling and design: dead or alive? In I.-Y. Song and P. Vassiliadis, editors, *DOLAP*, pages 3–10. ACM, 2006.
30. J. Schiefer, B. List, and R. Bruckner. A holistic approach for managing requirements of data warehouse systems. In *Americas Conf. on Information Systems*, pages 77–87, 2002.
31. E. Soler, J. Trujillo, E. Fernández-Medina, and M. Piattini. Building a secure star schema in data warehouses by an extension of the relational package from CWM. *Computer Standards & Interfaces*, In press (doi:10.1016/j.csi.2008.03.002).
32. E. Soler, J. Trujillo, E. Fernández-Medina, and M. Piattini. A framework for the development of secure data warehouses based on MDA and QVT. In *ARES*, pages 294–300. IEEE Computer Society, 2007.
33. J. Trujillo, M. Palomar, J. Gómez, and I.-Y. Song. Designing data warehouses with OO conceptual models. *IEEE Computer*, 34(12):66–75, 2001.
34. N. Tryfona, F. Busborg, and J. G. B. Christiansen. starer: A conceptual model for data warehouse design. In *DOLAP*, pages 3–8. ACM, 1999.
35. J. Vanderdonckt. A mda-compliant environment for developing user interfaces of information systems. In O. Pastor and J. F. e Cunha, editors, *CAiSE*, volume 3520 of *Lecture Notes in Computer Science*, pages 16–31. Springer, 2005.
36. R. Winter and B. Strauch. A method for demand-driven information requirements analysis in data warehousing projects. In *HICSS*, page 231, 2003.
37. E. Yu. *Modelling Strategic Relationships for Process Reengineering*. PhD thesis, University of Toronto, Canada, 1995.
38. J. J. Zubcoff, J. Pardillo, and J. Trujillo. Integrating clustering data mining into the multi-dimensional modeling of data warehouses with UML profiles. In I. Y. Song, J. Eder, and T. M. Nguyen, editors, *DaWaK*, volume 4654 of *Lecture Notes in Computer Science*, pages 199–208. Springer, 2007.
39. J. J. Zubcoff and J. Trujillo. A UML 2.0 profile to design association rule mining models in the multidimensional conceptual modeling of data warehouses. *Data Knowl. Eng.*, 63(1):44–62, 2007.

Chapter 4
Personalization and OLAP Databases

Franck Ravat and Olivier Teste

Abstract This paper focuses on the integration of personalization in a multidimensional context. We provide (i) a conceptual model, (ii) a query language and (iii) a personalized multidimensional database system. (i) The model we provide is based on multidimensional concepts (fact, dimension, hierarchy, measure, parameter or weak attribute) as well as personalization rules. These rules are based on Event-Condition-Action formalism and assign priority weights to attributes of a multidimensional schema. (ii) We also define OLAP operators adapted to the personalization context. Weights are taken into account during OLAP analyses; e.g. data with higher weights are displayed thus reducing the number of multidimensional operations a decision-maker executes during an analysis. (iii) This solution has been implemented in a prototype, which allows users both to define personalized rules and to query the personalized database. The system integrates user interfaces on top of an R-OLAP database.

4.1 Introduction

OLAP (On-Line Analytical Processing) systems allow analysts to improve the decision-making process by consulting and analysing aggregated data. These data are extracted from operational systems and are stored into multidimensional databases (MDB); data are modelled as points in a multidimensional space with the use of the cube (or hypercube) metaphor. Figure 4.1a illustrates through a cube representation, *sale amounts* according to *time*, *stores* and *products*. In an MDB a cube is defined according to an analysis subject (fact) associated to analysis axes (dimensions). Each dimension contains one or several analysis viewpoints (hierarchies) and each hierarchy organises various data granularities of analysis data. For exam-

Franck Ravat, Olivier Teste
IRIT (UMR5505), Université de Toulouse, 118 rte de Narbonne, F-31062 Toulouse Cedex 9, France, e-mail: {ravat,teste}@irit.fr

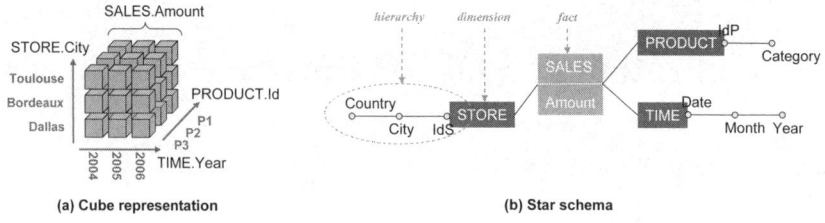

Fig. 4.1 MDB modelling.

ple, along the *store* dimension, a hierarchy could group *individual stores* into *cities*, themselves grouped into *countries*. Figure 4.1b shows the corresponding schema of the cube presented in Figure 4.1a; i.e. the fact named '*SALES*' is associated to three dimensions named '*PRODUCT*', '*STORE*', and '*TIME*'.

As observed by [5] "*the acceptance of technology by end users depends on the extent to which end users perceive the new technology will be useful and easy to use.*" Moreover, user-adaptive (or personalized) systems take individual characteristics of their current users into account and adapt their behaviour accordingly. Based on models that capture important user characteristics, personalized systems customize the generated content or its presentation for different individuals [9]. In this way, we argue that a personalized MDB could reduce the required effort to use OLAP systems, thus, this paper addresses the problem of defining a personalized MDB system.

4.1.1 Paper Issue and Related Works

Decision-makers use OLAP systems to improve their management by analysing aggregated historical data. In order to improve their decisions, they require adequate data and tools that facilitate their analysis. Adequate data are MDB subsets commonly manipulated by the decision-makers. Moreover, such subsets may change in order to support source data changes as well as user requirement changes. In order to avoid frequently adapting the MDB schema and to facilitate the analysis processes, decision-makers require a personalized approach. This solution allows users to find the right information at the right time, at the right level of detail and with the right presentation format.

Personalization is intensively studied in the context of Information Retrieval (IR), Web or DataBases (DB) [9]. These works focus on three issues: user modelling, user profiling and content personalization methods.

1. User models regroup two domains. *IR preference models* are defined for unstructured data whereas *DB user models* are defined for structured data. These latter have two approaches: qualitative and quantitative. The qualitative ap-

proach is based on binary preference relations while the quantitative approach consists in assigning a preference score to tuples.

2. User profiling refers to the process of collecting user cognitive characteristics to generate a relevant profile based on a user model. User profiling is based on several approaches: relevance feedback, machine learning, web mining ...

3. Content personalization methods regroup several approaches: information filtering systems, recommender systems, continuous queries and personalized searches.

More recently, some personalization techniques have been developed in MDB context. User modelling is based on several approaches. The first one is related to **multidimensional data presentation**. The approach developed in [3] consists in adapting displayed data into a constraint-based adaptable data cube. This approach is based only on a select operation. The displayed dimensions are only composed of a unique attribute. The second approach consists in specifying **pre-established dashboards**. The solutions studied in [17, 16] have presented active data warehouses. This approach aims at modelling pre-established scenarios using automatic mechanisms; for example, the authors illustrate their approach by weekly dashboards. Others researches [4], in the field of recommender systems, aim at **integrating decision-makers' expertise in an MDB**. This approach consists in associating zero or more superimposed information called annotations to every piece of multidimensional data. Annotations store decision-makers' remarks. These annotations assist users during their analyses by materialising their personal comments (personal use). Also, annotations can be shared decision-makers' expertises to facilitate collaborative analyses and decisions.

Nevertheless, all these solutions are based only on data presentation or data explanation. They do not specify a data subset dedicated to a specific decision-maker. Our objective is not to complete decisional data with comments but we intend to develop a solution for specifying relevant data according to user preferences. We aim at facilitating analysis processes by firstly visualizing information with the highest degree of importance. The approach we present is related to the user modeling domain. More precisely, we adopt a quantitative approach [9] that has the advantage of specifying absolute preferences in order to influence multidimensional query relevance.

4.1.2 Contributions and Paper Outline

The main contribution of the paper consists in providing personalization capabilities for multidimensional databases. The approach we present consists in modelling user preferences by weights associated to multidimensional database components. This preference model is used during the analysis process: the multidimensional database management system displays relevant data according to these user preferences. Moreover, this preference model impacts OLAP (On-Line Analytical Processing) operators [15] and the classical execution of OLAP operators must be adapted to support a personalized approach.

Our approach is more complete than [3] as it allows users to personalize all multidimensional database components. It is not limited to presentation aspects and the visualisation structure is not limited to dimensions with only one attribute. We also study the personalization behaviour with regard to OLAP operations. In [17, 16] the approach is based on established scenarios whereas our approach consists in personalising multidimensional databases independently of the analysis scenarios. The solution based on information explanation (annotations) [4] does not specify an MDB data subset and it does not influence the data visualisation as well as OLAP analysis process. As a consequence this solution must be combined with our solution.

This paper is organised as follows: section 4.2 defines the personalized multidimensional model. This model is based on both constellation concepts, which regroup facts, dimensions and hierarchies, and personalization rules, which specify priority weights to MDB attributes. In section 4.3, we study the impact of the personalization on multidimensional analyses and we extend OLAP operators to provide a personalized data visualisation. Finally, section 4.4 describes the R-OLAP implementations we developed.

4.2 Personalized Multidimensional Modelling

In this section, we firstly define a conceptual multidimensional model [14, 15]. This model has the advantage of being close to users' point of view and is independent of implementation choices. MDB are modelled according to a constellation of facts and dimensions, which are composed of hierarchies. This model facilitates correlations between several subjects of analysis and it supports several data granularities according to which subjects may be analysed.

Secondly personalization rules are associated to the constellation. We introduce personalization rules allowing users to define their preferences; *e.g.* users indicate the relevant attributes of the constellation by specifying weights. The model, we define, separates data and multidimensional structures and this approach allows attaching user preferences to data as well as structures.

4.2.1 Concepts and formalisms

A constellation regroups several subjects of analysis (facts), which are studied according to several analysis axes (dimensions) possibly shared between facts.

Definition 4.1. A *constellation* noted C is defined as $(N^C, F^C, D^C, Star^C, Rule^C)$ where

- N^C is a constellation name,
- $F^C = \{F_1, \ldots, F_m\}$ is a set of facts,
- $D^C = \{D_1, \ldots, D_n\}$ is a set of dimensions,
- $Star^C : FC \rightarrow 2^{D^C}$ associates each fact to its linked dimensions[1]. The notation $D_i \in Star^C(F_j)$ expresses that the dimension D_i is linked to the fact F_j.
- $Rule^C = \{R_1, \ldots, R_{nr}\}$ is a set of rules, which personalize the constellation. These rules are explained in section 4.2.2.

A dimension reflects information according to which measures will be analyzed. A dimension is composed of attributes, which are organised through hierarchies.

Definition 4.2. A *dimension*, noted $D_i \in D^C$, is defined as $(N^{D_i}, A^{D_i}, H^{D_i}, I^{D_i})$ where

- N^{D_i} is a dimension name,
- $A^{D_i} = \{a_1^{D_i}, \ldots, a_u^{D_i}\} \cup \{id^{D_i}, All\}$ is a set of attributes,
- $H^{D_i} = \{H_1^{D_i}, \ldots, H_v^{D_i}\}$ is a set of hierarchies,
- $I^{D_i} = \{i_1^{D_i}, \ldots, i_p^{D_i}\}$ is a set of dimension instances.

Within a dimension, attribute values represent several data granularities according to which measures could be analyzed. In a same dimension, attributes may be organised according to one or several hierarchies.

Definition 4.3. A *hierarchy*, noted $H_j^{D_i} \in H^{D_i}$, is defined as $(N^{H_j}, Param^{H_j}, Weak^{H_j})$ where

- N^{H_j} is a hierarchy name,
- $Param^{H_j} = \langle id^{D_i}, p_1^{H_j}, \ldots, p_{v_j}^{H_j}, All \rangle$ is an ordered set of attributes, called parameters, which represent useful graduations along the dimension, $\forall k \in [1..v_j], p_k^{H_j} \in A^D$,
- $Weak^{H_j} : Param^{H_j} \rightarrow 2^{A^{D_i} - Param^{H_j}}$ is a function associating weak attributes to parameters.

All hierarchies start with a same parameter, noted id^{D_i}, called *root parameter* and end with a same parameter, noted All, called *extremity parameter*. Weak attributes complete the parameter semantic; i.e., weak attributes *Lastname* and *First-name* complete parameter *IdC* in dimension *CUSTOMERS* (see figure

We represent dimensions and their hierarchies using a graphical formalism which extends notations introduced in [6]. Each path starting from idDi and ending by All represents a hierarchy.

A fact reflects information that is to be analyzed through one or several indicators, called measures.

Definition 4.4. A fact, noted $F_i \in F^C$, is defined as $(N^{F_i}, M^{F_i}, I^{F_i}, IStar^{F_i})$ where

- N^{F_i} is a name of fact,

---

[1] The notation 2^E represents the *powerset* of E.

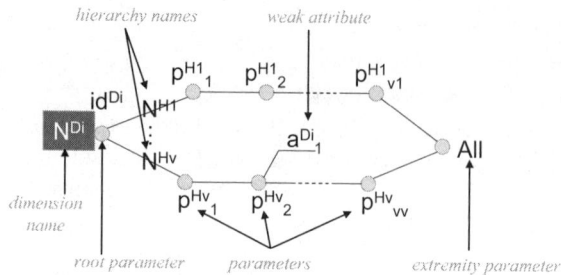

Fig. 4.2 Graphical notations of dimensions and hierarchies.

- $M^{F_i} = \{f_1(m_1^{F_i}), \ldots, f_w(m_w^{F_i})\}$ is a set of measures, each associated with an aggregation function,
- $I^{F_i} = \{i_1^{F_i}, \ldots, i_q^{F_i}\}$ is a set of fact instances,
- $IStar^{F_i} : I^{F_i} \rightarrow I^{D_1} \times \ldots \times I^{D_n}$ is a function $(\forall k \in [1..n], D_k \in Star^C(F_i))$, which respectively associates fact instances to their linked dimension instances.

To represent facts, we introduce graphical notations. Figure 4.3 illustrates graphical notations of facts.

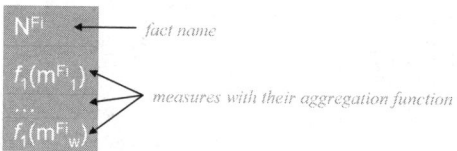

Fig. 4.3 Graphical notations of facts.

Example. The case study is taken from the banking domain. We define a multi-dimensionnal database that allows users to analyze accounts of bank customers as well as their loan amounts. More precisely, decision-makers want to analyze account numbers and account balance according to customers, branches and time. In the same MDB, they also intend to analyze loan amounts according to loan types and time. Figure 4.4 shows the schema of the constellation previously depicted. This notation is an extension of graphical notations defined by [6].

This constellation, called *BANK*, is composed of 2 facts and 4 dimensions. It is defined as $(N^{BANK}, F^{BANK}, D^{BANK}, Star^{BANK}, Rule^{BANK})$ where

- $N^{BANK} = {}'BANK'$,
- $F^{BANK} = \{F^{ACCOUNTS}, F^{LOANS}\}$,
- $D^{BANK} = \{D^{CUSTOMERS}, D^{DATES}, D^{BBRANCHES}, D^{LOANTYPES}\}$,
- $Star^{BANK} : Star^{BANK}(F^{ACCOUNTS}) \rightarrow (D^{DATES}, D^{CUSTOMERS}, D^{BBRANCHES})$, $Star^{BANK}(F^{LOANS}) \rightarrow (D^{CUSTOMERS}, D^{DATES}, D^{LOANTYPES})$,
- $Rule^{BANK} = \{R_1, \ldots, R_n r\}$.

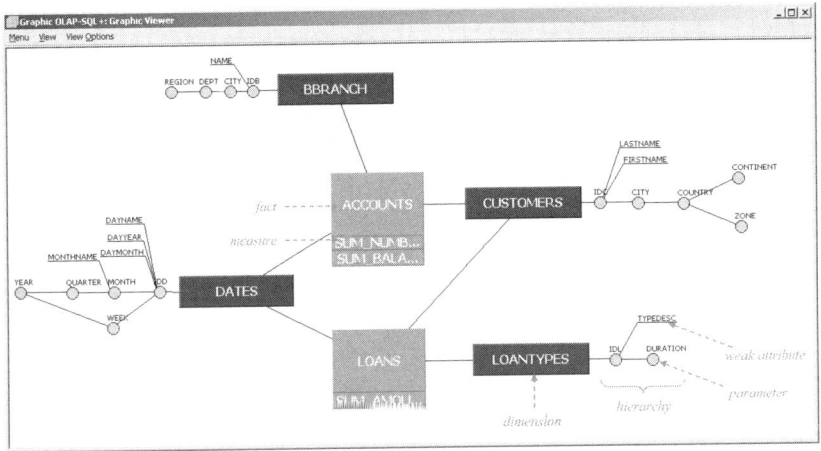

Fig. 4.4 Example of constellation schema.

The dimension noted $D^{CUSTOMERS}$ is defined as $(N^{D_{CUSTOMERS}}, A^{D_{CUSTOMERS}}, H^{D_{CUSTOMERS}}, I^{D_{CUSTOMERS}})$ where

- $N^{D_{CUSTOMERS}} = 'CUSTOMERS'$,
- $A^{D_{CUSTOMERS}} = \{IdC, Firstname, Lastname, City, Country, Continent, Zone, All\}$,
- $H^{D_{CUSTOMERS}} = \{H_1^{D_{CUSTOMERS}}, H_2^{D_{CUSTOMERS}}\}$,
- $I^{D_{CUSTOMERS}} = \{i_1^{D_{CUSTOMERS}}, i_2^{D_{CUSTOMERS}}, \ldots\}$; Table 4.1 displays some instances of this dimension.

Table 4.1 Example of dimension instances.

	IdC	Firstname	Lastname	City	Country	Zone	Continent
$i_1^{D_{CUSTOMERS}}$	c1	Franck	Ravat	Toulouse	France	Mediterranean	Europe
$i_1^{D_{CUSTOMERS}}$	c2	Olivier	Teste	Toulouse	France	Mediterranean	Europe

The hierarchies noted $H_1^{D_{CUSTOMERS}}$ and $H_2^{D_{CUSTOMERS}}$ are respectively defined by

- $N_1^{H_{CUSTOMERS}} = 'HGeo'$
- $Param_1^{H_{CUSTOMERS}} = \langle IdC, City, Country, Continent, All \rangle$
- $Weak_1^{H_{CUSTOMERS}} = \{(IdC, \{Firstname, Lastname\})\}$
- $N_2^{H_{CUSTOMERS}} = 'HZn'$
- $Param_2^{H_{CUSTOMERS}} = \langle IdC, City, Country, Zone, All \rangle$
- $Weak_2^{H_{CUSTOMERS}} = \{(IdC, \{Firstname, Lastname\})\}$

The fact noted $F^{ACCOUNTS}$ is defined as $(N^{F_{ACCOUNTS}}, M^{F_{ACCOUNTS}}, I^{F_{ACCOUNTS}}, IStar^{F_{ACCOUNTS}})$ where

- $N^{F_{ACCOUNTS}} = \text{'}ACCOUNTS\text{'}$,
- $M^{F_{ACCOUNTS}} = \{SUM(Balance), SUM(Number)\}$,
- $I^{F_{ACCOUNTS}} = \{i_1^{F_{ACCOUNTS}}, i_2^{F_{ACCOUNTS}}, \ldots\}$; Table 4.2 describes some fact instances.
- $IStar^{F_{ACCOUNTS}} = \{(i_1^{F_{ACCOUNTS}}, (i_1^{D_{CUSTOMERS}}, i_{x_1}^{D_{DATES}}, i_{y_1}^{D_{BBRANCHES}})),$
  $(i_2^{F_{ACCOUNTS}}, (i_2^{D_{CUSTOMERS}}, i_{x_2}^{D_{DATES}}, i_{y_2}^{D_{BRANCHES}})), \ldots\}$.

Table 4.2 Example of fact instances.

	SUM(Balance)	SUM(Number)
$i^{F_{ACCOUNTS}}{}_1$	43500.00	5
$i^{F_{ACCOUNTS}}{}_2$	60000.00	8

4.2.2 Personalization Rules

In order to personalize the constellation schema with regards to user needs, we introduce a rule-based mechanism. A personalized constellation is a constellation where users have attached priority weights to elements of the constellation through a set of rules. The attributes are displayed with regards to their weights (defined priorities).

These weights are materialized through a real between 0 (the lowest degree of interest) and 1 (the highest degree of interest).

Definition 4.5. A rule, noted R, is defined as $(N^R, S^R, E^R, C^R, A^R)$ where

- N^R is the rule name,
- S^R is the rule scope. It may be a fact name (N^F), a dimension name (N^D) or a hierarchy name (N^{H_i}).
- E^R is the event according to which the rule is triggered. In the personalized MDB context, events are limited to manipulation events such as 'displayed', 'rotated', 'drilled-down', 'rolled-up', etc.
- C^R is an optional condition. If a condition is specified, the rule is triggered if and only if the condition is true when the event happens. We introduce a function current(obj) : Boolean determining if an element obj is currently displayed in an OLAP analysis (obj$\in \{N^D, N^D.N^{H_i}, N^D[.N^{H_i}].p_k, N^F, N^F.f_i, N^F[.f_i].m_k\}$).[2]
- A^R is a set of actions to be executed when the rule is triggered. The main action consists in assigning weights, noted w_i, to dimension attributes and measures. Note that if obj is a dimension, then the affected weight w_i is valid in all hierarchies, whereas if obj is a hierarchy, the weight w_i is only used in this hierarchy.

---

[2] We note $[E]$ an optional expression E.

Example. A decision-maker usually defines dashboards customers' cities and countries. The decision-maker also uses frequently the last name and the first name of customers, but he/she thriftily uses customer identifiers. A decision-maker customises the MDB through the rule noted $R_1 = (N^{R_1}, S^{R_1}, E^{R_1}, C^{R_1}, A^{R_1})$ where

- $N^{R_1} =$ 'Customer_Rule',
- $S^{R_1} =$ 'CUSTOMERS',
- $E^{R_1} = Displayed \lor Rotated$
- $C^{R_1} = Current($'ACCOUNTS'$)$,
- $A^{R_1} = \{IdC \leftarrow 0.5; Firstname \leftarrow 0.8; Lastname \leftarrow 0.8; City \leftarrow 1; Country \leftarrow 1; Continent \leftarrow 0; Zone \leftarrow 0.5\}$.

This rule, named 'Customer_Rule', is associated to the CUSTOMERS dimension. It is triggered when users operate a display or rotate operations if and only if the fact named ACCOUNTS is currently displayed. The rule's actions assign weights as follows:

- At the root parameter, IdC is not very important whereas its weak attributes (Firstname and Lastname) have stronger weights ($IdC \leftarrow 0.5; Firstname \leftarrow 0.8; Lastname \leftarrow 0.8$).
- Intermediate parameters (City and Country) are considered more important ($City \leftarrow 1; Country \leftarrow 1$) than the highest parameters named Continent and Zone ($Continent \leftarrow 0; Zone \leftarrow 0.5$).

Note that these rules are associated to various constellation elements, and could conflict with others rules; for example, a rule associated to a dimension can affect weights whereas another rule associated to a hierarchy of this dimension can affect the same weights. Our current solution forbids different weights for one attribute.

4.3 Personalized OLAP Manipulations

The personalization we provide consists in associating weights to dimension attributes and measures to reflect the priority level of user interests. The OLAP system uses weights to monitor the OLAP manipulations, which are formally defined through OLAP algebra.

4.3.1 Multidimensional Table

Constellation schemas depict MDB structures whereas user analyses are based on tabular representations [8] where structures and data are displayed together. The visualization structure that we define is a Multidimensional Table (MT) and it displays data from one fact and two of its linked dimensions.

Definition 4.6. A multidimensional table T is defined as (S, L, C, R) where

- $S = (F^S, M^S)$ represents the analysed subject through a fact $F^S \in F^C$ and a set of projected measures $M^S = \{f_1(m_1), \ldots, f_x(m_x)\}$ where $\forall i \in [1..x], m_i \in M^F$.
- $L = (D^L, H^L, P^L)$ represents the horizontal analysis axis where $PL = \langle All, p_{max}^{H^L}, \ldots p_{min}^{H^L} \rangle$, $H^L \in H^{D_L}$ and $D^L \in Star^C(F^S)$, H^L is the current hierarchy of D^L.
- $C = (D^C, H^C, P^C)$ represents the vertical analysis axis where $P^C = \langle All, p_{max}^{H^C}, \ldots p_{min}^{H^C} \rangle$, $H^C \in H^{D_C}$ and $D^C \in Star^C(F^S)$, H^C is the current hierarchy of D^C.
- $R = pred_1 \wedge \ldots \wedge pred_t$ is a normalized conjunction of predicates (restrictions on dimension data and fact data).

Example. The next figure displays an example of a multidimensional table supporting an analysis about accounts according to customers (geographic informations) and dates.

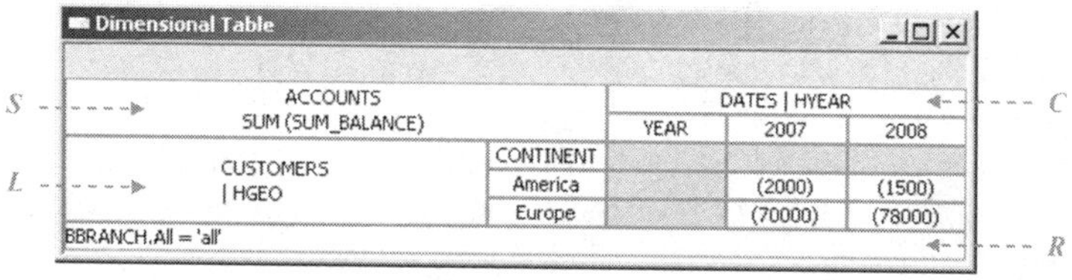

Fig. 4.5 Example of multidimensional table.

We introduce the DISPLAY operator to construct a multidimensional table (TRES) from a constellation C.

Definition 4.7. The display operator is expressed by $DISPLAY(F, M, D^L, H^L, D^C, H^C) = T_{RES}$ where

- F is the fact from which data must be displayed,
- $M = \{f_1(m_1), \ldots, f_x(m_x)\}$, $i \in [1..x]$, $m_i \in M$, M is the set of aggregated measures to be displayed
- $D^L \in Star^C(F)$ and $D^C Star^C(F)$ are respectively the horizontal and vertical dimensions,
- $H^L \in H^{D^L}$ and $H^C \in H^{D^C}$ are selected hierarchies, which are used to display parameters.

$T_{RES} = (S_{RES}, L_{RES}, C_{RES}, R_{RES})$ is the output multidimensional table, where:

- $S_{RES} = (F, M)$,
- $L_{RES} = (D^L, H^L, \langle All, p_{max}^{H^L} \rangle)$,
- $C_{RES} = (D^C, H^C, \langle All, p_{max}^{H^C} \rangle)$,
- $R_{RES} = \bigwedge_{\forall i, D_i \in Star^C(F^S)} D_i.ALL = 'all'$

Example. The multidimensional table illustrated in the previous figure (see figure 4.5) is calculated from the following algebraic expression.

$DISPLAY(Accounts, SUM(Balance), Customers, HGeo, Dates, HYear) = T_{RES}$

The resulting table, noted $T_{RES} = (S_{RES}, L_{RES}, C_{RES}, R_{RES})$, is defined as

- $S_{RES} = (Accounts, \{SUM(Balance)\})$,
- $L_{RES} = (Customers, HGeo, \langle All, Continent \rangle)$,
- $C_{RES} = (Dates, Year, \langle All, Year \rangle)$,
- $R_{RES} = Customers.All = $ 'all' $\wedge Dates.All = $ 'all' $\wedge BBranch.All = $ 'all'.

Note that the resulting multidimensional table in Fig. 4.5 does not display the internal attribute All along the current dimensions, as this attribute tends to confuse users [12].

4.3.2 Extended OLAP Algebra

Multidimensional OLAP analyses consist in exploring interactively constellation data through a multidimensional table. Several propositions have been made in the scientific literature [7, 2, 8, 13]. Although there is no consensus on a common set of operations for a multidimensional algebra, most papers offer a partial support of the following OLAP operation categories [1, 15, 18].

- **Drilling**: these operations allow navigating through the hierarchical structure along analysis axes, in order to analyze measures with more or less precision. Drilling upwards (ROLLUP) consists in displaying the data with a coarser level of detail [13]. Drilling downwards (DRILLDOWN) consists in displaying the data with a finer level of detail.
- **Rotations**: these operations allow changing an analysis axis by a new dimension (ROTATE) or changing an analysis perspective by a new hierarchy as well as changing the subject of analysis by a new fact.
- **Selections**: these operations allow the specification of restriction predicates on fact or dimension data. This operation is also known as "slice/dice" [2].
- **Dimension modification**: these operations allow more flexibility in analyses. They allow converting a dimensional element into a subject, thus "pushing" a parameter into the subject (fact); or converting a measure into a dimensional element, thus "pulling" a measure out of the subject. They also allow nesting. It is a structural reordering operation. This changes the order of parameters in a hierarchy but it also allows adding in a hierarchy a parameter from another dimension. The consequence is to be able to display in the multidimensional table more than two dimensions. This compensates for the 2D limitation of the multidimensional table.
- **Ordering**: these operations allow changing the order of the values of dimension parameters or inserting a parameter in another place in a hierarchy. Switching is an operation that eases analysis allowing regrouping columns or lines together independently of the order of the parameter values in lines or columns. It is a

value reordering operation. Notice that switching as well as nesting may "break" hierarchies' visual representation in the multidimensional table. Contrarily to commercial software which allows these operations without warning the user, the use of these specific operators enables a query system to warn the user of analysis incoherence risks.

- **Fact modification**: These operations allow the modification of the set of selected measures. They allow adding (ADDM) or removing (DELM) a measure to the current analysis.
- **Aggregation**: This operation allows the process of totals and subtotals of the displayed data. If applied to all displayed parameters, it is equivalent to the Cube operator [7].

We formally define a query algebra [14, 15] for allowing manipulations and retrieval of data through nested expressions of algebraic operators. Our approach is user-oriented whereas others previous approaches are system-oriented. The OLAP algebra we define provides a minimal core of operators; all operators may not be expressed by any combination of other core operators.

We extend our OLAP operators in order to take into account the personalized elements of constellations. We describe only extended operators (DISPLAY, ROTATE, DRILLDOWN, ROLLUP). The personalization impacts their classical execution because it changes the displayed attributes in order to improve analysed data relevance. To ensure closure of the algebra, each operator takes as input a source multidimensional table (T_{SRC}) and produces as output a resulting multidimensional table (T_{RES}).

$$T_{SRC} = (S_{SRC}, L_{SRC}, C_{SRC}, R_{SRC}) \text{ where}$$

- $S_{SRC} = (F^S, M^S) withM^S = f_1(M_1), \ldots, f_x(M_x)$,
- $L_{SRC} = (DL, HL, PL) withPL = \langle All, p^L_{max}, \ldots, p^L_{min} \rangle$,
- $C_{SRC} = (DC, HC, PC)$ with $PC = \langle All, p^C_{max}, \ldots, p^C_{min} \rangle$, and
- $R_{SRC} = (pred_1 \wedge \ldots \wedge pred_t)$.

Compared with classical definitions of OLAP operators, our extension consists in adding a threshold as input. This threshold specifies relevant measures, parameters and weak attributes to be displayed (S_{RES}, P^L_{RES}, P^C_{RES}) in the resulting multidimensional tables; more details are given in section 4.4.4.

Example. A decision-maker intends to build a dashboard with the data of the constellation previously presented in figure 4.4. More precisely, he/she wants to analyze the balance accounts according to customers and dates.

Figure 4.6 illustrates the display operator in classical and personalized contexts.

1. In the classical approach, the threshold noted is not specified. Fig. 4.6 shows the algebraic expression and the resulting multidimensional table. Each dimension is graduated by the highest granularity parameter according to the current hierarchy.

    a. $L_{RES} = (Customers, HGeo, \langle All, Continent \rangle)$,
    b. $C_{RES} = (Dates, Year, \langle All, Year \rangle)$.

Table 4.3 Syntax of OLAP operators.

Operator	Input	Output
DISPLAY	F, M, D^L, H^L, D^C, H^C	$T_{RES} = (S_{RES}, L_{RES}, C_{RES}, R_{RES})$ $-S_{RES} = (F, M),\ M = \{f_1(m_1), \ldots, f_x(m_x)\},$ $\forall i \in [1..x], m_i \in M$ $-L_{RES} = (D^L, H^L, \langle All, p_{max}^{H^L} \rangle)$ $-C_{RES} = (D^C, H^C, \langle All, p_{max}^{H^C} \rangle)$ $-R_{RES} = \bigwedge_{\forall i, D_i \in Star^C(F^S)} D_i.ALL = \text{'all'}$

ROTATE	$T_{SRC}, D_{old}, D_{new}, H_{new}$
	 $- D_{old} \in \{D_{SRC}^C, D_{SRC}^L\}$
	 $- D_{new} \in Star^C(F_{SRC})$
	 $- H_{new} \in H^{D_{new}}$
		$T_{RES} = (S_{SRC}, L_{RES}, C_{RES}, R_{SRC})$
		 if $D_{old} = D_{SRC}^L$ then
		 $- L_{RES} = (D_{new}, H_{new}, \langle All, p_{max}^{H_{new}} \rangle)$
		 $- C_{RES} = C_{SRC}$
		 if $D_{old} = D_{SRC}^C$ then
		 $- L_{RES} = L_{SRC}$
		 $- C_{RES} = (D^C, H^C, \langle All, p_{max}^{H_{new}} \rangle)$

DRILLDOWN	T_{SRC}, D, p_{inf}
	 $- D \in \{D_{SRC}^C, D_{SRC}^L\}$
	 $- p_{inf} \in Param^{H_i}, H_i \in D^D$
		$T_{RES} = (S_{SRC}, L_{RES}, C_{RES}, R_{SRC})$
		 if $D = D_{SRC}^L$ then
		 $- L_{RES} = (D_{SRC}^L, H_{SRC}^L, P_{SRC}^L + \langle p_{inf} \rangle)$
		 $- C_{RES} = C_{SRC}$
		 if $D = D_{SRC}^C$ then
		 $- L_{RES} = L_{SRC}$
		 $- C_{RES} = (D_{SRC}^C, H_{SRC}^C, P_{SRC}^C + \langle p_{inf} \rangle)$

ROLLUP	T_{SRC}, D, p_{sup}
	 $- D \in \{D_{SRC}^C, D_{SRC}^L\}$
	 $- p_{sup} \in Param^{H_i}, H_i \in H^D$
		$T_{RES} = (S_{SRC}, L_{RES}, C_{RES}, R_{SRC})$
		 if $D = D_{SRC}^L$ then
		 $- L_{RES} = (D_{SRC}^L, H_{SRC}^L, \langle All, p_{max}^{H^L}, \ldots, p_{sup} \rangle)$
		 $- C_{RES} = C_{SRC}$
		 if $D = D_{SRC}^C$ then
		 $- L_{RES} = L_{SRC}$
		 $- C_{RES} = (C_{SRC}^C, H_{SRC}^C, \langle All, p_{max}^{H^C}, \ldots, p_{sup} \rangle)$

2. In the personalized approach, the threshold =1 is specified in the example illustrated in Fig. 4.6. Each dimension is graduated according to relevant parameters; a parameter is considered relevant if its weight is equal or higher than the specified threshold. In this example,

    a. $L_{RES} = (Customers, HGeo, \langle All, Country, City \rangle)$,
    b. $C_{RES} = (Dates, Year, \langle All, Year \rangle)$.

The personalized approach simplifies the decision-maker's task. In a classical approach, to obtain the multidimensional table displayed in figure 4.6b, the decision-maker cannot use a single OLAP operation but a combination of different operations. This operation set is defined as follows:

- $T_1 = DISPLAY(Accounts, \{(SUM(Balance)\}, Customers, HGeo, Dates, HYear)$
- $T_2 = ROLLUP(T_1, Customers, All)$
- $T_3 = DRILLDOWN(T_2, Customers, Country)$
- $T_{RES} = DRILLDOWN(T_3, Customers, City)$

In this example, if the threshold is fixed to 0.75, the resulting table displays data using others relevant attributes.

$DISPLAY(Accounts, \{SUM(Balance)\}, Customers, HGeo, Dates, HYear, 0.75) = T_{RES2}$ where

- $L_{RES} = (Customers, HGeo, \langle All, Country, City, (Firstname, Lastname) \rangle \rangle)$,
- $C_{RES} = (Dates, Year, \langle All, Year \rangle)$.

The decision-maker's analysis combines several algebraic operators to display relevant decisional data. Using a personalized context, the algebraic expression is simplified; *e.g.*, relevant attributes are displayed according to user preferences, which were expressed thought rules. In the previous example, the roll-up and drill-down operations are not required in the personalized context as attributes with higher weights than the threshold (> 0.75) are directly displayed.

Note that the selected attributes depend on the threshold as well as on the user preferences (weights). In two user contexts, the same operation may display relevant data according to different attributes.

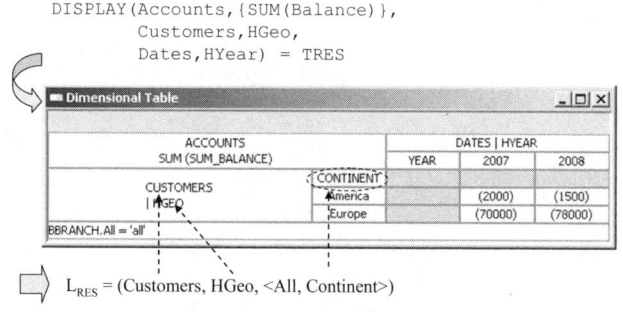

(a) Classical context

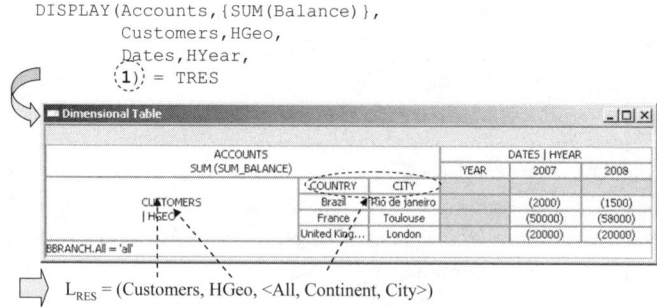

(b) Personalized context

Fig. 4.6 Example of multidimensional tables.

4.3.3 Discussion

The personalization approach we presented is a quantitative approach [9]; we define absolute user preferences through weights associated to the relevant components of a constellation. These weights impact multidimensional query process. The multidimensional system calculates the relevant attributes to be displayed using user preferences (weights). The algebraic query expressions are simplified: drilling operations (drill-down and roll-up) are reduced.

This paper aims at studying the influence of the user personalization on the multidimensional querying process. Nevertheless, this paper offers new perspectives:

- Firstly, the expression of rules may be a tedious task and defining weights is not easy for users. We plan to generate these rules according to decision-maker usage of the MDB. This approach will consist in defining an adaptative multidimensional system where rules are automatically generated according to user queries and their frequency.
- Secondly, beyond the simplification of algebraic queries, the user personalization may influence technical aspects by minimizing execution cost of multidimensional queries [11] and materialized view refreshment [19]. More precisely, we plan to materialize views in internal lattices according to user preferences.

4.4 A Personalized Multidimensional Database System

This section describes the prototype we developed. It presents the prototype architecture and shows the R-OLAP implementations of a personalized constellation.

4.4.1 Database System Architecture

We developed a prototype using Java JDK 1.6 on top of the Oracle 10*g* DBMS. It allows the definition and the manipulation of a personalized R-OLAP constellation as well as visualizing and querying the multidimensional data. The system is based on several components:

- Several **user interfaces** allow users to interact with a MDB. Users define personalized constellation through a textual commands (the rule definition language). Users display a constellation schema using graphical notations from which they build multidimensional tables. The constellation depicted in figure 4.4 as well as the multidimensional tables presented in figures 4.5 and 4.6 are screenshots from this interface.
- The **R-OLAP database** implements multidimensional data into relational tables according to a constellation organisation.

- The **R-OLAP metabase** describes the constellation structures of the R-OLAP database and it contains structures to manage the personalization mechanism.
- The **pre-compiler** consists in storing configuration rules into meta-tables called META_RULE, META_RULE_EVENT and META_RULE_CONDI-TION. These tables store weights attached to measures and dimension attributes of the constellation (parameters and weak attributes).
- The **query analyser** translates user interactions and extracts relevant data to be displayed through multidimensional tables. This component is based on the internal meta-tables.

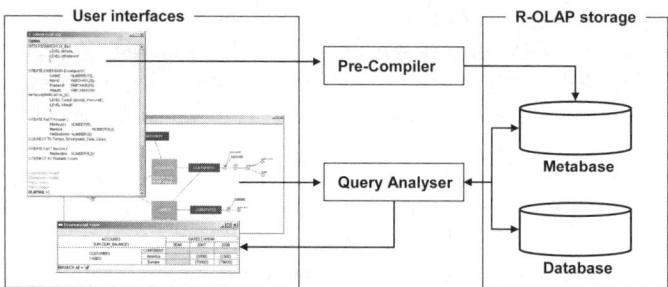

Fig. 4.7 System architecture.

4.4.2 R-OLAP storage

The system is based on an R-OLAP implementation. The constellation structures are described through metadata whereas analysed data are stored according to relations.

We store multidimensional data into an R-OLAP context using fact tables, dimension tables as well as pre-aggregated tables for optimisations. The multidimensional structures are described from meta-tables. Note that pre-aggregated tables will not be detailed in the following examples.

Example. From the constellation schema illustrated in Figure 4.4, the system we implemented, stores R-OLAP data as illustrated in figure 4.8.

The system stores facts and dimensions into tables according to principles defined in [10]. Figure 4.8 depicts a fact and a dimension R-OLAP storage.

- The fact named ACCOUNTS is translated in R-OLAP context as a table. Its schema is composed of attributes representing measures as well as one attribute with a foreign key for each relationship between a fact and a dimension. Its schema is completed by an internal primary key attribute.
- The dimension named CUSTOMERS is translated in R-OLAP context as a table. Its schema is composed of attributes from the dimension attributes (param-

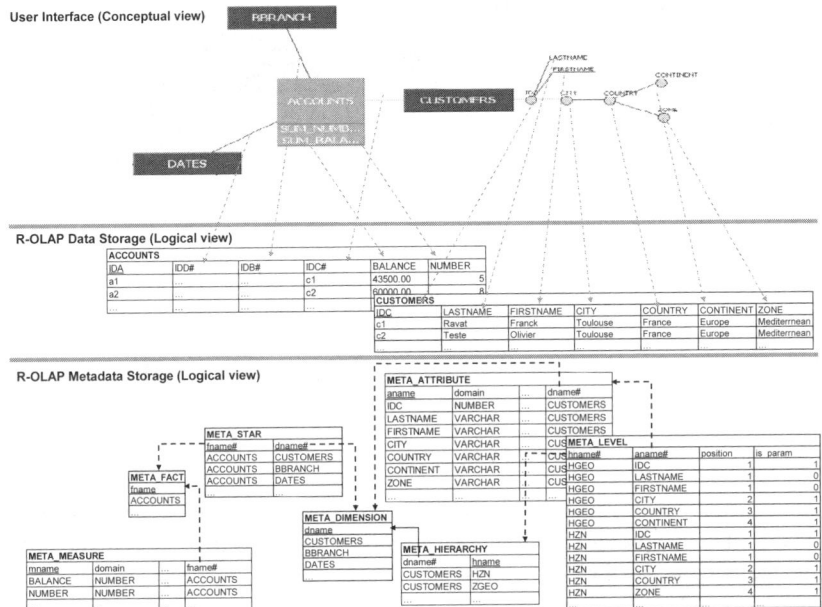

Fig. 4.8 Example of R-OLAP storage.

eters and weak attributes). The root parameter is translated as a primary key attribute.

Each conceptual element is described into meta-tables. Facts are described into META-FACT and META-MEASURE whereas dimensions and their hierarchies are described into META-DIMENSION, META-ATTRIBUTE, META-HIERARCHY and META-LEVEL. Relationships between facts and dimensions of the constellation are depicted into the table named META-STAR.

The personalization process is based on two steps:

- the definition of rules through a textual language,
- the manipulation of the constellation and the multidimensional tables using graphical manipulations.

4.4.3 A Rule Definition Language

The personalization consists in associating weights to dimension attributes and measures to reflect the priority level of user interests, whereas the OLAP system manages these weights to monitor OLAP manipulations. The personalization is based on the definition of rules. A rule allows users to fix weights to measures and dimen-

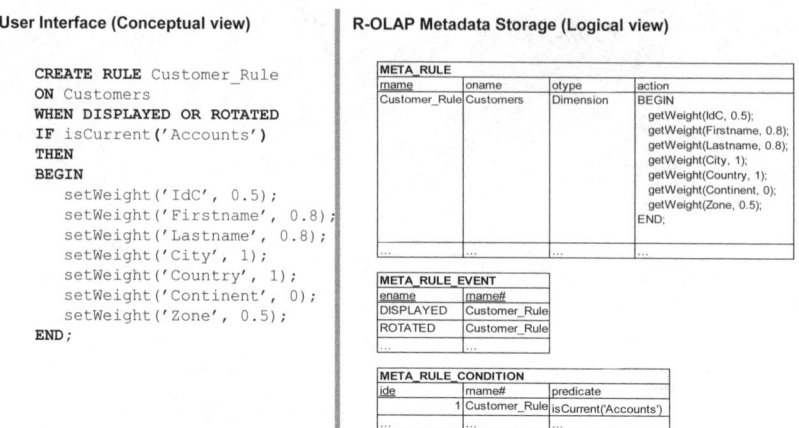

Fig. 4.9 Rule definition and associated rule metadata.

sion attributes. We provide an ECA-like customisation language. The rule definition command is based on the following syntax.

Definition 4.8. The syntax of the rule definition command is :
$$\text{CREATE RULE } N^R$$
$$\text{ON } S^R$$
$$\text{WHEN } E^R \text{ [IF } C^R\text{] THEN } A^R;$$

Example. We consider the rule named 'Customer_Rule' (see section 4.2.2). The rule is expressed through the following textual command. Each rule command is analyzed and stored into meta-tables.

4.4.4 Personalization Process

In this section we show how to perform extended OLAP operators with regard to a personalized constellation. The personalization aims at impacting the OLAP manipulations to improve displayed data with regard to user needs. Among the OLAP operators we defined, four operators are impacted.

- The display operation performs data extractions from the multidimensional database for displaying these extracted data into a multidimensional table ($DISPLAY(F,M,D^L,H^L,D^C,H^C,\tau) = T_{RES}$).
- The rotate operation allows the change of an analysis axis by a new dimension ($ROTATE(T_{SRC},D_{old},D_{new},H_k^{D_{new}},\tau) = T_{RES}$) as well as an analysis perspective by a new hierarchy ($ROTATE(T_{SRC},D_{old},D_{old},H_k^{D_{new}},\tau) = T_{RES}$).
- The drilling operations allow navigating through the hierarchical structure along analysis axes, in order to analyze measures with more ($ROLLUP(T_{SRC},D,p_{sup},\tau) = T_{RES}$) or less ($DRILLDOWN(T_{SRC},D,p_{inf},\tau) = T_{RES}$) precision.

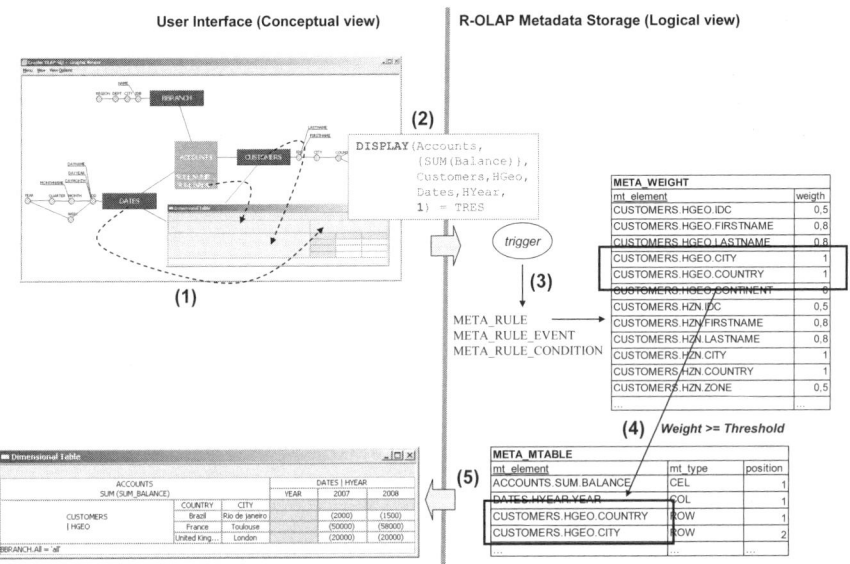

Fig. 4.10 Example of a personalized display operation.

When users make a query, the resulting multidimensional table is displayed. The system stores the multidimensional table descriptions into the meta-base. To calculate the displayed multidimensional table, the system triggers relevant rules for associating weights to the constellation elements (parameters, weak attributes or fact measures) into the meta-table called META_WEIGHT.

From META_WEIGHT the system choose elements to be displayed according to the specified threshold. Note that this table contains only impacted elements of the current user query.

Example of DISPLAY. We consider the Multidimensional Table (MT) depicted in figure 4.6b. This MT is build after the execution of the following steps:

1. A user displays a multidimensional table according to graphical interactions on the constellation graph. More precisely, the user specifies the DISPLAY operation using drag and drop actions or contextual menus; more details may be found in [15].
2. These manipulations are translated in an internal algebraic expression:
   $DISPLAY(Accounts, \{SUM(Balance)\}, Customers, HGeo, Dates, HYear, 1) = T_{RES_1}$.
3. From the algebraic expression, the system triggers relevant rules to populate the meta-table META-WEIGHT. This table contains properties of facts and dimensions which are currently displayed or impacted by the current operation.
4. The threshold τ determines the displayed properties according to the used operator. The multidimensional table is described in the meta-table noted META-MTABLE.

5. From META-MTABLE the final multidimensional table is displayed.

Moreover, the user interface supports incremental On-Line Analytical Processing; *e.g.*, MT components may be removed, replaced and new components may be added. The MT display adapts itself after each manipulation. We illustrate these concepts in the following example.

Example of ROTATE. This example is based on the two following rules associated to the hierarchies of the CUSTOMERS dimension.

<table>
<tr><td>

CREATE RULE HGeo_Rule
ON Customers.HGeo
WHEN DISPLAYED OR ROTATED
IF isCurrent('Accounts')
THEN
BEGIN
    setWeight('IdC', 0.5);
    setWeight('Firstname', 0.8);
    setWeight('Lastname', 0.8);
    setWeight('City', 1);
    setWeight('Country', 1);
    setWeight('Continent', 0);
END;

</td><td>

CREATE RULE HZn_Rule
ON Customers.HZn
WHEN DISPLAYED OR ROTATED
IF isCurrent('Accounts')
THEN
BEGIN
    setWeight('IdC', 0.5);
    setWeight('Firstname', 0.8);
    setWeight('Lastname', 0.8);
    setWeight('City', 1);
    setWeight('Country', 1);
    setWeight('Zone', 1);
END;

</td></tr>
</table>

The user intends to change in the MT previously displayed, the current hierarchy of the dimension named Customers. Its graphical interactions are translated into the following operation: $ROTATE(T_{RES_1}, Customers, HGeo, HZn, 1) = T_{RES_2}$.

The ROTATION operation used in the personalisation context has the advantage of directly displaying all the attributes having the highest degree of interest for the hierarchy 'HZN'.

4.5 Concluding Remarks

This paper focuses on a personalization approach dedicated to multidimensional databases. Firstly, we provide a personalized multidimensional model. This model integrates constellation concepts (facts with multiple measures, dimensions with multiple hierarchies, parameters with weak attributes) and a rule-based mechanism for specifying priority weights on constellation attributes. Secondly, we provide OLAP operators adapted to the personalization context. This algebra is based on the multidimensional table concept and offers drilling, rotations, selection, ordering, aggregation and modification operators. The personalization impacts their classical execution because it changes the displayed attributes in order to improve the relevance of the analysed data. Thirdly, we provide a personalized multidimensional database system. This system integrates user interfaces, a R-OLAP database, a metabase, a

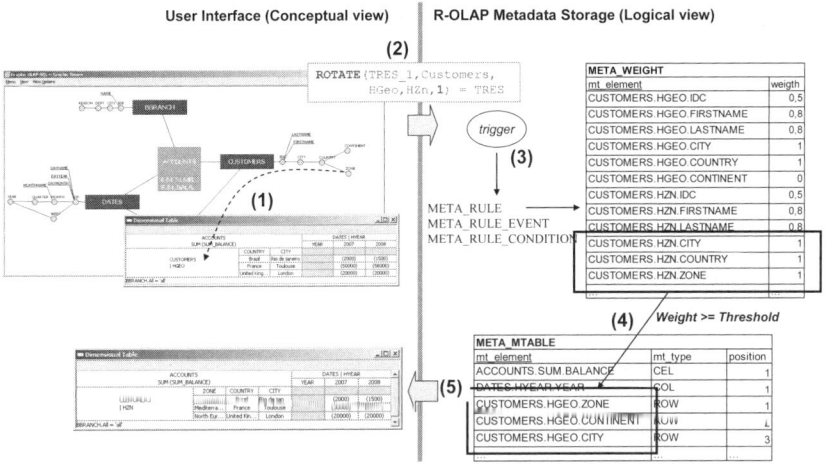

Fig. 4.11 Example of a personalized rotate operation.

pre-compiler and a query analyser. In this system, the rules are expressed with an ECA-like language.

This personalization approach is the first step for a more complete framework. We intend to define adaptive OLAP databases where the constellation customization (rule definitions) may be automatically generated from data access frequencies according to user manipulations. Moreover this solution must be combined with an annotation management system. This extension may explain MDB data displayed during the OLAP analyses.

Acknowledgements. The authors wish to thank greatly Ronan Tournier for his assistance in writing this paper. His comments were able to help us finish this work.

References

1. A. Abelló, J. Samos, and F. Saltor. YAM²: a multidimensional conceptual model extending UML. *Inf. Syst.*, 31(6):541–567, 2006.
2. R. Agrawal, A. Gupta, and S. Sarawagi. Modeling multidimensional databases. In *ICDE '97: Proceedings of the 13th International Conference on Data Engineering*, pages 232–243, Washington, DC, USA, 1997. IEEE Computer Society.
3. L. Bellatreche, A. Giacometti, P. Marcel, H. Mouloudi, and D. Laurent. A personalization framework for OLAP queries. In *DOLAP '05: Proceedings of the 8th ACM international workshop on Data warehousing and OLAP*, pages 9–18, New York, NY, USA, 2005. ACM.
4. G. Cabanac, M. Chevalier, F. Ravat, and O. Teste. An annotation management system for multidimensional databases. In I. Y. Song, J. Eder, and T. M. Nguyen, editors, *DaWaK*, volume 4654 of *Lecture Notes in Computer Science*, pages 89–98. Springer, 2007.
5. R. J. Goeke and R. H. Faley. Leveraging the flexibility of your data warehouse. *Commun. ACM*, 50(10):107–111, 2007.

6. M. Golfarelli, D. Maio, and S. Rizzi. Conceptual design of data warehouses from E/R schemes, 1998.
7. J. Gray, A. Bosworth, A. Layman, and H. Pirahesh. Data cube: A relational aggregation operator generalizing group-by, cross-tab, and sub-total. In *ICDE '96: Proceedings of the Twelfth International Conference on Data Engineering*, pages 152–159, Washington, DC, USA, 1996. IEEE Computer Society.
8. M. Gyssens and L. V. S. Lakshmanan. A foundation for multi-dimensional databases. In *VLDB '97: Proceedings of the 23rd International Conference on Very Large Data Bases*, pages 106–115, San Francisco, CA, USA, 1997. Morgan Kaufmann Publishers Inc.
9. Y. Ioannidis and G. Koutrika. Personalized systems: models and methods from an ir and db perspective. In *VLDB '05: Proceedings of the 31st international conference on Very large data bases*, pages 1365–1365. VLDB Endowment, 2005.
10. R. Kimball and M. Ross. *The Data Warehouse Toolkit: The Complete Guide to Dimensional Modeling*. John Wiley & Sons, Inc., New York, NY, USA, 2002.
11. Y. Kotidis and N. Roussopoulos. Dynamat: a dynamic view management system for data warehouses. In *SIGMOD '99: Proceedings of the 1999 ACM SIGMOD international conference on Management of data*, pages 371–382, New York, NY, USA, 1999. ACM.
12. E. Malinowski and E. Zimányi. Hierarchies in a multidimensional model: from conceptual modeling to logical representation. *Data Knowl. Eng.*, 59(2):348–377, 2006.
13. T. B. Pedersen, C. S. Jensen, and C. E. Dyreson. A foundation for capturing and querying complex multidimensional data. *Inf. Syst.*, 26(5):383–423, 2001.
14. F. Ravat, O. Teste, R. Tournier, and G. Zurfluh. Graphical querying of multidimensional databases. In Y. E. Ioannidis, B. Novikov, and B. Rachev, editors, *ADBIS*, volume 4690 of *Lecture Notes in Computer Science*, pages 298–313. Springer, 2007.
15. F. Ravat, O. Teste, R. Tournier, and G. Zurfluh. Algebraic and graphic languages for OLAP manipulations. *International Journal of Data Warehousing and Mining*, 4(1):17–46, January 2008.
16. T. Thalhammer and M. Schrefl. Realizing active data warehouses with off-the-shelf database technology. *Softw. Pract. Exper.*, 32(12):1193–1222, 2002.
17. T. Thalhammer, M. Schrefl, and M. Mohania. Active data warehouses: complementing olap with analysis rules. *Data Knowl. Eng.*, 39(3):241–269, 2001.
18. L. Tininini. Querying multidimensional data (chapter 9). In M. Rafanelli, editor, *Multidimensional Databases*, pages 252–281. Idea Group, 2003.
19. Y. Zhuge, H. Garcia-Molina, and J. L. Wiener. Consistency algorithms for multi-source warehouse view maintenance. *Distrib. Parallel Databases*, 6(1):7–40, 1998.

Chapter 5
A Metamodel for the Specification of Geographical Data Warehouses

Valéria Cesário Times, Robson do Nascimento Fidalgo, Rafael Leão da Fonseca, Joel da Silva, and Anjolina Grisi de Oliveira

Abstract The decision-making processes can be supported by many tools such as Data Warehouse (DW), On-Line Analytical Processing (OLAP) and Geographical Information System (GIS). Much research found in literature is aimed at integrating these technologies, although most of these approaches do not provide formal definitions for a Geographical Data Warehouse (GDW) nor there is a consensus regarding the design of spatial dimensional schemas for GDW. To address this, GeoDWFrame was proposed as a set of guidelines to design spatial dimensional schemas. However, there is not a metamodel that implements its specifications, nor there is a metamodel that integrates GDW concepts with some standards. Then, in this paper we propose GeoDWM, which is a formally specified metamodel, that extends GeoDWFrame with spatial measures. We have instantiated our formal metamodel based on CWM and OGC standards to assist the conceptual modelling needs found in the development of GDW applications. Finally, some issues concerning the development of a CASE tool that is based on the GeoDWM metamodel and that provides a means of validating the application conceptual data model are given together with a discussion on GDW conceptual design aspects and some descriptions for future work.

5.1 Introduction

Support to the process of decision-making may involve the use of technologies, such as DW (Data Warehouse) [14], OLAP (On-Line Analytical Processing) [2] and GIS (Geographical Information Systems) [16]. DW is a typical database to support decisions that is usually implemented with the star model, which is organized through fact tables and dimension tables. OLAP is a specific software category for multidimensional processing of data extracted from the DW and can be interpreted by different perspectives and levels of details. Finally, the GIS are specific systems

Center for Informatics, Federal University of Pernambuco, P.O. Box 7851, Recife - PE, Brazil, 50.732-970, e-mail: {vct,rdnf,rlf,js,ago}@cin.ufpe.br

for supporting geographical decisions that help acquiring, manipulating, visualizing, and analyzing spatial objects. For the last years, several researchers from the Information Technology community have thoroughly investigated the problem of integrating these technologies [26, 13, 1, 19, 18]. However, because they were originally conceived for different purposes, this integration is not trivial and as a result, a consensus has not been reached yet about the most appropriate way to do so.

Nevertheless, it is known that conventional and geographical data must be integrated in one sole database, which corresponds to a GDW (Geographical Data Warehouse). Thus, a GDW represents a data structure that facilitates the application of both GIS and OLAP functionalities so that the use of them is integrated and synchronized. This provides a means of applying spatial and multidimensional operators to the GDW data by generating different cross tabulations in different levels of aggregation and analysis views. By implementing a GDW on the top of a SDBMS, allows users to run spatial queries, including the verification of spatial relationships between geographical features (e.g. touch, intersects and contains), that are useful for spatial analysis.

Hence, building a GDW is characterized as an important issue in supporting multidimensional and geographical queries. According to Fidalgo et al. [9], a GDW can be defined as an extension of the traditional DW approach, added by a geographical component. Basically, this consists in extending the star model through the insertion of geographical properties (descriptive and geometrical), which can be defined as GDW dimensions and/or measures. Regarding the dimensions, they can store the geometries and the descriptions of the geographical objects, whilst the spatial measures can only store the geometries. Prominently a GDW must maintain the traditional characteristics of a DW [14], i.e., directed to the subject, integrated, nonvolatile and varying in time. Besides that, a GDW must offer support to the storage, the indexing, the aggregation, and the spatial analysis, in maps or tables. Some examples of GDW data visualization using maps, tables and charts are detailed in [4] and [6].

Although there is research about the use of GDW [13, 15, 26, 9, 7] there still is not any standard about the data model to be specified in its conceptual and logical project phases. The main objective of this research area is to provide an open and extensible environment with integrated functionalities for manipulation, queries and analysis not only of conventional data, but of geographical data as well. This new type of environment benefits the strategic decision-making process by widening the analysis universe that may be done about the business of an organization. This type of environment has been referred to as SOLAP (Spatial OLAP) [25]. Nevertheless, to this moment, this integration has not yet been totally achieved or makes use of proprietary technologies, which often raises expenses and makes both the development and re-usage of the proposed solution more difficult.

Therefore, in order to provide a satisfactory SOLAP environment, the GOLAPA *(Geographical Online Analytical Processing Architecture)* project [4] has studied ways to formally define a GDW. The work presented in this article includes: 1) formal definitions of a metamodel for specifying GDW schemas and extending GeoDWFrame with spatial measures; 2) an instanciation of this metamodel based on

CWM and OGC standards; 3) results derived from the implementation of a CASE tool for the modelling of GDW schemas and 4) a discussion regarding some existing GDW modelling approaches that are based on concepts proposed by our metamodel.

The remainder of this paper is organized as follows. Section 5.6 provides a brief overview about some related work. Then, the formal definitions for our metamodel are given in section 5.2. Next, section 5.3, discusses some implementation results related to our metamodel and based on OGC and CWM standards. Following this, GeoDWCASE, which is a CASE tool for helping in the GDW modelling tasks, is presented in section 5.4. Then, some GDW schema modelling approaches that are based on both our metamodel and are CASE tool are discussed in section 5.5. Finally, section 5.7 presents some conclusions and indications for future work.

5.2 Formal Definitions for a Geographical Data Warehouse Metamodel

Despite the wide interest in DW formalization in the field of DB research, little attention has been devoted to providing formal specifications for a GDW by researchers. This section formally defines a GDW by extending the high-level GeoD-WFrame specifications [9] to take into account the concept of spatial measures. GeoDWFrame provides a set of guidelines aiming to direct the definition of the dimensional and geographical schema of a GDW. There are several good reasons for using the GeoDWFrame approach in our work, including: (i) the geometrical data referred to the spatial objects may be normalized; (ii) more than one spatial dimension may be managed; (iii) spatial objects may be used in any dimensional level and (iv) descriptions of the spatial objects locations may be stored in the GDW. The gain in using the GeoDWFrame dimension taxonomy has further been discussed in [9].

In our approach, a data model for a dimensional geographical warehouse is based on two finite sets of tables: (i) *dimension* and *fact* tables, where columns are associated to a *type* . We assume the existence of two finite sets of types: (i) the base types T_B, such as *integer, real,* and *string* ; and (ii) the geographic types T_G, whose elements are *Point, LineString, Polygon, GeometryCollection, MultiPoint, Multi-LineString,* and *MultiPolygon* . The base types can be a *common description* or *geographic description*. While the geographic description type can just be used to describe the geographical properties, such as *country name*, *state government type* and *city major*, the common description type can be used to describe any other property of a DW.

Definition 1 (micro/macro geographic description type) *When the geographic object has a low granularity,* i.e. *it can be rarely shared, we say that the geographic description type is micro. Otherwise, if its granularity is high, the geographic description type is macro. Examples of micro geographic description type include the location of a car accident and a customer address, while districts, cities and states are considered as instances of macro geographic description types.*

When a column is associated to a given type, for example consider the type *integer* $\in T_B$, then we can say that the column is of type *integer*, or that the column is of type T_B. Additionally, we can also say that the column is of a common description or geographic description type.

Definition 2 (Dimension table) *A dimension table is an n-ary relation over* $K \times S_1 \times \ldots \times S_r \times A_1 \times \ldots \times A_m \times G_1 \times \ldots \times G_p$, *where*
(i) $n = 1 + r + m + p$;
(ii) K is the set of attributes representing the primary key of the dimension table;
(iii) each S_i, $0 \leq i \leq r$ *is a set of foreign keys to a dimension table;*
(iv) each column A_j *(called attribute name or attribute for short),* $0 \leq j \leq m$, *is a set of attribute values of type* T_B;
(v) and each column G_k *(called geometry),* $0 \leq k \leq p$, *is a set of geometric attribute values (or geometries values for short) of type* T_G.

Moreover, the dimension table can be *Geographic, Conventional*, or *Hybrid* as following defined.

Definition 3 (Geographic Dimension) *A geographic dimension table can be primitive or composite as following defined:*
Primitive: *A primitive geographic dimension table has the schema* $K \times \ldots \times G_1 \times \ldots \times G_p$, *where*
(i) $p \geq 1$, *i.e. there is at least one column geometry;*
(ii) and there is no foreign key neither attribute.
Composite: *A composite geographic dimension table has the schema* $K \times S_1 \times \ldots \times S_r \times A_1 \times \ldots \times A_m$, *where:*
(i) $r \geq 1$, *i.e. there is at least one column of foreign keys. Also, each foreign key is associated to a primitive dimension table;*
(ii) $m \geq 1$, *i.e. there is at least one attribute;*
(iii) and there is no geometry.

Figure 5.1 shows an example of a GDW schema based on meteorological data that has been created to illustrate our formalization ideas. In this example, we consider that precipitation data are acquired by data collect platforms (dcp) that are located in certain cities and within some hydrographic basins. Also, as shown in this figure, the tables *pgd_state, pgd_city, pgd_basin_localization* and *pgd_dcp_localization* are primitive geographical dimensions because all of them have at least one column of type geometrical (e.g. *polygon* and *point*). Realize that without the primitive geographical dimensions a dimension with spatial data would have to store their geographical descriptions and coordinate data together. Considering the intrinsic redundancy of dimensional data, this would probably result in high costs of storage.

For the composite geographical dimension, consider as an example the table *cgd_localization* shown in figure 5.1. This is a composite table because it does not contain any columns of type geometrical, but it does have two foreign keys, namely *city_fk* and *state_fk*, that references two primitive geographical dimensions (i.e.

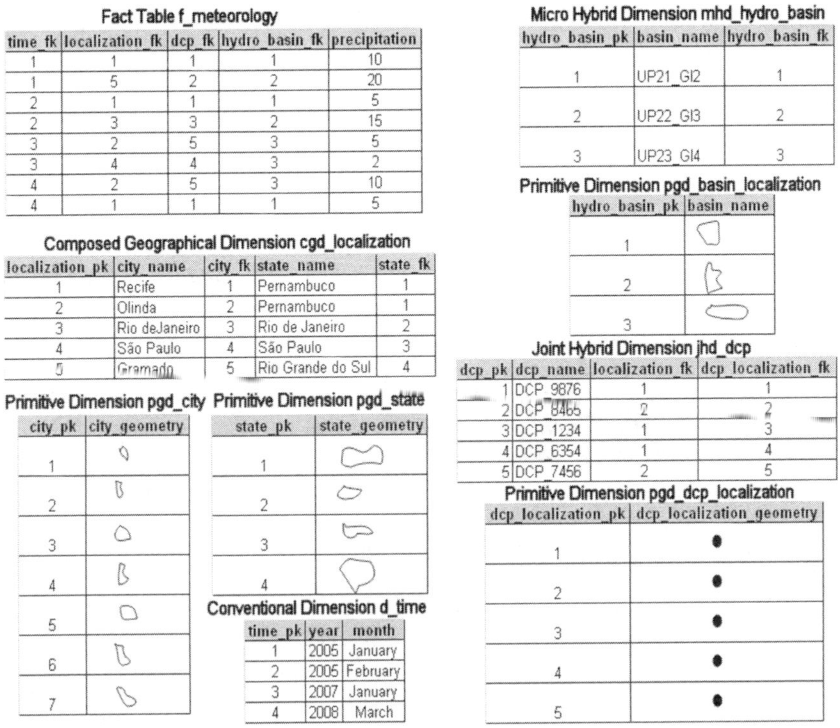

Fact Table f_meteorology

time_fk	localization_fk	dcp_fk	hydro_basin_fk	precipitation
1	1	1	1	10
1	5	2	2	20
2	1	1	1	5
2	3	3	2	15
3	2	5	3	5
3	4	4	3	2
4	2	5	3	10
4	1	1	1	5

Composed Geographical Dimension cgd_localization

localization_pk	city_name	city_fk	state_name	state_fk
1	Recife	1	Pernambuco	1
2	Olinda	2	Pernambuco	1
3	Rio deJaneiro	3	Rio de Janeiro	2
4	São Paulo	4	São Paulo	3
5	Gramado	5	Rio Grande do Sul	4

Primitive Dimension pgd_city

city_pk	city_geometry
1	
2	
3	
4	
5	
6	
7	

Primitive Dimension pgd_state

state_pk	state_geometry
1	
2	
3	
4	

Conventional Dimension d_time

time_pk	year	month
1	2005	January
2	2005	February
3	2007	January
4	2008	March

Micro Hybrid Dimension mhd_hydro_basin

hydro_basin_pk	basin_name	hydro_basin_fk
1	UP21_GI2	1
2	UP22_GI3	2
3	UP23_GI4	3

Primitive Dimension pgd_basin_localization

hydro_basin_pk	basin_name
1	
2	
3	

Joint Hybrid Dimension jhd_dcp

dcp_pk	dcp_name	localization_fk	dcp_localization_fk
1	DCP_9876	1	1
2	DCP_8465	2	2
3	DCP_1234	1	3
4	DCP_6354	1	4
5	DCP_7456	2	5

Primitive Dimension pgd_dcp_localization

dcp_localization_pk	dcp_localization_geometry
1	●
2	●
3	●
4	●
5	●

Fig. 5.1 An Example of a GDW Schema

pgd_city and *pgd_state*, respectively). This allows us to represent the spatial objects geographical descriptions by normalizing their geometries.

Definition 4 (Conventional dimension table) *A conventional dimension table has the schema $K \times S_1 \times \ldots \times S_r \times A_1 \times \ldots \times A_m$, where*
(i) $r \geq 0$. i.e. there are zero or more columns of foreign keys. Also, there is no foreign key to a primitive dimension table;
(ii) $m \geq 1$ (there is at least one attribute) and all attributes are of common description type;
(iii) and there is no geometry.

An example of a conventional dimension is the table *d_time* with just traditional data as shown in figure 5.1. With regards to hybrid dimensions, that is, micro, macro and joint, these are exemplified as follows. Figure 5.1 also shows the table *mhd_hydro_basin* which is an example of a micro hybrid dimension. This table has a foreign key (*hydro_basin_fk*) that refers to the primitive geographical dimension *pgd_basin_localization*. A micro hybrid dimension handles conventional and geographical data, but the geographical ones represent the finest geo-granularity of the dimension (e.g., addresses and plots of land). Note that due to the small spatial granularity, other dimensions rarely share these geo-referenced data. In contrast, a macro hybrid dimension, different to a micro hybrid dimension, handles geographical data that are usually shared (e.g., Countries, Regions, States, and Cities).

Also in the Figure 5.1, a joint hybrid dimension example is represented by the table *jhd_dcp*, with two foreign keys: 1) *dcp_localization_fk*, that links its table to the primitive geographical dimension table *pgd_dcp_localization* and 2) *localization_fk*, that provides a means of relating its table to the composed geographical dimension *cgd_localization*. A good reason for using the hybrid dimension specializations is that an increase in the data model semantic expressiveness may be gained. However, for some applications, we consider that there will be no need for such specialization and the use of the generic hybrid dimension will suffice.

Definition 5 (Hybrid dimension table) *A hybrid dimension table has the schema* $K \times S_1 \times \ldots \times S_r \times A_1 \times \ldots \times A_m$, *where:*
(i) $r \geq 1$, i.e. there is at least one column of foreign keys. Also, the foreign keys are keys for a primitive and/or composite dimension tables;
(ii) $m \geq 1$ in such way that there is at least one attribute of type common description and one attribute of type geographic description;
(iii) and there is no geometry.
Moreover the hybrid dimension table can be micro, macro or joint as following defined:
micro: *the attributes of type geographic description are micro (finest geo-granularity);*
macro: *the attributes of type geographic description are macro (highest geo-granularity);*
joint: *the attributes of type geographic description can be micro and macro.*

Definition 6 (Fact table) *A fact table is an n-ary relation over $K \times A_1 \times \ldots \times A_m \times M_1 \times \ldots M_r \times MG_1 \times \ldots \times MG_q$, where*
(i) $n = 1 + m + r + q$;
(ii) K is the set of attributes representing the primary key of the table, formed by $S_1 \times S_2 \times \ldots \times S_p$, where each S_i, $1 \leq i \leq p$ is a foreign key to a dimension table;
(iii) each attribute A_j, $0 \leq j \leq m$, is a set of attribute values of type T_B;
(iv) each column M_k, $0 \leq k \leq r$ is a set of measures of type T_B;
(v) and each column MG_l, $0 \leq l \leq p$, is a set of measures of type T_G.

For the fact table example, see the figure 5.1 and consider the table *f_meteorology* having four foreign keys (i.e. *time_fk, localization_fk, dcp_fk* and *hydro_basin_fk*) and a measure (i.e. *precipitation*) that represents the rain falls rates derived from all the data collect platforms.

Obviously, depending on the project decision, a GDW may be modeled on other ways, with schemas different from that presented in the Figure 5.1. One of these possible variations consists in the creation of a GDW with a facts table which stores geometries, what are called geographic measures. We also may define a schema having a facts table with no facts and degenerated dimensions.

In order to exemplify a facts table containing geographic measures we shall now consider the GDW schema built for helping in the distribution analysis of the agricultural products plantations showed in the Figure 5.2. In the figure 5.2-(A) we have the facts table *f_agriculture_distribution* which stores numerical and geographic data on the agricultural plantations distribution in a certain region. This table has three foreign keys: 1) *time_fk*, linking to a conventional dimension table *d_time* showed in the Figure 5.1; 2) *localization_fk*, linking to the composed geographic dimension table *cgd_localization* from the figure 5.1 and 3) *product_fk*, relating the facts table to the dimension table *d_product* (Figure 5.2-(B)), which is in turn related to the table *d_cultivation_category* (Figure 5.2-(C)). As observed, the facts table *f_agriculture_distribution* has two measures: 1) *planting_quantity*, which is of type numerical and 2) *planting_area*, being of type geographic. The aggregation functions commonly present at a traditional DW will be applied for the measure *planting_quantity*. However, as a differential, we have spatial functions being applied on the measure *planting_quantity*, as for instance the geometries union.

(A)
Fact Table f_agriculture_distribution

time_fk	localization_fk	product_fk	planting_quantity	planting_area
1	1	6	100	
1	5	1	20	
2	1	3	130	
2	3	6	30	
3	2	4	70	
3	4	5	40	
4	2	2	80	
4	1	5	140	

(B)
Conventional Dimension d_product

product_pk	product_name	cultivation_category_fk
1	Corn	2
2	Soy	2
3	Cane of Sugar	1
4	Cotton	1
5	Rice	2
6	Banana	1

(C)
Conventional Dimension d_cultivation_category

cultivation_category_pk	category_name
1	Permanent
2	Temporary

(D)
Fact Table f_meteorology2

time_fk	localization_fk	dcp_fk	dcp_localization	precipitation
1	1	1	●	10
1	5	2	●	20
2	1	1	●	5
2	3	3	●	15
3	2	5	●	5
3	4	4	●	2
4	2	5	●	10
4	1	1	●	5

(E)
Fact Table f_dcp_registration

time_fk	localization_fk	dcp_fk	hydro_basin_fk
1	1	1	1
1	5	2	1
2	1	1	2
2	3	3	3
3	2	3	2

(F)
Fact Table f_dcp_registration2

time_fk	localization_fk	dcp_fk	registration_number
1	1	1	2005011
1	5	2	2005012
2	1	3	2005013

Fig. 5.2 Additional Examples for the GDW Formal Definitions

The fact table *f_meteorology2*, presented in the Figure 5.2-(D) is an alternative modelling for the *f_meteorology* fact table showed in the Figure 5.1. The main difference is that, in the table *f_meteorology2* the geographical localization of the dcp (*dcp_localization*) is stored in a column of the fact table. Thus, the foreign key *dcp_fk* links this table with a conventional dimension table that has descriptive data only.

In the Figure 5.2-(E), an example of facts table (*f_dcp_registration*) without numerical or geographical measures is showed. At this example, the purpose is to register the installation date of data collection platforms located within hydrographic basins of a certain region. Thus, as no geographical or spatial measure is being registered, the analysis on the facts table may be performed using the COUNT function, for instance, on the foreign keys columns. Another possibility of modelling a facts table consists in creating degenerated dimensions which is represented by the column *registration_number* from the table *f_dcp_registration2* (Figure 5.2-(F)).

Definition 7 (Schema of Geographical Data Warehouse) *An schema of a Geographical Data Warehouse is a two-tuple GDW = (DT,FT), where DT is a nonempty finite set of dimension tables and FT is a nonempty finite set of fact tables.*

Finally, the set of tables shown in the Figure 5.1 may be seen as an example of a geographical data schema formally defined above.

5.3 A Metamodel for GDW

In this section, the GeoDWM metamodel is presented, which results from an implementation work related to the formal model discussed in the section 5.2. In order to allow the other studies to use and extend our metamodel, GeoDWM is based on the Relational patterns of CWM (Common Warehouse Metamodel) [24] and SFS (Simple Feature Specification) for SQL of the OGC [3]. GeoDWM is a metamodel which: 1) is specified using OCL restrictions (Object Constraint Language)[12] and UML (Unified Modeling Language) [20] classes diagram so that its specification is not ambiguous and is easy to understand; 2) is based on the Relational package of the CWM and SFS for SQL of the OGC to facilitate its usage and extension by other studies; 3) defines how the concepts (e.g., measures and conventional and geographical dimensions) of a dimensional and geographical model can be organized and related to describe a GDW; 4) provides a set of stereotypes with pictograms that are meant to assist and guide the project designer in the GDW modelling activity; 5) serves as a basic metamodel for CASE tools that aims the conceptual modelling and the automatic generation of logical GDW schemas; and finally, 6) enable, through its OCL restrictions, to verify the consistency of the models generated. The GeoDWM metamodel is showed in the Figure 5.3 and detailed as follows.

The *Schema*, *Table*, *Column*, *PrimaryKey* and *ForeignKey* classes are part of the CWM Relational package. The *Schema* class is a base for navigation in GeoDWM, hence, representing the dimensional and geographical schema of a DWG. A schema is a named set of zero or more tables, described by the *Table* class. Tables are composed of zero or more columns (*Column*) by at least one primary key restriction (*PrimaryKey*) and zero or more foreign keys (*ForeignKey*). These associate columns of a table with columns of another table. Tables can be specialized in fact tables (*FactTable*) and dimension tables (*DimensionTable*), whilst the columns are specialized in attributes of a table (*TAttribute*), degenerated dimensions (*Degenerated*)

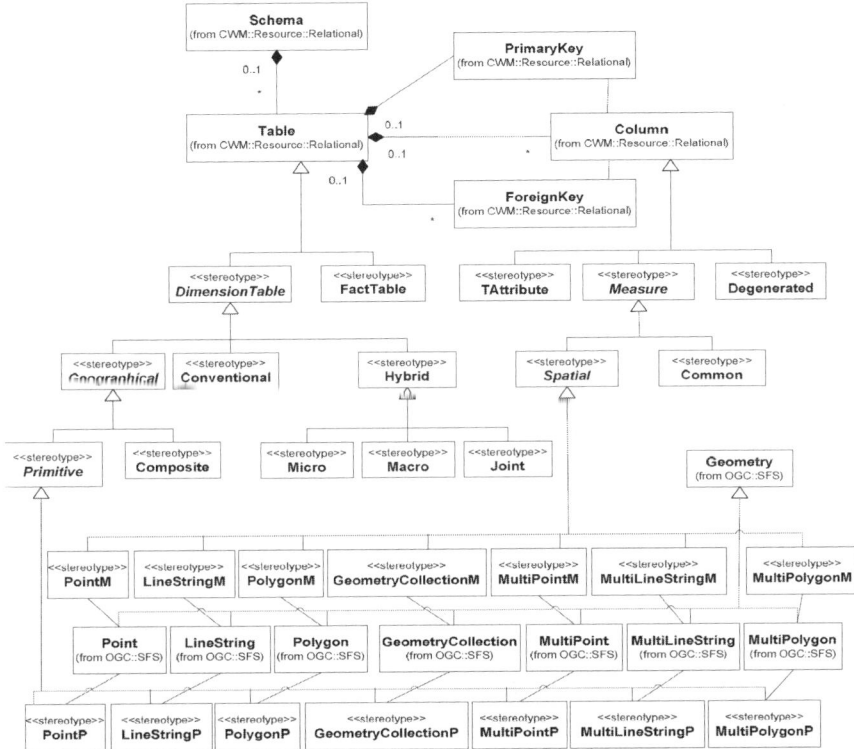

Fig. 5.3 The GeoDWM Metamodel

and measures (*Measure*). The latter can be specialized in common measures (*Common*) and spatial measures (*Spatial*). Spatial measures are specialized in classes that are associated with a SFS class to standardize and represent geometries of the point (*PointM*), line strings (*LineStringM*), polygon (*PolygonM*), geometry collections (*GeometryCollectionM*), multiple points (*MultiPointM*), multiple line strings (*MultiLineStringM*) and multiple polygons (*MultiPolygonM*) types.

A dimension table (*DimensionTable*) can be specialized in three different dimensions: *Conventional*, *Geographical* and *Hybrid*. In the first case, as in a traditional DW, a DWG also provides support for dimensions that store only conventional data (e.g., a dimension product). The other two types of dimensions model the concepts of the GeoDWFrame proposal. Geographical Dimensions are specialized in Composite (Composite) and Primitive (Primitive). These are also specialized in classes which are associated with a SFS class to standardize and represent geometries of the point (*PointP*), line strings (*LineStringP*), polygon (*PolygonP*), geometry collections (*GeometryCollectionP*), multiple points (*MultiPointP*), multiple line strings (*MultiLineStringP*) and multiple polygons (*MultiPolygonP*) types.

Hybrid Dimensions are specialized in Micro (Micro), Macro (Macro) and Joint (Joint). It is important to point out that the use of micro, macro and joint dimensions is not compulsory, being recommended when a project designer wishes to express details about the geographical granularity of each hybrid dimension. For that reason, if the GDW project does not request such level of detail, the *Hybrid* super class may be used in representing a generic hybrid dimension.

Stereotype	Pictogram	Description
FactTable	$\mathcal{F}$	Fact Table
TAttibute	a	Table Attribute
Degenerated	d	Degenerated Dimension
Measure		Abstract Measure
Common	$\$$	Conventional Measure
Spatial		Abstract Spatial Measure
PointM		Spatial Measure with a Point geometry
LineStringM		Spatial Measure with a Line String geometry
PolygonM		Spatial Measure with a Polygon geometry
GeometryCollectionM		Spatial Measure with a Geometry Collection geometry
MultiPointM		Spatial Measure with a Multiple Points geometry
MultiLineStringM		Spatial Measure with a Multiple Line Strings geometry
MultiPolygonM		Spatial Measure with a Multiple Polygons geometry

Fig. 5.4 GeoDWM Stereotypes related to facts

Stereotype	Pictogram	Description
DimensionTable		Abstract Dimension Table
Conventional	$\mathcal{D}$	Conventional Dimension
Geographical		Abstract Geographical Dimension
Composite		Composite Geographical Dimension
Primitive		Primitive Abstract Dimensão Geographical Dimension
PointP	●	Primitive Geographical Dimension with a Point geometry
LineStringP		Primitive Geographical Dimension with a Line String geometry
PolygonP		Primitive Geographical Dimension with a Polygon geometry
GeometryCollectionP		Primitive Geographical Dimension with a Geometry Collection geometry
MultiPointP		Primitive Geographical Dimension with a Multiple Points geometry
MultiLineStringP		Primitive Geographical Dimension with a Multiple Line Strings geometry
MultiPolygonP		Primitive Geographical Dimension with a Multiple Polygons geometry
Hybrid	$g\mathcal{H}$	Generic Hybrid Dimension
Micro	$\mu\mathcal{H}$	Micro Hybrid Dimension
Macro	$M\mathcal{H}$	Macro Hybrid Dimension
Joint	$\cup\mathcal{H}$	Joint Hybrid Dimension

Fig. 5.5 GeoDWM Stereotypes related to dimensions

In order to give more semantics and improve the graphic representation of a dimensional and geographical model, GeoDWM uses UML [20] stereotypes to enlarge its expression and visualization capacity. In our work, stereotypes are used to classify the metamodel elements, enabling its semantic abstraction and extension. Besides that, so as to enrich the model's visualization elements, GeoDWM uses pictograms (i.e., icons) for its stereotypes. In GeoDWM, the stereotypes are used to manipulate conventional and geographical properties of dimensions and measures (e.g., to represent different types of geographical dimensions and measures). Figures 5.4 and 5.5 specify, respectively, the GeoDWM stereotypes related to facts and dimensions of a GDW. These show tables with the following columns: 1) Stereotype: the name of the stereotype; 2) Pictogram: the icon associated with the stereotype (empty when non-existent) and 3) Description: the stereotype textual description.

In summary, the dimension table taxonomy aims to organize, normalize and give more semantic to the GDW schema. This is so because semantically related data are structured according to their respective dimension tables and the dimension tables with geographic data have their geometries normalized through the use of primitive dimensions to minimize storage costs. Moreover, the hybrid dimension table classification may be useful to explicitly indicate which tables share geographic data with each other (i.e. macro hybrid dimension tables) and which do not share (i.e. micro hybrid dimension tables). In doing this, the GDW database administrator is able to visualize, through pictograms, which dimension tables depend on each other and thus, is able to identify from these, which of them need amore effective physical management. Finally, the schema semantic improvements derived from the use of the GeoDWM stereotypes and pictograms may be useful to visually guide the GDW data analysis. By using these, users will be able to clearly identify the explicit semantics of each dimension table data, simplifying the analysis tasks and making them easy and friendly.

5.4 A CASE Tool for Modelling Geographical Data Warehouses

GeoDWCASE is a tool that: 1) offers a friendly interface (GUI) and has graphic resources which permit to abstract implementation details to that from the GDW schema, aiding both the designers and users to understand their geographic and dimensional model; 2) is implemented in Java on the open platform Eclipse [23] and thus, guarantying its portability to several operational systems; 3) is based on XMI pattern (XML Metadata Interchange) [11] for storage, manipulation, recuperation and exchange of metadata, 4) offers support to model UML classes using the stereotypes with pictograms of GeoDWM; 5) permits that the GDW model in developing is validated through OCL restrictions (Object Constraint Language) [12] of GeoDWM; 6) provides the automatic transformation between a conceptual model and a logical schema compatible to the SDBMS (Spatial DBMS) that will be used and 7) aims to offer support to the reverse engineering of logical schemas based on

GeoDWM. Figure 5.6 shows the GeoDWCASE tool architecture. The main components found in this architecture are detailed as follows.

Graphical Editor: Represents the modelling interface by which the user interacts with its schemas. This module was developed using the Eclipse GMF (Graphical Modelling Framework) [8] framework.

Metadata Manager: The GeoDWM metamodel guides this component to permit the storage and manipulation of metadata from the stored GDW schemas. Here, XMI [11] is used for metadata storing, importation and exportation.

Schema Validator: Uses the OCL restrictions defined in GeoDWM to verify the consistence of the GDW schema.

Schema Generator: Makes the transformation (SQL scripts generation), importation (reverse engineering) and exportation (using XMI) of schemas.

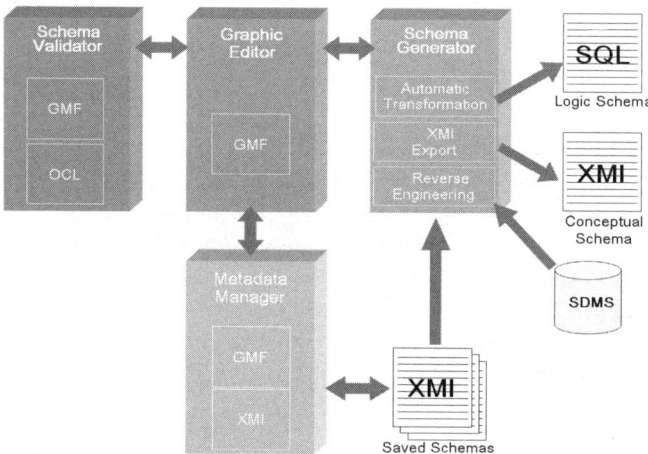

Fig. 5.6 GeoDWCASE Architecture

GeoDWCASE implements the stereotypes defined by GeoDWM, which were presented in the section 5.3. With the use of GeoDWCASE, the designer is able to perform manipulations on the elements which represent facts and dimensions of a GDW, such as: 1) insert. 2) exclude; 3) edit (e.g. colors and fonts); 4) visualize at different zoom levels; 5) organize (e.g. auto-organize and align); 6) export the data model as figure (e.g. JPG, GIF, SVG). Figure 5.7 presents the modelling environment of GeoDWCASE. In the area 1 shown in this figure, the designer has a tree view of all his GDW projects, with their respective models organized in folders. The edition area (Figure 5.7-(2)) exhibits the fact tables and dimensions tables, and their respective attributes which compose a GDW schema. For instance, the GDW schema for data taken from the DataSUS (Database from the Brazilian Health Unique System) is presented in the Figure 5.7-(2)).

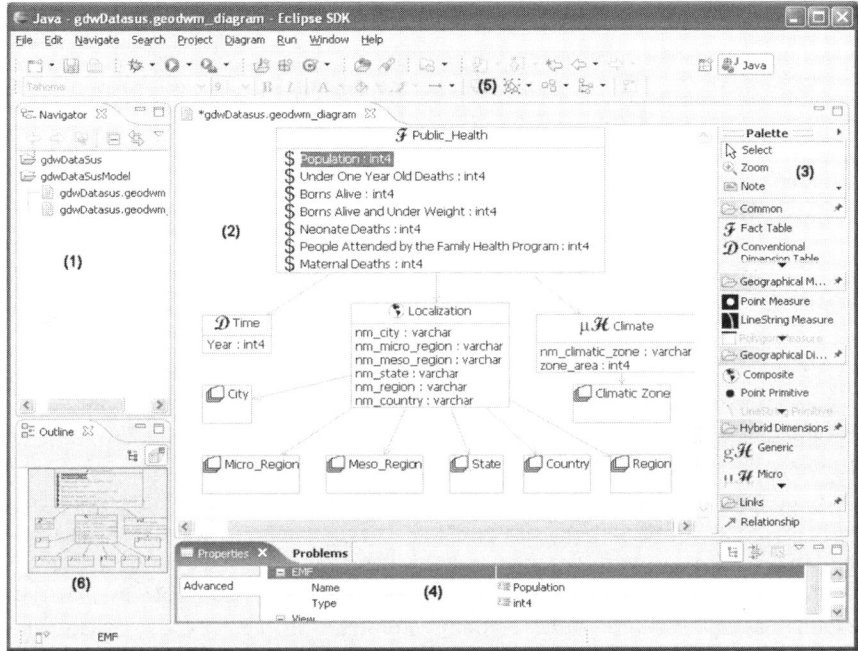

Fig. 5.7 The GeoDWCASE Tool

The elements palette of the GeoDWCASE (Figure 5.7-(3)) has constructers for the stereotypes used in the GDW modelling and defined by GeoDWM. Note that the semantics of each type of element is easily perceived by its stereotype with its pictogram. The task of modelling a GDW consists in clicking on the chosen palette element and putting it on the diagram. In the GDW schema from the Figure 5.7, we have the facts table *Public_health*, which has several conventional measures (e.g. population, under one year old deaths, births alive, births alive under weight and neonate's deaths). There are three dimension tables related to this facts table: *Time, Localization* and *Climate*, which are used to represent, respectively, the data when a certain fact occurred, its localization on the map and the climatic zones of a given region. *Localization* is a composed geographical dimension and its attributes represent the descriptive information of the geographical objects contained in the related primitive dimensions (e. g. *Country, Region, State, Meso Region, Micro Region* and *City*). In turn, *Climate* is a micro hybrid dimension, being related to the composed dimension *Localization* and the primitive dimension *Climatic Zone*. It is worth to emphasize that for using the GeoDWCASE, the definition of primary and foreign keys, at modelling time is not necessary once these keys are automatically generated at the moment of transformation into the logical model. Thus, in the case of primary key, a column with the name of the own table plus the prefix "PK" is inserted in the table which is suffering the transformation, whilst, for the foreign key, a field having the name of the destiny table plus the prefix "FK" is inserted in the relationship origin table.

The properties edition of each element of a schema may be performed through the view *Properties* exhibited in the area 4 illustrated in the Figure 5.7. These properties may be related to the element's appearance (e.g. font style, font size, font color, line color, filling) or element's metadata (e. g. name, type). The interface still has a bar with buttons for the selection of all elements, automatic organization and element's alignment (area 5 from the Figure 5.7). Further, there is a view which permits the outline view of the data model (area 6 from the Figure 5.7), allowing the user to navigate through the schema by dragging the mouse and thus, facilitating the visualization of big schemas.

As shown in the area 1 from the Figure 5.7, each schema being designed is composed by two files: a file containing the graphical representations of the model (extension *.geodwm_diagram*) and another containing the GeoDWM metadata used in the model (extension *.geodwm*). The content of these files is stored in XMI, in which each element is delimited by a tag (i.e. markup) which contains its name, its stereotype, its type and its relationships. The tag *table* stores the table stereotype with its name and the elements references for which the table has foreign keys (based on the relationships defined in the data model). The internal tag *column* stores the column stereotype, its name and its data type. These two files for the GDW schema shown in the Figure 5.7 can be found at http://www.cin.ufpe.br/~golapware/geodwcase/gdwDatasus.geodwm_diagram and http://www.cin.ufpe.br/~golapware/geodwcase/gdwDatasus.geodwm, respectively.

With GeoDWCASE, the designer may, at any instant, check its model consistence (i.e. verify if the same respects the rules defined by the GeoDWM). It may be done, accessing the *Diagram* menu and selecting the option *Validate*. The validation component performs a model checking based on the GeoDWM OCL restrictions and then, all the modelling inconsistencies found are listed in the view *Problems* shown in the area 4 from the Figure 5.7. For example, to enforce the geometries normalization, we must guarantee that a primitive geographical dimension table will not contain foreign keys to other dimension tables or fact tables. In this case the OCL restriction *(self.allOppositeAssociationEnds_- forAll* `(not participant.oclIsKindOf(DimensionTable) or not participant.oclIsTypeOf(FactTable))` is applied at validation time. A complete list of the OCL restrictions can be obtained by accessing the following address http://www.cin.ufpe.br/~golapware/geodwcase/geodwmoclrestrictions.pdf.

When finalizing the modelling tasks and validating the model, the designer may transform the GDW conceptual schema into its respective logical schema. GeoDW-CASE facilitates this task generating the logical schema to be implemented, automatically. This implementation is Java codified and makes the transformation of the XMI elements (conceptual schema) into tables and their respective columns (logical schema) according to the DDL syntax (Data Definition Language) of the target SDBMS. Because each spatial DBMS has a particular instructions set for the geometries treatment, the GeoDWCASE tool needs to implement an automatic transformation module specific for each spatial DBMS. Three of these modules have already been implemented and transform GeoDWM schemas into DDL of the following SDBMS: PostgreSQL with PostGIS, Oracle Spatial and MySQL. Each of these modules must implement a set of transformation rules according to its target SDBMS. For example, for the PostGIS module, each element with the stereotype *FactTable* generates a relational table. The primary key restriction is automatically generated based on the table's foreign keys. Another example is the treatment of *PointP, LineStringP, PolygonP, GeometryCollectionP, MultiPointP, MultiLnestringP* or *MultiPolygonP* primitive dimensions. Each of these dimensions generates a relational table with an identifier column that is automatically generated based on the element's name. The primary key restriction is also generated based on this column. On the other hand, the column that will store the geometry is automatically generated based on the element's stereotype, the SRID (Spatial Reference Identifier) and the number of dimensions defined by the designer at design time. After executing the transformation, a file *.sql* is generated with the logical model. This file may be accessed in the current project and its content may be visualized in GeoDWCASE, without being needed the use of an extern editor. In http://www.cin.ufpe.br/~golapware/geodwcase/gdwDatasusPostGIS.sql can be found the SQL script generated by the GeoDWCASE Tool for the GDW schema presented in the Figure 5.7, according to the PostgreSQL/PostGIS SDBMS syntax.

5.5 Design Issues

To demonstrate the application of the concepts related to GeoDWM and the practical use of GeoDWCASE, it will be presented here different approaches for modelling a GDW. First, we will discuss on some possible ways of modelling a GDW with meteorological data. This GDW has been specified from data taken from LAMEPE (Meteorological Laboratory from the State of Pernambuco, in Brazil). This laboratory counts on a meteorological DCP net (Data Collection Platform) and has the monitoring of atmospheric conditions as objective.

In the Figure 5.8, the "unique joint" approach was used for a composed geographic dimension *Localization*. In this figure, it can be noted a facts table and some dimension tables. Note that all these tables are easily identified through the GeoDWM stereotypes. The facts table *Meteorology* has precipitation, air temperature, air relative humidity, atmospheric pressure, wind velocity and solar radiation as conventional measures. *Time* is a conventional dimension and has attributes to store the year, semester, trimester, month of the year, name of the month, fortnight of the year, week of the year, name of the day, number of the day in the month, number of the day in the year and a date. *Localization* is a compose geographical dimension having attributes to store the location descriptions for the *State, Micro Region, Meso Region* and *City*. This latter is a primitive geographical dimension and provides a means of normalizing geometries.

The composed geographic dimension *Localization* is shared with the *DCP* and *Hydrographic Basins* dimensions where, *DCP* is a conjunct hybrid dimension be-

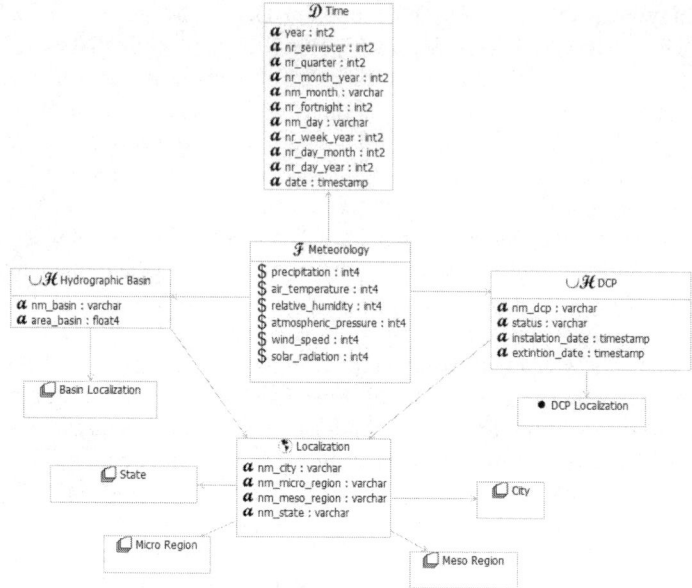

Fig. 5.8 GDW Schema with unique joint approach

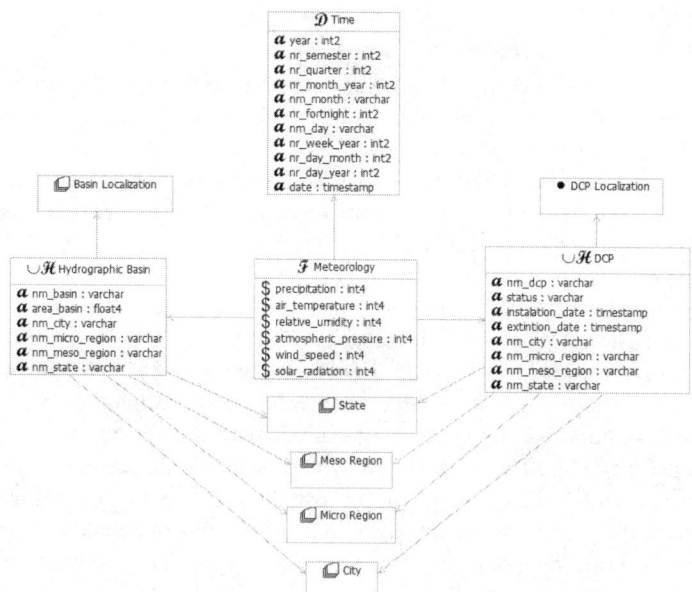

Fig. 5.9 GDW Schema with multiple junctions

cause manipulates both the conventional data and the geographical data of higher or lower granularity. *DCP* has fields to store conventional data as DCP name (i.e. identification), DCP status (i.e. if it is operating or not), DCP installation date and DCP extinction date. The geographical data of higher granularity are obtained from Localization, while those of lower granularity are represented by the primitive geographic dimension *DCP Localization*, which stores the geometry of the DCP localization as a point. *Hydrographic Basin* is also a conjunct hybrid dimension, storing the basin name and its area. This dimension shares the *Localization* geographical data of higher granularity and is related to the primitive geographic dimension *Basin localization* which stores the basin's geometry as multiple polygons, normalizing it.

Next, Figure 5.9 presents a second approach of the meteorological GDW modelling. A multiple junctions approach for several primitive geographic dimensions (i.e. City, *Micro Region, Meso Region* and *State*) was used in this figure. At this approach, the shared composed geographic dimension is not used. Each conjunct hybrid dimension is directly related to the primitive dimensions which store geometries of higher granularity, preserving the geometries' normalization. However, the geographic localization descriptions are stored in the conjunct hybrid dimension resulting in redundancy and a higher storage cost, once these descriptions would be stored for each register. Also, note that these attributes would be stored in both conjunct hybrid dimensions.

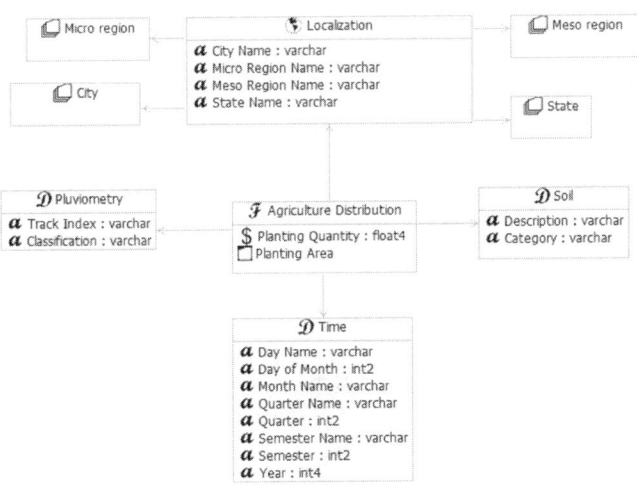

Fig. 5.10 GDW Schema with spatial measures for the agriculture field

To exemplify another possibility of GDW modelling containing spatial measures, we present in the Figure 5.10 a GDW schema containing a facts table *agriculture_distribution* which contains a conventional measure called *planting_quantity* and another spatial measure called planting area whose values stored will be geometries of polygon class. In the schema of the Figure 5.10, the facts table is related to three conventional dimensions (i.e. *Pluviometry*, *Time* and *Soil*) and to a composed geographic dimension *Localization*. The use of stereotypes and pictograms helps in clarifying the understanding about the application of spatial dimensions and spatial measures. This guides users in defining queries for data analysis as it helps them in visually distinguishing: 1) which kinds of aggregation functions are applicable to each spatial measure type and 2) what kinds of spatial queries are properly specified to each GDW dimension type (e.g. both Figures 5.8 and 5.9 differ from Figure 5.10 in that they do not have spatial measures and then, spatial aggregation functions are clearly not applicable.)

As previously discussed, there is more than one approach to design dimensional and geographic schemas of a GDW. First of the schemas showed here stands out by favoring the geometries' normalization (decreasing the storage cost) and the reduction in the amount of junctions to be performed (optimizing the query processing). Another point deserving attention is the gain in expression and semantic capacity provided by the GeoDWCASE and GeoDWM. Further, the great advantage in using them is the fact that the alterations in the conceptual schema of the GDW may be easily and quickly performed. Several approaches may be still analyzed at modelling time and the schemas created may be validated at every instant. The corresponding logical schemas may be automatically generated, analyzed and tested in order to identify which ones are better applied for each case.

5.6 Related Work

In this section, some relevant studies related to the modelling of GDW are discussed. Stefanovic et al. [28] have defined three types of dimensions based on the members of a hierarchy's spatial references: non-spatial, spatial-to-non-spatial and totally spatial. They also differ numerical and spatial measures. In addition, a method for constructing and materializing spatial cubes, as well as the efficiency and the efficacy of some algorithms for materializing cubes are also investigated.

Then, Rivest et al. [25] discussed the importance of new tools which enable exploring the potential of the spatial and temporal dimensions of a GDW in a space-temporal analysis process. They have extended the previous definition of spatial measures to address spatial measures that are computed by metric or topological operators. Further, the authors emphasized the need for more advanced querying capabilities to provide end users with topological and metric operators.

Another important work was carried out by Pedersen and Tryfona [22] who presented a data model formal definition given at the conceptual level for a GDW. This model is based on the work performed by Han et al. [13] that considers spatial measures as a collection of geometries whilst dimensions are always seen as non-spatial. However, this data model has a limited expressiveness capability because of the restricted number of spatial objects types that are taken into account.

More recently, Malinowski and Zimanyi [17] presented a GDW data model that is based on the MADS spatiotemporal conceptual model [21] which is in turn an object based entity- relationship approach (ERC+) [27] that uses pictograms to represent the geographical objects properties and topological relationships. According to this model, a dimension may contain one or more related levels to represent a geometrical hierarchy. Moreover, the fact table is represented as an existing n-ary relationship among these dimensions. The fact table attributes consist of measures and a spatial measure is seen as a geometry or function that computes a geometrical property, such as a spatial object length or surface. Further details on this metamodel formalization can be found in [27].

In [7] the data model MuSD (multigranular spatial data warehouse) is proposed, which is based on concepts of spatial fact, spatial dimension and multi-level spatial measure. According to this, a spatial fact registers a geographical event that is relevant to be known and analyzed. Also, a spatial dimension describes the geometrical properties of facts having a geographical meaning, while a multi-level spatial measure registers multiple geometries at different levels of details (e.g., an accident may be represented by a point along a road, a road segment or the whole road). Thus, the innovation issue related to this model is the representation of spatial measures according to multiple levels of geometrical granularity.

Zghal et al. [29] have proposed a metamodel and the CASME tool. The metamodel is based on class diagram of UML and also approaches spatial dimensions, spatial hierarchies and spatial measures. Four types of dimensions have been identified: non-geometrical spatial dimension, geometrical to non-geometrical spatial dimension, entirely geometrical dimension and temporal dimension. In thus, a measurement is numerical when it contains only numerical data and spatial when it corresponds to a collection of pointers to spatial objects.

As shown in this section, there are several GDW modelling approaches. However, their formalization work are not based on a friendly graphical language, such as ER and UML, that facilitates the daily activities of a GDW designer, except for the studies found in [17] and Zghal et al. [29]. Regarding the work described in [17], although using pictograms and a graphical language as well, the latter is based on the ERC+ data model semantic and syntax, which is not a pattern nor is in widespread use by researchers like a ER schema or a UML class diagram. Moreover, the metamodel outlined in [17] does not take into account the use of reference patterns, such as CWM [24] for DW and OGC for GIS [3] and defines concepts for a geographical data cube schema (e.g. hierarchy and level). With regards to the results given by Zghal et al. [29], their graphical language is based on UML, but pictograms are not used to increase the GDW schema expressiveness and also defines concepts for geographical data cube schema. In addition, reference patterns found in the DW and GIS areas are not used in [29] as well.

In comparing our data model proposal with the work presented in [29] and [17], it is worth to note that we focus on the GDW dimensional schema design by leaving the use of multidimensional constructors (e.g. hierarchies and levels) to the geographical cube schema design phase. With regards to the GDW dimensional schema design, the definitions for the different types of hybrid dimensions are not mandatory, but are useful for explicitly specifying the geographical granuralities of these dimension types and the dimension table dependences. This allows us to identify that while macro hybrid dimensions have high granularity and for this reason, they are associated with any other GDW schema dimensions. Thus, the micro dimensions have low granularity and rarely are associated with any other GDW schema dimensions. Finally, because of the intrinsic dimensional redundancy found in any DW and the high costs of storing coordinate data, the use of primitive dimensions optimizes the building of GDW schemas by normalizing geometries.

5.7 Conclusions and Future Work

Much research addresses the use of DW with GIS, but still lacks a consensus about the dimensional model of GDW. In this article, mathematical formalizations for a GDW data model are presented. These extend the GeoDWFrame framework to take into account the concept of spatial measures and to provide a data model definition that aims to be free from ambiguities. We have presented the GeoDWM, which is a metamodel that specifies how different types of dimensions and measures (conventional and geographical) can be organized and associated to model a dimensional and geographical model of a DWG. Besides that, GeoDWM details a set of stereotypes, pictograms and restrictions meant to describe and guarantee that the model's consistency can be verified. In order to facilitate its use and extension to other studies, GeoDWM is based on CWM and SFS for SQL of the OGC Relational patterns and on the GeoDWFrame proposal. Because it is a metamodel for DWG dimensional and geographical schemas, GeoDWM does not define concepts such as hierarchy and hierarchic levels, which are pertinent to the context of multidimensional modelling of a geographical cube (i.e. several geographical cubes can be created from a DWG). GeoDWM is also part of a larger project that proposed a software architecture, called GOLAPA [10, 4, 5].

UML and OCL were chosen to specify GeoDWM because: 1) UML is a pattern language for the metamodelling activity, easily extendable and well accepted by the data base community; 2) the UML classes diagram provides a detailed and easily understood graphic notation and 3) OCL has a good set of expressions which allow specifying high-level restrictions on models. Besides that, the CWM and SFS for SQL of an OGC Relational specifications were also conceived by UML.

In order to validate the proposal and offer the immediate application of GeoDWM, a GeoDWCASE tool was developed, which enables a DWG project designer to make a conceptual model based on the model proposed in this article, and afterwards, automatically create its compatible logical model with a spatial SGBD. As previously mentioned in section 5.4, currently, this functionality is only available for SGBD PostgreSQL with the PostGIS extension, Oracle Spatial and MySQL, therefore, in future studies other spatial SGBD will also be contemplated. Other indications of future studies are: 1) extending GeoDWM and GeoCASE to provide support to matrix type geographical data and 2) defining a methodology of a metamodel for the implementation (conceptual project, logical and physical) of DWG according to GeoDWM.

In summary, one of the main advantages of GeoDWM is to enrich the UML Classes Diagram by applying of a set of stereotypes and pictograms that have been proposed to guide and facilitate the GDW designers in their daily data modeling activities. These help in identifying the dimension types and data types that can be used in the conceptual data model representations. Another advantage of this data model is the possibility of making use of a CASE tool by providing a means of developing conceptual data modeling activities that are totally visual and easy of understanding. Also, it provides automatic generation facilities for creating GDW logical schemas together with schemas consistency verification tools through the use of OCL restrictions.

References

1. Sandro Bimonte, Anne Tchounikine, and Maryvonne Miquel. Towards a spatial multidimensional model. In *DOLAP '05: Proceedings of the 8th ACM international workshop on Data warehousing and OLAP*, pages 39–46, New York, NY, USA, 2005. ACM.
2. Surajit Chaudhuri and Umeshwar Dayal. An overview of data warehousing and olap technology. *SIGMOD Rec.*, 26(1):65–74, 1997.
3. Open Geospatial Consortium. Simple features specification for sql - http://portal.opengeospatial.org/files/?artifact_id=829. Technical report, 1999.
4. Joel da Silva, Valéria C. Times, and Ana Carolina Salgado. An open source and web based framework for geographic and multidimensional processing. In *SAC '06: Proceedings of the 2006 ACM symposium on Applied computing*, pages 63–67, New York, NY, USA, 2006. ACM.
5. Joel da Silva, Valéria Times, Robson Fidalgo, and Roberto Barros. Providing geographic-multidimensional decision support over the web. In *APWeb 2005*, pages 477–488, 2005.
6. Joel da Silva, Ausberto Castro Vera, Anjolina Oliveira, Robson Fidalgo, Ana Carolina Salgado, and Valéria Times. Querying geographical datawarehouses with geomdql. In *Brazilian Symposium on Databases(SBBD)*, pages 223–237, 2007.
7. Maria Luisa Damiani and Stephano Spaccapietra. Spatial data warehouse modelling. In Jérôme Darmont and Omar Boussaïd, editors, *Processing and Managing Complex Data for Decision Support*, pages 21–27. Idea Group Publishing, Hershey, PA, USA, April 2006.
8. Eclipse. Graphical modeling framework, http://www.eclipse.org/gmf/, Jan 2008.
9. Robson Fidalgo, Valéria Times, Joel da Silva, and Fernando Fonseca. Geodwframe: A framework for guiding the design of geographical dimensional schemas. In *Data Warehousing and Knowledge Discovery (DaWaK)*, pages 26–37, 2004.
10. Robson Fidalgo, Valéria Times, Joel da Silva, and Fernando Fonseca. Providing multidimensional and geographical integration based on a gdw and metamodels. In *Brazilian Symposium on Databases (SBBD)*, pages 148–162, 2004.
11. Object Modeling Group. Xml metadata interchange (xmi) specification, http://www.omg.org/docs/formal/03-05-02.pdf, May 2003.
12. Object Modeling Group. *Object Constraint Language Specification*. Object Modeling Group, June 2005.
13. Jaiwei Han, Krzysztof Koperski, and Nebojsa Stefanovic. Geominer: a system prototype for spatial data mining. *SIGMOD Rec.*, 26(2):553–556, 1997.
14. William H. Inmon. *Building the Data Warehouse*. John Wiley and Sons, 2 edition, 1997.
15. Zdenek Kouba, Petr Miksovský, and Kamil Matousek. On geographical on-line analytical processing (golap). In *ISAS-SCI '01: Proceedings of the World Multiconference on Systemics, Cybernetics and Informatics*, pages 201–205. IIIS, 2001.

16. Paul Longley, Michael Goodchild, David Maguire, and David Rhind. *Geographical Information Systems: Principles, Techniques, Applications and Management*. John Wiley and Sons, New York, 2 edition, May 2005.
17. Elzbieta Malinowski and Esteban Zimányi. Representing spatiality in a conceptual multidimensional model. In *ACM GIS*, pages 12–22, NY, USA, 2004.
18. Elzbieta Malinowski and Esteban Zimányi. Spatial hierarchies and topological relationships in the spatial multidimer model. In *BNCOD*, pages 17–28, 2005.
19. Elzbieta Malinowski and Esteban Zimányi. Requirements specification and conceptual modeling for spatial data warehouses. In *Proc. of the On The Move Federated Conferences and Workshops, OTM*, pages 1616–1625, 2006.
20. OMG. *Unified Modeling Language: Superstructure*. Object Modeling Group, 2004.
21. Christine Parent, Stefano Spaccapietra, and Esteban Zimányi. Spatio-temporal conceptual models: data structures + space + time. In *GIS '99: Proceedings of the 7th ACM international symposium on Advances in geographic information systems*, pages 26–33, New York, NY, USA, 1999. ACM.
22. Torben Bach Pedersen and Nectaria Tryfona. Pre-aggregation in spatial data warehouses. In *SSTD '01: Proceedings of the 7th International Symposium on Advances in Spatial and Temporal Databases*, pages 460–480, London, UK, 2001. Springer-Verlag.
23. Eclipse Plataform. http://www.eclipse.org/. http://www.eclipse.org/., 2007.
24. John Poole and David Mellor. *Common Warehouse Metamodel: An Introduction to the Standard for Data Warehouse Integration*. John Wiley & Sons, Inc., New York, NY, USA, 2001.
25. Sonia Rivest, Yvan Bédard, Marie-Josée Proulx, Martin Nadeau, Frederic Hubert, and Julien Pastor. Solap technology: Merging business intelligence with geospatial technology for interactive spatio-temporal exploration and analysis of data. *Journal of Photogrammetry e Remote Sensing*, pages 17–33, November 2005.
26. Shashi Shekhar, Chang-Tien Lu, X. Tan, Sanjay Chawla, and Ranga Raju Vatsavai. Map cube: A visualization tool for spatial data warehouses. In Harvey Miller and Jiawei Han, editors, *Geographic Data Mining and Knowledge Discovery*, pages 74–109. Taylor and Francis, 2001.
27. Stefano Spaccapietra and Christine Parent. ERC+: An Object based Entity Relationship Approach. In *Conceptual Modelling, Database and Case: An integrated View of Information Systems Development*. John Wiley, 1992.
28. Nebojsa Stefanovic, Jiawei Han, and Krzysztof Koperski. Object-based selective materialization for efficient implementation of spatial data cubes. *IEEE Trans. on Knowl. and Data Eng.*, 12(6):938–958, 2000.
29. Hajer Bâazaoui Zghal, Sami Faïz, and Henda Ben Ghézala. Casme: A case tool for spatial data marts design and generation. In *Design and Management of Data Warehouses (DMDW)*, Berlin, Germany, September 2003.

Chapter 6
Pushing Theoretically-Founded Probabilistic Guarantees in Highly-Efficient OLAP Engines

Alfredo Cuzzocrea and Wei Wang

Abstract Efficient aggregate query processing is a main requirement for Decision Support Systems (DSS), due to the very large size of the multidimensional data stored in the underlying Data Warehouse Server (DWS). Approximate aggregate query processing is able to provide fast answers to aggregate queries by trading off accuracy for efficiency, and has become a useful tool to many DSS-based applications. Researchers have devoted a great deal of attention to the problem of efficiently compressing data cubes in order to retrieve approximate answers having low query errors. However, few works only focus on the problem of deriving *theoretical bounds* over these errors, which is indeed a critical aspect for any database/datacube approximation technique. Starting from these considerations, in this chapter we propose a new approach for efficiently compressing data cubes while ensuring *probabilistic guarantees* over the degree of approximation of the retrieved answers. The final compressed data structure, called **T**unable **P**artition-Tree (*TP-Tree*), is obtained by sampling and separately handling outliers and non-outliers data, with also embedding efficient indexing data structures. The main novelty of TP-Tree consists in being building in dependence on typical *query-workloads* against the target data cube. Another contribution of this chapter is represented by the wide and comprehensive experimental assessment of our proposed data structure, whose performance outperforms state-of-the-art similar techniques.

Alfredo Cuzzocrea
Department of Electronics, Computer Science and Systems, University of Calabria, Italy, e-mail: cuzzocrea@si.deis.unical.it

Wei Wang
School of Computer Science and Engineering, University of New South Wales, Sydney 2052, Australia, e-mail: weiw@cse.unsw.edu.au

6.1 Introduction

Range aggregate queries [28] are one of the most typical and important forms of queries for OLAP applications [23], as they support several perspectives of analysis based on the multidimensional and multi-resolution nature of data. Range aggregate queries apply a SQL aggregation operator (e.g., SUM, AVG, MIN, MAX) over a set of selected contiguous ranges in the domain defined by the Cartesian product of dimension attributes. Range aggregate queries are usually intrinsically resource-intensive, as they introduce high computational overheads in terms of spatial and temporal needs.

Consider the application scenario defined by a Data Warehouse Server (DWS) interacting with an OLAP engine. In this context, due to (i) the large size of underlying data, and (ii) the analytical and interactive nature of client applications that issue OLAP queries, computing approximate answers is a widely-recognized solution to overcome limitations deriving from evaluating OLAP queries against massive data cubes (e.g., see [17]). *Approximate Query Processing* (AQP) allows us to speed-up the throughput of Decision Support Systems (DSS), and shorten the response time by orders of magnitude without decreasing the quality or the effectiveness of answers significantly. Basically, AQP techniques aim at obtaining synopsis data structures, which are succinct representations of the original data cubes, in order to obtain approximate answers to resource-intensive OLAP queries.

In order to tame these overheads, a popular solution is to use sampling-based data cube compression techniques. This because sampled data can be used effectively instead of original data without significantly compromising the accuracy of approximate answers. Besides, sampling-based techniques have gained popularity as they introduce a very low additional computational cost with respect to the one required by a conventional query optimizer. Skewed datasets represent a serious problem for sampling-based techniques [14, 17], because they are characterized by the presence of outliers (i.e., valid data whose values are significantly different from the rest of the data values) that can degrade the accuracy of the approximate answers substantially. In fact, when data distributions are skewed, it is highly likely that sampling will exclude these outliers, hence their contribution will not appear in the final approximate answers. Furthermore, sampling become more problematic when range aggregate queries are processed as it is possible that no sampled data satisfies the aggregation predicate. In turn, this enlarges the probability of excluding outliers' contribution to the final approximate answer. According to these analyses, it is highly advantageous to managing outliers separately from non-outliers in approximate query processing. However, previous work mainly focuses on the choice of outliers, and does not address this critical issue of how to organize those outliers to support efficient approximate query processing.

Our approximation technique focuses on answering range-sum queries on OLAP data cubes, which apply the SUM aggregation operator over a set of selected contiguous ranges in the domain defined by the Cartesian product of dimension attributes. Range-sum queries are very useful for a wide range of DSS-based applications, as they can be used (i) to obtain other basic aggregation operators (e.g., range-count queries are a special instance of the range-sum queries, and range-avg queries can be obtained by combing the results of range-sum and range-count queries), and (ii) as low-level functionalities for implementing more complex aggregation operators, such as standard deviation. Range-sum query answering has been widely investigated mainly by the so-called chunk-based techniques that aim at decomposing data cubes into a set of pre-aggregate chunks of multidimensional data in order to speed-up query processing. Obviously, this approach can be very useful when dealing with range-sum queries since the SUM operation is additive and, consequently, any range-sum query can be efficiently evaluated by summing-up the partial results computed on chunks instead of accessing the set of all the involved data cells. For instance, chunk-based techniques have been efficiently applied for (i) answering range-sum queries by building Prefix-Sum Arrays [28], (ii) caching multidi-mensional queries in OLAP [19], and (iii) designing highly efficient data cube storage managers [32].

Multidimensional OLAP (MOLAP) systems [25] store data cubes explicitly in the form of multidimensional arrays. For this reason, MOLAP data cubes require specialized software components for generating, manipulating, and querying multidimensional data. The advantage of MOLAP systems is that mathematical techniques, stemmed from different research areas and designed for different application purposes (such as data compression for images, data coding for telecommunication systems etc), allow additional data management functionalities and potential performance gains, as first reported in [42, 45]. Our approach for supporting range-sum approximate query answering is targeted at MOLAP data cubes since our basic technique for obtaining data cube compression is designed and tailored to multidimensional arrays. This allows us to efficiently access and process data, and ensures low computational overheads at query time.

In this paper, we address the issue of providing fast approximate answers to range-sum queries on data cubes. We propose a query-workload adaptive, tree-like synopsis data structure, called *Tunable Partition-Tree* (TP-Tree), against which queries are evaluated to obtain approximate answers. Given a data cube A, the data structure $TP\text{-}Tree(A)$ for A contains sampled data *and* outliers from partitions of A. Samples and outliers are efficiently organized by means of a high-performance data structure retaining a hierarchical nature that facilitates query processing. Furthermore, our approach enjoys probabilistic guarantees on the quality of approximate answers, which is a desideratum for any Approximate Query Engine (AQE). An important novelty of our proposal is the proposal of separating carefully-chosen outliers from the rest of the data and managing them using a quad-tree-based indexing data structure that further speeds-up approximate query processing. To derive theoretical guarantees, we exploit the well-known Hoeffding's inequality [29], in a similar spirit to the technique proposed by Hellerstein et al. for supporting online aggregation [27].

Finally, to facilitate query processing, TP-Tree codifies a tunable and hierarchical partition of the target data cube, i.e. a partition that varies over time according to the query-workload. As a consequence, TP-Tree is self-adjusting in that a trigger-like procedure updates it, hence updating the underlying partitions according to the current query-workload. In such a way, the natural application field of TP-Tree is a middleware system that sits between a DWS and OLAP clients, similarly to the well-known AQUA system [2, 5, 6, 22], and allows the latter to establish a communication protocol about the degree of approximation of the answers.

The organization of the remainder of the paper is as follows. First, in Sec. 2, we provide an overview of previous work on approximate query processing. In Sec. 3, we outline our proposed technique. In Sec. 4, we describe our solution for managing outliers. Then, in Sec. 5 we present in detail the data structure TP-Tree. In Sec. 6, we describe our query model, while in Sec. 7 we give an experimental validation of the effectiveness of our technique, considering both synthetic and real data cubes. Finally, in Sec. 8 we draw conclusions and discuss future work.

6.2 Related Work

Many techniques for compressing data cubes and evaluating range queries over their compressed representation have been proposed in the literature. Several compression models, originally defined in different contexts, have been used to this end. In the following, we focus on several popular techniques underlying these approaches.

Ioannidis and Poosala [30] introduced histograms for providing approximate answers to set-valued queries. Histograms are data structures obtained by partitioning a data domain into a number of mutually disjoint blocks, called *buckets*, and then storing for each bucket some aggregate information, such as the sum of items they contain. Many techniques for building multidimensional histograms have been proposed in literature, each of them based on particular properties of the data distributions characterizing input domains. Typically, statistical and error metrics-based properties are taken into account. Among all the alternatives, we focus on the following histograms that are most relevant to our problem setting: Equi-Depth [36], MHist [40], and GenHist [24] histograms.

Given a k-dimensional data domain D, the Equi-Depth histogram $H_{ED}(D)$, proposed by Muralikrishna and DeWitt [36], is built as follows: (i) fix an ordering of the d dimensions $d_0, d_1, \ldots, d_{k-1}$; (ii) set $\alpha \approx k^{\text{th}}$ root of the desired number of buckets (which is bounded by the storage space available for storing $H_{ED}(D)$); (iii) initialize $H_{ED}(D)$ to the input data distribution of D; (iv) for each i in $[0, k-1]$, split each bucket of $H_{ED}(D)$ into equi-depth partitions along d_i; finally, (v) return resulting buckets to $H_{ED}(D)$. This technique has several limitations: fixed α and fixed dimension ordering may result in poor partitions, and, consequently, there could be a limited level of bucketization, which decreases query answering performance.

The MHist histogram $H_{MH}(D)$ was proposed by Poosala and Ioannidis [40]. The MHist build procedure depends on the parameter p (specifically, such histograms are denoted by *MHist-p* histograms): contrarily to the previous technique, at each step the bucket b in $H_{MH}(D)$ containing the dimension d_i whose marginal is the most in need of partitioning is chosen, and it is split along d_i into p (e.g., $p = 2$) buckets.

Gunopulos et al. propose GenHist histograms [24], which are significantly different from previous ones with respect to the nature of the build procedure. The key idea is the following: given an histogram H with h_b buckets on an input data domain D, the proposed technique builds the output GenHist histogram $H_{GH}(D)$ via finding n_b overlapping buckets on H (n_b is an input parameter). To this end, the technique individuates the number of distinct regions that is much larger than the original number of buckets h_b, thanks to a greedy algorithm that considers increasingly-coarser grids. At each step, the algorithm selects the set of cells J of highest density and moves enough randomly-selected items from J into a bucket to make J and its neighbors "close-to-uniform".

Another related approach is STHoles [10]. STHoles computes the final histogram based on the analysis of the query-workload on the target data cube. Similarly to GenHist, STHoles considers the tuple density concept, and, differently from previous proposals, STHoles allows bucket nesting, thus achieving the definition of the so-called bucket tree. By means of the abstraction on "holes" in the nodes of the bucket tree, STHoles computes the final histogram via minimizing differences among tuple densities of buckets. With respect to GenHist, STHoles efficiently exploits the nice abstraction of generating and/or pruning nodes of the bucket tree to arrange the tuple density homogenization process.

Wavelets [43] are a mathematical transformation that defines a hierarchical decomposition of functions (representing signals or data distributions) into a set of coefficients, called wavelet coefficients. Wavelets were originally applied to the image and signal processing problems [38, 43]. Recent studies have shown the applicability of wavelets to selectivity estimation [35], as well as to the approximation query processing, such as range queries [44, 45], and queries with join operators over data cubes [12]. Specifically, the compressed representation of data cubes via wavelets is obtained by means of two steps [45]. First, a wavelet transform is applied to the data cube, thus generating a sequence of N coefficients. At this step no compression is obtained (the number of wavelet coefficients is the same as the number of data items in the target distribution), and no approximation is introduced (the original data distribution can be reconstructed exactly by applying the inverse of the wavelet transform to the sequence of coefficients). Next, among the N wavelet coefficients, only the $m \ll N$ most significant ones are retained, with the rest of the coefficients set to zero implicitly. The set of retained coefficients defines the compressed representation, called wavelet synopsis. In order to execute the wavelet decomposition procedure for a given data domain D, first a wavelet basis function set must be chosen. Haar Wavelets [12, 44, 45] are conceptually the simplest wavelet basis functions, and are widely used in literature.

It has been shown that wavelet-based techniques improve the histogram-based ones in the summarization of multidimensional data [44, 45], and they were also used for approximate query answering [12]. Wavelets and histograms have also been successfully mixed to combine the positive aspects of both the techniques. The deriving technique is known as wavelet-based histogram [35].

Random sampling-based methods map the original multidimensional data domain to a smaller data domain via sampling. This allows a more compact representation of the original data to be achieved. Query performance can be significantly improved by pushing sampling to Query Engines, with very low computational overheads [8, 21, 22]. Sampling-based methods features a very low computational requirements. Hellerstein et al. [27] propose a system for effectively supporting on-line aggregate query answering, which also provides probabilistic guarantees on the accuracy of answers in terms of confidence intervals. Such system allows a user to issue an aggregate query and to observe its evaluation in a graphical interface that shows both the partial answer and the corresponding confidence interval. Users can stop the query evaluation when the answer has achieved the desired degree of approximation. Therefore, the whole process is interactive. No synopsis is maintained since the system is based on a random sampling of tuples involved by the query, and this operation occurs at query time. Random sampling allows an unbiased estimator for the answer to be built, and the associated confidence interval is computed by applying the Hoeffding's inequality [29]. The drawback of this proposal is that response time needed to compute answers can increase significantly depending on the selectivity of queries, since sampling is done at query time. The absence of synopsis ensures that no additional computational overheads are introduced as no maintenance task needs to be performed.

Recently, Ganti et al. [21] develop a weighted sampling scheme that exploits workload information to continuously tune a representative sample of data. Chaudhuri et al. [14] extend this novel approach towards a more accurate scheme taking special care of data skews and low selectivity queries. Their experimental results show that the accuracy of the approximate answers can be outperformed by taking into account a more adaptive scheme. Babcock et al. [8] exploit the previous work by arguing that, for many aggregate queries, appropriately constructed biased samples can provide more accurate approximation than uniform samples and, consequently, propose an improved technique that dynamically constructs an ad-hoc biased sample for each query by combining samples selected from a family of non-uniform samples built during the pre-processing phase.

6.3 TP-Tree Overview

Fig. 6.1 shows an overview of our solution to approximate range-sum query processing. Given the input data from an OLAP server, we separate outliers from non-outliers and manage them differently. Outliers are organized into a quad-tree based indexing data structure within a given space limit. For non-outliers, uniform samples are extracted and preserved within the a dynamic tree-like structure named TP-Tree.

The idea underlying the TP-Tree is to superimpose on the input data cube A a hierarchical partition Φ that evolves over time, according to the query-workload against A. Φ is used at query time to evaluate (with approximation) range-sum queries by exploiting the pre-aggregate sums stored in its buckets, thus reducing the processing time effectively. In more detail, the approximate answer to a range-sum query Q, de-noted by $\widetilde{A}(Q)$, involving a set of buckets $I_Q = \{b_{Q,0}, b_{Q,1}, \ldots, b_{Q,W-1}\}$

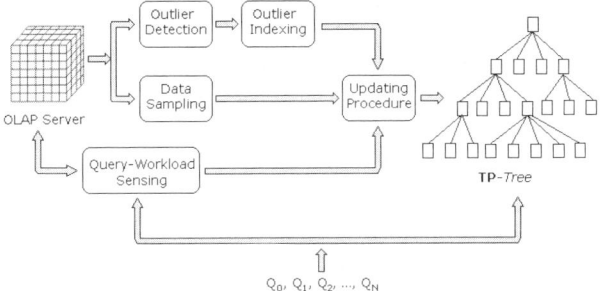

Fig. 6.1 Technique overview

in Φ is evaluated by summing-up the answers from probing the non-outliers contained in the TP-Tree, and the outliers in the quad-tree, as follows:

$$\widetilde{A}(Q) = \sum_{i=0}^{W-1} \widetilde{A}(b_{Q,i}) + \widetilde{A}_{QT}(Q)$$

where $\widetilde{A}(b_{Q,i})$ and $\widetilde{A}_{QT}(Q)$ are the portions of answer evaluated on the bucket $b_{Q,i}$ and the quad-tree, respectively. A tighter theoretical guarantee on $\widetilde{A}(Q)$ can be obtained because errors due to "problematic" outliers are non-existent. This approach aims at capturing and isolating buckets with reasonably uniform data distributions in order to minimize the query error. As a consequence, such a partition can also be regarded as a multidimensional histogram on A. However, our "histogram" is dynamic in that buckets will be changing according to the query-workload, and, above all, are computed by means of efficient update algorithms that do not need to access the underlying data. In this sense, we name the partition as *tunable*, i.e. varying according to the query-workload. As we will explain shortly, using tunable partitions on data cubes allows us to overcome well-known limitations inherent in most multidimensional histogram methods on very large data cubes, such as scalability of the techniques with respect to data size and number of dimensions.

As mentioned above, such a partition varies over time, so that, formally, at each timestamp t_k, the TP-Tree data structure codifies the current partition Φ_k. The Φ_k configuration, and, consequently, the TP-Tree data organization, is updated in a batch mode by monitoring the query-workload within a time window, which is the period of the query-workload sensing process (see Fig. 1).

The details of the detection, indexing and querying outliers are covered in Sec. 4. Construction, update, and query of non-outliers organized in the TP-Tree are presented in Sec. 5. We illustrate how to obtain the approximate answers to range-sum queries in Sec. 6.

Before going into details, we first introduce some notations. Let $A = \langle D, M \rangle$ be a data cube such that $D = \{d_0, d_1, \ldots, d_{N-1}\}$ is the set of dimensions. For simplicity, we deal with one measure (denoted as $M = \{m_0\}$) in this paper. We also assume that A is stored according to an MOLAP data organization, so that A is an N-dimensional array of size $S(A) = \Pi_{i=0}^{N-1} |d_i|$, where $|d_i|$ is the size of the dimension d_i. Our basic task is to provide an approximate answer to the following multidimensional range-sum query Q over A:

$$Q(l_0 : u_0, l_1 : u_1, \ldots, l_{N-1} : u_{N-1}) = \sum_{i_0=l_0}^{u_0} \cdots \sum_{i_{N-1}=l_{N-1}}^{u_{N-1}} A[i_0, i_1, \ldots, i_{N-1}] \qquad (6.1)$$

where $l_k : u_k$ is the range defined on the dimension d_k, and $A[i_0, i_1, \ldots, i_{N-1}]$ is the data cell located at the multidimensional entry $(i_0, i_1, \ldots, i_{N-1})$ of A.

6.4 Efficiently Detecting, Indexing, and Querying Outliers of Multidimensional Data Cubes

Outlier detection and management strongly depend on: (i) the space budget B, and (ii) the strategy for detecting and manage them. Traditionally, outlier detection has been widely investigated in Statistics [9, 13, 26], Data Mining [31, 34, 41], and, more recently, as an efficient method for improving the degree of accuracy of answers in the context of approximate query processing [14].

In our approach, we adopt an approximate query answering technique similar to that in [14]. Compared with [14], our approach differs in that we further use a quad-tree-based index to support querying the outliers efficient. Indexing outliers is important to our problem, as otherwise it could degrade the performance of any AQE. The major benefit of managing outliers separately is that the overall approximation error is mitigated as the error due to the outliers is zero, and the quality of answers only depend on the sampling of relatively uniform non-outliers.

Our solution for detecting outliers of the input data cube A consists of the following steps:

1. **Detection of the (whole) outlier set Ω inside the data cube**. Determine all the outliers of A that deviate from the absolute average value of the data cells of A, denoted by Y_m, by at least $\alpha \cdot Y_m$. Compared with [9], our method is more efficient yet highly effective for most real datasets.
2. **Extraction of a subset Ω_B from Ω within the space limit B**. If $|\Omega| \leq B$ then $\Omega_B = \Omega$; otherwise, determine the subset Ω_B by minimizing the standard deviation of its complement, $A \setminus \Omega_B$. This is the optimal set of outlier for a given space limit [9].

These two steps are codified in algorithm outlierDetection (Algorithm 1), which takes as input a data cube A, the space limit B, and the parameter α, and returns the optimal set of outliers Ω_B.

outlierDetection makes use of the following procedures: (i) computeAbsAvg-Value, which returns the absolute average value of data cells; (ii) sel, which selects the maximum number of outliers in Ω sequentially that can be stored within B.

Algorithm 1: outlierDetection

---

1   $Y_m \leftarrow$ computeAbsAvgValue(A);
2   **foreach** *cell* $P \in A$ **do**
3   **if** $|P - Y_m| \geq \alpha \cdot Y_m$ **then**
4   add($\Omega, |P - Y_m|$);

5   **if** $|\Omega| > B$ **then**
6      $\Omega \leftarrow$ sort(Ω, DESC);
7      $\Omega_B \leftarrow$ sel(Ω, B);
8   **else**
9      $\Omega_B \leftarrow \Omega$;

10   **return** Ω_B;

Note that selecting the outlier set in descendent order of the deviations gives the optimal set of outliers Ω_B with respect to B, in the sense that the standard deviation of $A \setminus \Omega_B$ is minimized [14].

Unlike previous approaches [14], we propose to index the potentially large set of outliers for efficient access at query time. To this end, we propose a fast and efficient multi-resolution indexing scheme based on the multidimensional quad-tree. We impose a hierarchical decomposition of a d-dimensional space into a set of hyper-blocks [20]. This decomposition naturally defines a 2^d-ary tree, such that each node is associated with a hyper-block. Given a d-dimensional data set D, a multidimensional quad-tree built for D (denoted as $QT(D)$, See Fig. 6.2), is a tree-like index such that each node (i) contains points (i.e., data items) in D, and (ii) can have at most 2^d children nodes. Each level l of $QT(D)$ represents a partition $P(l)$ of D in $|P(l)|$ buckets, such that each bucket b of $P(l)$ is recursively split into a number r of children buckets, with r belonging to the set $\{0, \ldots, 2^d\}$. In our implementation, each node n of the quad-tree contains the following information: (i) the bounding box of the multi-dimensional region it represents (MBR); (ii) the sum of the outliers contained in this MBR and the pointers to its children nodes, if n is not a leaf node; and (iii) pointer to the disk block that contains the outliers belonging to n, if n is a leaf node.

Given a d-dimensional data cube A and its outlier set Ω_B generated during the outlier detection phase, we can incrementally build the multidimensional quad-tree $QT(\Omega_B)$ using the following heuristic bound over its maximum depth $l_{\max}$:

$$l_{\max} = \frac{1}{d} \cdot \log_2 \frac{f \cdot |\Omega_B|}{F} \tag{6.2}$$

where f is the storage size for an outlier, and F is the size of a disk block. This heuristic implies that outliers contained in the bucket represented by a leaf node are mostly likely to be contained in a single disk block, thus taking advantages during accessing the outliers. Furthermore, in order to minimize the overall computational overheads due to the possible great fan-out of each node of $QT(\Omega_B)$, nodes repre-

senting buckets without outliers are not stored in $QT(\Omega_B)$, so that both the space
and time complexities can be reduced to a minimum.

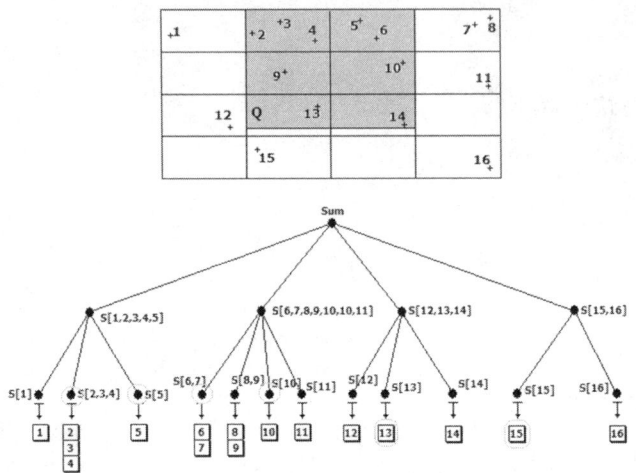

Fig. 6.2 The indexing data structure $QT(\Omega_B)$ for a 2D data cube

We assume that the resulting $QT(\Omega_B)$ can be maintained in main memory. This
allows us to devise a multi-resolution approach in the evaluation of a given range-
sum query Q on $QT(\Omega_B)$. Note that storing the pre-calculated sums of outliers contained in each bucket of $QT(\Omega_B)$ save many disk I/Os. Algorithm evalQueryOnQT
(Algorithm 2) computes the exact portion of answer due to outliers of the input data
cube A.

In Algorithm 2, we use the following routines: (i) getReg returns the multidimensional region corresponding to a node n; (ii) getInter computes the interesection
of two input regions.

Under the constraint represented by Equation (6.2), we can calculate the number
of disk I/Os needed to evaluate a query Q on the quad-tree $QT(\Omega_B)$ as follows. Let
$P(l_{\max})$ be the partition of the leaf level of $QT(\Omega_B)$, we have that, if

$$\sum(Q) = \{ b \mid b \in P(l_{\max}) \wedge b \cap Q \neq \phi \wedge b \nsubseteq Q \} \tag{6.3}$$

is the set of nodes that are partially "touched" by Q, then we need $|\sum(Q)|$ disk I/Os
to evaluate Q on $QT(\Omega_B)$ in the expected case.

Algorithm 2: evalQueryOnQT(Q)

1 *sum* ← 0;   *currNode* ← **NULL**;
2 *nodesToBeProcessed* ← ϕ;
3 *nodesToBeProcessed.add($QT(\Omega_B)$.getRoot());*
4 *intReg* ← **NULL**;
5 **while** *nodesToBeProcessed.size()* > 0 **do**
6 | *currNode* ← *nodesToBeProcessed.getFirstElement();*
7 | **if** *currNode.getReg()* ∩ Q ≠ ϕ **then**
8 | | **if** *currNode.getReg()* ⊆ Q **then**
9 | | | *sum* ← *sum* + *currNode.getSum();*
10 | | **else**
11 | | | **if** *currNode.isLeaf()* = ***TRUE*** **then**
12 | | | | *intReg* ← *Util.getInter(currNode.getReg(),Q);*
13 | | | | *sum* ← *sum* + *Util.getSum(currNode.getDiskBlockAddr(),intReg);*
14 | | | **else**
15 | | | | *nodesToBeProcessed.add(currNode.getChildren());*
16 | *nodesToBeProcessed.removeFirstElement();*
17 **return** *sum*;

6.5 TP-Tree: A Tree-Like, "Self-Adjusting" Synopsis Data Structure for Approximate Query Answering in OLAP

6.5.1 Tunable Partitions of Data Cubes

A fundamental issue in approximate range query processing based on pre-computation is how to determine the partitioning of the target data cube. Finding a set of *typical* queries as the basis to drive the synopsis building task is the core issue of pre-computation-based techniques. This derives from the widely-accepted assumption claiming that typical queries must be defined starting from some probable partition of the data cube, e.g. computed starting from frequency and locality issues.

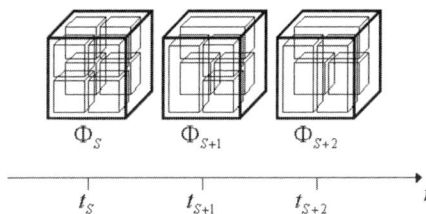

Fig. 6.3 Tunable partition of a 3D data cube

It is well-known that finding the optimal partitioning for a d-dimensional data domainy is NP-Hard when $d \geq 2$ [33, 37]. As a result, many initiatives, like the one from Poosala and Ioannidis [40], propose greedy solutions to deal with this problem efficiently. We propose a different solution that (i) avoids computing partitions on the basis of some statistical properties (or metrics) on data, and (ii) considers the analysis of the target query-workload only, thus sensibly reducing computational overheads. Our proposal is named *tunable workload-aware partition*. Since the underlying problem is NP-Hard, we propose a systematic, workload-aware partitioning scheme on the basis of which, given a data cube A, its current partition Φ_k *only* depends on the query-workload against it. This way, in a certain time window starting at a given timestamp t_S and having width M, $\{t_S, t_{S+1}, \ldots, t_{S+M-1}\}$, we model a set of corresponding partitions $\{\Phi_S, \Phi_{S+1}, \ldots, \Phi_{S+M-1}\}$, such that Φ_k is the partition at timestamp t_k. For instance, in Fig. 6.3, the initial partition Φ_S at the timestamp t_S of a three-dimensional data cube A evolves towards other configurations according to the query-workload against A, namely Φ_{S+1} at the timestamp t_{S+1}, and Φ_{S+2} at the timestamp t_{S+2}.

We denote the time window between two timestamps t_h and t_k ($t \leq k$) as $TW(t_h, t_k)$. It is the period of the query-workload sensing process (see Fig. 6.1), i.e. the period during which input queries are collected and stored to be analyzed at timestamp t_k in order to update the TP-Tree. Therefore, we have: $\Phi_k = TW(t_h, t_k)$.

We highlight that, at the current state of development of our work, the width of the time window TW is fixed. A more accurate scheme could take into account the query-workload to determine the most appropriate width.

6.5.2 TP-Tree Data Organization

TP-Tree is the codification of the current partition Φ_k, and its configuration evolves as Φ_k evolves. In this sense, TP-Tree is a self-adjusting data structure, meaning that it is periodically updated by a trigger-like procedure re-configuring its bucket set according to the query-workload. The period of the update procedure is defined by the width of the time window $TW(t_h, t_k)$; the query-workload taken into account is formed by the set of queries executed against the target data cube during the time interval $[t_h, t_k]$.

The major difference of our approach from [27] is that [27] proposes computing queries in an online fashion — without storing any data structure, while in our solution we store samples and outliers in an offline fashion. Sampling offline does not affect performance at query time, and its storage requirement is modest when compared with the size of the target data cube.

In order to manage samples in a query-friendly manner, we propose the following tree-like data organization for TP-Tree (see Fig. 6.4). Each node $n(b)$ of TP-Tree, such that b is the corresponding bucket in Φ_k, contains the following information:

- For internal nodes, it contains: (i) the multidimensional region $R(b)$, which can be stored in many efficient ways — for instance, we could store its multidi-

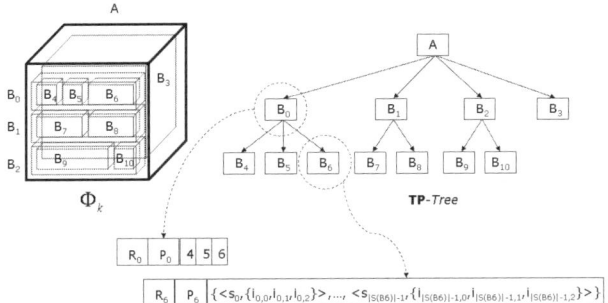

Fig. 6.4 TP-Tree data organization for a 3D data cube

mensional boundary points; (ii) the sum $P(b)$ of all the samples extracted from buckets in Φ_k and contained in $R(b)$. Specifically, each internal node $n(b)$ contains the sum of all the samples stored in the leaf nodes of the TP-Tree sub-tree rooted at $n(b)$; (iii) pointers to children nodes.

• For leaf nodes, it contains: (i) the multidimensional region $R(b)$; (ii) the sum $P(b)$ of all the samples extracted from b; (iii) the sampled data set $S(b)$ extracted from b and, for each sample s belonging to $S(b)$, the set of coordinates of s in the original representation. This is because, at query time, we could then determine samples that is contained in a query Q (See Sec 6 for further details).

6.5.3 Updating the TP-Tree

Existing approaches in self-tuning databases literature adopt the idea of adjusting data organization on the basis of the query-workload in an online manner [4, 7, 10, 15]. We use the same idea with the different aim of efficiently supporting approximate query processing.

When the current time window $TW(t_h, t_k)$ expires, we activate the update procedure by collecting queries issued the time window $TW(t_h, t_k)$. We use the following simple yet efficient criterion: given a query-workload QWL, we consider, for each bucket b of the current partition Φ_k, the number of times $T(b)$, for which b has been involved by queries in QWL. Then, taking into account the most frequently accessed buckets of k during $TW(t_h, t_k)$, and bounding such a number with an empirically-determined threshold U over the frequency, the criterion decides if b has to be (i) erased from, or (ii) restructured in, or (iii) unchanged in the next partition Φ_{k+1}.

Obviously, both the building and the update procedures depend on the available storage space B. For instance, this issue can be faced off by assigning a proportional portion of B to each node $n(b)$ of the TP-Tree according to the statistical properties of data distributions of b. A heuristic solution is to take into account the variance of each bucket b_i in Φ_k, denoted by $\sigma^2(b_i)$, and to assign to each b_i an space budget

$B(k, b_i)$ proportional to its variance, i.e.,

$$B(k, b_i) = \frac{\sigma^2(b_i)}{\sum_{j=0}^{|\Phi_k|-1} \sigma^2(b_j)} \cdot B \qquad (6.4)$$

Variance is widely-recognized as an important indicator for discovering if a given data domain contains clusters [16]. Due to this nice property, variance analysis has been often used to build multidimensional histograms, which just aim at finding data blocks having a low value of variance, in order to summarize them using a given method, such as storing the most frequent value or the average value of buckets. We highlight that, for simplicity, we do not consider in Equation (6.4) the amount of storage space needed for representing the information on (i) the geometry of buckets, (ii) the number of samples extracted from buckets, and (iii) topological issues of TP-Tree (see Sec. 5.2).

Algorithm 3: updateCurrPartition(Φ_k, QWL, U)

1 $\Phi_{k+1} \leftarrow \phi$; $newRegionArray \leftarrow [0, 0, \ldots, 0]$;
2 **foreach** *bucket b in* Φ_k **do**
3   **foreach** *query q* $\in QWL$ **do**
4   **if** $b \cap q \neq \phi$ **then**
5              $b.frequncy \leftarrow b.frequency + 1$;
6              $newRegionArray[b] = b \cap (b \cap q)$;

7 **foreach** *bucket b in* Φ_k **do**
8   **if** $b.frequency > U$ **then**
9          $P \leftarrow createParts(b, newRegionArray[b], B(b))$;
10         $\Phi_{k+1}.add(P)$;
11         $b.frequency \leftarrow 0$;

12 **return** Φ_{k+1};

The approach above is implemented by algorithm updateCurrPartition (Algorithm 3), where (i) *newRegionArray* is an array of objects storing candidate multidimensional regions for an existing partition (specifically, such regions originate buckets in the next partition Φ_{k+1}); (ii) function $B(\cdot)$ is due to Equation (6.4); (iii) procedure createParts takes as input a bucket b, a list of multidimensional regions ϕ, and a storage space bound $B(b)$, and creates new partitions of b by individuating in ϕ a set of multidimensional regions which entirely cover b, and can be stored within $B(b)$;

After the next partition Φ_{k+1} is computed, TP-Tree is updated consequentially. Although we limit the possible over-adaptation to the query-workload using the parameter U in the algorithm above, we still need to consider the rare case in which there are too many partitions in the TP-Tree, possibly due to a change in the query-workload characteristics. Our proposed solution is to merge partitions that affect least the accuracy of TP-Tree, in a similar spirit as the STHoles histogram approach [10]. The difference is that we use samples to calculate the estimates before and after the merge, thus obtaining the penalty value for a particular merge. Contrary to this, [10] only stores the frequency of each partition and has to resort to often unrealistic uniform distribution assumption to calculate the penalty values.

6.5.4 Deriving the Theoretical Bound

In order to provide probabilistic guarantees on the degree of approximation, we exploit the Hoeffding's inequality [29]. Specifically, we apply the Hoeffding's inequality via uniformly sampling each bucket b of the current partition Φ_k. This allows us to obtain probabilistic bounds over the (approximate) value of the aggregation operator AVG defined on b. Starting from the value of the aggregation operator AVG on b, we can easily derive the value of the SUM one by multiplying the former by the size of the sampled data set, thus answering any given range-sum query Q against b. By iterating this procedure for each bucket b belonging to Φ_k and having a nonempty intersection with Q, we provide the approximate answer to Q, denoted by $\widetilde{A}(Q)$, along with probabilistic guarantees. We recall that sampling introduces approximation, whereas query processing on the outlier set does not introduce any approximation.

The Hoeffding's inequality asserts the following. Let (i) $Z = \{Z_0, Z_1, \ldots, Z_{M-1}\}$ be a set of independent random variables, (ii) C be a scalar such that $0 \leq Z_k \leq C$ for $k \in [0, M-1]$, (iii) $\bar{Z} = \frac{1}{M} \cdot \sum_{k=0}^{M-1} Z_k$ be the sample mean of the set Z, and (iv) μ be the (unknown) average value of the set Z. Then, for every $\varepsilon > 0$, we have:

$$P(|\bar{Z} - \mu| \leq \varepsilon) \geq 1 - 2 \cdot \exp\left(\frac{-2M\varepsilon^2}{C^2}\right) \qquad (6.5)$$

Therefore, it gives a probabilistic bound for the event $\mu \in \bar{Z} \pm \varepsilon$. If P_Q is a given probability threshold, we can obtain the corresponding error value ε_Q as:

$$\varepsilon_Q = C \cdot \left(\frac{1}{2M} \cdot \ln \frac{2}{1 - P_Q}\right)^{\frac{1}{2}} \qquad (6.6)$$

This means that we can compute the error for a requested probability. This nice theoretical property provides the probabilistic bounds for our approximate query answering model. By exploiting such a theoretical property, we could design an AQE that is able to support a communication protocol between the target OLAP server and client/user applications (see Sec. 1) in order to mediate the degree of approximation of the retrieved answers, according to the guidelines drawn by the well-known Quality of Service (QoS) deploying paradigm of the service-oriented architectures and systems. An existent solution following this paradigm can be found in [18].

In order to adopt the Hoeffding's inequality in our setting, an independent random variable set Z must be introduced. We obtain Z by uniform random sampling over each bucket b of the current partition Φ_k. We note that this probabilistic model ensures that each data cell of b has the *same* probability $P_u = 1/N(b)$ to be selected as a sample, where $N(b)$ is the total number of data cells of b.

More specifically, in our proposal, the following probabilistic formal model is the theoretical support for the *multidimensional data sampling*, i.e. sampling on multidimensional buckets of the current partition Φ_k. We introduce the random variable set $Z(k) = Z_{\Phi_k}$ defined on the current partition Φ_k as follows. For each bucket b belonging to Φ_k, we define the random variable $Z^0(k,b)$ that returns a data cell of the bucket b by applying a uniform sampling in $[0, |d_i| - 1]$ over each dimension of A. Each uniform sampling on $[0, |d_i| - 1]$ provides a sampled coordinate s_i, and the set $\{s_0, s_1, \ldots, s_{N-1}\}$ is obtained via iterating this step for each dimension of A. Therefore, the sampled data cell is $A[s_0, s_1, \ldots, s_{N-1}]$. Furthermore, let $S(k,b)$ be the sample number for a given bucket b in Φ_k, the random variable set $Z_S(k,b)$ on b is defined as:

$$Z_S(k,b) = \{Z_0^0(k,b), Z_1^0(k,b), \ldots, Z_{S-1}^0(k,b)\} \tag{6.7}$$

That is, $Z_S(k,b)$ is composed of all the random variables $Z^0(k,b)$ defined on b. Note that the uniform sampling task ensures that the random variables belonging to the set $Z_S(k,b)$ are independent, as required by the Hoeffding's inequality. Finally, the random variable set $Z(k)$ on Φ_k is composed of all the random variables $Z_S(k,b)$ defined on buckets of Φ_k. For instance, if A is a 3×3 two-dimensional data cube and the current partition is $\Phi_0 = \{A\}$, then the random variable $Z^0(0,A)$ is defined as:

$$Z^0(0,A) = \{A[unif(0,2), unif(0,2)]\}$$

where $unif(a,b)$ is the uniform distribution on the range $[a,b]$, and the random variable set $Z_4(0,A)$ is:

$$Z_4(0,A) = \{Z_0^0(0,A), Z_1^0(0,A), Z_2^0(0,A), Z_3^0(0,A)\}$$

In conclusion, given a range-sum query Q on the bucket b of the current partition Φ_k, the probabilistically-bounded approximate answer to Q can be obtained as:

$$\widetilde{A}(Q,k,b) = |S(k,b)| \cdot \bar{Z}(k,b) \tag{6.8}$$

by introducing an error of at most $\varepsilon(Q)$ that is probabilistically-bounded by Equation (6.5).

6.6 Querying the TP-Tree

The approximate answer to a given query Q is evaluated by summing-up the partial (approximate) answer to Q against TP-Tree and the partial (exact) answer to

Q against $QT(\Omega_B)$. We note that the query error $\varepsilon(Q)$ is solely due to the error in estimating the aggregate of non-outliers

In more detail, let Q be a range-sum query involving the bucket set $I_Q = \{b_{Q,0}, b_{Q,1}, \ldots, b_{Q,K-1}\}$ (i.e., $b_{Q,k} \cap Q \neq \phi$ for each k in $[0, K-1]$; the approximate answer to Q, $\widetilde{A}(Q)$, is obtained according to the following steps:

1. **Aggregate outliers.** Apply Q to the involved outliers accessed via the index $QT(\Omega_B)$; this step provides the *exact* portion of answer due to the outliers, denoted by $A_O(Q)$.
2. **Aggregate non-outliers.** Apply Q to the involved sampled data; this step provides the *approximate* portion of answer due to the sampled data, denoted by $\widetilde{A}_S(Q)$.
3. **Combine aggregates.** Obtain the approximate answer to Q by combining the portions of answer given by steps 1 and 2 as follows: $\widetilde{A}(Q) = A_O(Q) + \widetilde{A}_S(Q)$.

Note that the error in estimating Q, $\varepsilon(Q)$ is only due to the approximate error from sampling. Therefore, $\varepsilon(Q) = \varepsilon_S(Q)$.

In Sec. 4, we provided algorithm evalQueryOnQT for computing $A_O(Q)$. Now, we can provide algorithm evalQueryOnTP (Algorithm 4) for evaluating $\widetilde{A}_S(Q)$. This portion of answer is evaluated against the TP-Tree by Equation (6.8), thus obtaining, thanks to the Hoeffding's inequality, probabilistic bounds over the degree of approximation of retrieved answers.

Algorithm 4: evalQueryOnTP(Q)

```
1  appxSum ← 0;    currNode ← NULL;
2  nodesToBeProcessed ← φ;
3  nodesToBeProcessed.add(TP-Tree.getRoot());
4  intReg ← NULL;
5  while nodesToBeProcessed.size() > 0 do
6  │   currNode ← nodesToBeProcessed.getFirstElement();
7  │   if currNode.getReg() ∩ Q ≠ φ then
8  │   │   if currNode.getReg() ⊆ Q then
9  │   │   │   sum ← sum + currNode.getSum();
10 │   │   else
11 │   │   │   if currNode.isLeaf() = TRUE then
12 │   │   │   │   intReg ← Util.getInter(currNode.getReg(), Q);
13 │   │   │   │   sum ← sum + hoeff(intReg.getSamples());
14 │   │   │   else
15 │   │   │   │   nodesToBeProcessed.add(currNode.getChildren());
16 │   nodesToBeProcessed.removeFirstElement();
17 return appxSum;
```

The main functions employed in the algorithm are: (i) the procedure getSamples, which, called on a multidimensional region R, returns the samples contained in R; (ii) the procedure hoeff, which takes a sampled data set I and returns the approximate answer to the range-sum query Q on I according to Equation (6.8).

Finally, the whole approximate answer to a range-sum query Q is to sum up the returned values from algorithms evalQueryOnTP and evalQueryOnQT.

6.7 Experimental Assessment

In this section, in order to prove the effectiveness of TP-Tree, we present our experimental results conducted on both synthetic and real data cubes. We also engineered two classes of queries: (i) synthetic ad hoc queries, and (ii) benchmark queries based on the popular OLAP benchmarks (TCP-H). These queries have been used to populated workloads considered in the experimental evaluation. We combine synthetic and real data cubes, and synthetic query-workloads and benchmark queries, thus developing a comprehensive experimental work that demonstrates the merits of TP-Tree performance, also in comparison with the following similar techniques based on multidimensional histograms: Equi-Depth [36], MHist [40], and GenHist [24].

To compare the TP-Tree with the other techniques on a common basis, we impose the same space budget for all the methods to generate their own compressed representation of the target data cube. In our experiments, we set the space budget to be about the 8–9% of the size of the data cube.

We used the *accuracy* as a metric to evaluate the goodness of a compression technique H on a given data cube A. We tried our best to tune and set the parameters of other methods considered in the experiment. Specifically, for Equi-Depth, for a fixed space budget, we derived from the number of buckets that minimized the query approximation error given the space constraint (see Sec. 2.1). For MHist, we considered $p = 2$ (see Sec. 2.1), as [40] indicates that this setting provides best results. For GenHist, we followed the guidelines given in [24] in order to obtain an optimal setting of all the input parameters.

Another metric we used is the *sensitivity* of TP-Tree in comparison with the other techniques, i.e. we study how the query approximation error varies with respect to the available space budget. A third metric is the *construction costs* of all the techniques.

All our experiments were conducted on a host equipped with a 4GHz Pentium IV processor and 2.5GB RAM, running Microsoft Windows 2000 Server. We used Microsoft SQL Server 2000 as the DBMS server, and Microsoft Analysis Services 2000 as the OLAP server.

6.7.1 Experiment Setup

6.7.1.1 Synthetic Data Cubes

Using synthetic data cubes allows us to study the performance of our algorithms on datasets with various controllable features, such as dimensionality, sparseness, size, and data distributions.

To generate synthetic data cubes, we followed the following steps: (i) define the dimension number of the target data cube and the cardinality of each dimension; (ii) randomly generate a set of points in the multi-dimensional space defined by the target data cube and use these points as the centers of cuboids (i.e., sub-data-cubes), and (iii) fill the cuboids according to a given data distribution. In the remainder of the paper, we denote each synthetic data cube by the tuple $\Lambda = \langle d, \zeta, s \rangle$, such that d is the number of dimensions, ζ is the data distribution used to fill the cuboids, and s is the sparseness coefficient of the data cube. Three data distributions are used: Uniform (denoted by U), Gaussian (denoted by G), and Zipf (denoted by Z). Specifically, we used a Uniform distribution U_{gen} to generate centers of cuboids inside the target data cube. In order to fill cuboids, Uniform distribution takes as input a range $[u_{min}, u_{max}]$, and generate values distributed uniformly within the ranges. Gaussian distribution instead takes as input the number of peaks p, the standard deviation of the peaks σ, and a set of non-negative integer values $M = \{m_0, m_1, \ldots, m_{P-1}\}$, such that each value m_k represents the percentage number of data cells contained in the k-th Gaussian bell with respect to the overall number of non-zero data cells of the data cube (note that the latter value depends on the value of the sparseness coefficient s). Finally, Zipf distribution takes as input a range $[z_{min}, z_{max}]$ to obtain the parameter z as uniformly distributed within the range.

We built the following synthetic data cube set: $DCS = \{A_0, A_1, A_2, A_3, A_4, A_5, A_6\}$. More statistics about the datasets are reported in Table 1.

Table 6.1 Synthetic Data Cubes

Data Cube	d	ζ	s [%]	Size [GB]
A0	6	$U(u_{min} = 25, u_{max} = 75)$	0.0010	1.00
A1	6	$G(p = 100, \sigma = 25, m_k = 0.01)$	0.0010	1.00
A2	6	$Z(z_{min} = 0.2, z_{max} = 1.2)$	0.0010	1.25
A3	10	$Z(z_{min} = 0.5, z_{max} = 1.5)$	0.0001	2.00
A4	10	$U(u_{min} = 15, u_{max} = 85)$	0.0001	1.75
A5	10	$G(p = 150, \sigma = 35, m_k = 0.006)$	0.0001	1.75
A6	10	$Z(z_{min} = 0.3, z_{max} = 1.0)$	0.0001	2.00

6.7.1.2 Real Data Cubes

Real data cubes are provided by (i) the popular benchmark TPC-H [3], (ii) the skewed benchmark TPC-H due to [1] (denoted by TPC-HS), and (iii) the data cube SALES, which is a real-life data cube derived as a portion of a large corporate sales database, and characterized by a star schema with a fact table containing about one million rows, and eight dimension tables with the largest containing about 400,000 rows.

Fig. 6.5 shows the TPC-H relational schema implemented on Microsoft SQL Server 2000. The TPC-H database holds data about the ordering and selling activities of a hypothetic large-scale business company. In the skewed version of the benchmark TPC-H, the data generation procedures have been altered in order to produce skewed data according to a Zipf distribution instead of the Uniform distribution as in the original benchmark specification, thus obtaining a more accurate modeling of real-life multi-dimensional databases [1]. The statistics of real data cubes used for our experiments are reported in Table 6.2.

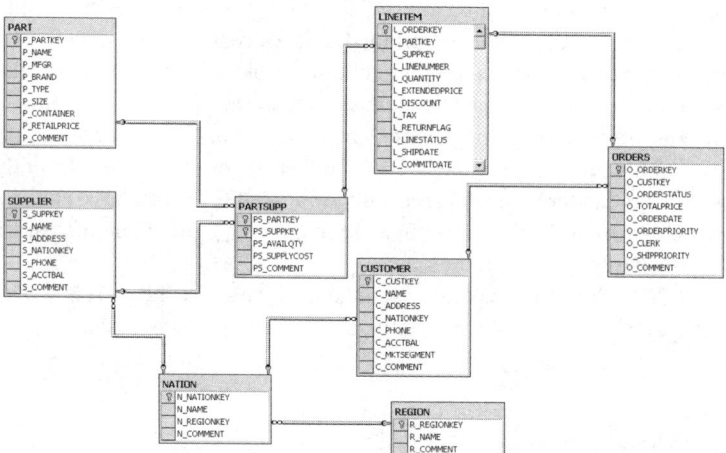

Fig. 6.5 The TPC-H relational schema implemented on Microsoft SQL Server 2000

Table 6.2 Real Data Cubes

Data Cube	Description	Size[GB]
TPC-H	TPC-H benchmark	1.0
TPC-HS	Skewed TPC-H benchmark	1.0
SALES	Corporate sales data cube	1.6

6.7.1.3 Synthetic Query-Workloads

We define a query-workload as a stream of queries, which are generated by setting the values of some parameters characterizing the query-workload. Query-workloads allow us to study the performance of our proposed technique in a controlled manner. We followed the same method used to generate query workloads in [39], as this method is able to efficiently capture users' behaviors as well as their dynamics. A query-workload is modeled as $QWL = \langle z_{min}, z_{max}, V[v] \rangle$, such that query ranges are obtained using a Zipf distribution with parameter z uniformly distributed within $[z_{min}, z_{max}]$, and $V[v]$ is a selectivity function that takes a positive integer value and returns the volume of the queries as the percentage value $v\%$ of the overall volume of the target data cube. We focus on the Zipf distribution as it models real-life phenomena most closely. By tuning the parameter z of the Zipf distribution, we obtain both *lowly skewed* and *highly skewed* query-workloads. In our experiments, we considered as lowly skewed query-workloads when $z \in [0, 1]$, and as highly skewed query-workloads when $z > 1$.

Table 6.3 Synthetic Query-Workloads (L="lowly skewed", H="highly skewed", S="sparse", and D="dense")

Query-Workload	z_{min}	z_{max}	v [%]	Skewness	Selectivity
QWL_0	0.2	0.9	1	L	S
QWL_1	0.5	1.4	1	H	S
QWL_2	0.8	1.7	1	H	S
QWL_3	0.5	1.5	$\{2,\dots,9\}$	H	S
QWL_4	0.2	0.9	15	L	D
QWL_5	0.5	1.4	15	H	D
QWL_6	0.8	1.7	15	H	D
QWL_7	0.5	1.5	$\{16,\dots,26\}$	H	D
QWL_8	0.5	1.5	$\{7,\dots,21\}$	H	S–D

Selectivity is another important feature of the query workload and is captured by the function $V[v]$. We can distinguish between *sparse* and *dense* query-workloads. In our experiments, we considered as sparse query-workloads when $v \in [1, 10]$, and as dense query-workloads when $v > 10$. To study the performance of our proposed technique with respect to the selectivity of queries, we also designed the class of query-workloads $QWL(v)$, which are parametric-with-respect-to-v query-workloads.

We built nine query-workloads: $QWLS = \{ QWL_0, \dots, QWL_8 \}$, and report their statistics in Table 6.3.

6.7.1.4 Benchmark Queries

Our technique has been also tested with benchmark queries. Specifically, we used the query set TPC-H, which includes frequent joins between two or more relations.

Among all the available queries (they are 22 in total), we selected the query set $QTPC$-$H = \{Q_6, Q_{14}, Q_{17}, Q_{19}\}$ as they are more similar to range-sum queries. See Table 6.4 for further details about the queries.

Table 6.4 Benchmark Queries

Query	Description	Involved Relations
Q_6	Forecasting Revenue Change Query	1
Q_{14}	Promotion Effect Query	2
Q_{17}	Small-Quantity-Order Revenue Query	2
Q_{19}	Discounted Revenue Query	2

6.7.1.5 Error Metrics

Since we need to compare different histogram-based data cube approximation techniques against same query-workloads, we use an error metrics similar to that in [10]. In [10], Bruno et al. take into account different features of query answers, like volume and size. On the contrary, we compare approximate and exact answers for all the queries belonging to the same query-workload. Thus, given a data cube A, a histogram H, and a query-workload QWL, we define the *Average Absolute Error* (AAE) $E(A,H,QWL)$ as

$$E(A,H,QWL) = \frac{1}{|QWL|} \sum_{Q \in QWL} |appx(H,Q) - A(Q)| \qquad (6.9)$$

where $appx(H,Q)$ is the approximate answer to Q evaluated on H and $A(Q)$ is the exact answer to Q. Nevertheless, the absolute error is not a reliable metrics in general and will vary across query sets and datasets. Therefore, we also introduce the *Normalized Absolute Error* (NAE) $\|E(A,H,QWL)\|$ as

$$\|E(A,H,QWL)\| = \sum_{Q \in QWL} \frac{appx(H,Q) - A(Q)}{appr_{CVA}(H,Q) - A(Q)} \qquad (6.10)$$

where $appx_{CVA}(H,Q)$ is the approximate answer to Q evaluated on H by assuming uniformity of the data under the Continuous Value Assumption (CVA) [16], and $appx(H,Q)$ and $A(Q)$ are the same as Equation (6.9). We choose the CVA-based technique for error normalization because it can be considered as the "neutral" method for approximate query answering [11, 16].

6.7.2 Synthetic Query-Workloads against Synthetic Data Cubes

In the first set of experiments, we considered the synthetic query-workload set $QWLS_1 = \{QWL_0, \ldots, QWL_6\}$ against the synthetic data cube set $DCS_1 = \{A_0, A_1, A_2, A_3\}$, and we compared the performance of TP-Tree with those of the other techniques by looking at the percentage NAE. As shown in Figs. 6.6–6.8, TP-Tree's performance is better when the size of the range $[z_{min}, z_{max}]$ is small, as expected. The error due to the sampling task is low when query ranges are small, since the number of samples involved by queries is small and the error due to the sampling has a negligible effect with respect to the error due to outliers. Compared with other techniques, TP-Tree's performance is almost comparable with GenHist, and much better than Equi-Depth and MHist.

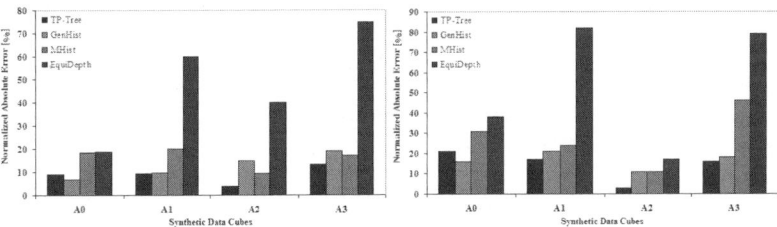

Fig. 6.6 Query performance for the query-workloads QWL_0 (left) and QWL_1 (right) on the data cube set DCS_1

Then, we tested the performance of all the methods by varying the selectivity (v) of query sets $QWL_3(v)$ and $QWL_7(v)$ against the synthetic data cube set $DCS2 = \{A_4, A_5, A_6\}$. As shown in Figs 6.9–6.11, TP-Tree's performance is almost always better than other techniques. Obviously, for all the techniques, performance is better when query selectivity is low.

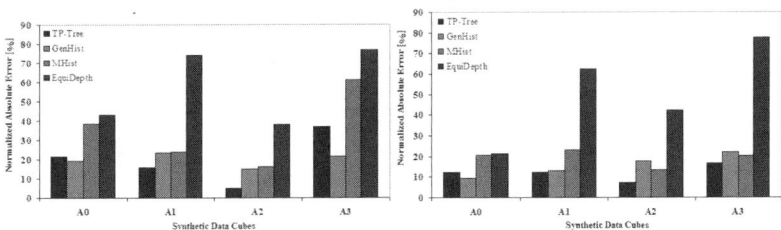

Fig. 6.7 Query performance for the query-workloads QWL_2 (left) and QWL_4 (right) on the data cube set DCS_1

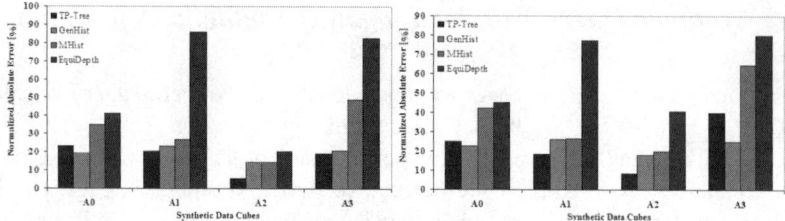

Fig. 6.8 Query performance for the query-workloads QWL_5 (left) and QWL_6 (right) on the data cube set DCS_1

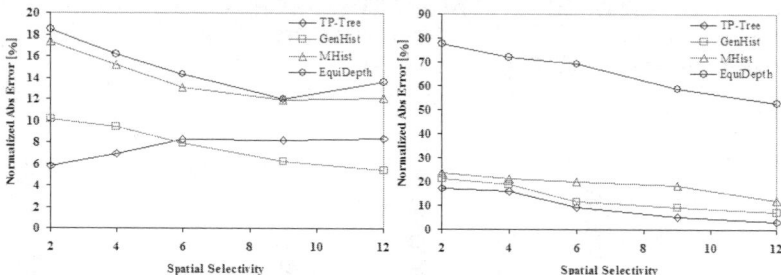

Fig. 6.9 Scalability w.r.t. the spatial selectivity for the query-workload QWL_3 on the data cubes A_4 (left) and A_5 (right)

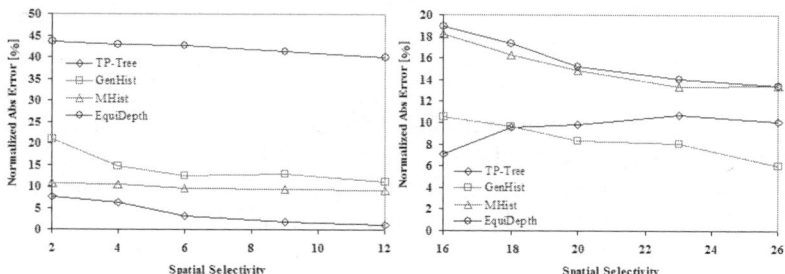

Fig. 6.10 Scalability w.r.t. the spatial selectivity for the query-workload QWL_3 on the data cube A_6 (left) and for the query-workload QWL_7 on the data cube A_4 (right)

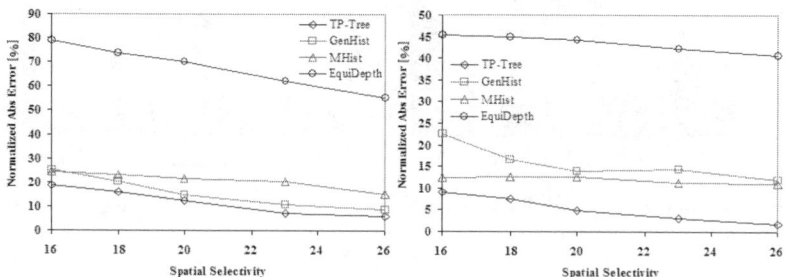

Fig. 6.11 Scalability w.r.t. the spatial selectivity for the query-workload QWL_7 on the data cube A_5 (left) and the data cube A_6 (right)

6.7.3 Synthetic Query-Workloads against Real Data Cubes

Similarly to what is done with synthetic data cubes, we engineered two kinds of experiments to study TP-Tree's performance when synthetic query-workloads are performed against the real data cubes TPC-H, TPC-HS, and SALES. In the first experiment, we considered the query-workload set $QWLS_2 = \{QWL_0, QWL_2, QWL_4, QWL_6\}$; in the second experiment, we test TP-Tree's scalability with respect to the spatial selectivity of the query-workload $QWL_8(v)$. The experimental results are presented in Figs. 6.12–6.15. We can see that TP-Tree achieve good performance on the benchmark TPC-H, as it has a uniform data distributions. TP-Tree works well on such kind of data, as the approximation error is negligible. As for the benchmark TPC-HS and the data cube SALES, performance is not so excellent as in the previous case, but it still remains good. This is due to the fact that skewed data distributions introduce higher approximation errors. However, TP-Tree performance on these data cubes still outperforms other techniques in many cases.

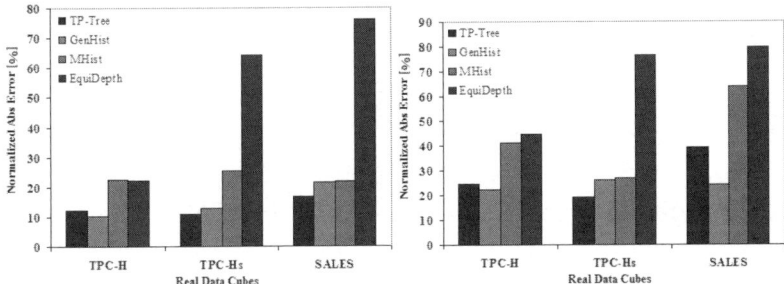

Fig. 6.12 Query performance for the query-workloads QWL_0 (left) and QWL_2 (right) on real data cubes

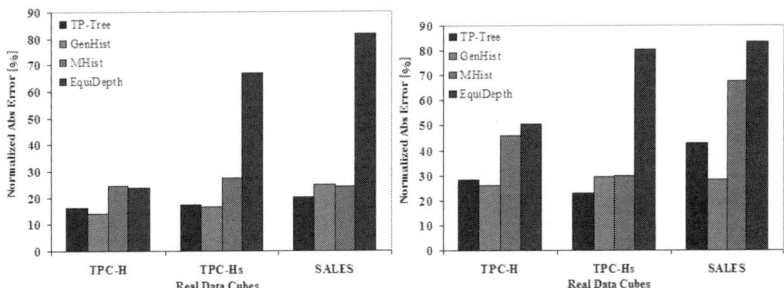

Fig. 6.13 Query performance for the query-workloads QWL_4 (left) and QWL_6 (right) on real data cubes

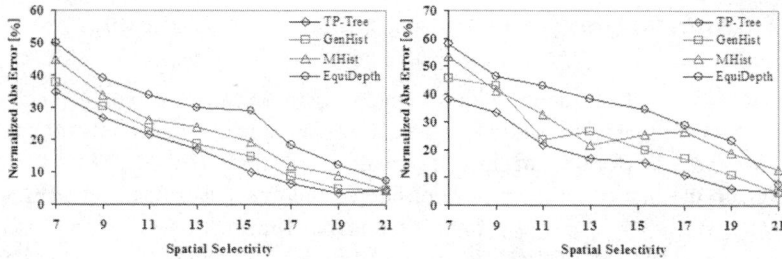

Fig. 6.14 Scalability w.r.t. the spatial selectivity for the query-workload QWL8 on the benchmark TPC-H (left) and on the benchmark TPC-HS (right)

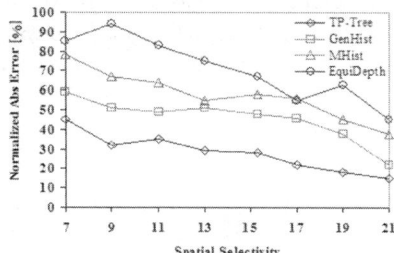

Fig. 6.15 Scalability w.r.t. the spatial selectivity for the query-workload QWL_8 on the data cube SALES

6.7.4 Benchmark Queries against Real Data Cubes

Fig. 6.16 shows the TP-Tree performance observed when the query set $QTPC$-H is performed against the benchmarks TPC-H and the TPC-HS. We can observe the similar trend that the performance on TPC-H is better than that on TPC-HS, as the latter has skewed data distribution and is hard to approximate.

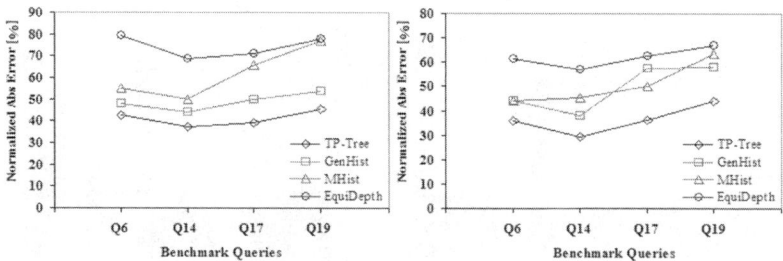

Fig. 6.16 Query performance for the query set QTPC-H on the on the benchmark TPC-H (left) and on the benchmark TPC-HS (right)

6.7.5 Sensitivity Analysis

In the sensitivity analysis, we study the impact of the storage space limit to the performance. We consider the synthetic data cubes A_0 and A_2, which have uniform and Zipf data distributions, respectively, and are both sparse. We use the query-workload QWL_0. We plot the change of the percentage NAE with respect to the available storage space B in Fig. 6.17.

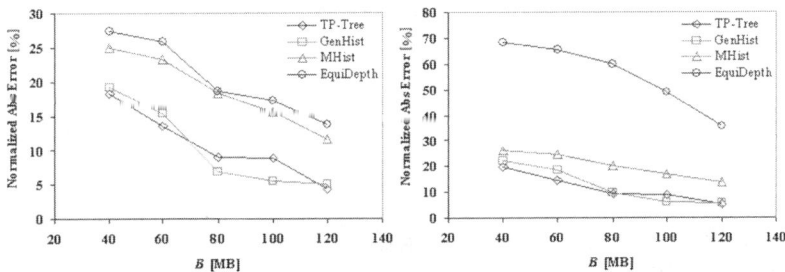

Fig. 6.17 Sensitivity for the query-workload QWL_0 on the data cube A_0 (left) and on the data cube A_1 (right)

From the figure, it can be observed that TP-Tree is less sensitive to the space limit B than MHist and Equi-Depth, and is comparable with GenHist. The general trend concerning better performances with uniform data cubes rather than skewed data cubes is also observed here.

6.7.6 Construction Cost with Synthetic Query-Workloads against Synthetic Data Cubes

Finally, Tables 6.5 and 6.6 show the construction cost of all methods. In this experiment, we considered the synthetic data cubes A_0 and A_2, thus representing both uniform and non-uniform distributions. We used the query-workload QWL_0.

We can see that the TP-Tree construction cost is comparable with those of alternative techniques. Specifically, performance of TP-Tree on data cube A_0 is better than performance on A_2 as A_2 is of the Zipf distribution and thus contains more outliers than A_0; as a result, (i) executions of algorithm outlierDetection are longer for A_2 than A_0, and (ii) building the quad-tree $QT(\Omega_B)$ also takes more time in A_2 than in A_0.

Table 6.5 Construction Costs For the Data Cube A_0 Under the Query-Workload QWL_0

Technique	Construction Time [sec]
TP-Tree	29
GenHist	35
MHist	32
Equi-Depth	30

Table 6.6 Construction Costs For the Data Cube A_2 Under the Query-Workload QWL_0

Technique	Construction Time [sec]
TP-Tree	45
GenHist	39
MHist	37
Equi-Depth	36

6.8 Conclusions and Future Research Efforts

In this paper, we presented TP-Tree, a tree-like, self-adjusting synopsis data structure for approximate range-sum query processing in OLAP. TP-Tree employs efficient outlier management, and provides probabilistic guarantees over the degree of approximation of answers. The main contributions of our proposal are: (i) low spatial and temporal computational overheads for building the TP-Tree; (ii) probabilistic guarantees on the approximate answers and accuracy control; and (iii) independence on any *a priori* assumption on the data distribution. Experimental results confirm the effectiveness of TP-Tree over a large range of data cubes and query workloads, outperforming alternative techniques.

Our future work will be focused on two directions. First, we want to make the TP-Tree update task adaptive, so that an intelligent agent near the OLAP client would be able to interact with the remote AQE server in order to drive the TP-Tree update task by taking into account only the portion of data which the user is interested in. Second, we will explore the possibility of using clustering methods together with our TP-Tree to further improve the performance.

References

1. Program for TPC-D Data Generation with Skew. In *ftp://ftp.research.microsoft.com/pub/users/viveknar/tpcdskew*.
2. The AQUA Project Home Page. In *http://www.bell-labs.com/project/aqua/*.
3. Transactions Processing Council Benchmarks. In *http://www.tpc.org*.
4. A. Aboulnaga and S. Chaudhuri. Self-Tuning Histograms: Building Histograms without Looking at Data. In *Proceedings of the 1999 ACM International Conference on Management of Data*, pages 181–192, 1999.

5. S. Acharya, P. Gibbons, and V. Poosala. AQUA: A Fast Decision Support System Using Approximate Query Answers. In *Proceedings of the 25th International Conference on Very Large Data Bases*, pages 754–757, 1999.

6. S. Acharya, P. Gibbons, and V. Poosala. AQUA: A Fast Decision Support System Using Approximate Query Answers. In *Proceedings of the 25th International Conference on Very Large Data Bases*, pages 275–286, 1999.

7. S. Agrawal, S. Chaudhuri, A. Das, and V. Narasayya. Automating Layout of Relational Databases. In *Proceedings of the 19th IEEE International Conference on Data Engineering*, pages 607–618, 2003.

8. B. Babcock, S. Chaudhuri, and G. Das. Dynamic Sample Selection for Approximate Query Answers. In *Proceedings of the 2003 ACM International Conference on Management of Data*, pages 539–550, 2003.

9. V. Barnett and T. Lewis. *Outliers in Statistical Data*. John Wiley, 1994.

10. N. Bruno, S. Chaudhuri, and L. Gravano. STHoles: A Multidimensional Workload-Aware Histogram. In *Proceedings of the 2001 ACM International Conference on Management of Data*, pages 211–222, 2001.

11. F. Buccafurri, F. Furfaro, D. Sacca, and C. Sirangelo. A Quad-Tree Based Multiresolution Approach for Two-Dimensional Summary Data. In *Proceedings of the 15th IEEE International Conference on Scientific and Statistical Database Management*, pages 127–140, 2003.

12. K. Chakrabarti, M. Garofalakis, R. Rastogi, and S. K. Approximate Query Processing Using Wavelets. In *Proceedings of the 26th International Conference on Very Large Data Bases*, pages 111–122, 2000.

13. C. Chatfield. *The Analysis of Time Series*. Chapman and Hall, 1984.

14. S. Chaudhuri, G. Das, M. Datar, R. Motwani, and R. Rastogi. Overcoming Limitations of Sampling for Aggregation Queries. In *Proceedings of the 17th IEEE International Conference on Data Engineering*, pages 534–542, 2001.

15. S. Chaudhuri and V. Narasayya. AutoAdmin "What-if" Index Analysis Utility. In *Proceedings of the 1998 ACM International Conference on Management of Data*, pages 367–378, 1998.

16. G. Colliat. OLAP, Relational, and Multidimensional Database Systems. *ACM SIGMOD Record*, 25(3):64–69, 1996.

17. A. Cuzzocrea. Overcoming Limitations of Approximate Query Answering in OLAP. In *Proceedings of the 9th IEEE International Database Engineering and Applications Symposium*, pages 200–209, 2005.

18. A. Cuzzocrea. Accuracy Control in Compressed Multidimensional Data Cubes for Quality of Answer-based OLAP Tools. In *Proceedings of the 18th IEEE International Conference on Scientific and Statistical Database Management*, pages 301–310, 2006.

19. P. Deshpande, K. Ramasamy, A. Shukla, and J. Naughton. Caching Multidimensional Queries using Chuncks. In *Proceedings of the 1998 ACM International Conference on Management of Data*, pages 259–270, 1998.

20. V. Gaede and O. Gunther. Multidimensional Access Methods. *ACM Computing Surveys*, 30(1):170–231, 1998.

21. V. Ganti, M. Lee, and R. Ramakrishnan. ICICLES: Self-Tuning Samples for Approximate Query Answering. In *Proceedings of the 26th International Conference on Very Large Data Bases*, pages 176–187, 2000.

22. P. Gibbons and Y. Matias. New Sampling-Based Summary Statistics for Improving Approximate Query Answers. In *Proceedings of the 1998 ACM International Conference on Management of Data*, pages 331–342, 1998.

23. J. Gray, A. Bosworth, A. Layman, and H. Pirahesh. Data Cube: a Relational Aggregation Operator Generalizing Group-By, Cross-Tab, and Sub-Totals. In *Proceeding of the 12th IEEE International Conference on Data Engineering*, pages 152–159, 1996.

24. D. Gunopulos, G. Kollios, V. Tsotras, and C. Domeniconi. Approximating Multi-Dimensional Aggregate Range Queries over Real Attributes. In *Proceedings of the 2000 ACM Conference on Management of Data*, pages 463–474, 2000.

25. J. Han and M. Kamber. *Data Mining: Concepts and Techniques*. Morgan Kaufmann Publishers, 2000.

26. D. Hawkins. *Identification of Outliers*. Chapman and Hall, 1980.
27. J. Hellerstein, P. Haas, and H. Wang. Online Aggregation. In *Proceedings of the 1997 ACM International Conference on Management of Data*, pages 171–182, 1997.
28. C.-T. Ho, R. Agrawal, N. Megiddo, and R. Srikant. Range Queries in OLAP Data Cubes. In *Proceedings of the 1997 ACM International Conference on Management of Data*, pages 73–88, 1997.
29. W. Hoeffding. Probability Inequalities for Sums of Bounded Random Variables. *Journal of the American Statistical Association*, 58(301):13–30, 1963.
30. Y. Ioannidis and V. Poosala. Histogram-based Approximation of Set-Valued Query Answers. In *Proceedings of the 25th International Conference on Very Large Data Bases*, pages 174–185, 1999.
31. H. Jagadish, N. Koudas, and S. Muthukrishnan. Mining Deviants in Times Series Database. In *Proceedings of the 25th International Conference on Very Large Data Bases*, pages 102–113, 1999.
32. N. Karayannidis and T. Sellis. SISYPHUS: The Implementation of a Chunk-Based Storage Manager for OLAP. *Data & Knowledge Engineering*, 45(2):155–180, 2003.
33. S. Khanna, S. Muthukrishnan, and M. Paterson. On Approximating Rectangle Tiling and Packing. In *Proceedings of 9th ACM SIAM Symposium on Discrete Algorithms*, pages 384–393, 1998.
34. E. Knorr and R. Ng. Algorithms for Mining Distance-based Outliers in Large Datasets. In *Proceedings of 24th International Conference on Very Large Data Bases*, pages 392–403, 1998.
35. Y. Matias, J. Vitter, and M. Wang. Wavelet-Based Histograms for Selectivity Estimation. In *Proceedings of the 1998 ACM International Conference on Management of Data*, pages 448–459, 1998.
36. M. Muralikrishna and D. DeWitt. Equi-Depth Histograms for Estimating Selectivity Factors for Multi-Dimensional Queries. In *Proceedings of the 1998 ACM International Conference on Management of Data*, pages 28–36, 1998.
37. S. Muthukrishnan, V. Poosala, and T. Suel. On Rectangular Partitioning in Two Dimensions: Algorithms, Complexity, and Applications. In *Proceedings of the 7th IEEE International Conference on Database Theory*, pages 236–256, 1999.
38. A. Natsev, R. Rastogi, and K. Shim. WALRUS: A Similarity Retrieval Algorithm for Image Databases. In *Proceedings of the 1999 ACM International Conference on Management of Data*, pages 395–406, 1999.
39. B.-U. Pagel, H.-W. Six, H. Toben, and P. Widmayer. Towards an Analysis of Range Query Performance in Spatial Data Structures. In *Proceedings of the 12th ACM Symposium on Principles of Database Systems*, pages 214–221, 1993.
40. V. Poosala and Y. Ioannidis. Selectivity Estimation without the Attribute Value Independence Assumption. In *Proceedings of the 23rd International Conference on Very Large Databases*, pages 486–495, 1997.
41. S. Ramaswamy, R. Rastogi, and K. Shim. Efficient Algorithms for Mining Outliers from Large Data Sets. In *Proceedings of the 2000 ACM International Conference on Management of Data*, pages 427–438, 2000.
42. J. Smith, V. Castelli, A. Jhingran, and C.-S. Li. Dynamic Assembly of Views in Data Cubes. In *Proceedings of the 7th ACM Symposium on Principles of Database Systems*, pages 274–283, 1998.
43. E. Stollnitz, T. Derose, and D. Salesin. *Wavelets for Computer Graphics*. Morgan Kauffmann, 1996.
44. J. Vitter and M. Wang. Approximate Computation of Multidimensional Aggregates of Sparse Data Using Wavelets. In *Proceedings of the 1999 ACM International Conference on Management of Data*, pages 194–204, 1999.
45. J. Vitter, M. Wang, and B. Iyer. Data Cube Approximation and Histograms via Wavelets. In *Proceeding of the 7th ACM International Conference on Information and Knowledge Management*, pages 96–104, 1998.

Chapter 7
Closed Cube Lattices

Alain Casali, Sebastien Nedjar, Rosine Cicchetti, and Lotfi Lakhal

Abstract In this paper we propose a lattice-based approach intended for summarizing the Data Cubes. With this intention, we introduce a novel concept: the cube closure over the cube lattice (multidimensional search space) of a categorical database relation. We introduce the cube connection, show that it is a Galois connection and derive a closure operator over the cube lattice. We introduce the concept of Closed Cube lattice which is a cover for Data Cube and show that it is isomorphic to, on one hand the Galois (concept) lattice and, on the other hand the Quotient Cube. Proposed by Lakshmanan *et al.*, the Quotient Cube is a succinct summary of a Data Cube preserving the Rollup/Drilldown semantics. We show that the Quotient Cube, provided with a closure-based characterization, can be derived from the Closed Cube. Thus these two structures have a similar expression power but the Closed Cube is smaller. Finally, we perform some experiments in order to measure the benefit of our approach.

Key words: Closed Cubes, Data Cubes, Lattices, Quotient Cubes.

7.1 Introduction

Precomputing Data Cubes [15, 9] is a widely recognised solution to efficiently answer OLAP queries and provide decision makers with required aggregated data at the desired granularity levels [28, 2, 14]. However, the Data Cube computation is extremely costly both in execution time and main memory size. Moreover, due to the well known problem of space explosion [8, 16], its storage on disk can be prohibitive. In such a context, various researches have proposed compact representa-

Laboratoire d'Informatique Fondamentale de Marseille (LIF), Aix-Marseille Université - CNRS, Case 901, 163 Avenue de Luminy, 13288 Marseille Cedex 9, France, e-mail: `firstname.lastname@lif.univ-mrs.fr`

tions of Data Cubes. We divide this related work in two great trends depending on the fact that the underlying representations are or not information lossless.

Related work

Approaches which do not choose to preserve exact or complete data claim that data warehouse users are interested in general trends among the studied "populations". Some of them are based on the statistic structure of data for computing density distributions and answering OLAP queries in an approximate way. The challenge is of course to obtain the best approximation [27, 37, 32, 10, 21, 11]. In the same trend, the algorithms BUC [2], HCUBING [14], CCUBE [19] and STAR-CUBING [39] compute exact but incomplete results: iceberg cubes. The underlying idea is to take into account, all along the cube computation, the anti-monotone constraints of future users (e.g. the iceberg or frequency constraint). This results in computing and storing only aggregates capturing trends sufficiently general to be relevant (at the risk of being enable to satisfy users searching exceptions or mean trends).

In contrast, approaches proposing lossless information representations can be divided in three categories:

- the ones which attempt to find the best compromise between OLAP query efficiency and storage optimisation. By materializing only certain aggregates (chosen according to their use frequency and size), these approaches favour the efficiency of frequent queries while being able to compute ad hoc queries. Thus, results can be directly yielded or take benefit of a partial precomputation. Various work about materialized views fits in this category [15, 17, 31, 36, 12];
- the second ones fitting in the information lossless trend are the following four methods: the Condensed Cube [38], the Dwarf Cube [30], the Partition Cube [6] and the CURE for Cubes [22]. They favor the optimization of storage space while preserving the capability to answer what ever query. The Condensed Cube, the Partition Cube and the CURE for Cubes have the same spirit: they condense tuples from different cuboids that are aggregated with the same set of tuples in a single tuple. The Dwarf Cube performs size reduction of data cubes by factorizing redundant prefixes and suffixes out of the data warehouse.
- the first lattice-based cover of Data Cubes: the Quotient Cube lattice [20] has the nice property of preserving the Rollup/Drilldown semantics of the cube. The main idea is to define a cover of a Data Cube as small as possible and from which it is possible to compute any OLAP query. Quotient Cube method partitions a cube into classes of tuples with identical aggregate values to save storage space.

In the spirit of the Quotient Cube lattice, we propose, within the groundwork of cube lattice (multidimensional search space [3]), a novel cover for Data Cubes.

Contribution

In this paper, we introduce a sound and well founded representation called Closed Cube lattice for summarizing the semantics of Data Cube. More precisely, the paper makes the following contributions.

- We introduce a novel concept for data mining problems over categorical database relations: the cube closure over the cube lattice. We introduce the concept of cube connection and show that it is a Galois connection between the cube lattice of a relation r and the powerset lattice of $Tid(r)$ (the set of tuple identifiers in r). Hence we derive from the cube connection a closure operator and obtain what we call the Closed Cube lattice of r, which is a cover of the original cube for any aggregative functions. Providing such a reduced representation is an important issue because of the well known problem of storage combinatorial explosion in data warehouse management [8, 9]. Each element of the Closed Cube lattice is a closed tuple and cube keys are minimal generators of closed tuples. We define a lattice-isomorphism for reusing algorithms devised in a binary context.
- We provide a sound characterization of the closure-based semantics of Quotient Cubes. The Quotient Cube lattice [20] is the first cover of the Data Cube preserving the ROLLUP/DRILLDOWN semantics of a Data Cube. It is a set of convex classes provided with a new order relation between them. Using the closure operator over the cube lattice, another contribution is to identify a new relationship between the Closed Cube lattice and the Quotient Cube by showing that the maximal tuple (*w.r.t.* generalization) of each convex class is a closed tuple and minimal elements of such classes are key tuples. By stating this relationship between the two representations, we can take benefit of the smart property of Quotient Cubes, *i.e.* navigating across various data granularity levels like with ROLLUP/DRILLDOWN operators.
- We show formally as well as experimentally that the size of the Closed Cube Lattice can never exceed the size of the Data Cube. When the Quotient Cube begins to meet its objective of reduced representation, our proposal still remains smaller.

The remainder of the paper is organized as follows. Cube lattice framework [3] is described in section 7.2 as a search space for categorical database mining and the Quotient Cube approach [20] is presented in appendix 7.7. Cube connection, the related closure operator and Closed Cube Lattice are presented in section 7.3. In section 7.4, we show the relationship between the Closed Cube lattice and the concept lattice, and in section 7.5 between the former and the Quotient Cube. Experimental results are given in section 7.6. We compare the sizes of our representation, the Quotient Cube and the Data Cube. Results are convincing: the size of the Closed Cube Lattice is always smaller than the ones of the Data Cube and the Quotient Cube. As a conclusion, we resume the strong points of our approach. Proofs are given in appendix.

7.2 Cube Lattice Framework

In this section, we describe the cube lattice framework: a search space for extracting knowledge from categorical database relations [3]. We introduce a novel vision of Data Cubes using this framework.

Throughout the paper, we make the following assumptions and use the introduced notations. Let r be a relation over the schema $\mathscr{R}$. Attributes of $\mathscr{R}$ are divided in two sets (i) $\mathscr{D}$ the set of dimensions, also called categorical or nominal attributes, which correspond to analysis criteria for OLAP, classification or concept learning [23] and (ii) $\mathscr{M}$ the set of measures (for OLAP) or class attributes (for classification or concept learning). Moreover, attributes of $\mathscr{D}$ are totally ordered (the underlying order is denoted by $<_{\mathscr{D}}$[1]) and for a dimension attribute A, $Dom(A)$ stands for the projection of r over A.

The multidimensional space of the categorical database relation r groups all the valid combinations built up by considering the value sets of attributes in $\mathscr{D}$, sets which are enriched with the symbolic value ALL. The latter, introduced in [9] when defining the operator CUBE-BY, is a generalization of all the possible values of any dimension.

The multidimensional space of r is noted and defined as follows: $Space(r) = \{\times_{A \in \mathscr{D}}(Dom(A) \cup ALL)\} \cup \{(\phi, \ldots, \phi)\}$ where $\times$ symbolizes the Cartesian product, and $(\phi, \ldots, \phi)$ stands for the combination of empty values. Any combination belonging to the multidimensional space is a tuple and represents a possible multidimensional pattern.

Example 1 *Table 7.1 presents the categorical database relation used all along the paper to illustrate the introduced concepts. In this relation, Location, Product and Time are dimensions and Sales is a measure attribute. Each tuple of the relation gives the number of products bought in a city on a given day.*

The following tuples (T, ALL, ALL), (T, B, ALL) and (T, F, d_2) are elements of $Space(r)$ and the semantics of the former is: the purchases of all the products on any day in the city of Toronto.

Table 7.1 Relation example r

Location	Product	Time	Sales
Vancouver (V)	Book (B)	99.1.1 (d_1)	9
Vancouver (V)	Food (F)	99.2.1 (d_2)	3
Toronto (T)	Book (B)	99.1.1 (d_1)	6

The multidimensional space of r is structured by the generalization / specialization order between tuples. This order is originally introduced by T. Mitchell [23]

---

[1] We can merely consider the lexicographical order or a more sophisticated order dictated by optimization reasons (such as dimension domain cardinality) [9].

in the context of machine learning. Let u, v be two tuples of the multidimensional space of r:

$$u \preceq_g v \Leftrightarrow \begin{cases} \forall A \in \mathscr{D} \text{ such that } u[A] \neq ALL, u[A] = v[A] \\ \text{or } v = (\phi, \ldots, \phi) \end{cases}$$

If $u \preceq_g v$, we say that u is more general than v in $Space(r)$. In other words, u captures a similar information than v but at a rougher granularity level. The covering relation of $\preceq_g$ is noted $<_g$ and defined as follows: $\forall t, t' \in Space(r), t <_g t' \Leftrightarrow t \prec_g t'$ and $\nexists t'' \in space(r)$ such that $t \prec_g t'' \prec_g t'$.

Example 2 - *In the multidimensional space of our relation example, we have: $(T, ALL, ALL) \preceq_g (T, B, d_2)$, i.e. (T, ALL, ALL) is more general than (T, B, d_2) and (T, B, d_2) is more specific than (T, ALL, ALL). Moreover, we have $(T, B, ALL) <_g (T, B, d_2)$ and any tuple generalizes the tuple (ϕ, ϕ, ϕ) and specializes the tuple (ALL, ALL, ALL).*

The two basic operators provided for tuple construction are: Sum (denoted by $+$) and Product (noted $\bullet$).

The Sum of two tuples yields the most specific tuple which generalizes the two operands. Let u and v be two tuples in $Space(r)$.

$$t = u + v \Leftrightarrow \forall A \in \mathscr{D}, t[A] = \begin{cases} u[A] \text{ if } u[A] = v[A] \\ ALL \text{ otherwise.} \end{cases}$$

We say that t is the Sum of the tuples u and v.

Example 3 - *In our example of $Space(r)$, we have $(V, B, d_1) + (V, F, d_2) = (V, ALL, ALL)$. This means that the tuple (V, ALL, ALL) is built up from the tuples (V, B, d_1) and (V, F, d_2).*

The Product of two tuples yields the most general tuple which specializes the two operands. If it exists, for these two tuples, a dimension A having distinct and real world values (i.e. existing in the original relation), then the only tuple specializing them is the tuple $(\phi, \ldots, \phi)$ (apart from it, the tuple sets which can be used to retrieve them are disjoint). Let u and v be two tuples in $Space(r)$, then:

$$t = u \bullet v \Leftrightarrow \begin{cases} t = (\phi, \ldots, \phi) \text{ if } \exists A \in \mathscr{D} \text{ such that } u[A] \neq v[A] \neq ALL, \\ \text{otherwise } \forall A \in \mathscr{D} \begin{cases} t[A] = u[A] \text{ if } v[A] = ALL \\ t[A] = v[A] \text{ if } u[A] = ALL. \end{cases} \end{cases}$$

We say that t is the Product of the tuples u and v.

Example 4 - *In our example of $Space(r)$, we have $(V, B, ALL) \bullet (ALL, ALL, d_1) = (V, B, d_1)$. This means that (V, B, ALL) and (ALL, ALL, d_1) generalize (V, B, d_1) and (V, B, d_1) participates to the construction of (V, B, ALL) and (ALL, ALL, d_1) (directly or not). The tuples (V, B, ALL) and (T, B, ALL) have no common point apart from the tuple of empty values.*

In order to state the relationship between our multidimensional space and the classical space which is the power set of attribute values, we introduce the function *Attribute*. Such a function yields for any tuple the set of attributes for which the value is different from the value ALL. Let t be a tuple of $Space(r)$, we have $Attribute(t) = \{A \in \mathscr{D} \text{ such that } t[A] \neq \text{ALL}\}$.

Example 5 - *In our example of $Space(r)$, we have $Attribute((V,B,ALL)) = \{ Location, Product\}$.*

By providing the multidimensional space of r with the generalization order between tuples and using the above-defined operators Sum and Product, we define an algebraic structure which is called cube lattice. Such a structure provides a sound foundation for several multidimensional data mining issues.

Theorem 1 - *Let r be a categorical database relation over $\mathscr{D} \cup \mathscr{M}$. The ordered set $CL(r) = \langle Space(r), \preceq_g \rangle$ is a complete lattice, called cube lattice in which Meet ($\bigwedge$) and Join ($\bigvee$) elements are given by:*

1. $\forall T \subseteq CL(r), \bigwedge T = +_{t \in T} t$
2. $\forall T \subseteq CL(r), \bigvee T = \bullet_{t \in T} t$

Through the following proposition, we characterize the order-embedding from the cube lattice towards the powerset lattice of the whole set of attribute values and analyze the number of elements (for a given level or in general) of the cube lattice. In order to avoid ambiguities, each value is prefixed by the name of the concerned attribute.

Proposition 1 - *Let $\mathscr{L}(r)$ be the powerset lattice of attribute value set, i.e. the lattice $\langle \mathscr{P}(\bigcup_{A \in \mathscr{D}} A.a, \forall a \in Dom(A)), \subseteq \rangle$, where $\mathscr{P}(X)$ stands for the powerset of X. Then it exists an order-embedding Φ:*

$$CL(r) \rightarrow \mathscr{L}(r)$$

$$t \mapsto \begin{cases} \bigcup_{A \in \mathscr{D}} A.a, \forall a \in Dom(A) \text{ if } t = (\phi, \ldots, \phi) \\ \{A.t[A] \text{ such that } \forall A \in Attribute(t)\} \text{ otherwise.} \end{cases}$$

The cube lattice framework provides also a precise definition of the Data Cube for aggregative functions f. Thus, a Data Cube is the set $\{(t, f(t)) \mid t \in CL(r)$ and $\text{COUNT}(t) > 0\}$. Each cuboid over $X \subseteq \mathscr{D}$ is the set $\{(t, f(t)) \mid t \in CL(r)$ and $Attribute(t) = X\}$.

Example 6 - *Figure 7.1 exemplifies the Data Cube of our relation example (Cf. Table 7.1) using the function SUM. The measure associated to a tuple is also given (e.g. $(V, ALL, d_2):3$). In this diagram, the tuples of the cuboid according to $\{Location, Time\}$ are in bold.*

Moreover, the cube lattice provides a sound basis for defining the search space to be explored when extracting semantics from the Data Cube such as Roll-Up dependencies [35], multidimensional associations [34], decision tables and classification

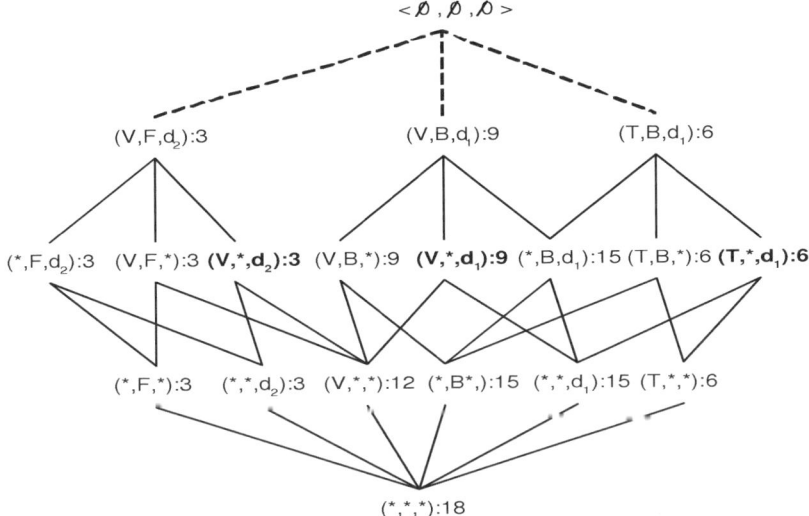

Fig. 7.1 Data Cube of r w.r.t. SUM ($'*' \Leftrightarrow$ ALL).

rules [18], iceberg cubes [2], [14], multidimensional constrained gradients [7], concise representation of hight frequency multidimensional patterns [5] and reduced cubes [20], [38].

7.3 Closed Cube Lattices

The Closed Cube, defined in this section, is a summary of Data Cube. We use the Birkhoff theorem [1] to construct a lattice associated to our closure operator. In contrast with Galois (concept) lattice [13], our resulting lattice is not unspecified: it remains coatomistic (meet elements of the lattice are the tuples of r).

The cube connection is a couple of functions (λ, σ), such that λ is defined from the cube lattice of r to the powerset lattice of $Tid(r)$ and σ is the dual function of λ. We show that (λ, σ) is a special case of Galois connection between two lattices [13]. Hence, we obtain a closure operator over $CL(r)$ under r.

Definition 1 *(Cube Connection)* - *Let Rowid* $: r \to \mathbb{N}^*$ *be a mapping which associates each tuple with a single positive integer and* $Tid(r) = \{Rowid(t)$ *such that* $t \in r\}$ *(i.e. the set of the tuple identifiers of the relation* r*). Let* λ *and* σ *be two functions defined as follows:*

$$\lambda : CL(r) \to \langle \mathscr{P}(Tid(r)), \subseteq \rangle$$
$$t \mapsto \cup \{Rowid(t') \in Tid(r) \text{ such that } t \preceq_g t' \text{ and } t' \in r\}$$
$$\sigma : \langle \mathscr{P}(Tid(r)), \subseteq \rangle \to CL(r)$$

$$P \mapsto \begin{cases} +\{t \in r \text{ such that } Rowid(t) \in P\} \\ (\phi,\ldots,\phi) \text{ otherwise.} \end{cases}$$

Proposition 2 - *The cube connection* (λ,σ) *is a Galois connection between the cube lattice of r and the powerset lattice of* $Tid(r)$.

Definition 2 *(Cube Closure)* - *Let us define the operator* $\mathbb{C} : CL(r) \to CL(r)$

$$t \mapsto \begin{cases} +_{t' \in r} t' \text{ such that } t \preceq_g t' \text{ if } \exists t' \in r \\ (\phi,\ldots,\phi) \text{ otherwise.} \end{cases}$$

By using the cube connection, the operator $\mathbb{C}$ can be defined as follows: let t be a tuple in $CL(r)$, then $\mathbb{C}(t) = \lambda \circ \sigma(t)$.

Example 7 - *Considering the multidimensional space of the relation example we have:*

- $\mathbb{C}((ALL,B,ALL)) = (V,B,d_1) + (T,B,d_1) = (ALL,B,d_1)$
- $\mathbb{C}((T,ALL,ALL)) = (T,B,d_1)$

Proposition 3 - $\mathbb{C}$ *is a closure operator over* $CL(r)$ *under r and thus it satisfies the following properties [1]:*

1. $t \preceq_g t' \Rightarrow \mathbb{C}(t) \geq_g \mathbb{C}(t')$ *(monotony)*
2. $t \preceq_g \mathbb{C}(t)$ *(extensity)*
3. $\mathbb{C}(t) = \mathbb{C}(\mathbb{C}(t))$ *(idempotency).*

The closure of each tuple is computed and results are gathered within a closure system. The minimal tuples w.r.t. $\preceq_g$ originating the very same closure are called cube keys.

Definition 3 *(Closure System)* - *Let us assume that* $\mathbb{C}(r) = \{ t \in CL(r) \text{ such that } \mathbb{C}(t) = t\}$. $\mathbb{C}(r)$ *is a closure system over r and its related closure operator is* $\mathbb{C}$. *Any tuple belonging to* $\mathbb{C}(r)$ *is a closed tuple.*

Example 8 - *Considering our relation example, we have:* $\mathbb{C}(r)=\{(ALL,ALL,ALL), (ALL,B,d_1), (V,ALL,ALL), (V,B,d_1), (V,F,d_2), (T,B,d_1), (\phi,\phi,\phi)\}$.

Definition 4 *(Cube Key)* - *Let t be a closed tuple.* $Key(t) = \min_{\preceq_g} (\{t' \in CL(r) \text{ such that } \mathbb{C}(t') = t\})$ *is the set of minimal generators of t. Each tuple of* $Key(t)$ *is a cube key.*

Example 9 - *By considering our relation example (cf. Table 7.1), we have:*

$$Key((ALL,B,d_1)) = \{(ALL,B,ALL),(ALL,ALL,d_1)\}$$

Since we have a closure operator and an order relation linking the closed tuples, we can use the Birkhoff theorem [1] for constructing a lattice associated to our closure operator.

Theorem 2 - *The partially ordered set $CCL(r) = \langle \mathbb{C}(r), \preceq_g \rangle$ is a complete lattice, with the coatomistic property, called Closed Cube of r. Moreover, we have:*

1. $\forall\, T \subseteq CCL(r),\, \bigwedge T = +_{t \in T}\, t$
2. $\forall\, T \subseteq CCL(r),\, \bigvee T = \mathbb{C}(\bullet_{t \in T}\, t)$

Example 10 - *Figure 7.2 exemplifies the Closed Cube of our relation example (cf. Table 7.1).*

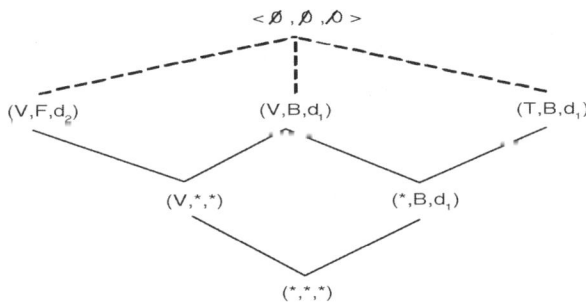

Fig. 7.2 Hasse diagram of the Closed Cube lattice of r ($'*' \Leftrightarrow$ ALL).

All the multidimensional patterns having the same closure generalize the same tuples of the relation. However, the patterns generalizing similar tuples have the same aggregated value (GROUP-BY property). Thus the Closed Cube is a cover for the Data Cube.

Theorem 3 - *The Closed Cube lattice is a cover for Data Cubes w.r.t. aggregative functions such that* COUNT, SUM, MIN, MAX *or* AVG.

Let us underline that, in contrast with the Quotient Cube, we have built a cover which is independent from the measure values. The resulting advantage is to generate a single cover for the Data Cube for any aggregative function. Once the Closed Cube lattice is built, the user can choose one of the quoted aggregative functions. The precomputed structure does not change, contrarily to the Quotient Cube. We just need to update the aggregated values of the measure.

7.4 Lattice Isomorphism and Algorithmic Aspects

Closed set computation has been widely addressed in a binary context. Defining the following lattice-isomorphism makes it possible to reuse results obtained in a binary context.

Definition 5 *(Lattice-Isomorphism) - Let P and Q be two lattices. $\forall X, Y \in P$, a mapping $m : P \rightarrow Q$ is a lattice-isomorphism if and only if it satisfies:*

1. $m(X \wedge_P Y) = m(X) \wedge_Q m(Y)$ *($\wedge$-morphism property)*
2. $m(X \vee_P Y) = m(X) \vee_Q m(Y)$ *($\vee$-morphism property)*
3. *m is bijective*

Let us assume that $Br = \{\Phi(t) \text{ such that } t \in r\}$, the mapping $h : \mathscr{L}(r) \rightarrow \mathscr{L}(r), X \mapsto \cap \{Y \subseteq I \text{ such that } X \subseteq Y\}$ is a closure operator on $I = \bigcup_{A \in D} A.a, \forall \, a \in Dom(A)$ over Br [13]. $Cl(Br) = \{h(X) \text{ such that } X \subseteq I\}$ is a closure system and $\mathscr{L}(Br) = \langle Cl(Br), \subseteq \rangle$ is a lattice called concept lattice of Br [13].

Theorem 4 - *The mapping $\Psi : CCL(r) \rightarrow \mathscr{L}(Br)$ is a lattice-isomorphism and we have $\forall t \in CCL(r), X \in \mathscr{L}(Br)$:*
$$\Psi(t) = \Phi(t)$$

$$\Psi^{-1}(X) = \begin{cases} (\phi, \ldots, \phi) \text{ if } \exists A \in \mathscr{D} \text{ and } a_1, a_2 \in Dom(A) \text{ such that} \\ \quad A.a_1 \text{ and } A.a_2 \in X \\ t \text{ such that } \forall A \in \mathscr{D}, t[A] = \begin{cases} a \text{ if } A.a \in X \\ ALL \text{ otherwise.} \end{cases} \end{cases}$$

Consequences of theorem 4 are specially attractive: when mining closed (frequent) tuples, we can use either binary algorithms like CHARM [41], CLOSE [24], CLOSET [26], TITANIC [33] or algorithms fitting into the cube lattice framework [20], [40].

7.5 Relationships between Closed Cubes and Quotient Cubes

Closed Cube is a small cover of Data Cube. Nevertheless this structure does not preserve the Rollup/Drilldown semantics of the cube whereas the Quotient Cube [20] preserves it. In such a context, it is specially interesting to state a sound relationship between the Closed Cube and the Quotient Cube. To meet this objective, we use results presented in [33] to construct equivalence classes: we merge within a single equivalence class tuples having the very same cube closure. Each equivalence class is then represented by its closed tuple (i.e. the maximal tuple w.r.t. $\preceq_g$) and by the cube keys related to this closed tuple (i.e. the minimal tuples w.r.t. $\preceq_g$). The result is a lattice of closed-equivalence classes which is a Quotient Cube. Finally we state a novel link between key tuples and closed tuples. Then we show that the Closed Cube lattice has the same expression power as the Quotient Cube lattice but its size is smaller. Thus the Closed Cube Lattice is a specially good candidate for an optimized representation of Quotient Cube lattice for the quoted aggregative functions. In the remainder of this section, we assume that f is an aggregative and monotone function.

Definition 6 *(Lattice of closed-equivalence classes) - Let θ be the following equivalence relation : $t\theta t'$ holds if and only if $\mathbb{C}(t,r) = \mathbb{C}(t',r)$. The equivalence class of*

t is given by $[t] = \{t' \in CL(r)$ such that $t \; \theta \; t'\}$. Thus we have $max_{\preceq_g}([t]) = \mathbb{C}(t,r)$ and $min_{\preceq_g}([t]) = Key(\mathbb{C}(t,r))$ (cf. [33] and theorem 4). The set of equivalence classes provided with the generalization order is a lattice (cf. [33] and theorem 4) called lattice of closed-equivalence classes. The order relation within equivalence classes is also the generalization. Let us underline that this lattice is isomorphic to the Closed Cube lattice (cf. [33] and theorem 4).

Example 11 - *The lattice of closed-equivalence classes of the relation illustrated in table 7.1 is given in figure 7.3. In this figure, each equivalence class is represented by its maximal tuple w.r.t. $\preceq_g$ and by its minimal elements w.r.t. $\preceq_g$. When an equivalence class encompasses a single element, it is represented only by this element.*

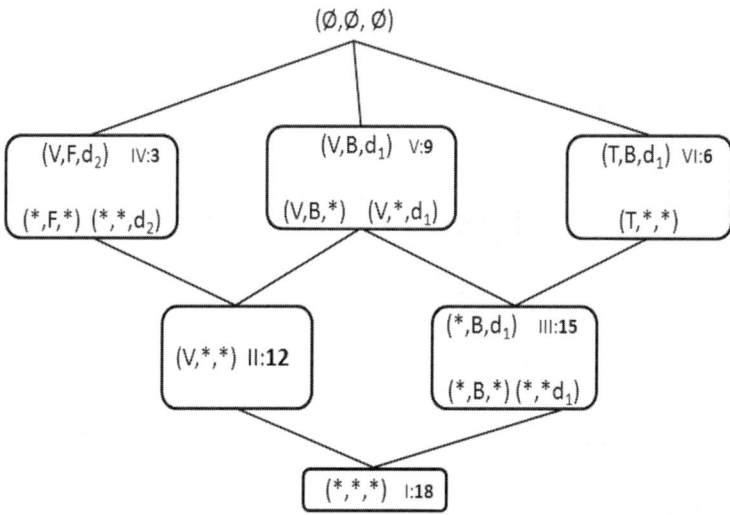

Fig. 7.3 Lattice of closed-equivalence classes ($'*' \Leftrightarrow$ ALL).

In the lattice of closed-equivalence classes like in the Quotient Cube, each equivalence class has a single maximal element and can have several minimal tuples. Based on the isomorphism between the lattice of closed-equivalence classes and the Closed Cube lattice, we introduce the following theorem which states that the latter lattice is isomorphic to the Quotient Cube.

Theorem 5 - *The lattice of closed-equivalence classes is a Quotient Cube and the Closed Cube lattice is isomorphic to the Quotient Cube.*

The Closed Cube lattice is the smallest representation of Data Cube (cf. theorem 4 and [33], [13]). As a consequence, the Quotient Cube has the smallest number of equivalence classes (due to theorem 5). For taking advantage of the lossless representation of the Quotient Cube, our aim is to show that the Closed Cube lattice has a similar expression power. In order to meet this objective, it is necessary to find the cube keys of a closed tuple, provided only with the other closed tuples.

The first method consists in retrieving the closure of all the tuples for which we want to know the value of the aggregative function. Since this value is similar to the one of its closure ($cf.$ theorem 3), we need to find the smallest closed tuple generalizing the considered pattern.

Nevertheless, we can use the following proposition in order to yield the key of a closed tuple while knowing only its direct predecessors ($w.r.t.$ $\preceq_g$). Thus we can retrieve the minimal tuples of any equivalence class in the Quotient Cube.

Proposition 4 - $\forall t \in CCL(r), Key(t) = min_{\preceq_g} \{t' \in CL(r) \text{ such that } t' \preceq_g t \text{ and } \nexists t'' \in DLB(t) \text{ such that } t'' \preceq_g t\}$, where $DLB(t) = max_{\preceq_g} \{t' \in CCL(r) \text{ such that } t' <_g t\}$.

Example 12 - *In the lattice given in figure 7.2, for the particular tuple (V, B, d_1), we have $DLB((V, B, d_1)) = \{(V, ALL, ALL), (ALL, B, d_1)\}$. The keys of this tuple are (V, B, ALL) and (V, ALL, d_1). We obtain results similar to the ones in figure 7.3.*

Proposition 4 proves that the Quotient Cube lattice for the aggregative functions can be obtained from the Closed Cube lattice. Thus the Closed Cube lattice has the same expression power as the Quotient Cube, moreover it is the smallest possible representation.

Let us underline that the previous concept is similar to the one of minimal cube transversal introduced in [4] with an efficient algorithm.

7.6 Experimental results

Our objective now is to compare, through various experiments, the sizes of the Data Cube, the Quotient Cube and the Closed Cube. In this section, we report a summary of our results. All experiments are conducted on a Pentium IV 2,4 GhZ with 1Go main memory and running on Windows XP. We use the algorithm CLOSE [24] in order to perform experimental comparisons between the three representations. We use real data sets to evaluate the validity of our approach. In our experiments, the Quotient Cube is stored by preserving both lower and upper bounds for each class.

We use the real dataset SEP85L containing weather conditions at various weather stations or lands from December 1981 through November 1991[2]. This weather dataset has been frequently used in calibrating various cube algorithms [20], [38]. Mushroom is a dataset widely known in frequent pattern mining. It provides various characteristics of mushrooms. Death is a dataset gathering information about patient decease with the date and cause. TombNecropolis and TombObjects are issued from archaeological excavation. They encompass a list of necropolises, their tombs and other properties like: the country, the funeral rite,

---

[2] http://cdiac.ornl.gov/ftp/ndp026b/SEP85L.DAT.Z

the objects discovered in the tombs and their description. Finally, Joint_Objects_Tombs results from the natural join between TombObjects and TombNecropolis according to the identifiers of necropolises and tombs.

Table 7.2 gives the datasets used for experiments. The columns #Attributes and #Tuples stand for the number of attributes and tuples respectively. In the last column, the size in bytes of the dataset is reported (each dimension or attribute is encoded as an integer requiring 4 bytes for any value).

Table 7.2 Datasets

Tables	# Attributes	# Tuples	Size
SEP85L	20	507 684	56 520
mushroom	23	8 124	747 408
death	5	389	7 700
TombNecropolis	7	1 846	51 688
TombObjects	12	8 278	397 344
Joint_Objects_Tombs	17	7 643	519 724

Figure 7.4 illustrates the size of the studied representations for the various datasets. Since the two datasets Mushroom and Joint_Objects_Tombs require too much main memory (> 4Go) when computing the Quotient Cube and the Closed Cube with a minimum threshold equal to 1 (all the possible tuples), we have to state a minimum threshold to 5% and 1% and to compute an iceberg cube [2].

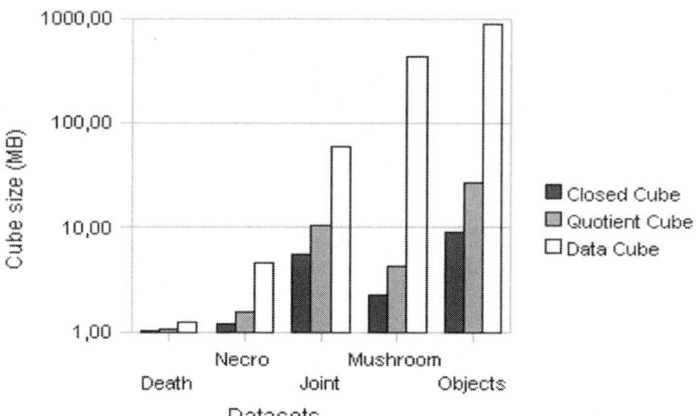

Fig. 7.4 Size of the generated cubes

These five datasets are only encompassing strongly correlated data. Thus we are in the most difficult cases. In this context, the Quotient Cube offers a significant reduction of the Data Cube size and the Closed Cube improves this result by requiring at least half (Joint_Objects_Tombs) or a third (all the others data sets) of the size of the Quotient Cube.

By using the SEP85L dataset, we have generated 9 datasets having from 2 to 10 dimensions by projecting the weather dataset on the first k dimensions ($2 \leq k \leq 10$). For commodity, we just compute the iceberg cube with a minimum support (*minsup*) equal to 0.01% for the aggregative function COUNT.

Whatever the number of dimensions is, the Closed Cube is the smallest representation. It is always significantly reduced when compared to the Data Cube itself. Figure 7.5 shows the size of the representations (in Megabyte). For instance, with ten dimensions, the size of the Closed Cube represents a third of the Data Cube size and a half of the Quotient Cube one. Figure 7.6 provides the zip factor between the size of (*i*) the Closed Cube and the data cube, (*ii*) the closed cube and the Quotient Cube and (*iii*) the Quotient cube and the data cube. As expected when compared to the datacube, the Closed Cube provides the best summary. It remains interesting when compared to the Quotient Cube.

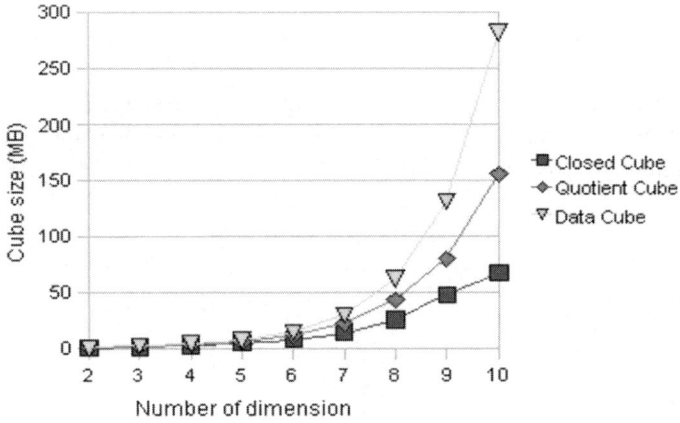

Fig. 7.5 Experimental results for SEP85L with *minsup* = 0.01%

7.7 Conclusion

The presented work is a contribution to the foundation of data mining and data warehouse. It is a cross-fertilization between the fields of discrete mathematics and databases. We introduce the concept of the cube closures of a categorical database relation. In the spirit of the Quotient Cube, we propose the new concept of Closed Cube lattice which is the most reduced summary of Data Cube. We state the iso-

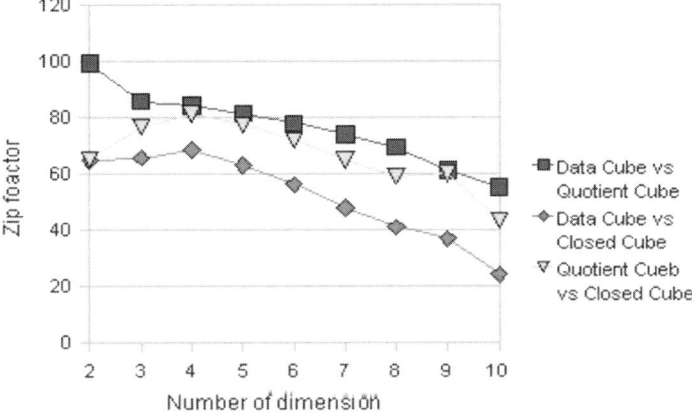

Fig. 7.6 Compression Ratio for SEP85L with *minsup* = 0.01%

morphisms on one hand between the Closed Cube lattice and the concept lattice for which many efficient algorithms are provided, and on the other hand between the Closed Cube lattice and the Quotient Cube lattice. We show both formally and experimentally that our representation is the smallest one and can never exceed the Data Cube size. For instance, the space occupied for storing the Closed Cube can be a third of the Data Cube size and a half of the Quotient Cube. In the context of disk explosion, the benefit is significant.

Defining set operations on constrained cube lattices (convex spaces) is an interesting future work. It could be a basis for providing a convex space algebra in the cube lattice framework (with arbitrary monotone and/or antimonotone constraints given in [25]).

References

[1] Garrett Birkhoff. *Lattice Theory*, volume XXV of *AMS Colloquium Publications*. American Mathematical Society, third (new) edition, 1970.
[2] Kevin Beyer and Raghu Ramakrishnan. Bottom-Up Computation of Sparse and Iceberg CUBEs. In *Proceedings of the International Conference on Management of Data, SIGMOD*, pages 359–370, 1999.
[3] Alain Casali, Rosine Cicchetti, and Lotfi Lakhal. Cube lattices: a framework for multidimensional data mining. In *Proceedings of the 3rd SIAM International Conference on Data Mining, SDM*, pages 304–308, 2003.
[4] Alain Casali, Rosine Cicchetti, and Lotfi Lakhal. Extracting semantics from datacubes using cube transversals and closures. In *Proceedings of the 9th ACM SIGKDD International Conference on Knowledge Discovery and Data Mining, KDD*, pages 69–78, 2003.
[5] Alain Casali, Rosine Cicchetti, and Lotfi Lakhal. Mining concise representations of frequent multidimensional patterns. In *Proceedings of the 11th International Conference on Concep-*

tual Structures, ICCS, pages 351–361, 2003.

[6] Alain Casali, Rosine Cicchetti, Lotfi Lakhal, and Noel Novelli. Lossless reduction of datacubes. In *Proceedings of the 17th International Conference on Database and Expert Systems Applications, DEXA*, pages 409–419, 2006.

[7] G. Dong, J. Han, Joyce M. W. Lam, J. Pei, and K. Wang. Multi-Dimensional Constrained Gradients in Data Cubes. In *Proceedings of 27th International Conference on Very Large Data Bases, VLDB*, pages 321–330, Italy, 2001.

[8] Prasad Deshpande, Jeffrey F. Naughton, Karthikeyan Ramasamy, Amit Shukla, Kristin Tufte, and Yihong Zhao. Cubing algorithms, storage estimation, and storage and processing alternatives for olap. In *Bulletin of IEEE*, volume 20(1), pages 3–11, 1997.

[9] Jim Gray, Surajit Chaudhuri, Adam Bosworth, Andrew Layman, Don Reichart, Murali Venkatrao, Frank Pellow, and Hamid Pirahesh. Data cube: A relational aggregation operator generalizing group-by, cross-tab, and sub-totals. In *Data Mining and Knowledge Discovery*, volume 1(1), pages 29–53, 1997.

[10] Anna Gilbert, Yannis Kotidis, S. Muthukrishnan, and Martin Strauss. Optimal and approximate computation of summary statistics for range aggregates. In *Proceedings of the 20th ACM SIGACT-SIGMOD-SIGART Symposium on Principles of Database Systems, PODS*, 2001.

[11] Anna Gilbert, Yannis Kotidis, S. Muthukrishnan, and Martin Strauss. Surfing Wavelets on Streams : One-Pass Summaries for Approximate Queries. In *Proceedings of 27th International Conference on Very Large Data Bases, VLDB*, pages 79–88, 2001.

[12] Himanshu Gupta and Inderpal Mumick. Selection of Views to Materialize in a Data Warehouse. In *IEEE Transactions on Knowledge and Data Engineering, TKDE*, volume 17 (1/2005), pages 24–43, 2005.

[13] Bernhard Ganter and Rudolf Wille. *Formal Concept Analysis: Mathematical Foundations*. Springer, 1999.

[14] Jiawei Han, Jian Pei, Guozhu Dong, and Ke Wang. Efficient Computation of Iceberg Cubes with Complex Measures. In *Proceedings of the International Conference on Management of Data, SIGMOD*, pages 441–448, 2001.

[15] Venky Harinarayan, Anand Rajaraman, and Jeffrey D. Ullman. Implementing data cubes efficiently. In *Proceedings of the International Conference on Management of Data, SIGMOD*, pages 205–216, 1996.

[16] Yannis Kotidis and Nick Roussopoulos. An alternative storage organization for rolap aggregate views based on cubetrees. In *Proceedings ACM SIGMOD International Conference on Management of Data, SIGMOD*, pages 249–258, 1998.

[17] Yannis Kotidis and Nick Roussopoulos. DynaMat: A Dynamic View Management System for Data Warehouses. In *Proceedings ACM SIGMOD International Conference on Management of Data, SIGMOD*, pages 371–382, 1999.

[18] H. Lu and H. Liu. Decision Tables: Scalable Classification Exploring RDBMS Capabilities. In *Proceedings of the 26th International Conference on Very Large Databases, VLDB*, pages 373–384, 2000.

[19] Marc Laporte, Noel Novelli, Rosine Cicchetti, and Lotfi Lakhal. Computing full and iceberg datacubes using partitions. In *Proceedings of the 13rd International Symposium on Methodologies for Intelligent Systems, ISMIS*, pages 244–254, 2002.

[20] Laks V. S. Lakshmanan, Jian Pei, and Jiawei Han. Quotient cube: How to summarize the semantics of a data cube. In *Proceedings of the 28th International Conference on Very Large Databases, VLDB*, pages 778–789, 2002.

[21] Rokia Missaoui, Cyril Goutte, Anicet Kouomou Choupo, and Ameur Boujenoui. A probabilistic model for data cube compression and query approximation. In Il-Yeol Song and Torben Bach Pedersen, editors, *DOLAP*, pages 33–40. ACM, 2007.

[22] Konstantinos Morfonios and Yannis E. Ioannidis. Cure for cubes: Cubing using a rolap engine. In *Proceedings of the 32nd International Conference on Very Large Databases, VLDB*, pages 379–390, 2006.

[23] Tom M. Mitchell. *Machine learning*. MacGraw-Hill Series in Computer Science, 1997.

[24] Nicolas Pasquier, Yves Bastide, Rafik Taouil, and Lotfi Lakhal. Discovering frequent closed itemsets for association rules. In *Proceedings of the 7th International Conference on Database Theory, ICDT*, pages 398–416, 1999.

[25] Jian Pei and Jiawei Han. Constrained Frequent pattern Mining: A Pattern-Growth View. In *SIGKDD Explorations*, volume 4(1), pages 31–39, 2002.

[26] Jian Pei, Jiawei Han, and Runying Mao. CLOSET: An Efficient Algorithm for Mining Frequent Closed Itemsets. In *Workshop on Research Issues in Data Mining and Knowledge Discovery, DMKD*, pages 21–30, 2000.

[27] Torben Pedersen, Christian Jensen, and Curtis Dyreson. Supporting Imprecision in Multidimensional Databases Using Granularities . In *Proceedings of the 11th International Conference on Scientific and Statistical Database Management, SSDBM*, pages 90–101, 1999.

[28] Kenneth A. Ross and Divesh Srivastava. Fast Computation of Sparse Datacubes. In *Proceedings of the 23rd International Conference on Very Large Databases, VLDB*, pages 116–125, 1997.

[30] Yannis Sismanis, Antonios Deligiannakis, Nick Roussopoulos, and Yannis Kotidis. Dwarf: shrinking the petacube. In Michael J. Franklin, Bongki Moon, and Anastassia Ailamaki, editors, *SIGMOD Conference*, pages 464–475. ACM, 2002.

[31] Theodoratos Sellis. Designing data warehouses. In *Data and Knowledge Engineering, DKE*, volume 31 (3/1999), pages 279–301, 2004.

[32] Jayavel Shanmugasundaram, Usama Fayyad, and Paul Bradley. Compressed Data Cubes for OLAP Aggregate Query Approximation on Continuous Dimensions . In *Proceedings of the 5th ACM SIGKDD International Conference on Knowledge Discovery and Data Mining, KDD*, pages 223–232, 1999.

[33] Gerd Stumme, Rafik Taouil, Yves Bastide, Nicolas Pasquier, and Lotfi Lakhal. Computing Iceberg Concept Lattices with Titanic. In *Data and Knowledge Engineering*, volume 42(2), pages 189–222, 2002.

[34] Anthony K. H. Tung, Hongjun Lu, Jiawei Han, and Ling Feng. Efficient Mining of Intertransaction Association Rules. In *IEEE Transactions on Knowledge and Data Engineering, TKDE*, volume 15(1), pages 43–56, 2003.

[35] Toon Calders and Raymond T. Ng and Jef Wijsen. Searching for Dependencies at Multiple Abstraction Levels. In *ACM Transactions on Database Systems, ACM TODS*, volume 27(3), pages 229–260, 2002.

[36] Dimitri Theodoratos and Wugang Xu. Constructing search spaces for materialized view selection . In *Proceedings ACM Seventh International Workshop on Data Warehousing and OLAP, DOLAP*, pages 112–121, 2004.

[37] Jeffrey Vitter and Min Wang. Approximate Computation of Multidimensional Aggregates of Sparse Data Using Wavelets . In *Proceedings ACM SIGMOD International Conference on Management of Data, SIGMOD*, pages 193–204, 1999.

[38] Wei Wang, Hongjun Lu, Jianlin Feng, and Jeffrey Xu Yu. Condensed Cube: An Effective Approach to Reducing Data Cube Size. In *Proceedings of the 18th International Conference on Data Engineering, ICDE*, pages 213–222, 2002.

[39] Dong Xin, Jiawei Han, Xiaolei Li, and Benjamin W. Wah. Star-cubing: Computing iceberg cubes by top-down and bottom-up integration. In *Proceedings of the 29th international Conference on Very Large Data Bases, VLDB*, pages 476–487, 2003.

[40] Dong Xin, Zheng Shao, Jiawei Han, and Hongyan Liu. C-cubing: Efficient computation of closed cubes by aggregation-based checking. In *ICDE*, page 4, 2006.

[41] Mohammed Javeed Zaki and Ching-Jui Hsio. CHARM: An Efficient Algorithm for Closed Itemset Mining. In *Proceedings of the 2nd SIAM International Conference on Data mining*, 2002.

Appendix

Quotient Cube Lattices

A Quotient Cube is a summary of Data Cube for aggregative functions like COUNT, MIN, MAX, AVG and TOP-k [20]. Moreover, the Quotient Cube preserves the semantics of the cube operators ROLLUP and DRILLDOWN.

When introducing a Quotient Cube, the authors use the concept of convex classes (i.e. sets of tuples). A class $\mathscr{C}$ is convex if and only if $\forall c, c' \in \mathscr{C}$ if $\exists c''$ such that $c \preceq_g c'' \preceq_g c'$ implies $c'' \in \mathscr{C}$.

Classes are built as follows. Given an aggregative function f, the equivalence relation $\equiv_f$ is defined as a transitive and reflexive closure of the following relation $\mathbf{R}$: let t, t' be two tuples, $t\mathbf{R}t'$ holds if and only if (i) $f(t) = f(t')$ and (ii) t is either a parent or a child of t'. Let us note by $[t]_{\equiv_f}$ the equivalence class of t ($[t]_{\equiv_f} = \{t' \in CL(r) \mid t\mathbf{R}t'\}$). Moreover, the relation $\equiv_f$ must satisfy the weak congruence property which can be expressed as follows: $\forall c, c', d, d' \in CL(r)$, if $c \equiv_f c', d \equiv_f d', c \preceq_g d$ and $d' \preceq_g c'$, thus $c \equiv_f d$ also holds. Weak congruence property induces convex property for each equivalence classes.

Definition 7 *(Quotient Cube Lattice) - Let $CL(r)$ be the cube lattice of the relation r and $\equiv_f$ an equivalence relation on $Space(r)$ satisfying the weak congruence property. The Quotient Cube lattice $QCL(r, f) = \{([t]_{\equiv_f}, f(t)) \mid t \in CL(r))\}$ encompasses equivalence classes induced by $\equiv_f$. For two equivalence classes $A, B \in QCL(r, f)$, we have $A \preceq B$ if $\exists a \in A, \exists b \in B$ such that $a \preceq_g b$.*

Example 13 *- The Quotient Cube lattice of the relation in table 7.1 for the aggregative function* SUM *is illustrated in figure 7.7. Classes are numbered and provided with the value of the* SUM *function (e.g. III:15).*

A particular focus is made on the class VI in order to show all its elements. Other classes are represented by their minimal and maximal tuples w.r.t. $\preceq_g$. This lattice is isomorphic to the lattice shown in figure 7.3.

Proof of lemmas, propositions and theorems

Proof of proposition 2: - In order to prove that (λ, σ) is a Galois connection, we show that $\forall t \in CL(r), X \in \langle \mathscr{P}(Tid(r)), \subseteq \rangle : t \preceq_g \sigma(X) \Leftrightarrow X \subseteq \lambda(t)$ [13].
($\Rightarrow$) Let $t \in CL(r)$ be a tuple and $X \in \langle \mathscr{P}(Tid(r)), \subseteq \rangle : t \preceq_g \sigma(X)$. Moreover, let us suppose that $\exists i \in Tid(r)$ such that $i \notin \lambda(t)$ and $i \in X$. Since $CL(r)$ is coatomistic, we know that $\exists t' \in r$ such that $\sigma(X) \preceq_g t'$ and $t' = t_i$. However, $i \notin \lambda(t)$, thus $t \npreceq_g t'$, which is impossible because $t \preceq_g \sigma(X)$. Thus the implication always holds.
($\Leftarrow$) dual to the previous case. $\square$
Proof of proposition 3: - Obvious because $\mathbb{C}(t, r) = \sigma \circ \lambda(t)$ where λ and σ are

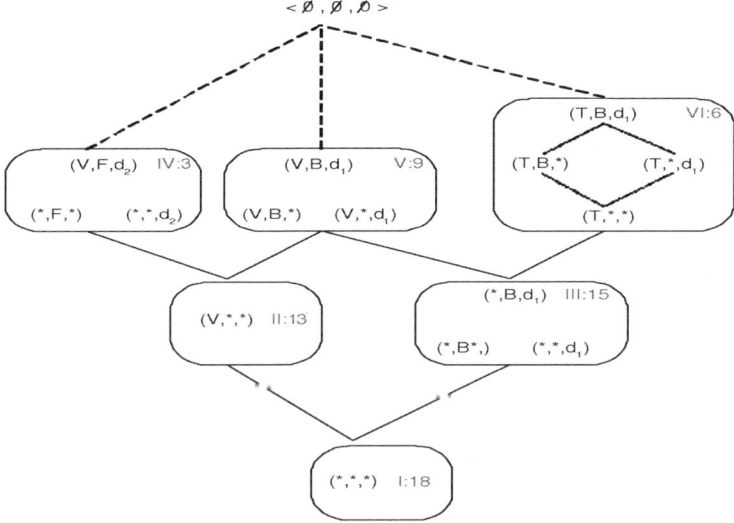

Fig. 7.7 Quotient Cube lattice for the aggregative function SUM.

the functions specified in definition 1 and $rc = (\lambda, \sigma)$ is a Galois connection, therefore $\sigma \circ \lambda$ is a closure operator on $CL(r)$ ($\mathbb{C}' = \lambda \circ \sigma$ is a closure operator on $\langle \mathscr{P}(Tid(r)), \subseteq \rangle$). Any closure operator verifies the properties of isotony, extensity and idempotency, thus $\mathbb{C}$ and $\mathbb{C}'$ satisfy these three properties. $\square$

Proof of proposition 2: - By definition of the closure operator $\mathbb{C}$ (*cf.* definition 3 and proposition 3) and applying Birkhoff theorem [1] on $\mathbb{C}(r)$, $CCL(r)$ is a complete lattice. Moreover, $CCL(r)$ is a coatomistic lattice by definition of $\mathbb{C}$. $\square$

Proof of proposition 3: - Let be t, $t' \in CL(r)$ and f an aggregative function. Due to the GROUP-BY property, we have:

$$f(t) = f(t') \Leftrightarrow \{t'' \in r \text{ such that } t \preceq_g t''\} = \{t'' \in r \text{ such that } t' \preceq_g t''\}$$
$$\Leftrightarrow \lambda(t) = \lambda(t') \ (cf. \text{ definition 1})$$
$$\Leftrightarrow \mathbb{C}(t) = \mathbb{C}(t') \ (cf. \text{ definition 2})$$

Thus $CCL(r)$ is a cover for any Data Cubes. $\square$

Proof of theorem 4: - In order to prove the theorem, we assume that $t_1, t_2 \in CCL(r)$ and $X, Y \in \mathscr{L}(Br)$.

1. Ψ is a $\bigwedge$-morphism:

$$\Psi(t_1 \bigwedge_{CCL(r)} t_2) = \{A.t[A] \text{ such that } t_1[A] = t_2[A]$$
$$\text{and } t[A] \neq \text{ALL}\}$$
$$= \{A.t[A] \text{ such that } A.t[A] \in \Psi(t_1) \text{ and }$$
$$A.t[A] \in \Psi(t_2)\}$$
$$= \Psi(t_1) \cap \Psi(t_2)$$
$$= \Psi(t_1) \bigwedge_{\mathscr{L}(Br)} \Psi(t_2)$$

2. Ψ is a $\bigvee$-morphism:

$$
\begin{aligned}
\Psi(t_1 \vee_{CCL(r)} t_2) &= \Psi(\mathbb{C}(t_1 \bullet t_2)) \\
&= \Psi(+t \in r \text{ such that } t_1 \bullet t_2 \preceq_g t) \\
&= \cap\{\Psi(t \in r \text{ such that } t_1 \bullet t_2 \preceq_g t)\} \\
&\qquad\qquad (\bigwedge -\text{morphism property}) \\
&= \cap\{\Psi(t) \in \Psi(r) \text{ such that } \Psi(t_1 \bullet t_2) \subseteq \Psi(t)\} \\
&= h(X) \text{ where } X = \{A.t[A], A \in \mathscr{D} \text{ such that} \\
&\qquad\qquad\qquad\qquad t_1[A] \neq \text{ALL or } t_2[A] \neq \text{ALL}\} \\
&= \Psi(t_1) \vee_{\mathscr{L}(Br)} \Psi(t2)
\end{aligned}
$$

3. Ψ is injective:
   obvious because if $t_1 \neq t_2$ then $\Psi(t_1) \neq \Psi(t_2)$.
4. Ψ is surjective:

   If $X = I$, then $\Psi^{-1}(X) = (\phi, \dots, \phi)$.
   Else $X = \cap\{Y \in \Psi(r) \text{ such that } X \subseteq Y\}$
   $\qquad\qquad = \Psi^{-1}(+t, t \in r \text{ and } \Psi^{-1}(X) \preceq_g (t))$
   $\qquad\qquad\qquad\qquad (\bigwedge -\text{morphism property})$
   $\qquad\qquad = \Psi^{-1}(t'), t' = +t, t \in r \text{ and } \Psi^{-1}(X) \preceq_g t \ \square$

Proof of theorem 5: - Since there is an isomorphism between Closed Cube lattice and lattice of closed-equivalence class, it is sufficient to show that lattice of closed-equivalence classes is isomorphic to Quotient Cube. We prove that the equivalence relation θ introduced in definition 6 satisfies the weak congruence property.
Let t and t' be two tuples such that $[t] \preceq_g [t'] \Rightarrow \exists u \in [t], v \in [t']$ such that $u \preceq_g v(1)$. We show that $\forall v' \in [t'], u' \in [t] : v' \npreceq_g u'$.
Let us assume that $\exists \ v_1 \in [t']$ and $u_1 \in [t]$ such that $v_1 \preceq_g u_1$. Thus we have $freq(v_1) \geq freq(u_1)(2)$. But $v_1 \in [t'] \Rightarrow freq(v_1) = freq(v)$ and $u_1 \in [t] \Rightarrow freq(u_1) = freq(u)$. Therefore $(1) + (2) \Rightarrow freq(v) = freq(u)$ which is impossible because $u \preceq_g v$ and $freq(u) = freq(v) \Rightarrow \mathbb{C}(u, r) = \mathbb{C}(v, r)$ ([33]) and thus u, v belong to the same equivalence class which is contradicting the initial assumption. $\square$

Proof of proposition 4: - In order to demonstrate the proposition, we need, firstly, to prove the following equivalence: let u be a tuple, v a closed tuple and $u \preceq_g v$, we have the following equivalence:

$$Freq(u) = Freq(v) \Leftrightarrow \nexists w \in DLB(v) : u \preceq_g w, (1)$$

where $DLB(t) = max_{\preceq_g}\{t' \in CCL(r) \text{ such that } t' \preceq_g t\}$.

Thus if $Freq(u) = Freq(v)$ and $\exists w \in DLB(t) : u \preceq_g w \Rightarrow u \preceq_g w \Rightarrow Freq(u) \geq Freq(w) \Rightarrow Freq(w) = Freq(v)$, which is impossible. So, the equivalence (1) always yields.

Let t be in $CCL(r)$, then we have:

$$
\begin{aligned}
Key(t) &= min_{\preceq_g}(\{u \preceq_g t \text{ such that } Freq(t) = Freq(u)\}) \\
&= min_{\preceq_g}(\{u \preceq_g t \text{ such that } \nexists w \in DLB(t) \text{ and such that } u \preceq_g w\}) \ (cf. \ (1)) \ \square
\end{aligned}
$$

Chapter 8
Design and Analysis of Index Structures in MultiVersion Data Warehouses

Khaled Jouini and Geneviève Jomier

Abstract A MultiVersion Data Warehouse (MVDW) is a Data Warehouse (DW) using versioning to cope with the slowly evolving nature of analysis dimensions as well as to support what-if analyses. In such a DW, several DW versions coexist. Each DW version is composed of data extracted from external data sources during a certain time period, or of computed hypothetical data, generated to analyze the outcomes of an hypothetical strategic decision. In a MVDW, data may evolve along different version branches and queries may span multiple DW versions. The efficiency of query processing is crucial in a DW environment and requires DW designers aware of tradeoffs among index structures. This paper defines a framework for understanding, designing, analyzing and comparing index structures for MVDW. First, the paper extends index structures designed for data with linear evolution to handle data with branched evolution. Next, the paper defines an analytical method for understanding the behavior of the different index structures. The analysis allows determining the most suitable index structure, for given data and application characteristics.

8.1 Introduction

Data Warehouses (DW) are databases built for strategic decision support: they are useful in domains were the past is supposed to throw light on the future. Thus, a DW stores time-series of multidimensional *facts*, which are to be analyzed, and the data describing the different *analysis dimensions*[19] used for analyzing facts. In a relational databases, it results in fact tables and dimensions tables [14].

This paper concerns time-series analyses in DWs under the framework of versions. More specifically, there are two kinds of versioning scenarios: (1) versioning of the analysis context (*i.e.* schema and dimension data) in order to handle its slowly

Université Paris Dauphine, Place du Maréchal de Lattre de Tassigny, Paris, France, e-mail:
{khaled.jouini,genevieve.jomier}@dauphine.fr

evolving nature; and (2) versioning of facts and dimensions, in order to analyze alternative hypothetical choices. A DW using versioning for such purposes is called MultiVersion Data Warehouse (MVDW) [16, 17, 2].

Under this research perspective, two families of analysis procedures can be performed. The first family consists in analyzing data harvested from external data sources, called *real data* in [2], using business intelligence applications (OLAP, data-mining etc.). In theory, the analysis of real data works only for a stable analysis context, *i.e.* for fixed dimension tables (schema and data). In practice, however, not only factual data change, but so do dimension tables. We consider that small changes in dimensions should not affect the analyses. It is up to the analysts to decide when a new analysis context is to be considered. Versioning for handling the slowly evolving nature of the analysis context, means keeping track of all versions of the analysis context [4, 13, 8, 5, 2, 9]. To this end, whenever the analysis context of the DW is updated, its old value is kept and a new version reflecting the update is inserted. Such an approach creates a sequence of analysis context versions. Each context version is associated with a semi-closed time interval expressing its time validity.

The second family of analysis tries to enlighten the decision process by evaluating the impact of alternative hypothetical strategic decisions, using for instance what-if analysis [1, 10]. Versioning for supporting what-if analysis means providing the ability to use business intelligence applications, not only on real data, but also on hypothetical computed data. For example, in a grocery DW devoted to business transactions, decision makers may need to investigate the impact on profits, if during the last three months a promotion campaign for some products have taken place. First, hypothetical sales are generated by computation as versions of real sales that should have been impacted by the promotion. Next, the outcomes of the promotion are explored by OLAP queries. The data generated for such hypothetical decision can be implemented as a version of the DW, partly composed of real data unconcerned with the promotion and partly composed of hypothetical data impacted by the promotion. As several such scenarios can be studied, the DW can be transformed, by inclusion of hypothetical data, as follows: (1) the real data constitute the so called *real DW version*; (2) an hypothetical DW version with the same content as the real DW version is created. Such a DW version is called *alternative DW version* [2]; (3) in the alternative DW version, hypothetical data generated by computation replaces the corresponding real data. As for real DW versions, an alternative DW version is associated to a semi-closed time interval expressing its time validity. The valid time interval of an alternative DW version is within the valid time interval of its parent DW version [2]. As the real fact table is a multidimensional time-series, the identifier of a fact includes a time-identifier. Thus, a fact has no temporal versions, but may only have alternative versions. Figure 8.1 depicts a MVDW composed by a sequence of two real DW versions and four alternative DW versions.

A distinctive feature of MVDWs is that data may evolve along different version branches (*i.e.* branched evolution) and queries may involve a single DW version (*i.e.* intra-version queries) or span multiple DW versions (*i.e.* inter-version or cross-version queries [9]). Although many index structures have been proposed to

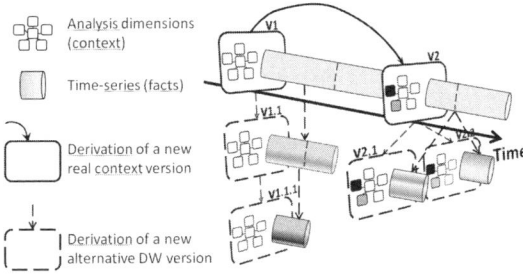

Fig. 8.1 The context versions v_1 and v_2 are created in order to handle the slowly evolving nature of the analysis context. $v_{1.1}$, $v_{1.1.1}$, $v_{2.1}$ and $v_{2.2}$ are created to simulate hypothetical strategic decisions.

optimize queries to data with linear evolution [21], little work has been carried out on indexing data with branched evolution [20]. This paper defines a framework for understanding, designing, analyzing and comparing index structures for such data. In particular, a mean value analysis method of the system at steady state, called *the Steady State Analysis* is proposed. It allows determining the most suitable index structure given data and application characteristics.

The paper is organized as follows. Section 8.2 introduces basic concepts. Section 8.3 describes different index structures. Section 8.4 presents the steady state analysis. Section 8.5 validates the analysis through simulations. Section 8.6 concludes the paper.

8.2 Basic Concepts

8.2.1 DW Versions and Entity Versions

A DW version is composed of an analysis context version (*i.e.* schema and dimension data) and a fact table instance limited to a predefined time interval. In the sequel, when no confusion is possible, we do not distinguish between a DW version and the version stamp v identifying it. The term *entity* is used to designate any persistent information (fact or dimension).

Let $\mathbb{E} = \{e\}$ and $\mathbb{V} = \{v\}$ be, respectively, the set of all entity identifiers (*i.e.* surrogates) and the set of all DW version stamps. An entity $e \in \mathbb{E}$ is represented in a DW version $v \in \mathbb{V}$ by a single entity version (e, v, val), where val is the value taken by the entity e in the DW version v. If e does not appear in v, val has the special value *nil*, meaning *does not exist* in that DW version. A DW version $v_i \in \mathbb{V}$ contains at most one version of each entity: $v_i = \{(e, v, val)$, such that, $e \in \mathbb{E}$ and $v = v_i\}$.

Except for the initial DW version v_1, a new DW version is always *derived* from an existing one. Thus, $\mathbb{V}$ is structured in a genealogical tree, called *DW version tree* [7]. In case of alternative DW versions, the initial DW version is composed of a context version and the part of real fact consistent with the context version (*c.f.* figure 8.1). These concepts are illustrated in figures 8.2.a and 8.2.b, where the following

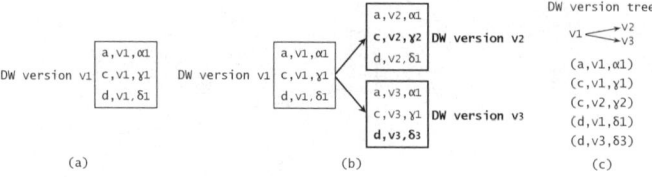

Fig. 8.2 (a) Initial DW version v_1. (b) DW versions v_2 and v_3 are derived from v_1. c is updated in v_2, d is updated in v_3 and a keeps the same value α_1 over v_1, v_2 and v_3. (c) Stored DW version tree and entity versions

notations are applied: entity versions identifiers are latin minuscules and entity versions values are greek minuscules. Figure 8.2.a shows the entity versions composing the initial DW version v_1. The entity version (e, v_1, α_1), shows for instance that a has the value α_1 in v_1. In figure 8.2.b, two DW versions v_2 and v_3 are derived from v_1 (*i.e.* v_1 is the parent of v_2 and of v_3). Entity c is updated in v_2 and entity d is updated in v_3.

Since a DW version usually differs only partially from its parent, an entity e can keep the same value through a set of DW versions. Thus, considerable space can be saved if an entity version is associated not merely to a single DW version, but to the set of DW versions over which the entity keeps the same value. For example, in figure 8.2.b, there are 3 DW versions, 3 entities and, hence, 9 entity versions. However, there are only 5 distinct entity version values. To store a value only once, the *implicit sharing* [7] is used: "if the value of (e, v_j) is not explicitly stored, its value is the value of (e, v_i), where the DW version v_i is the closest ancestor of v_j, such that, (e, v_i) is explicitly stored". The entity version (e, v_i) is said to be *alive* in DW version v_j and in each DW version v, such that:

1. DW version v_i is an ancestor of DW version v; and
2. there is no DW version v_k, such that: (*a*) the value of (e, v_k) is explicitly stored; (*b*) v_k is an ancestor of v; and (*c*) v_k is closer to v than v_i.

Figure 8.2.c depicts the content of the data warehouse of figure 8.2.b. The value of (a, v_2) is not explicitly stored. Implicit sharing allows to deduce that (a, v_1) is alive in v_2, hence, the value of (a, v_2) is α_1.

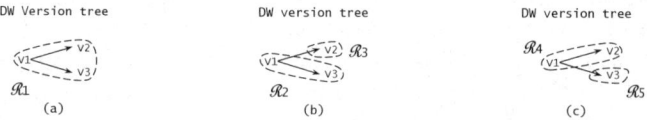

Fig. 8.3 (a) DW version range of (a, v_1): $\mathscr{R}_1 = (v_1, \phi)$. (b) DW version range of (c, v_1) and (c, v_2): respectively, $\mathscr{R}_2 = (v_1, \{v_2\})$ and $\mathscr{R}_3 = (v_2, \phi)$. (c) DW version range of (d, v_1) and (d, v_3): respectively, $\mathscr{R}_4 = (v_1, \{v_3\})$ and $\mathscr{R}_5 = (v_3, \phi)$.

8.2.2 DW Version Range

The set of DW versions over which an entity version is alive, and the edges between them, forms a tree included in the DW version tree. Such an included tree is called *DW version range*. Figures 8.3.a, 8.3.b and 8.3.c depict, respectively, the DW version ranges corresponding to the versions of entities *a*, *c* and *d* of figure8.3.c.

A DW version range $\mathscr{R}$ is represented by a pair $(v_{start}, \{v_{end}\})$, where v_{start} is the DW version root of $\mathscr{R}$ and $\{v_{end}\}$ a set of DW versions [20]. A version v_e appearing in $\{v_{end}\}$ does not belong to $\mathscr{R}$, but its parent does. Thus, v_e explicitly terminates a branch starting at v_{start}. This is illustrated in figures 8.3.b, where the DW version range corresponding to the entity version (c, v_1) is $(v_1, \{v_3\})$. A particular value of a DW version range $\mathscr{R}$ is (v, ϕ), meaning that $\mathscr{R}$ is the subtree of the DW version tree rooted at *v*.

8.3 Indexing Data in MultiVersion Data Warehouses

Indexes devoted to multiversion data use either values to search entity versions identifiers or entity versions identifiers to search values. In the sequel, the term *primary index* is used if the index is on identifiers of entity versions and controls the physical placement of entity versions (clustered indexes). The term *secondary index* is used if the index is on an attribute. In the remainder, we focus mainly on primary indexes. Secondary indexes are discussed briefly in subsection 8.3.2.

8.3.1 Primary Indexes

In this paper, index structures are categorized in three families according to whether entity versions are clustered: (1) by entity, and then by DW version; (2) by DW version, and then by entity; or (3) by the pair (entity identifier, version stamp). The first family is represented by the B+V-tree proposed in this paper. The second family is represented by the Overlapping B+Trees structure (OB+tree) [23] that we modify to handle data with branched evolution. The third family is represented by the Branched and Temporal tree (BT-tree) [11, 12, 20]. These index structures have in common that leaf nodes contain data and internal nodes are used to direct search. In the sequel, I_i denotes an internal node and D_i a leaf node. For internal nodes, we use the term *entry* to designate a reference of a child node and the associated search information. To simplify examples, we assume that each internal node (*resp.* leaf node) of an index structure contains at most three entries (*resp.* entity versions).

8.3.1.1 B+V-tree

The use of the B+tree to index entity versions with linear evolution has been proposed in [18]. In our work, we extend the B+tree to handle data with branched evolution and call the resulting structure the B+V-tree.

The B+V-tree clusters entity versions by entity, and then by DW version. Consequently, when a leaf D_i overflows, it is split into D_i and D_j, according to entity identifiers. This is shown in figure 8.4.c, where the update of d in v_3 causes D_2 to overflow: c's versions remain in D_2 and d's versions are moved to D_3.

If D_i only contains versions of a single entity e (figure 8.5.a), it is split according to a version stamp v_s appearing in D_i: the (e,v) of D_i moved to the newly allocated node D_j are, such that, v_s is an ancestor of v. The motivation behind this splitting policy is as follows. Let $\mathscr{R}_i$ be the DW version range corresponding to the versions of e stored in D_i before the split (in figure 8.5.a, $\mathscr{R}_i = (v_1, \phi)$). v_s divides $\mathscr{R}_i$ in two DW version ranges $\mathscr{R}_i$ and $\mathscr{R}_j$, where $\mathscr{R}_i$ corresponds to the versions of e remaining in D_i and $\mathscr{R}_j$ to the versions of e moved to D_j (in figure 8.5.b, $v_s = v_3$, $\mathscr{R}_i = (v_1, \{v_3\})$ and $\mathscr{R}_j = (v_3, \phi)$). The value of any (e,v), such that $v \in \mathscr{R}_j$, should be found in D_j, because (e, v_s) is explicitly stored and v_s is closer to v than any DW version belonging to $\mathscr{R}_i$ (i.e. appearing in D_i). Conversely, the value of any (e,v), such that $v \in \mathscr{R}_i$, should be found in D_i. Note that it is not necessary to represent the sets $\{v_{end}\}$ of $\mathscr{R}_i$ and $\mathscr{R}_j$ in the parent node of D_i. Accordingly, if a search for (e,v) is directed to an internal node I_j containing more than one entry where e appears, we must look at all the entries of I_j where e appears and choose among them the one where the closest ancestor of v appears. Consider figure 8.5.b and assume that we are searching for the value of (e,v_5). In I, the search is directed to D_j, because v_3 is closer to v_5 than v_1. In D_j, the implicit sharing allows to deduce that (e,v_3) is alive in v_5, thus the value of (e,v_5) is ε_3.

8.3.1.2 Overlapping B+Trees Structure

The Overlapping B+trees structure (OB+tree) [6, 23] has been proposed for data with linear evolution. This section reviews it and shows how it can be extended to handle data with branched evolution.

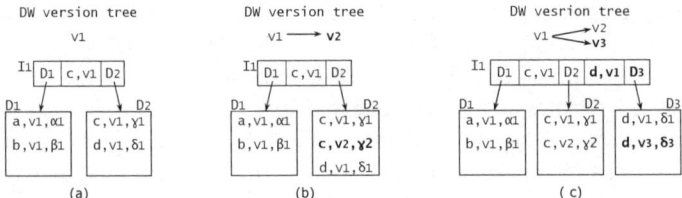

Fig. 8.4 (a) B+V-tree at v_1. (b) Derivation of DW version v_2, then update of c in v_2. (c) Derivation of DW version v_3, then update of d in v_3.

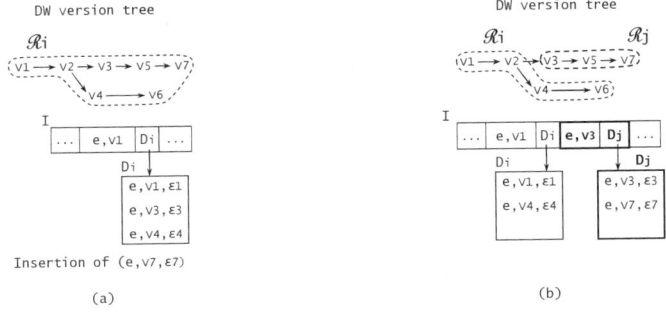

Fig. 8.5 Split of a leaf containing versions of the same entity

Whereas in the B+V-tree the granularity of versioning is an entity in the OB+tree the granularity of versioning is a B+tree node. More precisely, the OB+tree builds a B+tree, denoted $B+(v)$, for each DW version v and allows consecutive B+trees to share nodes, as long as the underlying entities do not change.

The initial B+tree $B+(v_1)$ is stored in its entirety. Then, when a new DW version v_j is derived from a DW version v_i, the root of $B+(v_j)$ is created. The content of the root of $B+(v_i)$ is *duplicated* in the root of $B+(v_j)$, so $B+(v_i)$ and $B+(v_j)$ share all their nodes, except their root. When a leaf D_k shared between $B+(v_i)$ and $B+(v_j)$ is affected by an entity modification, its sharing is broken and a new version of D_k is created: D_k is duplicated in a new node D_l where the modification is performed. After the duplication, I_m, the parent node of D_k, is modified to point to D_l: the sharing of I_m between $B+(v_i)$ and $B+(v_j)$ is also broken. The break of node sharing continue up to the update of the root of $B+(v_j)$.

Figure 8.6.a shows the initial B+tree $B+(v_1)$. The update of c in v_2 affects the leaf D_2. In order not to overwrite the previous version of c, D_2 is duplicated in a new leaf D_3, where the update is performed. The parent node of D_2, I_1, must be modified to point to D_3. Thus, in order not to affect $B+(v_1)$, I_1 is duplicated into I_2, where the modification is applied (figure 8.6.b).

The work of [23] proposes an improvement of the OB+tree. In this approach, if a node D_{i+1} is created by duplication from a node D_i, D_i and D_{i+1} are chained using pointers. The goal of chaining is to improve OB+tree performance for inter-version queries.

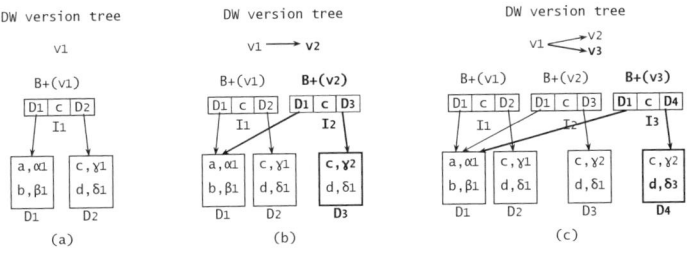

Fig. 8.6 (a) Initial B+tree $B+(v_1)$. (b) Derivation of $B+(v_2)$, update of c in v_2. (c) Derivation of $B+(v_3)$, update of d in v_3.

The OB+tree was proposed for data with linear evolution. We extend it to data with branched evolution by storing a DW version range $(v_{start}, \{v_{end}\})$ in the header of each node D: v_{start} is the DW version where D was created and $\{v_{end}\}$ indicates the DW versions where the sharing of D is broken. The DW version range $(v_{start}, \{v_{end}\})$ allows: (*i*) to detect if D is shared (*ii*) to find out the DW version range of the entity versions stored in D; this is useful for inter-version queries.

8.3.1.3 Branched and Temporal Tree

Similar to the B+V-tree, the Branched and Temporal Tree (BT-Tree) [11, 20] uses implicit sharing. However, unlike the B+V-tree, during a node split, some of the data from the overflowing node are duplicated in the newly allocated node. The motivation for duplication is to cluster entity versions alive in a given DW version into a small number of leaves (as opposed to B+V-tree where the entity versions alive in a given DW version are scattered among the leaves).

The BT-tree is a bi-dimensional index structure clustering entity versions on the pair (entity identifier, version stamp). The nodes of the BT-tree at a given level partition the bi-dimensional space entity-DW version. An entry of an internal node is a triple $([e_{min}, e_{max}[, (v_{start}, \{v_{end}\}), ref)$, where $[e_{min}, e_{max}[$ is an interval of entity identifiers; $(v_{start}, \{v_{end}\})$ a DW version range; and *ref* the reference of a child node I_j. Such an entry indicates that the underlying leaves contain entity versions (e, v), such that: $e \in [e_{min}, e_{max}[$ and $v \in (v_{start}, \{v_{end}\})$. The node I_j is said to be *alive* for each DW version $v \in (v_{start}, \{v_{end}\})$.

Figure 8.7.a shows the initial BT-tree. In figure 8.7.b, the insertion of (c, v_2, γ_2) is directed to the leaf whose interval of entity identifiers contains c and whose DW version range contains v_2; hence to D_2. As D_2 is not full, (c, v_2, γ_2) is inserted in it. In figure 8.7.c, the insertion of (d, v_3, δ_3) causes D_2 to overflow. Consequently, a split occurs and a new leaf D_3 is allocated. D_3 is associated to the DW version range (v_3, ϕ) and the same interval of entity identifiers as D_2. In addition to the insertion of (c, v_3, γ_3) in D_3, (d, v_1, δ_1), which is still alive in v_3, is duplicated in D_3. Duplication allows not to visit D_3 when searching for data alive in v_2 and not to visit D_2 when searching for data alive in v_3. Accordingly, the $\{v_{end}\}$ of D_2 is set to $\{v_3\}$ indicating that D_2 is no longer alive in v_3 (and for each future DW version descendant of v_3).

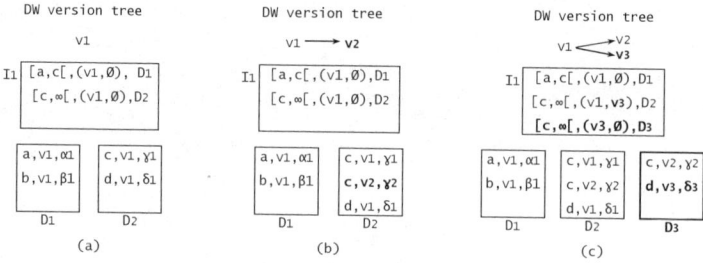

Fig. 8.7 (a) Initial BT-tree. (b) The BT-tree after the update of c in DW version v_2. (c) The BT-tree after the update of d in DW version v_3.

More precisely, the different split types in the BT-tree are: *version split, entity identifier split* and combination of both [20]. An entity identifier split is similar to a split in a B+tree. It occurs when the overflowing leaf only contains entity versions alive in the DW version which triggers the split (figure 8.7.a). A version split of a leaf D_i separates its entity versions according to the DW version v which triggers the split: (1) v is added to the $\{v_{end}\}$ of D_i; (2) a new leaf D_j with DW version range (v, ϕ) is allocated; and (3) entity versions whose DW version range intersects both the DW version range of D_i and D_j are copied in D_j (figure 8.7.c). After a version split, if the newly created leaf is almost full, only few modifications would be sufficient to trigger a new split on it. To prevent such situation, if the number of entity versions copied in D_j exceeds a threshold $\theta \times B$, where B is the node capacity, the version split is followed by an entity identifier split.

The split of an internal node is similar to the split of a leaf. A version split copies alive entries in a new node. If the proportion of copied entries exceeds θ, an entity identifier split is performed.

8.3.1.4 Conclusion

Shared data granularity, sharing mechanisms and data clustering, are among the criteria that differentiate indexing approaches. Figure 8.8 synthesizes these differences.

Index	Favored queries	Clustering	Granularity of sharing
B+V-tree	Historical	By entity then by DW version	Entity versions. No redundancy
OB+tree	Version slice	By DW version then by entity	B+tree nodes. Redundancy
BT-tree	Rectangle in the entity-DW version space	by the pair (entity,DW version)	BT-tree nodes and entity versions. Redundancy

Fig. 8.8 Qualitative comparison of the index structures

8.3.2 Secondary Indexes

The B+V-tree, the OB+tree and the BT-tree can be used as secondary indexes. For the OB+tree, the entries of the index are of the form: (k,e), where k is the value of an attribute and e an entity identifier. For the B+V-tree and the BT-tree, each attribute value must be explicitly associated to the DW version range over which the value is valid. Thus, an entry has the form $(k, (v_{start}, \{v_{end}\}), e)$, where v_{start} indicates in which DW version the entity e takes the value k and $\{v_{end}\}$ indicates the DW versions where e takes a value different than k.

An important difference between primary and secondary indexes is the type of queries handled. Indeed, the efficient support of *range queries* (*i.e.* queries involving consecutive attribute values) is crucial for secondary indexes but is useless for primary indexes (in general, we do not search for intervals of surrogates). In a primary index, searches will mainly be for *perfect match* (*i.e.* queries searching for the values associated to a given set of entity identifiers).

8.4 Analysis and Comparison

This section analyzes and compares the performance of the different index structures. The goal is not to definitively settle the question of wether an index structure is better than the others, but to determine the conditions under which an index structure outperforms the others. In the remainder, subsection 8.4.1 surveys existing analyses of temporal indexes. Subsection 8.4.2 defines our steady state analysis for primary indexes. Subsections 8.4.3 through 8.4.5 apply the analysis to the B+V-tree, the OB+tree and the BT-tree. Subsection 8.4.6 discusses secondary indexes.

8.4.1 Previous Work

Many kinds of analyses and comparisons have been performed to be able to adapt the choice of index structures to applications and data characteristics [15][21][22]. Paper [21] focuses on the asymptotic optimality of temporal index structures. Asymptotic analysis provides an order of magnitude for query and storage costs, but does not accurately reflect the actual costs [22]. This is insufficient in practice, since it does not allow a good discrimination among the distinct indexing policies.

The work of [15] analyzes different splitting policies for the *TSB-tree* (an index structure similar to the BT-tree, designed for data with linear evolution). [15] uses Markov chains to classify the leaves of an index according to the number of distinct entity identifiers appearing in a leaf. The goal is to determine the proportion of leaves in each class and then, to deduce storage and query costs. [15] does not discuss inter-version queries.

The work of [22] proposes an analysis based on the concept of *agility of temporal datasets*, which is the proportion of entities modified in each DW version. This analysis is the first one which shows the close connection between the performance of temporal indexes and the dataset agility. [22] does not discuss data with branched evolution and primary indexes.

8.4.2 Steady State Analysis

8.4.2.1 Principle and assumptions

A multiversion data warehouse at *steady state* is modeled by a set of $E=card(\mathbb{E})$ entities and $V=card(\mathbb{V})$ DW versions. Each entity e is subject to updates; each update occurring in a DW version v, generates a new entity version (e,v), whose value is stored in the data warehouse. The proportion a of entity versions updated in each DW version, called *data agility* in [22], is assumed to be constant. The total number of distinct entity versions is:

$$\mathscr{E} = E + aE(V-1). \tag{8.1}$$

The $\mathscr{E}$ entity versions are indexed by a B+V-tree, an OB+tree and a BT-tree. Given a, E, V and the node capacity B, the purpose is to predict the amount of redundancy, the storage and the query costs of the different index structures.

The number of internal nodes is usually much smaller than the number of leaf nodes. To simplify the analysis we focus on leaves. Moreover, we make the assumption that in each DW version, all entities are equally likely to be updated and that all entity version values have the same size.

8.4.2.2 Comparison Items

The storage cost is estimated by two elements giving complementary results: N, the *number of leaf nodes in the final index*, and r, the *redundancy factor*.

Let n be the *number of leaves in the initial index* and m be the *average number of new leaves* created when aE entities are updated in a DW version. N is estimated by:

$$N = n + m(V-1), \tag{8.2}$$

r is estimated by: $r = \frac{\mathscr{E}_r - \mathscr{E}}{\mathscr{E}}$, where $\mathscr{E}_r$ is the *number of stored entity versions*:

$$r = \frac{\mathscr{E}_r}{\mathscr{E}} - 1, \tag{8.3}$$

a	data agility.
V	total number of DW versions represented in the data warehouse. $V = card(\mathbb{V})$.
E	total number of entities represented in the data warehouse. $E = card(\mathbb{E})$.
$\mathscr{E}$	total number of distinct entity versions. $\mathscr{E} = E + aE(V-1)$
$\mathscr{E}_r$	total number of stored entity versions.
r	redundancy factor. $r = \frac{\mathscr{E}_r}{\mathscr{E}} - 1$.
n	average number of leaves created in the first DW version v_1.
m	average number of new leaves created in the index structure, when aE entities are updated in a DW version.
N	total number of leaf nodes in the final index structure. $N = n + m(V-1)$.
A	for the OB+tree (respectively, the BT-tree) A is the probability for a leaf node belonging to a B+tree $B + (v_i)$ (respectively alive in a DW version v_i) to be duplicated (version split) in a DW version v_j, child of v_i. $A = \frac{m}{n}$.
q_v	number of consecutive DW versions involved in a query q.
q_e	number of entities involved in a perfect match query q.
q_{val}	number of consecutive values involved in a range query q.
p	average number of leaves accessed to retrieve the values of q_e entities in a single DW version v.
P	average number of leaves accessed by a query q.
B	leaf node capacity.
b	for the B+V-tree and the OB+tree, b is average number of entity versions stored in a leaf node. $b \approx B \ln 2$.
θ	in the BT-tree, θ is threshold above which a version split is followed by an entity identifier split.
b'	Let D be a leaf of the BT-tree alive in a DW version v. b' is the average number of entity versions stored in D and alive in v. $b' \approx \theta B \ln 2$

Fig. 8.9 List of used symbols

The cost of a query q is estimated by P, the *number of visited leaves*. q is assumed to be a perfect match query involving q_e entities, and for each entity q_v consecutive DW versions (range queries are discussed in subsection 8.4.6).

In the remainder, N, r and P are estimated for each index structure. Table 8.9 lists the used symbols.

8.4.3 The B+V-tree as primary index

8.4.3.1 Estimation of N, number of leaf nodes

- Estimation of n

Let b be the average number of entity versions stored in a leaf node. In a B+tree, the commonly adopted value for b is $b \approx B\ln 2$. Initially the B+V-tree indexes E entity versions. As a result: $n = \frac{E}{b}$

- Estimation of m

In each DW version v, aE entities are updated. As a result, the average number of new leaves created in v is: $m = \frac{aE}{b}$

- Estimation of N

As $N = n + m(V - 1)$,

$$N = \frac{E}{b} + \frac{aE}{b}(V - 1) \Rightarrow N = \frac{E}{B\ln 2}(1 + a(V - 1)) \qquad (8.4)$$

8.4.3.2 Estimation of r, redundancy factor

Since there is no redundancy ($\mathcal{E}_r = \mathcal{E}$), r=0.

8.4.3.3 Estimation of P, number of visited leaves

P varies according to whether or not all versions of an entity fit on a single leaf. An entity has $1 + a(V - 1)$ versions on average. If all versions fit on a single leaf, then: $1 + a(V-1) \leq B \Leftrightarrow a \leq \frac{B-1}{V-1}$. Else, $a > \frac{B-1}{V-1}$.

Let us first consider the case where $a \leq \frac{B-1}{V-1}$. In this case, q_v has no incidence on the query cost, since a single leaf is visited for retrieving one or all versions of an entity. The average number of leaves in the B+V-tree is N. Thus, given a search for version(s) of an entity, each leaf has a probability $\frac{1}{N}$ to be visited and a probability $1 - \frac{1}{N}$ not to be visited. As all searches are independent, the probability for a leaf not to be visited while searching for versions of q_e entities, is $\left(1 - \frac{1}{N}\right)^{q_e}$. As a result, the probability for a leaf to be visited by at least one search, is $1 - \left(1 - \frac{1}{N}\right)^{q_e}$. Thus,

the average number of leaves to visit for retrieving the versions of q_e entities, is
$P = N \left(1 - \left(1 - \frac{1}{N} \right)^{q_e} \right) \Rightarrow$

$$P = \frac{E}{B \ln 2} (1 + a(V-1)) \left(1 - \left(1 - \frac{B \ln 2}{E} \frac{1}{1 + a(V-1)} \right)^{q_e} \right) \qquad (8.5)$$

Let us consider the case where $a > \frac{B-1}{V-1}$. For q_v DW versions, an entity has $1 + a(q_v - 1)$ versions on average. To retrieve $1 + a(q_v - 1)$ versions of an entity, $\frac{1 + a(q_v - 1)}{b}$ leaves are accessed. Thus, for q_e entities, $P = q_e \frac{1 + a(q_v - 1)}{B \ln 2}$.

8.4.4 The OB+tree as primary index

8.4.4.1 Estimation of N, number of leaf nodes

- Estimation of n

The first B+tree $B + (v_1)$ indexes E entity versions, thus: $n = \frac{E}{b}$.

- Estimation of m

As the model only considers entity updates, each B+tree indexes E entity versions. Thus, each B+tree has the same structure and the same number of leaves as $B + (v_1)$.

Let $B + (v_i)$ and $B + (v_j)$ be two consecutive overlapping B+trees. When an entity is updated in v_j, each leaf of $B + (v_j)$ has a probability $1 - \frac{1}{n}$ not to be affected (hence, to remain shared between $B + (v_i)$ and $B + (v_j)$). In v_j, aE entity are updated. Thus, the probability for a leaf not to be affected by any of these updates is $(1 - \frac{1}{n})^{aE}$. Conversely, the probability that a leaf is affected by at least one update is $1 - (1 - \frac{1}{n})^{aE}$. As a result, the number of leaves affected by at least one update is:
$m = n \left(1 - \left(1 - \frac{1}{n} \right)^{aE} \right)$.

- Estimation of N

As $N = n + m(V-1)$, then

$$N = \frac{E}{B \ln 2} \left(1 + (V-1) \left(1 - \left(1 - \frac{B \ln 2}{E} \right)^{aE} \right) \right) \qquad (8.6)$$

Note that the OB+tree degenerates into independent B+trees when $\left(1 - \left(1 - \frac{B \ln 2}{E} \right)^{aE} \right)$ approaches 1, hence, when: $a \approx \frac{-2}{E \log(1 - \frac{B \ln 2}{E})}$.

8.4.4.2 Estimation of r, redundancy factor

Each leaf stores b entity versions on average. Accordingly, $\mathcal{E}_r = b \times N$. As a result:
$r = \frac{\mathcal{E}_r}{\mathcal{E}} - 1 \Rightarrow r = \frac{((1 - \frac{B \ln 2}{E})^{aE} - a)(V-1)}{1 + a(V-1)}$.

8.4.4.3 Estimation of P, number of visited leaves

Let v_i and v_j be two consecutive DW versions involved in query q and p be the average number of leaves to visit in $B + (v_i)$ to retrieve the values of q_e entities. Part of the leaves visited in $B + (v_i)$ is shared with $B + (v_j)$. These leaves are not visited in $B + (v_j)$: in $B + (v_j)$ only unshared leaves are visited. Thus, the average number of leaves to visit in $B + (v_j)$ equals $p \times A$, where A is the probability that a leaf belonging to $B + (v_i)$ is modified in $B + (v_j)$. Extending the reasoning to q_v versions, implies: $P = p(1 + A(q_v - 1))$.

Reasoning as in subsection 8.4.3.3 (changing N to n and P to p), p can be estimated by: $p = n\left(1 - \left(1 - \frac{1}{n}\right)^{q_e}\right)$. A is the ratio of m to n: $A = \frac{m}{n} \Rightarrow A = 1 - \left(1 - \frac{1}{n}\right)^{aE}$. Consequently, $P = \frac{E}{b}\left(1 - \left(1 - \frac{b}{E}\right)^{q_e}\right)\left(1 + \left(1 - \left(1 - \frac{b}{E}\right)^{aE}\right)(q_v - 1)\right) \Rightarrow$

$$P = \frac{E}{B\ln 2}\left(1 - \left(1 - \frac{B\ln 2}{E}\right)^{q_e}\right)\left(1 + \left(1 - \left(1 - \frac{B\ln 2}{E}\right)^{aE}\right)(q_v - 1)\right) \qquad (8.7)$$

8.4.5 The BT-Tree as primary index

8.4.5.1 Estimation of N, number of leaf nodes

- Estimation of n

Let D be a leaf of the BT-tree alive in a DW version v, and b' be the average number of entity versions stored in D and alive in v. At steady state, b' has been estimated by $\approx \theta B \ln 2$ [11]. Initially the BT-tree indexes E entity versions, thus: $n = \frac{E}{b'}$.

- Estimation of m

As each DW version v is composed by E entity versions, the average number of leaves alive in v equals $\frac{E}{b'}$. Thus, when aE entities are updated in v, each leaf alive in v receives $\frac{aE}{\frac{E}{b'}} = ab'$ entity versions on average. When a leaf D is created due to a version split at a DW version v_{start}, it initially contains b' entity versions. Thus, D is version split after the insertion of $B - b'$ entity versions. As D receives on average ab' entity versions from each DW version descendant of v_{start}, D is version split after the generation of $\frac{B-b'}{ab'}$ DW versions (starting from v_{start}). Thus, after the generation of $\frac{B-b'}{ab'}$ DW versions, on average, $\frac{E}{b'}$ new leaves are created in the BT-tree. Consequently, the average number of new leaves created in a DW version is $m = \frac{\frac{E}{b'}}{\frac{B-b'}{ab'}} \Rightarrow m = \frac{aE}{B-b'}$.

- Estimation of N

$$N = \frac{E}{b'}\left(1 + \frac{ab'}{B - b'}(V - 1)\right) \Rightarrow N = \frac{E}{\theta B \ln 2}\left(1 + \frac{a\theta \ln 2}{1 - \theta \ln 2}(V - 1)\right) \qquad (8.8)$$

8.4.5.2 Estimation of r, redundancy factor

When a leaf node is split, b' entity versions are copied on average. The total number of leaf splits is $m(V-1)$. Consequently, $\mathcal{E}_r = \mathcal{E} + b'm(V-1) \Rightarrow r = \frac{ab'(V-1)}{(B-b')(1+a(V-1))}$. If V is sufficiently large, such that $1 \ll a(V-1)$, then: $r \approx \frac{b'}{B-b'} \Rightarrow r \approx \frac{\theta \ln 2}{1-\theta \ln 2}$. Note here that the redundancy factor of the BT-tree is highly dependant on the value chosen for θ: greatest is θ and greatest is the amount of redundancy.

8.4.5.3 Estimation of P, number of visited leaves

The estimation of P for the BT-tree follows the same principle as for the OB+tree: $P = p(1+A(q_v-1))$, where p is the average number of leaves visited to retrieve q_v entity versions alive in a DW version v_i and A the probability that a leaf alive in v_i is version split in a DW version v_j, child of v_i (D is no longer alive in v_j).

A is the ratio of m to $n \Rightarrow A = \frac{ab'}{B-b'}$. Reasoning as in subsection 8.4.3.3 (changing N to $\frac{E}{b'}$ and P to p), p can be estimated by: $p = \frac{E}{b'}\left(1-\left(1-\frac{b'}{E}\right)^{q_e}\right)$. Consequently,

$P = \frac{E}{b'}\left(1-\left(1-\frac{b'}{E}\right)^{q_e}\right)\left(1+\frac{ab'}{B-b'}(q_v-1)\right) \Rightarrow$

$$P = \frac{E}{\theta B \ln 2}\left(1-\left(1-\frac{\theta B \ln 2}{E}\right)^{q_e}\right)\left(1+\frac{a\theta \ln 2}{1-\theta \ln 2}(q_v-1)\right) \qquad (8.9)$$

Note here the impact of the value chosen for θ on the query cost. For intra-version queries ($q_v = 1$), greater is θ and smaller is $P = \frac{E}{\theta B \ln 2}\left(1-\left(\frac{E-\theta B \ln 2}{E}\right)^{q_e}\right)$, hence better is the performance. Conversely, smaller is θ and smaller is $\left(1+\frac{a\theta \ln 2}{1-\theta \ln 2}(q_v-1)\right)$, hence better is the performance for inter-version queries.

8.4.6 Secondary indexes

This section applies the steady state analysis to secondary indexes. Due to lack of space, only the cost of range queries is discussed.

Let K be an entity attribute. In the first DW version v_1, there are E values of K. Then, in each newly derived DW version, attribute K is updated for $a \times E$ entities. The update of an entity e inserts a new K value for e and invalidates the previous K value of e. The E values of K valid at a given DW version are assumed to be uniformly distributed in the space of values.

A range query q is assumed to involve q_v consecutive DW versions and an interval of values, denoted S. Let q_{val} be the number of values inserted in the first DW version v_1 and belonging to S. The hypotheses of the cost model help to do that, at any DW version, the number of values belonging to S equals q_{val}.

8.4.6.1 The B+V-tree as secondary index

Since the distribution of values is assumed to be the same in any DW version, the total number of values belonging to S is: $q_{val}(1 + a(V - 1))$. To retrieve $q_{val}(1 + a(V - 1))$ values, the average number of leaves to be visited is:

$$P = \frac{q_{val}(1 + a(V - 1))}{b} \tag{8.10}$$

8.4.6.2 The OB+tree as secondary index

Let $B + (v_i)$ and $B + (v_j)$ be two consecutive B+trees involved in the query q. P can be estimated by: $P = \frac{q_{val}}{b}(1 + A(q_v - 1))$, where $\frac{q_{val}}{b}$ is the average number of leaves to visit in $B + (v_i)$ to extract q_{val} consecutive values and A the probability that a leaf belonging to $B + (v_i)$ is duplicated in $B + (v_j)$.

The estimation of A for a secondary OB+tree differs from its estimation for a primary OB+tree. Indeed, for a dataset with agility a the total number of modifications equals $2aE$, because each entity update involves one insertion and one deletion [22]. In a primary OB+tree, the insertion and the deletion occur in the same node. In a secondary OB+tree, the deletion and the insertion may occur in different nodes. Thus, following the same reasoning as in subsection 8.4.4, for a secondary OB+tree, A is estimated by: $A = 1 - \left(\frac{E-b}{E}\right)^{2aE}$. As a result:

$$P = \frac{q_{val}}{b}\left(1 + (q_v - 1)\left(1 - \left(\frac{E-b}{E}\right)^{2aE}\right)\right) \tag{8.11}$$

8.4.6.3 The BT-tree as secondary index

P is estimated by:

$$P = \frac{q_{val}}{b'}\left(1 + \frac{ab'}{B - b'}(q_v - 1)\right), \tag{8.12}$$

where $\frac{q_{val}}{b'}$ is the average number of leaves to be visited to extract q_{val} values valid in a DW version v_i and $\frac{ab'}{B-b'}$ the probability that a leaf alive in v_i is version split in a DW version v_j, child of v_i.

8.5 Simulation

We performed a large number of experiments to prove the accuracy of the steady state analysis. However, due to lack of space, only a few results are presented herein. For the presented simulation, data are generated as follows. E and V are fixed respectively to $200K$ entities and 200 DW versions. E entities are inserted in the first DW version. Then, in each newly derived DW version, aE entities randomly selected, are updated. Each DW version is derived from a randomly selected DW version, with the only restriction that the distance between the DW version root and any DW version leaf of the final DW version tree is ≥ 20 DW versions. The data page capacity is set to $B=101$ entity versions for the OB+tree and $B=92$ for the B+tree and the BT-tree (the difference correspond to DW versions stamps). To appreciate the impact of θ on the performance of the BT-tree, we consider two values of θ: $\frac{2}{3}$ and $\frac{4}{5}$ (these values are adopted, respectively, in [20] and in [3])

8.5.1 Storage Cost of Primary Indexes

Figure 8.10 depicts the estimated sizes provided by equations (8.4),(8.6) and (8.8) and the experimental sizes provided by simulation, as function of the agility a. Initially, the size of the OB+tree grows very quickly as the agility increases. As predicted in subsection 8.4.4.1, from an agility bordering $\frac{-2}{E\log(\frac{E-b}{E})} \approx 6\%$, the OB+tree degenerates into independent B+trees and its size stabilizes (since there are 200 B+trees with the same size). Figure 8.10 shows also that even when the OB+tree does not degenerate, it occupies much more space than the other index structures. For example, when the agility approaches 1% the OB+tree occupies nearly 34 times more storage space than the corresponding B+V-tree.

The sizes of the B+V-tree and the BT-tree grow linearly with a higher growth rate for the BT-tree. The growth rate is higher for the BT-tree when θ is larger. According to the value of θ, the BT-tree occupies two to three times the space occupied by the corresponding B+V-tree.

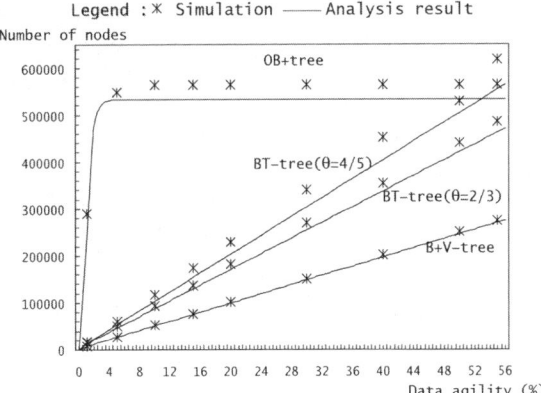

Fig. 8.10 Storage cost as function of the data agility

8.5.2 Query Cost of Primary Indexes

The analytical analysis highlights three parameters impacting the query cost: a, q_e and q_v, respectively the data agility, the number of entities and the number of consecutive DW versions involved in the query. To evaluate the estimation of the query costs provided by equations (8.5), (8.7) and (8.9), we consider a dataset with low agility, $a = 0.5\%$ and a moderately agile dataset, $a = 5\%$. For each dataset three values of q_e are considered: $q_e = 1000(= 0.5\%E)$, $q_e = 5000(= 2.5\%E)$ and $q_e = 10000(= 5\%E)$. The q_e entities are randomly selected. For each dataset and each value of q_e, q_v is gradually increased from 1 to 25 DW versions (=12.5%V).

Figure 8.11 depicts the estimated and experimental costs of perfect match queries. As illustrated in this figure, the OB+tree justifies its use only when intra-version queries are the sole type of queries. In general the B+V-tree presents good performance. The BT-tree outperforms the B+V-tree only when the query involves a great number of entities and a relatively low number of DW versions.

8.5.3 Query Cost of Secondary Indexes

Following the same procedure used for perfect match queries, we consider two datasets and three values for q_{val}: $q_{val} = 1000$, $q_{val} = 5000$ and $q_{val} = 10000$. For

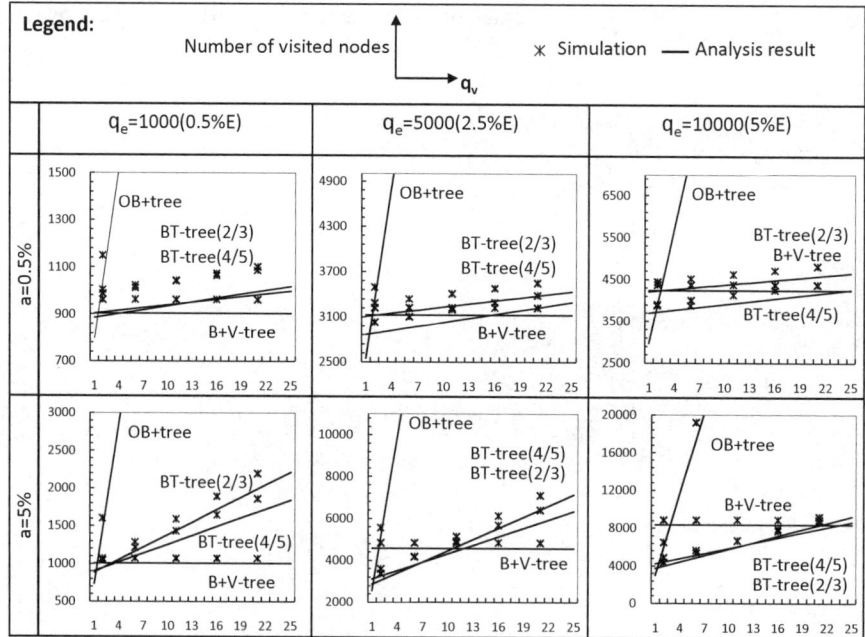

Fig. 8.11 Primary indexes: cost of perfect match queries

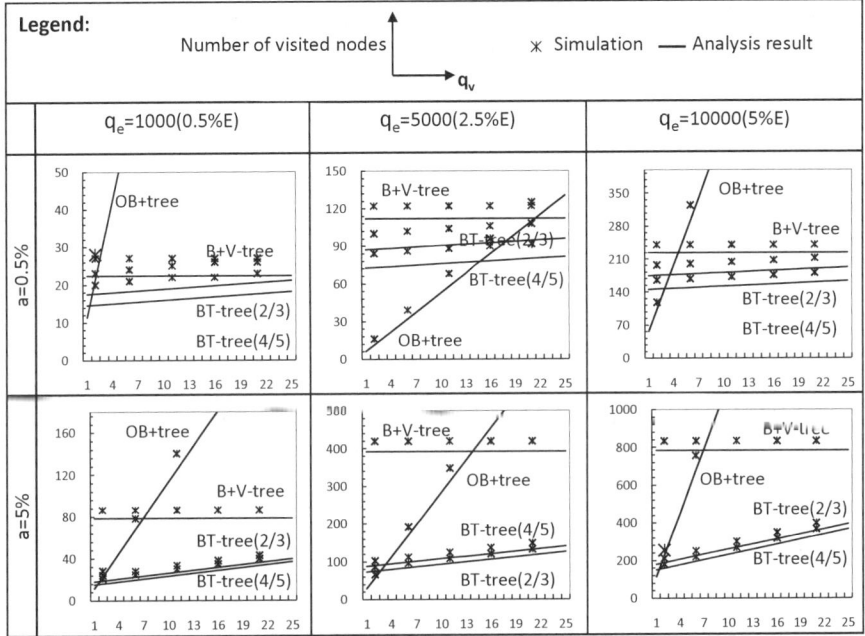

Fig. 8.12 Secondary indexes: cost of range queries

each dataset and each value of q_{val}, q_v is gradually increases from 1 to 25 DW versions. As noticed in subsection 8.4.6.2, when used as secondary index, the OB+tree degenerates into independent trees with lower agility than if it is used as primary index. For this reason, the values considered for agility are: $a = 0.5\%$ and $a = 3\%$.

Figure 8.12 depicts the estimated and experimental costs of range queries. As shown in this figure, the BT-tree outperforms the B+V-tree and the OB+tree. Once again, the OB+tree justifies its use only when intra-version queries are frequent. Figure 8.12 confirms that the steady state analysis allows to predict with accuracy the conditions under which an index structure outperforms another. Due to the fact that the analysis only considers leaf nodes, the steady state analysis slightly underestimates the actual costs.

8.6 Conclusion

Efficient query processing is crucial in a DW environment and requires DW designers that are aware of tradeoffs among different index structures. This paper studies the problem of efficiently indexing data in a MVDW. Its main contributions are: (*i*) the extension of indexes designed for data with linear evolution to handle data with branched evolution; (*ii*) the steady state analysis method, which brings to light fundamental properties of different index structures, accurately predicts their behavior and provides guidelines for the selection of the most appropriate one; and (*iii*) experimental simulations validating these results. Another important result of our work is that it allows to tune variable θ for the BT-tree, according to the tolerated redundancy and to the frequent query type.

The studied index structures can be used for facts, dimensions and as join indexes. Moreover, they can be used orthogonally to other storage techniques (*e.g.* partitioning, materialized views). Although our framework only focuses on index structures derived from the B+tree, it can serve as the basis for other index types.

8.7 Acknowledgments

We would like to thank Claudia Bauzer Medeiros for many helpful discussions and reviews that improved this paper.

References

1. A. Balmin, T. Papadimitriou, and Y. Papakonstantinou. Hypothetical Queries in an OLAP Environment. In *VLDB'00*, pages 220–231, 2000.
2. B. Będel, J. Eder, C. Koncilia, T. Morzy, and R. Wrembel. Creation and Management of Versions in Multiversion Data Warehouse. In *ACM SAC '04*, pages 717–723, 2004.
3. B. Becker, S. Gschwind, T. Ohler, B. Seeger, and P. Widmayer. An Asymptotically Optimal Multiversion B-tree. *The VLDB Journal*, 5(4):264–275, 1996.
4. M. Bellosta, G. Jomier, and W. Cellary. Consistent Versioning of OODB Schema and its Extension. In *Bases de Données Avancées*, 1998.
5. M. Body, M. Miquel, Y. Bédard, and A. Tchounikine. A Multidimensional and Multiversion Structure for OLAP Applications. In *DOLAP*, pages 1–6, 2002.
6. M. Carey, D. DeWitt, J. Richardson, and J. Shekita. Object and File Management in the EXODUS Extensible Database System. In *VLDB*, pages 91–100, 1986.
7. W. Cellary and G. Jomier. Consistency of Versions in Object-Oriented Databases. In *VLDB '90*, pages 432–441, 1990.
8. J. Eder and C. Koncilia. Changes of Dimension Data in Temporal Data Warehouses. In *DaWaK*, pages 284–293, 2001.
9. M. Golfarelli, J. Lechtenbörger, S. Rizzi, and G. Vossen. Schema Versioning in Data Warehouses. *DKE*, 59(2):435–459, 2006.
10. M. Golfarelli, S. Rizzi, and A. Proli. Designing What-If Analysis: Towards a Methodology. In *DOLAP '06*, pages 51–58, New York, NY, USA, 2006. ACM.
11. L. Jiang, B. Salzberg, D. Lomet, and M. Barrena. The BT-tree: A Branched and Temporal Access Method. In *VLDB '00*, pages 451–460, 2000.
12. L. Jiang, B. Salzberg, D. Lomet, and M. Barrena. The BTR-Tree: Path-Defined Version-Range Splitting in a Branched and Temporal Structure. In *SSTD'03*, pages 28–45, 2003.
13. G. Jomier and W. Cellary. The Database Version Approach. *Networking and Information Systems Journal*, 3(1):177–214, 2000. Hermes Science Publications.
14. R. Kimball. *The Data Warehouse Toolkit*. Wiley Computer Publishing, 1996.
15. D. Lomet and B. Salzberg. The Performance of a Multiversion Access Method. In *ACM SIGMOD'90*, pages 353–363. ACM Press, May 1990.
16. A. Mendelzon and A. Vaisman. Temporal Queries in OLAP. In *VLDB*, pages 242–253, 2000.
17. T. Morzy and R. Wrembel. Modeling a Multiversion Data Warehouse: A Formal Approach. In *ICEIS (1)*, pages 120–127, 2003.

18. M. Nascimento and M. Dunham. Indexing Valid Time Databases via B+-Trees. *IEEE TKDE*, 11(6):929–947, 1999.

19. T. Pedersen and C. Jensen. Multidimensional Databases. In *The Industrial Information Technology Handbook*, pages 1–13. 2005.

20. B. Salzberg, L. Jiang, D. Lomet, M. Barrena, J. Shan, and E. Kanoulas. A Framework for Access Methods for Versioned Data. In *EDBT'04*, pages 730–747, 2004.

21. B. Salzberg and V. Tsotras. Comparison of Access Methods for Time-Evolving Data. *ACM Comput. Surv.*, 31(2):158–221, 1999.

22. Y. Tao, D. Papadias, and J. Zhang. Cost Models for Overlapping and Multiversion structures. *ACM Trans. Database Syst.*, 27(3):299–342, 2002.

23. T. Tzouramanis, Y. Manolopoulos, and N. Lorentzos. Overlapping B+-Trees: An Implementation of a Transaction Time Access Method. *DKE'99*, 29(3):381–404, 1999.

Chapter 9
Using Bitmap Index for Joint Queries on Structured and Text Data*

Kurt Stockinger, John Cieslewicz, Kesheng Wu, Doron Rotem, and Arie Shoshani

Abstract The database and the information retrieval communities have been work-ing on separate sets of techniques for querying structured data and text data, but there is a growing need to handle these types of data together. In this paper, we present a strategy to efficiently answer joint queries on both types of data. By using an efficient compression algorithm, our compressed bitmap indexes, called FastBit, are compact even when they contain millions of bitmaps. Therefore FastBit can be applied effectively on hundreds of thousands of terms over millions of documents. Bitmap indexes are designed to take advantage of data that only grows but does not change over time (append-only data), and thus are just as effective with append-only text archives. In a performance comparison against a commonly used database sys-tem with a full-text index, MySQL, we demonstrate that our indexes answer queries 50 times faster on average. Furthermore, we demonstrate that integrating FastBit with a open source database system, called MonetDB, yields similar performance gains. Since the integrated MonetDB/FastBit system provides the full SQL func-tionality, the overhead of supporting SQL is not the main reason for the observed performance differences. Therefore, using FastBit in other database systems can of-fer similar performance advantages.

K. Stockinger, K. Wu, D. Rotem and A. Shoshani
Computational Research Division, Lawrence Berkeley National Laboratory, University of California, e-mail: `kurt.stockinger@gmail.com`, {`KWu,D_Rotem,AShoshani`}@ `lbl.gov`

J. Cieslewicz
Department of Computer Science, Columbia University, e-mail: `johnc@cs.columbia.edu`

* This work was supported by the Director, Office of Science, Office of Advanced Scien-tific Computing Research, of the U.S. Department of Energy under Contract No. DE-AC03-76SF00098. Part of the funding was provided by a US Department of Homeland Security Fellow-ship administered by Oak Ridge Institute for Science and Education. We also thank the MonetDB Team at CWI, Netherlands for their great support of the integration effort.

9.1 Introduction

The records in data warehouses are usually extracted from other database systems and therefore contain only what is known as structured data [10, 8, 29]. In these cases, most vendors are reusing existing database techniques to perform analysis tasks. However, data warehouses and database systems are starting to include a large amount of text documents, and the existing database techniques are inadequate for processing efficiently joint queries over structured data and text data.

Data warehouses typically contain records that are not modified once added to the collection [8, 9, 14]. This is very similar to most text collections, but different from transactional data, where the records are frequently modified. For this reason, techniques developed for data warehouses are likely also useful for queries on text, provided that they can be used effectively over thousands or even millions of terms.

Bitmap indexes are designed to take advantage of data that only grows but does not change over time (append-only data). Recent work on compressed bitmap indexing has shown that they can be applied to attributes (columns) with high cardinality; i.e., attributes that have a large number of possible distinct values. In particular, our compressed bitmap indexes, called FastBit, are compact and perform extremely well even when the index contains millions of bitmaps [43, 44]. It was therefore natural to investigate whether such indexes could be applied to searches over append-only text data containing hundreds of thousands of terms over millions of documents. If successful, this would enable efficient joint queries over structured and text data.

In this paper, we extend FastBit for searches over text data. We show that our proposed approach can significantly speed up joint queries on structured data and text data. An additional advantage is that we achieve this high performance gains by using the same indexing technique for both structured data and text data. We demonstrate that this can be done with minimal modification to the existing FastBit code. A number of database systems already implement various bitmap indexes, and the same modification can be made there too.

Originally, database management systems (DBMS) only handle structured data as tables, rows and columns, where each column value must be an atomic data type. Recently, many DBMSs have removed this limitation and allowed more complex data, such as date and time. Some of them even allow text. This enables text data to be stored together with the structured data. However, to support efficient searching operations on text, additional indexing data structures are introduced, e.g., the inverted index [4, 25, 49]. Among the popular database systems, MySQL is reputed to have an efficient implementation of an inverted index. Therefore, we chose to compare FastBit against MySQL to evaluate the merit of our approach. This comparison showed a large performance difference, with FastBit being 50 times faster in answering an average joint query on structured and text data.

To better understand whether the performance gain was due to difference in the indexing data methods or the system overhead, we integrated FastBit into an open-source database system called MonetDB [5, 20]. The integrated MonetDB/FastBit system has full SQL support and is much closer to MySQL in overall functionality than FastBit alone. We found that the integrated MonetDB/FastBit system has similar performance as FastBit alone. This confirms the performance advantage of FastBit over the full-text index in MySQL and indicates that our bitmap index is a valid approach for handling joint queries on structured data and text data.

The paper is organized as follows. In Section 2, we review related work on indexing data structures for structured data and text data. We also discuss the advantages of compressed bitmap indexes for querying both structured data and text data. In Section 3, we briefly describe the test dataset, referred to as the Enron dataset, that has been used in a number of studies on social networks. This dataset is particularly attractive since it contains a natural mixture of structured data and text data. In Section 4, we describe our framework for indexing text data with our bitmap index implementation, called FastBit. The challenges of integrating FastBit into MonetDB are briefly described in Section 5. An experimental evaluation of the combined MonetDB/FastBit system is presented in Section 6, with MySQL as the reference point. We summarize the findings of our studies in Section 7 and point out open research topics on using bitmap indexes for text searches.

9.2 Related Work

9.2.1 Indexing techniques for structured data

In the database community, a general strategy to reduce the time to answer a query is to devise an auxiliary data structure, or an index, for the task. Earlier database systems were more commonly used for transaction type applications, such as banking. For this type of applications, indexing methods such as B^+-tree and hash-based indexes are particularly efficient [10, 22]. One notable characteristic of data in these applications is that they change frequently and therefore their associated indexes must also be updated quickly.

As more data are accumulated over time, the need to analyze large historical data sets gained more attention. A typical analysis on such data warehouses is known as On-Line Analytical Processing (OLAP). For these operations, bitmap indexes are particularly efficient since they take advantage of the stable nature of the data (i.e., permitting efficient append operations, but not updates) [21, 46, 42, 44]. OLAP queries typically return a relative large number of selected values (also known as hits). In these cases, a bitmap index answers the queries much faster than a B^+-tree, but it takes longer to modify a bitmap index to update an existing record. However, for most data warehouses, existing records are not updated, and the only change to a data warehouse is the addition of a large number of new records. Appending new records to a bitmap index usually takes less time than updating a B^+-tree because the time to append to bitmap indexes is a linear function of the number of new records while the time to update a B^+-tree is always a superlinear function due to sorting involved. For these reasons, bitmap indexes are well-suited for data warehousing applications.

In Fig. 9.1, we show a small example of a bitmap index for an integer column **A** that takes its value from 0, 1, 2, and 3. In this case, we say that the *column cardinality* of **A** is 4. The basic bitmap index consists of four bitmaps, b_1, b_2, b_3, and b_4. Each bitmap corresponds to one of the four possible values of **A** and contains as many bits (0 or 1) as the number of rows in the table. In the basic bitmap index, a bit is set to 1 if the value of **A** in the given row equals the value associated with the bitmap.

		bitmap index			
RID	**A**	=0	=1	=2	=3
1	0	1	0	0	0
2	1	0	1	0	0
3	3	0	0	0	1
4	2	0	0	1	0
5	3	0	0	0	1
6	3	0	0	0	1
7	1	0	1	0	0
8	3	0	0	0	1
		b_1	b_2	b_3	b_4

Fig. 9.1 A example bitmap index, where RID is the record ID and **A** is an integer column with values in the range of 0 to 3.

Let N denote the number rows in a table and C denote the column cardinality. It is easy to see that a basic bitmap index contains CN bits in the bitmaps for the given column. As the column cardinality increases, the basic bitmap index requires correspondingly more storage space. In the worst case where each value is distinct, $C = N$, the total number of bits is N^2. There are a number of different strategies to reduce this maximum index size; we organize them into three orthogonal strategies: binning, encoding, and compression.

Binning: Instead of recording each individual value in a bitmap, the strategy of binning is to associate multiple values with a single bitmap [17, 30, 45]. For example, to index a floating-point valued column **B** with a domain between 0 and 1, we may divide the domain into 10 equi-width bins: $[0,0.1)$, $[0.1,0.2)$, ..., $[0.9,1]$. In this case, only 10 bitmaps are used. Binning can control the number of bitmaps used. However, the index is no longer able to resolve all queries accurately. For example, when answering a query involving the query condition "**B** < 0.25," the information we get from the above binned index is that the entries in bins $[0,0.1)$ and $[0.1,0.2)$ definitely satisfy the query condition, but the records in bin $[0.2,0.3)$ have to be examined to determine whether they actually satisfy the condition. We call the records in bin $[0.2,0.3)$ candidates. The process of examining these candidates, called *candidate check*, can be expensive [24, 34]. For this reason, all commercial bitmap indexes do not use binning[21, 35].

Encoding: We can view the output from binning as a set of bin numbers. The encoding procedure translates these bin numbers into bitmaps. The basic bitmap index [21] uses an encoding called *equality encoding*, where each bitmap is associated with one bin number and a bit is set to 1 if the value falls into the bin, 0 otherwise.

Other common encoding strategies include range encoding and interval encoding [6, 7]. In range encoding and interval encoding, each bitmap corresponds to a number of bins that are ORed together. They are designed to answer one-sided and two-sided range queries efficiently. The three basic encoding schemes can also be composed into multi-level and multi-component encodings [6, 31, 40]. One well-known example of a multi-component encoding is the binary encoding scheme [39, 23], where the jth bitmap of the index represents the value 2^j. This encoding produces the fewest number of bitmaps, however, to answer most queries, all bitmaps in the index are accessed. In contrast, other encodings may access a few bitmaps to answer a query, for example, an interval encoded index only need to access two bitmaps to answer any query.

Compression: Each bitmap generated from the above steps can be compressed to reduce the storage requirement. Any compression technique may be used, however, in order to reduce the query response time, specialized bitmap compression methods are preferred. Bitmap compression is an active research area [32, 44]. One of the best-known bitmap compression methods is the Byte-aligned Bitmap Code by Antoshenkov [3, 15]. A more efficient bitmap compression method is the Word-Aligned Hybrid (WAH) code [42, 44]. In multiple timing measurements, WAH was shown to be about 10 times faster then BBC [41]. As for the index size, the basic bitmap index compressed with WAH is shown to use at most $O(N)$ words, where N is the number of records in the dataset [42, 44]. In most applications, a WAH compressed basic bitmap index is smaller than a typical B-tree implementation.

Given a range condition that can be answered with a WAH compressed index, the total response time is proportional to the number of hits [44]. This is optimal in terms of computational complexity. In addition, compressed bitmap indexes are in practice superior to other indexing methods because the result from one index can be easily combined with that of another through bitwise logical operations. Therefore, bitmap indexes can efficiently answer queries involving multiple columns, a type of query we call the multi-dimensional query.

9.2.2 Database Systems for Full-Text Searching

Traditionally, DBMS treat text attributes as strings that have to be treated as a whole, or as opaque objects that can not be queried. However, users frequently need to identify text containing certain keywords. Supporting such keyword based text retrieval in database systems is an important research topic. The research literature discusses incorporating text retrieval capabilities into different types of database systems such as relational database systems [16], object oriented databases [47], and XML databases [1]. Our approach follows the general theme of combining relational databases with text searching capabilities [38, 18]. In this context, it is crucial to address the modeling issues, query languages and appropriate index structures for such database systems [27, 26]. A recent prototype of such a system, called QUIQ [16]. The engine of this system, called QQE, consists of a DBMS that holds all the base data and an external index server that maintains the unified index. Inserts and updates are made directly to the DBMS. The index server monitors these updates to keep its indexes current. It can also be updated in bulk-load mode. Another recent paper describes a benchmark called TEXTURE which examines the efficiency of database queries that combine relational predicates and text searching [12]. Several commercial database systems were evaluated by this benchmark.

Another approach for combining text retrieval and DBMS functionality is to use the external function capability of object oriented databases. Combining the structured-text retrieval system (TextMachine) with an object-oriented database system (OpenODB) has also been explored before [47].

As XML document is able to represent a mix of structured and text information, a third approach that is recently gaining some popularity is to combine text retrieval with XML databases. For example, there are proposals to extend the XQuery language with complex full-text searching capabilities [1].

Supporting text in databases requires appropriate index structures. One type of index proposed for text searching is called Signature files [13]. The space overhead of this index (10%-20%) is lower than that of inverted files, but any search always accesses the whole index sequentially. This index uses a hash function that maps words in the text to bit masks consisting of B bits called signatures. The text is then divided into blocks of b words each. The bit mask for each block is obtained by ORing the signatures of all the words in the block. A search for a query word is conducted by comparing its signature to the bit mask of each block. In case that at least one bit of the query signature is not present in the bit mask of a block, the word cannot be present in this block. Otherwise, the block is called a *candidate block* as the word may be present in it. All candidate blocks must be examined to verify that they indeed contain the query word.

Another common structure for indexing text files, found in commercial database systems and text search engines, is the inverted file index [49]. This data structure consists of a vocabulary of all the terms and an inverted list structure [36]. For each term t the structure contains the identifiers (or ordinal numbers) of all the documents containing t as well as the frequency of t in each document. Such a structure can also be supplemented with a table that maps ordinal document numbers to disk locations. As inverted files are known to require significant additional space (up to 80% of the original data) [50], we next review the compression issue.

9.2.3 Compressing Inverted Files

The inverted indexes commonly used for text searching are usually compressed [19, 37, 48]. The primary use of the compressed data in an inverted index is to reconstruct the document identifiers. Reducing the amount of time required to read the compressed data into memory is key to reducing the query response time. For this reason, the compression methods used to be measured exclusively by their compressed sizes. However, recently there has been some emphasis on compute efficiency as well [2, 37]. In particular, Anh and Moffat have proposed a Word-Aligned Binary Compression for text indexing, which they call slide [2], even though their primary design goal was to reduce the compressed sizes rather than improving the search speed. Making the decompression (i.e., reconstruction of the document identifiers) more CPU friendly is only a secondary goal. They achieve this by packing many code words that require the same number of bits into a machine word. Because all these code words require the same number of bits, they save space by only representing their sizes once. In contrast, WAH imposes restrictions on lengths of the bit patterns that can be compressed so that the bitwise logical operations can be performed on compressed words directly [42, 44]. In particular, a WAH code word is always a machine word. These properties yield efficient computations.

Because of their differences, it is usually not efficient to use a bitmap compression method to compress document identifiers or a compression method for the inverted index to compress bitmaps. What we propose to do in this paper is to turn a term-document matrix (a version of the inverted index) into a bitmap index, then compress the bitmap index. This approach allows us to make the maximum use of the efficient bitmap compression method WAH and reuse the bitmap indexing software for keyword searches.

The approach we take in this paper is to use compressed bitmaps to represent inverted files, an approach that is efficient for relatively small number of distinct terms. However, recently WAH-compressed indexes have been shown to be very efficient for high cardinality numerical data [44]. The strength of this particular work is to demonstrate that the compressed bitmap approach is efficient for text data with a large number of distinct terms. Using a compressed bitmap index, the results of processing a query condition is a compressed bitmap. The bitmaps representing the answers to different query conditions can be efficiently combined to form the final answer to the user query through logical operations. Since WAH compressed bitmaps can participate in logical operations efficiently without decompression, we anticipate this to be a great advantage of our approach.

For performance comparison, we choose to use MySQL for two reasons. The first reason is that MySQL implements an inverted index for full-text searches and its full-text search capability is well-regarded by the user community. The second reason is that MySQL is widely available, and has one of the most commonly used inverted indexes [49].

9.3 Case Study: The Enron Data Set

The Enron dataset, a large set of email messages, is used by various researchers in the areas of textual and social network analysis. The dataset was made public by the US Federal Energy Regulatory Commission during the criminal investigation into Enron's collapse in 2002. This dataset is particularly attractive for studies of index data structures since it contains numerical, categorical, and text data. Our case study is based on the data prepared by Shetty and Adibi [28] and contains

252,759 email messages stored in four MySQL tables, namely `EmployeeList`, `Message`, `RecipientInfo` and `Reference Info`.

In early performance experiments comparing FastBit with MySQL, we showed that FastBit greatly outperformed MySQL for queries over structured data, including all *numerical* and *categorical* values [33]. One of the key findings of these experiments was that materializing some tables to avoid expensive join operations can significantly reduce query response time. We plan to use the same dataset for our study of querying combined structured data and text data. Following the above observation, we combined six tables into two tables called `Headers` and `Messages` (see Tables 9.1 and 9.2), where the first contains primarily structured data and the second contains primarily text data.

Table 9.1 Schema of database table Headers.

Column Name	Explanation
mid	Message ID
senderFirstName	First name of the sender (only Enron employees)
senderLastName	Last name of the sender (only Enron employees)
senderEmail	Email address of the sender
recipientFirstName	First name of the recipient (only Enron employees)
recipientLastName	Last name of the recipient (only Enron employees)
recipientEmail	Email address of the recipient
day	Day email was sent
time	Time email was sent
rtype	Receiver type: "TO," "CC," and "BCC"

Table 9.2 Schema of database table Messages.

Column Name	Explanation
mid	Message ID
subject	Subject of email message
body	Body of email message
folder	Name of folder used in email client

The table `Headers` contains both numerical and categorical values, whereas `Messages` contains only text data. Table `Headers` is a materialization of the parts from the three original tables `EmployeeList`, `Messages` and `RecipientInfo`. Table `Messages` contains a subset of the columns of the original table `Messages`. The advantage of this schema design is to use bitmap indexes for query processing for both tables. The column `mid` in `Messages` is a foreign key to the column of the same name in `Headers` and is used to join message text columns with the corresponding numerical and categorical data.

9.4 Extending Bitmap Indexes to Support Full Text Search

FastBit compressed bitmap index technology was originally designed to speed up queries on numerical data. In this section we describe how to extend bitmap indexes to support keyword queries over text data. Indexing text usually requires the following two steps: text parsing and term extraction and index generation.

In our framework we use Lucene [11] for text parsing and term extraction. The output of Lucene is a *term-document list* which is an inverted index that contains all identified terms across all documents and a set of document identifiers (IDs) of each document containing the term. Once the term-document list is obtained, we convert the term-document list into a bitmap index consisting of a dictionary of terms and a set of compressed bitmaps. Note that the use of a dictionary is not essential to the approach, but it is a convenient way to reuse the existing software for indexing integer data.

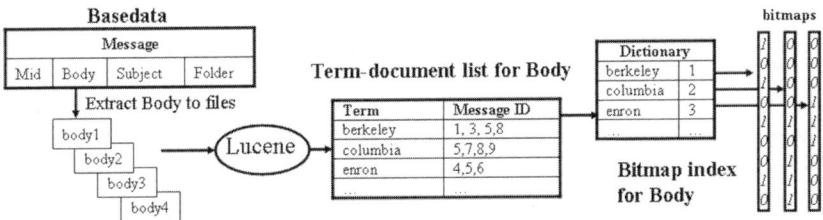

Fig. 9.2 Framework for Indexing Text with FastBit. This illustration use the column "Body" as the example.

As illustrated in Figure 9.2, assuming a database table called `Messages` containing four columns `mid`, `body`, `subject` and `folder`, we proceed to build our bitmap index as follows. We first extract each text value, say from column `body`, into a file named after the `mid` column. Note that the Message IDs, `mid`, are the same as used in the MySQL version of the Enron e-mail message dataset [28]. In Figure 9.2, these files are indicated by "body1," "body2," etc.. Next, we pass this set of files to Lucene to identify terms in the files. The output from Lucene is a list of terms, and for each term a list of files containing the term. Since the file names are the `mid`s, we effectively produce a list of `mid` values for each term. For instance, the term "Berkeley" appears in the messages with the IDs 1, 3, 5 and 8. Similarly, the term "Columbia" appears in the messages with the IDs 5, 7, 8 and 9. These lists are the core content of a typical inverted index. Additional content typically include term frequencies [4, 25]. Since other inverted indexes contains more information than the term-document list, they take more space than the term-document list without compression.

The next step is to convert the term-document list into a bitmap index. However, before we can index the identified terms with bitmaps, we need to introduce an auxiliary data structure, called a *dictionary*, that provides a mapping between the terms and the bitmaps. In our example, "Berkeley" is represented by the numerical value 1, "Columbia" by the value 2 and "Enron" by the value 3 (see "dictionary" in Figure 9.2). Next, the message IDs originally stored in the term-document lists can be encoded with bitmaps. For instance, the bitmap representing "Berkeley" contains the bit string 101010010 to indicate that "Berkeley" is contained in the messages 1, 3, 5 and 8. Similarly, the bitmap representing "Columbia" contains the bit string 000010111 to indicate that "Columbia" is contained in the message 5, 7, 8, and 9. In other words, a bit is set to 1 if the respective term is contained in a message, otherwise the bit is set to 0[2].

Using compressed bitmap indexes for storing term-document lists supports keyword searches efficiently. For instance, finding all emails where `body` contains the terms "Berkeley" and "Columbia" requires reading two bitmaps and combining them with a logical AND operation. As showed in the past, such basic bitmap operations are very efficient [41].

9.5 Integrating FastBit into MonetDB

We decided to integrate FastBit into a relational database system for two reasons. First, as part of a relational database management system, FastBit would benefit from the system's ability to undertake tasks beyond indexing and querying, such as performing joins between tables and enforcing consistency in the records. Second, by adding FastBit to a relational database system, relational data can benefit from FastBit's high performance indexes. With the addition of text searching to Fast-Bit, adding FastBit to a relational system also provides a high performance tool for keyword searches. The database system we chosen is MonetDB, an open source database system developed by CWI [20]. In this section we begin by describing MonetDB and our reasons for choosing it, then briefly describe our integration of FastBit with MonetDB.

9.5.1 Why MonetDB?

MonetDB is our target relational database system for FastBit integration because of its data layout. Unlike most databases, such as MySQL or Oracle, that use horizontal or row-based storage, MonetDB uses vertical partitioning also known as a decomposed storage model (DSM) [5]. See Figure 9.3 for an illustration of the storage techniques. In a database with row-based storage, entire records are stored contiguously, thus making access to entire records efficient, but wasting I/O and memory

---

[2] In general, the document identifiers may not be directly used as row numbers for setting the bits in the bitmaps. We may actually need an additional step of mapping the document identifiers to row numbers. This additional level of operational detail is skipped for clarity.

bandwidth when only a small subset of columns is required [5, 29, 35]. For instance, in Figure 9.3b the records are read right to left, top to bottom during a scan even if the query is interested in only column $a2$ in each record. That is, the entire record is loaded even though only a small part of it is needed. With a DSM, single columns are stored contiguously (Figure 9.3c) resulting in efficient I/O for queries that involves only a subset of the columns. MonetDB's data layout is analogous to FastBit indexing, where each column is indexed and stored separately.

$a1$	$a2$	$a3$
a_{11}	a_{21}	a_{31}
a_{12}	a_{22}	a_{32}
$\vdots$	$\cdot$	$\vdots$
a_{1n}	a_{2n}	a_{3n}

(a) Logical View. Each row has three columns

$$\begin{array}{l} \{a_{11}, a_{21}, a_{31}\} \\ \{a_{12}, a_{22}, a_{32}\} \\ \vdots \\ \{a_{1n}, a_{2n}, a_{3n}\} \end{array}$$

(b) Horizontal Partitioning. Store values from the same row contiguously

$$\begin{pmatrix} a_{11} \\ a_{12} \\ \vdots \\ a_{1n} \end{pmatrix} \begin{pmatrix} a_{21} \\ a_{22} \\ \vdots \\ a_{2n} \end{pmatrix} \begin{pmatrix} a_{31} \\ a_{32} \\ \vdots \\ a_{3n} \end{pmatrix}$$

(c) Vertical Partitioning Store values from the same column contiguously

Fig. 9.3 An illustration of horizontal and vertical Partitioning.

The MonetDB SQL Server is a two-layer system [20]. On the bottom is the MonetDB kernel that manages the actual data. At this layer, the data is not stored as a complete relational table, but is decomposed into separate Binary Association Tables (BAT)–one for each column. Each entry in the BAT is a two-field record containing an object identifier (OID) and a column data value. All column values for the same relational tuple have the same OID even though they are stored in separate BATs. Interaction with these BATs is accomplished via the Monet Interpreter Language (MIL), that can be extended with new commands which we make use of as outlined next.

The SQL module sits atop the MonetDB kernel and provides an SQL interface for client applications. Though the relational tables are actually decomposed into many BATs, the SQL module allows users to interact with the data in the normal relational manner. The SQL module is responsible for transaction and session management as well as transforming SQL queries into MIL code to be executed by the MonetDB kernel. With the help of the MonetDB developers at CWI, we decided it would be best to integrate FastBit into the SQL module rather than the underlying MonetDB kernel. In the following sections we give an overview of the changes required to integrate FastBit into MonetDB/SQL. Note that all changes described occurred within the SQL module; the MonetDB kernel was left unchanged. The MonetDB kernel was version 4.12 and the SQL module was version 2.12. Both are available from the MonetDB website at http://monetdb.cwi.nl/.

9.5.2 Integrating MonetDB and FastBit

Integrating FastBit into MonetDB's SQL module (MonetDB/SQL) required four tasks: (1) addition of the `FASTBIT` keyword to MonetDB's SQL parser, (2) functionality to allow MonetDB to send data to a FastBit library for index construction, (3) rules to recognize subqueries that are FastBit eligible during query optimization, and (4) integration of FastBit and MonetDB execution so that a unified query result is produced by MonetDB. We next briefly describe each of these tasks.

Overall, users continue to interact with MonetDB/SQL as the front end. To allow MonetDB to invoke FastBit index creation functions, we need to do two things: first to inform the MonetDB system that it needs to invoke FastBit indexing creation functions, and then to prepare the necessary base data for index creation. We modified the parser in the SQL module to recognize the keyword `FASTBIT` in the index creation command. This keyword informs MonetDB to invoke FastBit for index creation.

In order for FastBit to create an index, it needs to know the raw data of the column to be indexed. This set of data is written to a specific directory under the data directory for MonetDB. MonetDB server then invokes the appropriate functions to create FastBit indexes. The metadata held by the MonetDB server is modified to reflect the existence of FastBit indexes and it has to update the FastBit indexes when the data is modified.

Since FastBit can only perform a subset of queries that MonetDB supports, recognizing which part of the query can take full advantage of FastBit indexes is critical. We achieve this by examining and modifying the query plan generated by the MonetDB SQL parser. All equality conditions and range conditions on variables that have FastBit indexes are recognized as suitable for FastBit processing, and they are combined together into a special node in the query plan. This special node along with its parameters are later passed to FastBit. To perform a keyword search, we overload the operator '=,' for example, the MySQL expression "MATCH(body) AGAINST('Berkeley')" would be expressed as "body = 'Berkeley'."

The special node in the query execution plan is translated into a command in Monet Interpreter Language called `fastbit_execute`. The MonetDB execution engine recognizes this command and composes the appropriate query string for FastBit. Following a typical evaluation command, the command `fastbit_-execute` also produces a list of OIDs. This allows other operations in MonetDB to proceed as usual.

9.6 Experiments

This section contains a discussion of our experimental results and demonstrates that adding compressed bitmap indexes to a relational database system enables high performance, integrated querying of structured data and text data.

The first two parts of this section (9.6.1 and 9.6.2) present some statistics about the term distribution in our text data as well as the size and cardinality of the bitmap indexes constructed for all columns in the Enron Data Set. The remainder of the section presents the timing results. The experiments compare MySQL, a popular open-source database management system supporting text searching, a stand-alone FastBit client, and MonetDB integrated with FastBit. The experiments are broken down into three groups: (1) queries over structured data, (2) queries over text data, and (3) queries over both structured data and text data.

Each query in the following experiments was issued both as a *count query* and as an *output query*. A *count query* returns only the number of hits, that is, the SQL SELECT clause starts with SELECT COUNT(*) FROM. An *output query* retrieves data values associated with the tuples in the result set. Note that all performance graphs are shown with a log-log scale.

All experiments were conducted on a server with dual 2.8 GHz Pentium 4 processors, 2 GB of main memory, and an IDE RAID storage system capable of sustaining 60 MB/sec for reads and writes. Before we executed each set of 1000 queries, we unmounted and remounted the file system containing the data and the indexes as well as restarted the database servers in order to ensure cold cache behavior.

9.6.1 Data Statistics

Figure 9.4 shows the term frequency distributions in the "body" and the "subject" of the Enron emails. The terms were extracted with Lucene. Both distributions match Zipf's law as commonly observed in many phenomena in nature. The total number of distinct terms in the message body is more than 1.2 million. The total number of distinct terms in the message subject is about 40,000.

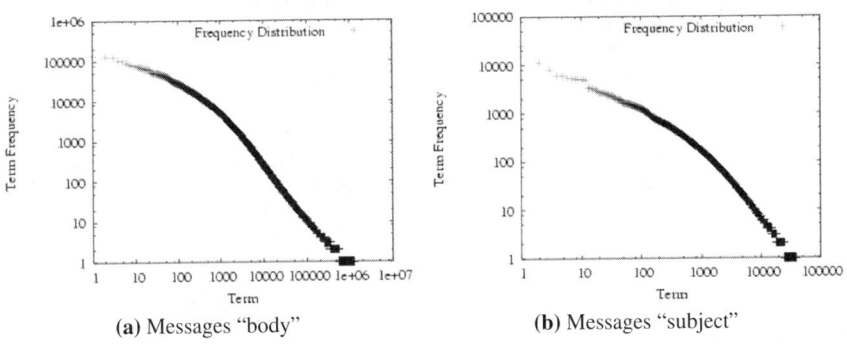

(a) Messages "body"   (b) Messages "subject"

Fig. 9.4 Term frequency distribution in the message "body" and "subject."

9.6.2 Size of Bitmap Indexes

Table 9.3 shows the size of raw data compared with the size of the compressed bitmap indexes for each column of table Headers. The column cardinalities of each columns are also given. Note that we have chosen not to index column mid because it is unique for every message and is therefore more efficient to directly work with the raw data to answer typical queries involving it. The sizes of the compressed bitmap indexes are much smaller than the raw data. For instance, the index size for column recipientEmail is about 20% or raw data even though this column has a very high column cardinality, about 70,000. For lower cardinality columns, such as senderEmail, the bitmap index sizes are only about 2~3% of the raw data.

Table 9.4 shows the size of the compressed bitmap indexes for the table Messages, i.e., the table that stores the text data. In addition to the size of the raw data, we also provide the size of the uncompressed term-document list. We see that the space required for table Messages is dominated by the column body. Since it contains more than 1.2 million distinct terms, its index is also the largest. In this case, the size of the compressed bitmap index is about half the size of the term-document list, which in turn is about half the size of the raw data. On average, we use less than 100 bytes per term indexed. Overall, the compressed bitmap indexes are smaller than the term-document lists, which are the minimal information in typical inverted indexes.

Table 9.3 Size of the raw data compared with the size of compressed bitmap indexes for each column of the table Headers. For the categorical values also the dictionary sizes are also given.

Column	Card.	Data [MB]	Dict. [MB]	Bitmap Index [MB]	[% Data]
mid	252,759	8.26			
senderFirstName	112	7.21	0.0007	0.14	1.9
senderLastName	148	7.70	0.0001	0.14	1.8
senderEmail	17,568	48.00	0.4336	1.41	2.9
recipientFirstName	112	7.20	0.0007	0.14	1.9
recipientLastName	148	7.52	0.0001	1.40	18.6
recipientEmail	68,214	47.78	1.5454	13.69	28.6
day	1,323	8.26		0.74	9.0
time	46,229	8.26		3.24	39.2
rtype	3	6.45	0.0001	0.49	7.6

From earlier analyses of the WAH compressed bitmap indexes [42, 44], we know that the upper bound of the total size of bitmaps is a linear function of the number of rows in the dataset. For typical high-cardinality data, the total size of bitmaps may be twice the size of the base data. The relative sizes shown in Tables 9.3 and 9.4 indicates that the actual index sizes are well within the predicted upper bounds. Note that the index sizes reported in Tables 9.3 and 9.4 include all information associated with the compressed bitmaps such as the dictionary for text data.

Table 9.4 Size of the raw data and the term-document list (td-list) compared with the size of compressed bitmap indexes including the dictionary for each column of table `Messages`.

Column	Card.	Data [MB]	td-list [MB]	Dict. [MB]	Bitmap Index Size [MB]	[% Data]	[% td-list]
mid	252,759	1.01					
subject	38,915	7.56	8.20	0.31	5.23	69.2	63.8
body	1,247,922	445.27	245.57	16.92	121.72	27.3	49.6
folder	3,380	20.98	8.09	0.04	0.14	0.7	1.7

9.6.3 Query performance on structured data

In this first set of timing measurements, we present the time required to answer queries on structured data from table `Headers`. We tested queries of one- and two-dimensions, with and without retrieving data values.

Table 9.5 Total time in seconds for running 1,000 queries against table `Headers`. This is a summary of the results presented in Figure 9.5.

	MySQL	FastBit	MonetDB/FastBit
Fig. 9.5a	5.17	0.17	1.53
Fig. 9.5b	51.56	1.29	2.73
Total time	56.72	1.46	7.45
Speedup		36.4	13.3
Fig. 9.5c	47.66	181.64	6.35
Fig. 9.5d	53.17	95.93	5.86
Total time	100.93	277.57	12.21
Speedup		0.36	8.27

Figure 9.5 shows the timing results of running 1000 one- and two-dimensional queries. In the query expressions, ":S" and ":D" denote the values that vary in the 1000 queries. In the one-dimensional queries, our queries use top 1000 senders as the value of ":S." To answer these count queries FastBit is clearly faster than MySQL. On average, FastBit is about a factor of 36 faster than MySQL as shown in Table 9.5.

For each count query, we also execute an output query with the same set of query conditions. The timing results for answering these queries are shown in Figure 9.5(c) and (d). On these queries, FastBit takes much longer to retrieve the selected values than the other two. This is because FastBit reconstruct the string values from the content of the dictionary and the bitmap representing the hits. In contrast, the combined system uses FastBit to retrieve the object identifiers and uses MonetDB to retrieve the values. Clearly, this is a better option. Overall, using MonetDB/FastBit is about eight times faster than using MySQL, see Table 9.5.

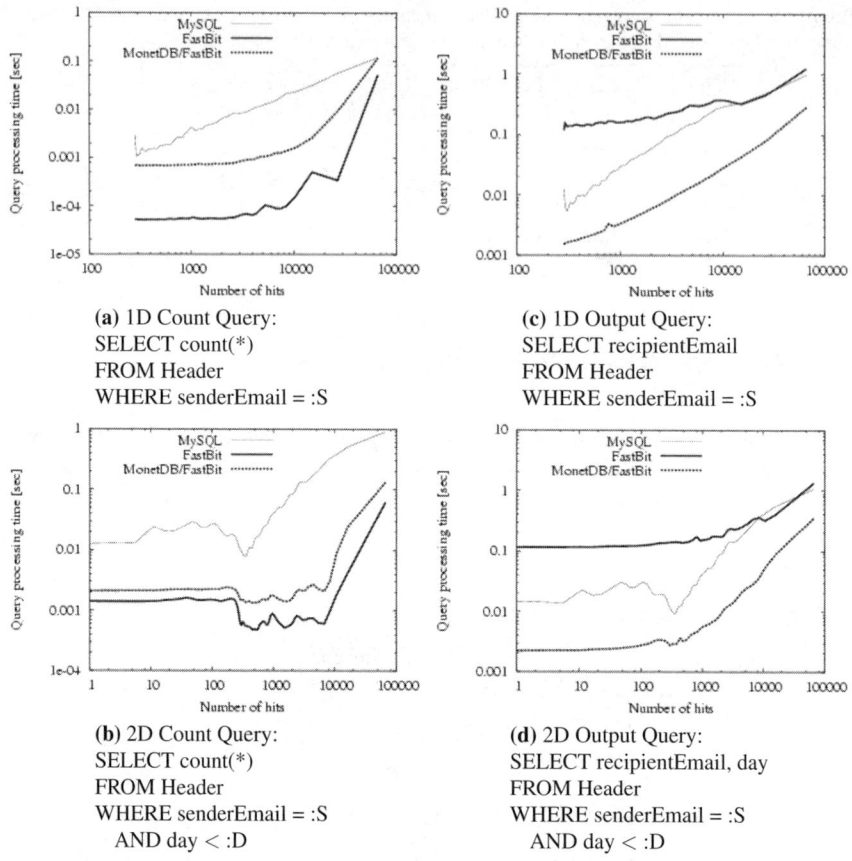

(a) 1D Count Query:
SELECT count(*)
FROM Header
WHERE senderEmail = :S

(c) 1D Output Query:
SELECT recipientEmail
FROM Header
WHERE senderEmail = :S

(b) 2D Count Query:
SELECT count(*)
FROM Header
WHERE senderEmail = :S
    AND day < :D

(d) 2D Output Query:
SELECT recipientEmail, day
FROM Header
WHERE senderEmail = :S
    AND day < :D

Fig. 9.5 Count and output queries on the table `Headers`. A summary of the performance measurements is given in Table 9.5.

When a WAH compressed bitmap index is used to answer a query, analyses show that the worst-case query response time is bounded by a linear function of the number of hits [42, 44]. This worst case can be achieved with uniform random data. Since the actual index sizes shown in Table 9.3 are much smaller than predicted worst-case sizes and the average query response time is proportional to the index size, the query response time should be proportionally less than in the worst case. This expectation is for one-dimensional queries shown in Figure 9.5(a). The answers to multi-dimensional queries are composed from answers to multiple one-dimensional queries. One average, the total query response time for a k-dimensional query is k times that of a one-dimensional query.

9.6.4 Query Performance for Text Searching

Next, we study the keyword searching capability of FastBit and compare it with that of MySQL. Figure 9.6 shows both the timing results and the queries used. As before, our actual queries replace the variables with top 1000 frequent terms from each of the text columns. Presumably, the most frequent terms are also "interesting" for text analysis since these terms are more discussed among people in Enron emails and might thus have a higher semantic meaning.

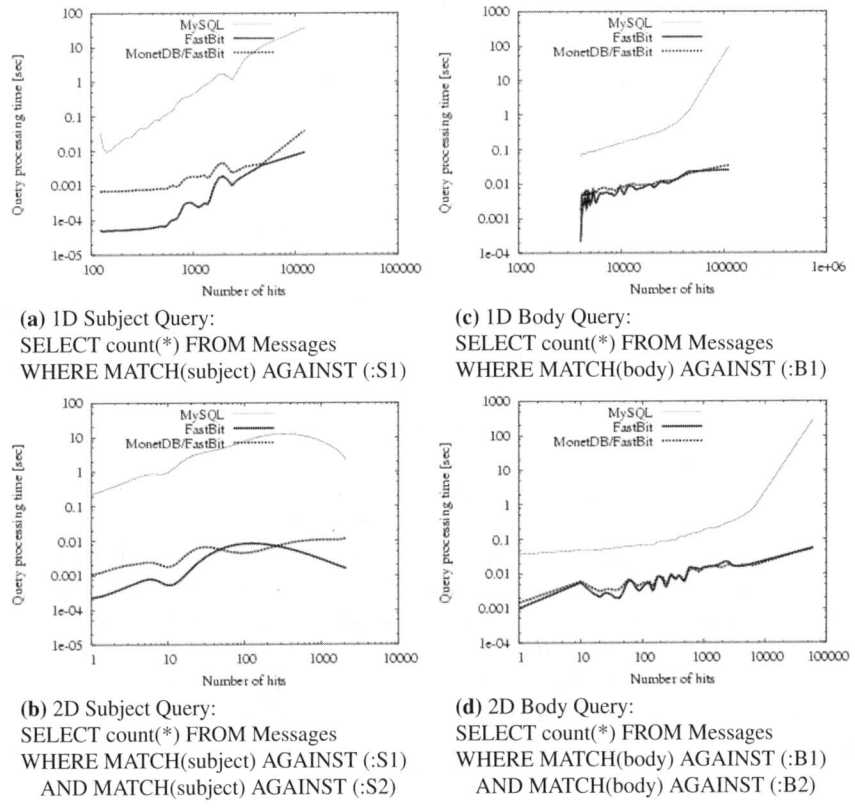

(a) 1D Subject Query:
SELECT count(*) FROM Messages
WHERE MATCH(subject) AGAINST (:S1)

(c) 1D Body Query:
SELECT count(*) FROM Messages
WHERE MATCH(body) AGAINST (:B1)

(b) 2D Subject Query:
SELECT count(*) FROM Messages
WHERE MATCH(subject) AGAINST (:S1)
AND MATCH(subject) AGAINST (:S2)

(d) 2D Body Query:
SELECT count(*) FROM Messages
WHERE MATCH(body) AGAINST (:B1)
AND MATCH(body) AGAINST (:B2)

Fig. 9.6 Count queries on the "subject" and "body" columns of the table `Messages`. A summary of the performance measurements is given in Table 9.6.

Figure 9.6 shows the response times for 1000 queries over the subject and the body of the email messages from the Enron data set. Table 9.6 shows a summary of timing information. For those queries containing one keyword, using FastBit as a stand-alone system, is more than 500 times faster than using MySQL. Since these queries need to pass a relatively larger number of OIDs from FastBit to MonetDB,

Table 9.6 Total time in seconds for running 1,000 count queries against the table Messages. This table is a summary of the results presented in Figure 9.6.

	MySQL	FastBit	MonetDB/FastBit
Fig. 9.6a	324.79	0.58	1.56
Fig. 9.6b	311.11	0.58	1.45
Fig. 9.6c	532.12	13.34	13.32
Fig. 9.6d	518.70	18.06	15.71
Total time	1706.72	32.56	32.04
Speedup		52.42	53.26

the combined MonetDB/FastBit takes longer time using FastBit alone. Nevertheless, the combined system still show very impressive speedup over MySQL, about 50.

9.6.5 Query Performance for both Numerical and Text Data

Our last set of experiments is the most challenging because it requires a join operation over the tables Headers and Messages. Since FastBit currently does not support join operations, we implemented a simple sort-merge join algorithm outside of FastBit. In particular, a join query over two tables consists of four FastBit queries. The first query evaluates the query condition on the table Headers. The second query evaluates the query condition on the table Messages. Next, the lists of resulting message IDs (mids) of both queries are sorted and intersected to find the common ones. The list of common mids is then sent back as two queries in the form of "mid IN (12, 35, 89, ...)." Finally, the desired columns are retrieved from the two tables. The count queries can skip the last step since they do not retrieve any values. Retrieving values through FastBit this way is likely to be slow because FastBit is not efficient at retrieving string values, and parsing the long query expression involving thousands of mids is also time consuming.

In Figures 9.7 and 9.8, we plot the query response time against the number of hits for the combined queries on both structured data and text data. In these tests, the combined MonetDB/FastBit uses FastBit to perform the filtering one each table and then perform the sort-merge join on mid. Since our external join algorithm essentially does the same thing, we see that FastBit and MonetDB/FastBit take about the same amount of time. Both of them are significantly faster than MySQL. Table 9.7 shows the total time to answer 1000 queries. Overall, we see that FastBit and MonetDB/FastBit are about 52 and 67 times faster than MySQL in answering these count queries.

Figure 9.8 shows the query response time of the output queries. Because retrieving string values using FastBit is slow, the overall speed of FastBit versus MySQL decreases to 16, but MonetDB/FastBit combined system remains about 64 times faster than MySQL.

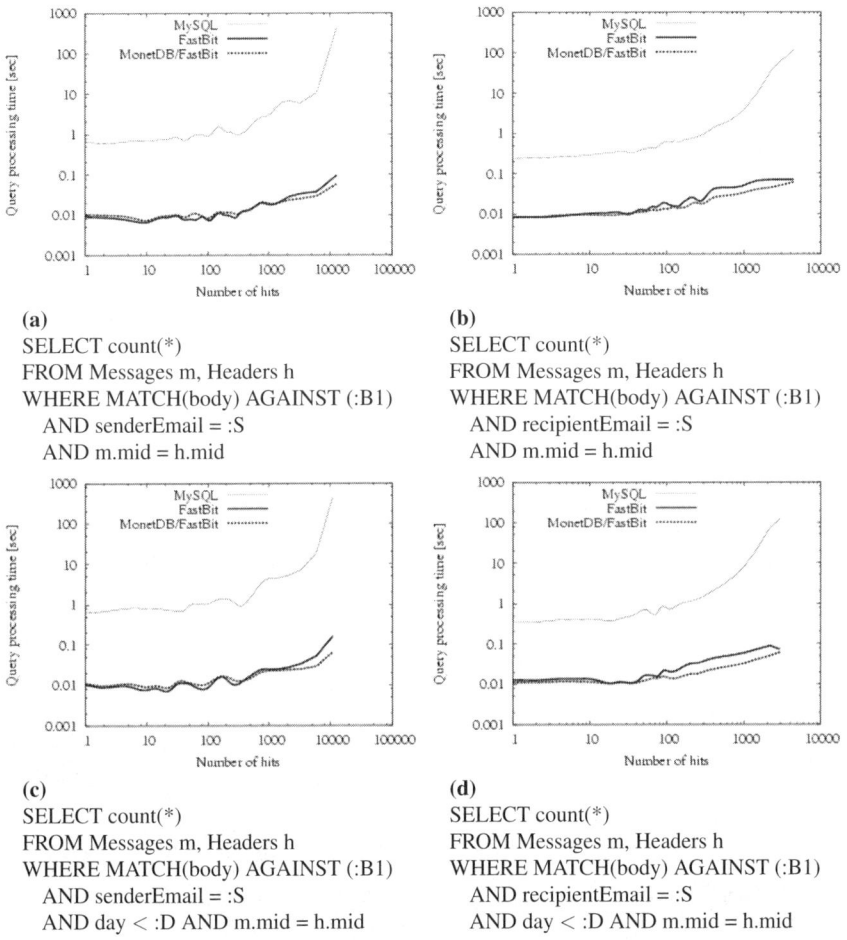

(a)
SELECT count(*)
FROM Messages m, Headers h
WHERE MATCH(body) AGAINST (:B1)
    AND senderEmail = :S
    AND m.mid = h.mid

(b)
SELECT count(*)
FROM Messages m, Headers h
WHERE MATCH(body) AGAINST (:B1)
    AND recipientEmail = :S
    AND m.mid = h.mid

(c)
SELECT count(*)
FROM Messages m, Headers h
WHERE MATCH(body) AGAINST (:B1)
    AND senderEmail = :S
    AND day < :D AND m.mid = h.mid

(d)
SELECT count(*)
FROM Messages m, Headers h
WHERE MATCH(body) AGAINST (:B1)
    AND recipientEmail = :S
    AND day < :D AND m.mid = h.mid

Fig. 9.7 Integrated numerical and text count queries. These queries are shown in the format used by MySQL. A summary of the performance measurements is given in Table 9.7.

9.7 Conclusions and Future Work

We propose a way of using compressed bitmaps to represent the commonly used term-document matrix to support keyword searches on text data. By using a compute-efficient compression technique, we are able to not only keep the indexes compact but also answer keyword queries very efficiently. In our detailed experimental study we show that our bitmap index technology called FastBit answers count queries over text data about 50 times faster than MySQL.

To provide the full functionality of SQL including text search, we integrated our text index technology with an open-source database management system called

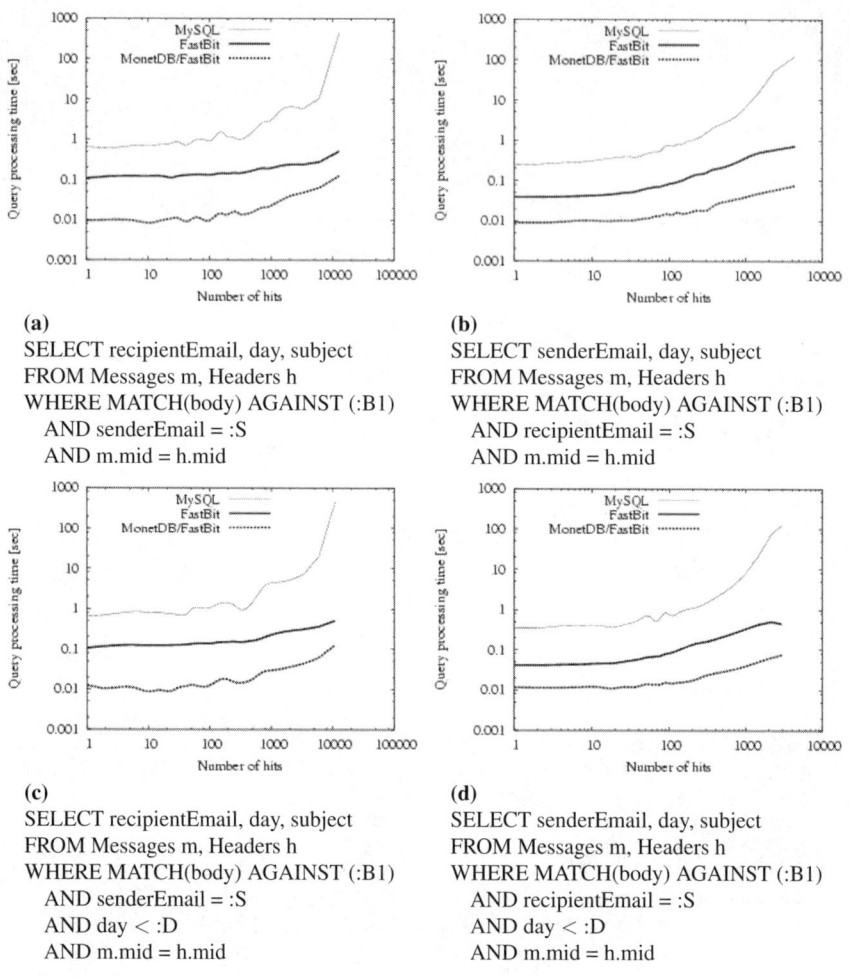

(a)

SELECT recipientEmail, day, subject
FROM Messages m, Headers h
WHERE MATCH(body) AGAINST (:B1)
    AND senderEmail = :S
    AND m.mid = h.mid

(b)

SELECT senderEmail, day, subject
FROM Messages m, Headers h
WHERE MATCH(body) AGAINST (:B1)
    AND recipientEmail = :S
    AND m.mid = h.mid

(c)

SELECT recipientEmail, day, subject
FROM Messages m, Headers h
WHERE MATCH(body) AGAINST (:B1)
    AND senderEmail = :S
    AND day < :D
    AND m.mid = h.mid

(d)

SELECT senderEmail, day, subject
FROM Messages m, Headers h
WHERE MATCH(body) AGAINST (:B1)
    AND recipientEmail = :S
    AND day < :D
    AND m.mid = h.mid

Fig. 9.8 Integrated numerical and text output queries. These queries are shown in the format used by MySQL. A summary of the performance measurements is given in Table 9.7.

MonetDB. This integration introduces text-search capability to MonetDB. Our performance experiments demonstrate that the integrated system significantly reduces the time needed to answer joint queries over structured data and text data. Compared with MySQL, the integrated system is 60 times faster on average at retrieving text values subject to multi-dimensional query conditions. This demonstrates that the demand of providing full SQL support does not necessarily diminish performance. It further validates our compressed bitmap approach as an efficient way of accelerating joint queries on structured data and text data.

Table 9.7 Total time in seconds for running 1,000 join queries against tables Headers and Messages. This table is a summary of the results in Figures 9.7 and 9.8.

	MySQL	FastBit	MonetDB/FastBit
Fig. 9.7a	1302.28	16.54	16.03
Fig. 9.7b	866.98	23.37	17.45
Fig. 9.7c	975.18	24.81	18.10
Fig. 9.7d	556.80	6.40	2.98
Total time	3701.24	71.12	54.56
Speedup		52.04	67.84
Fig. 9.8a	1303.24	82.55	18.24
Fig. 9.8b	970.31	78.64	18.51
Fig. 9.8c	977.99	53.00	19.17
Fig. 9.8d	557.27	21.24	3.35
Total time	3808.81	235.43	59.27
Speedup		16.18	64.26

The work presented in this paper only supports Boolean queries over the text data, i.e., without ranking the results. Future versions of bitmap indexes may include ranking information, as well as proximity of terms in text documents.

References

1. AmerYahia, S., Botev, C., Shanmugasundaram, J.: TeXQuery: A FullText Search Extension to XQuery. In: WWW2004. New York, New York, USA (2004)
2. Anh, V.N., Moffat, A.: Improved Word-Aligned Binary Compression for Text Indexing. IEEE Transactions on Knowledge and Data Engineering **18**(6), 857–861 (2006)
3. Antoshenkov, G.: Byte-aligned Bitmap Compression. Tech. rep., Oracle Corp. (1994). U.S. Patent number 5,363,098
4. Baeza-Yates, R.A., Ribeiro-Neto, B.: Modern Information Retrieval. Addison-Wesley Longman Publishing Co., Inc., Boston, MA, USA (1999)
5. Boncz, P.A., Manegold, S., Kersten, M.L.: Database Architecture Optimized for the New Bottleneck: Memory Access. In: The VLDB Journal, pp. 54–65 (1999)
6. Chan, C.Y., Ioannidis, Y.E.: Bitmap Index Design and Evaluation. In: SIGMOD. ACM Press., Seattle, Washington, USA (1998)
7. Chan, C.Y., Ioannidis, Y.E.: An Efficient Bitmap Encoding Scheme for Selection Queries. In: SIGMOD. ACM Press., Philadelphia, Pennsylvania, USA (1999)
8. Chaudhuri, S., Dayal, U.: An Overview of Data Warehousing and OLAP Technology. ACM SIGMOD Record **26**(1), 65–74 (1997)
9. Chaudhuri, S., Dayal, U., Ganti, V.: Database Technology for Decision Support Systems. Computer **34**(12), 48–55 (2001)
10. Comer, D.: The Ubiquitous B-tree. Computing Surveys **11**(2), 121–137 (1979)
11. Doug Cutting, e.a.: Apache Lucene. http://lucene.apache.org.
12. Ercegovac, V., DeWitt, D.J., Ramakrishnan, R.: The Texture Benchmark: Measuring Performance of Text Queries on a Relational DBMS. In: VLDB, pp. 313–324 (2005)
13. Faloutsos, C., Christodoulakis, S.: Signature Files: an Access Method for Documents and Its Analytical Performance Evaluation. ACM Trans. Inf. Syst. **2**(4), 267–288 (1984)

14. Inmon, W., Hackathorn, R.: Using the Data Warehouse. Wiley-QED Publishing, Somerset, NJ, USA (1994)
15. Johnson, T.: Performance Measurements of Compressed Bitmap Indices. In: International Conference on Very Large Data Bases. Morgan Kaufmann., Edinburgh, Scotland (1999)
16. Kabra, N., Ramakrishnan, R., Ercegovac, V.: The QUIQ Engine: A Hybrid IR-DB System. In: ICDE, pp. 741–743. IEEE (2003)
17. Koudas, N.: Space Efficient Bitmap Indexing. In: CIKM 2000, McLean, Virginia, USA. ACM Press. (2000)
18. L.V. Saxton, V.R.: Design of an Integrated Information Retrieval/Database Management System. IEEE Transactions on Knowledge and Data Engineering **2**, 210–219 (1999)
19. Moffat, A., Zobel, J.: Self-Indexing Inverted Files for Fast Text Retrieval. ACM Transactions on Information Systems **14**(4), 349–379 (1996)
20. MonetDB: Query Processing at Light-Speed. http://monetdb.cwi.nl.
21. O'Neil, P.: Model 204 Architecture and Performance. In: 2nd International Workshop in High Performance Transaction Systems. Springer-Verlag, Asilomar, California, USA (1987)
22. O'Neil, P., O'Neil, E.: Database: Principles, Programming, and Performance, 2nd edn. Morgan Kaugmann (2000)
23. O'Neil, P., Quass, D.: Improved Query Performance with Variant Indexes. In: Proceedings ACM SIGMOD International Conference on Management of Data. ACM Press, Tucson, Arizona, USA (1997)
24. Rotem, D., Stockinger, K., Wu, K.: Optimizing Candidate Check Costs for Bitmap Indices. In: CIKM (2005)
25. Salton, G.: Automatic Text Processing: the Transformation, Analysis, and Retrieval of Information by Computer. Addison-Wesley Longman Publishing Co., Inc., Boston, MA, USA (1989)
26. Schek, H.J.: Nested Transactions in a Combined IRS-DBMS Architecture. In: SIGIR'84, Cambridge, England. pp. 55–70. (1984)
27. Schek, H.J., Pistor, P.: Data Structures for an Integrated Data Base Management and Information Retrieval System. In: VLDB'82, Mexico City, Mexico. Morgan Kaufmann. (1982)
28. Shetty, J., Adibi, J.: The Enron Email Dataset, Database Schema and Brief Statistical Report. Tech. rep., Information Sciences Institute, Marina del Rey, California (2006). http://www.isi.edu/\~adibi/Enron/Enron_Dataset_Report.pdf
29. Shoshani, A.: OLAP and Statistical Databases: Similarities and Differences. In: PODS, pp. 185–196 (1997)
30. Shoshani, A., Bernardo, L.M., Nordberg, H., Rotem, D., Sim, A.: Multidimensional indexing and query coordination for tertiary storage management. In: SSDBM'99, Cleveland, Ohio, USA, 28-30 July, 1999, pp. 214–225. IEEE Computer Society (1999)
31. Sinha, R.R., Winslett, M.: Multi-resolution bitmap indexes for scientific data. ACM Trans. Database Syst. **32**(3), 16 (2007)
32. Stabno, M., Wrembel, R.: RLH: Bitmap Compression Technique Based on Run-Length and Huffman Encoding. In: DOLAP'07, pp. 41–48. ACM, New York, NY, USA (2007). DOI http://doi.acm.org/10.1145/1317331.1317339
33. Stockinger, K., Rotem, D., Shoshani, A., Wu, K.: Bitmap Indexing Outperforms MySQL Queries by Several Orders of Magnitude. Tech. Rep. LBNL-59437, Berkeley Lab, Berkeley, California (2006)
34. Stockinger, K., Wu, K., Shoshani, A.: Evaluation Strategies for Bitmap Indices with Binning. In: DEXA. Springer-Verlag., Zaragoza, Spain (2004)
35. SybaseIQ. http://www.sybase.com/products/informationmanagement/sybaseiq.
36. Tomasic, A., Garcia-Molina, H., Shoens, K.A.: Incremental Updates of Inverted Lists for Text Document Retrieval. In: SIGMOD'94. Minneapolis, Minnesota, USA (1994)
37. Trotman, A.: Compressing Inverted Files. Information Retrieval **6**, 5–19 (2003)
38. de Vries, A., Wilschut, A.: On the Integration of IR and Databases. In: IFIP 2.6 DS-8 Conference. Rotorua, New Zealand (1999)

39. Wong, H.K.T., Liu, H.F., Olken, F., Rotem, D., Wong, L.: Bit transposed files. In: Proceedings of VLDB 85, Stockholm, pp. 448–457 (1985)
40. Wu, K., Otoo, E., Shoshani, A.: Compressed Bitmap Indices for Efficient Query Processing. Tech. Rep. LBNL-47807, LBNL, Berkeley, CA (2001)
41. Wu, K., Otoo, E., Shoshani, A.: Compressing Bitmap Indexes for Faster Search Operations. In: SSDBM, pp. 99–108 (2002)
42. Wu, K., Otoo, E., Shoshani, A.: On the performance of bitmap indices for high cardinality attributes. In: VLDB 2004, Toronto, Canada, pp. 24–35. Morgan Kaufmann (2004)
43. Wu, K.: FastBit: an Efficient Indexing Technology for Accelerating Data-Intensive Science, *J. Phys.: Conf. Ser.*, vol. 16, pp. 556–560. Institute of Physics (2005). Software available at http://sdm.lbl.gov/fastbit/.
44. Wu, K., Otoo, E., Shoshani, A.: An Efficient Compression Scheme for Bitmap Indices. ACM Transactions on Database Systems **31**, 1–38 (2006)
45. Wu, K.L., Yu, P.: Range-based bitmap indexing for high cardinality attributes with skew. Tech. Rep. RC 20449, IBM Watson Research Division, Yorktown Heights, New York (1996)
46. Wu, M.C., Buchmann, A.P.: Encoded bitmap indexing for data warehouses. In: ICDE '98, pp. 220–230. IEEE Computer Society (1998)
47. Yan, T.W., Annevelink, J.: Integrating a Structured-Text Retrieval System with an Object-Oriented Database System. In: VLDB'94 Santiago, Chile, pp. 740–749. (1994)
48. Ziviani, N., de Moura, E.S., Navarro, G., Baeza-Yates, R.: Compression: a Key for Next-Generation Text Retrieval Systems. IEEE Computer **33**, 37–44 (2000)
49. Zobel, J., Moffat, A.: Inverted Files For Text Search Engines. ACM Computing Serveys **38**(2) (2006)
50. Zobel, J., Moffat, A.: Inverted Files for Text Searching. ACM Computing Surveys **38**(3) (2006)

Chapter 10
HP&BJI: A Combined Selection of Data Partitioning and Join Indexes for Improving OLAP Performance

Kamel Boukhalfa, Ladjel Bellatreche, and Zaia Alimazighi

Abstract Data warehouses tend to be extremely large. With terabytes and petabytes of data in the warehouse, complex queries can slow down performance for all decision makers and the task of managing this warehouse becomes difficult. To optimize these queries, many optimization techniques were proposed: materialized views, advanced indexing schemes, data partitioning, parallel processing, etc. The problem of selecting any of these techniques is a very crucial decision for the performance of the data warehouse. Two main modes for selecting optimization techniques exist: sequential and combined. In the first mode, the selection is done in isolation. The main drawback of this mode is its ignorance of the interactions between different optimization techniques. In the combined mode, a joint searching is performed directly in the combined search space of optimization techniques. This selection gives better performance than the sequential selection, since it takes into account interdependencies between optimization techniques, but it requires a high complexity. In this paper, we concentrate on the combined mode, where two optimization techniques are considered: horizontal partitioning and bitmap join indexes. The use of horizontal partitioning prunes the search space of bitmap join index selection problem. We first show the strong similarities between these two techniques. Secondly, we propose a new approach of selecting simultaneously these two techniques. Genetic and greedy algorithms are used for selecting horizontal partitioning schema and bitmap join indexes, respectively. Finally, we conduct intensive experimental studies using a theoretical cost model and the obtained optimization techniques are validated on ORACLE10g using dataset of an APB-1 benchmark.

Kamel Boukhalfa and Ladjel Bellatreche
LISI/ENSMA Poitiers University, Futuroscope 86960 France, e-mail: {boukhalk, bellatreche}@ensma.fr

Zaia Alimazighi
USTHB University, Algiers, Algeria, e-mail: alimazighi@wissal.dz

10.1 Introduction

A data warehouse (DW) integrates huge amount of data of detailed and current data across entire organizations and enables different forms of decision making from the same database. DWs tend to be extremely large, for instance, the DW of General Motors Corporation modelled using a star schema exceeds 1.5 terabytes, and its fact table has more than 2 *billions of instances* [9]. With terabytes and petabytes of data in the warehouse, complex queries can slow down performance for all decision makers and the task of managing this warehouse becomes difficult. A DW is usually modelled with a relational schema (star schema, snow flake schema). A star schema consists of a single fact table that is related to multiple dimension tables via foreign key joins. Dimension tables are relatively small compared to the fact table and rarely updated. They are typically *denormalized* so as to minimize the number of joins required to evaluate OLAP queries. Note that each dimension table contains *several attributes* usually used by OLAP queries. Queries defined on star schemas are called, *star join queries*, are characterized by: (i) a *multi-table* join among a *large fact table* and dimension tables, (ii) each of the dimension tables involved in the join operation has *multiple* selection predicates [1] on its descriptive attributes and (iii) no joins between dimension tables. These queries are time consuming, since they are performed using complex operations like joins, selections and aggregations. Joins are well known to be expensive operations, especially, when the involved relations are substantially larger than the main memory [17], which is usually the case of data warehouse applications [12].

To speed up these star join queries, many optimization techniques were proposed that we classified into two main types [5]: (i) *redundant techniques* like materialized views, advanced indexing schemes (bitmap indexes, bitmap join indexes, etc.) and vertical partitioning (where the primary key is replicated in each fragment) and (ii) non redundant techniques like horizontal partitioning [20, 3, 22] and parallel processing [23]. To select optimization techniques, two modes exist: *sequential* and *combined*. In the sequential mode, selecting optimization techniques is done in isolation, where each technique is selected one at a time. The main drawback of this approach is its ignorance of the interactions between different optimization techniques. In the combined mode, a joint searching is performed directly in the combined search space of optimization techniques [27]. This selection gives better performance than the sequential selection, since it takes into account interdependencies between optimization techniques [21, 27, 25, 16, 23]. But it requires a high complexity since the problem of selecting any optimization technique is a NP-complete problem [6, 14, 20]. An interesting issue to combine optimization techniques is to use one of these techniques to prune search space(s) of other technique(s). This issue is considered in this paper.

---

[1] A selection predicate has the following form: $D_i.A_j \ \theta \ value$, where A_j is an attribute of dimension table D_i and θ is one of five comparison operators $\{=, <, >, \leq, \geq\}$, and value is the predicate constant belonging to domain value of A_j.

To perform a combined mode, an identification of similar optimization techniques is required. For instance, Sanjay et al. [21] identified interaction between materialized views and indexes which are two redundant optimization techniques. They are fundamentally similar – they are used to speed up query execution, compete for the same resource representing storage, and incur maintenance overhead in the presence of updates. Furthermore, indexes and materialized views can interact with one another, i.e., the presence of an index can make a materialized view more attractive and vice versa [21]. Another work done by [23] proposed an approach combining horizontal partitioning (a non redundant optimization technique) and bitmap join indexes (a redundant optimization technique) in parallel data warehousing environment, where generated fragments and bitmap join indexes are allocated over nodes of a shared disk machine. To elaborate the allocation process, Stöhr et al. [23] partitioned fact table of a relational data warehouse schema based on the fragmentation schemas[2] of dimension tables. This work considered only *point fragmentation* of each dimension table, where each value range consists of exactly one attribute value of a fragmentation attribute[3]. The authors imposed that each fragmentation attribute shall belong to a hierarchy of a dimension table. The proposed fragmentation approach selected a set of fragmentation attributes from the dimension attributes, *at most one attribute per dimension table* [24]. This approach is very restricted, since in the context of relational data warehouse, dimension tables may be fragmented using several attributes belonging or not to a hierarchy. Recently, most of commercial database systems (e.g., Oracle 11g) offer a variety of partitioning modes, where a table may be fragmented using *more than one attribute*. In order to ensure a high performance of queries, [23] selected bitmap join indexes on fragmented data warehouse. This selection is done using non fragmentation attributes. Since the fragmentation process is done using at most one attribute for each dimension table, the number of non fragmentation attribute candidates for indexing may be very large.

In this paper, we propose an approach combining horizontal partitioning and bitmap join indexes by exploiting their similarities. It allows dimension tables to be partitioned using several attributes without any restriction on their belonging to hierarchy. The fragmentation schemas of dimension tables are used to horizontally partition the fact table. The data warehouse administrator (DBA) has the freedom to materialize the partitioning of different dimension tables or consider them as virtual. Another interesting functionality offered by our partitioning approach is the possibility for DBA to control the number of generated fragments of the fact tables. This number represents the constraint of our horizontal partitioning selection problem. Since we offer a multiple fragmentation (where several dimension attributes may participate on fragmenting a dimension table), search space of bitmap join indexes may be pruned. This is because horizontal partitioning and bitmap join indexes compete for the same resource representing selection attributes of dimension tables.

---

[2] Fragmentation schema of a table is the result of partitioning process.

[3] A fragmentation attribute is an attribute participating in the fragmentation process.

This paper is divided in seven sections: Section 2 reviews the problem of select-ing horizontal partitioning schema for a given data warehouse, its complexity its advantages and drawbacks. Section 3 reviews the problem of selecting bitmap join indexes (BJIs) and its formalization as an optimization problem. Section 4 shows the strong similarities between bitmap join indexes and horizontal partitioning by con-sidering an example. Section 5 proposes our approach (HP&BJI) that combines hor-izontal partitioning and BJIs in order to reduce query processing cost and minimize storage and maintenance costs. Section 6 gives the experimental results comparing different optimization approaches using a mathematical cost model. A validation of our findings is done using Oracle10g with data of an adaptation of the APB-1 benchmark. Section 7 concludes the paper by summarizing the main results and suggesting future work.

10.2 Data Partitioning

Data partitioning [4] is an important aspect of physical database design and in fa-cilitating *manageability* process of very large databases [22, 20]. In the context of relational data warehouses, it allows tables, indexes and materialized views to be partitioned into disjoint sets of rows and columns that are physically stored and accessed separately [20]. Two main types of data partitioning are available [19]: vertical and horizontal partitioning. Vertical partitioning allows tables and mate-rialized views to be decomposed into disjoint sets of columns. Note that the key columns are duplicated in each vertical fragment to allow "reconstruction" of an original table (that's why it is considered as a redundant optimization technique). Vertical partitioning has been used for selecting materialized views. [11] proposed an approach for materializing views in vertical fragments, each including a subset of measures possibly taken from different cubes, aggregated on the same grouping set. This approach may unify two or more views into a single fragment.

On the other hand, horizontal partitioning allows tables, materialized views and indexes to be decomposed into disjoint sets of rows (called fragments) physically stored and usually accessed separately. Contrary to redundant structures, horizontal partitioning does not replicate data, thereby reducing storage requirement and min-imizing maintenance overhead. Most of today's commercial database systems offer native DDL (data definition language) support for defining horizontal partitions of a table [20].

There are two versions of horizontal partitioning [19]: *primary* and *derived*. Pri-mary horizontal partitioning of a relation is performed using attributes defined on that relation. This fragmentation may reduce query processing cost of selections. Derived horizontal partitioning, on the other hand, is the fragmentation of a relation using attribute(s) defined on another relation(s). In other word, the derived horizon-tal partitioning of a table is based on the fragmentation schema of another table(s)

---

[4] We use fragmentation and partitioning words interchangeably.

[5]. The derived partitioning of a table R based on the fragmentation schema of S is feasible if and only if there is a join link between R and S (R contains a foreigner key of S). Derived horizontal partitioning optimizes joins [3]. Therefore, horizontal partitioning is a serious candidate for optimizing star join queries (characterized by selection and join operations) using *partition elimination* [22]: if a query includes a partition key as a predicate in the WHERE clause, the query optimizer will automatically route the query to only relevant partitions.

Recall that horizontal partitioning is supported by most of commercial database systems. The first horizontal partitioning mode supported by Oracle was *Range* partitioning (in Oracle 8). It is defined by a tuple (c, V), where c is a column type and V is an ordered sequence of values from the domain of c. In Range partitioning, an access path (table, view, index) is split according to a range of values of a given set of columns. Oracle 9 and 9i added other modes, like Hash, List and Composite (Range-Hash, Range-List). Hash mode decomposes data according to a hash function (provided by the system) applied to the values of the partitioning columns. List partitioning splits a table according list values of a column. The point fragmentation may be performed using List mode. Composite partitioning is supposed by using PARTITION - SUBPARTITION statement [6]. Range, List and Hash are the *basic methods* supported by most of commercial database systems. [23] did not consider composite partitioning which is a strong limitation of their work.

Recently, Oracle 11g offers a great evolution of horizontal partitioning, where several fragmentation modes were supported. For instance, the Composite partitioning method has been enriched to include all possible combinations of basic methods: List-List, Range-Range, List-Range, List-Hash, etc. Two other interesting modes were supported: (1) *Virtual Column partitioning*, where a table is decomposed using a virtual attribute defined by an expression, using one or more existing columns of a table, and storing this expression as meta data only and (2) *Referential partitioning* that allows to partition a table by leveraging an existing parent-child relationship [22]. This partitioning is similar to derived horizontal partitioning. But, it can be applied using *only one table*.

10.2.1 Methodology to Horizontal Partition Relational Data Warehouse

In the context of relational data warehouses, we proposed in [2], a methodology to partition different tables of star schema (dimension and fact):

1. Partition some/all dimension tables using the primary horizontal partitioning and then

---

[5] the fragmentation schema is the result of the partitioning process of a given table

[6] These modes are also supported by other commercial databases like SQL Server, Sybase, DB2, etc.

2. Partition the facts table using the fragmentation schemas of the fragmented dimension tables. This methodology takes into consideration the *star join queries requirements*, but it may generate an important number of horizontal fragments of the fact table (denoted by N) $N = \prod_{i=1}^{g} m_i$, where m_i and g are the number of fragments of the dimension table D_i and the number of dimension tables participating in the fragmentation process, respectively. This fragmentation technique generates a large number of fragments of the fact table. For example, suppose we have: *Customer* dimension table partitioned into 50 fragments using the State attribute [7], *Time* into 36 fragments using the Month attribute, and *Product* into 80 fragments using Package_type attribute, therefore the fact table will be fragmented into 144 000 fragments ($50 \times 36 \times 80$). Consequently, instead of managing one star schema, we will manage 144 000 sub star schemas. It will be very hard for DBA to maintain all these sub-star schemas.

To ovoid the explosion of this number, we formalize the problem of selecting horizontal partitioning schema as an optimization problem [2]: Given a representative workload $Q = \{Q_1, Q_2, ..., Q_n\}$ defined on a data warehouse schema $\{D_1, ..., D_d, F\}$, and a constraint (maintenance bound W) representing the number of sub star schemas (fragments) that DBA can maintain, horizontal partitioning selection consists in identifying dimension table(s) used for derived fragmenting the fact table F into N fragments, such that $\sum_{Q_j \in Q} f_{Q_j} \times Cost(Q_j)$ is minimized and $N \leq M$, where f_{Q_j} and $Cost(Q_j)$ represent the access frequency of the query Q_j and the cost of evaluating Q_j, respectively.

10.2.2 Horizontal Partitioning Selection Process

Note that every fragmentation algorithm needs application information defined on the tables that have to be partitioned. The information is divided into two categories [19]: quantitative and qualitative. Quantitative information gives the selectivity factors of selection predicates and the frequencies of queries accessing these tables ($Q = \{Q_1, ..., Q_n\}$). Qualitative information gives the selection predicates defined on dimension tables. Before performing fragmentation, the following tasks should be done [2]:

1. Extraction of all simple predicates defined on dimension tables used by the n queries,

2. Assignment to each dimension table $D_i (1 \leq i \leq d)$, its set of simple predicates ($SSPD_i$),

---

[7] case of 50 states in the U.S.A.

3. Each dimension table D_i having $SSPD_i = \phi$ cannot participate on the partitioning process. Let $D_{candidate}$ be the set of dimension tables having a non-empty $SSPD_i$. Let g be the cardinality of $D_{candidate}$ $(g \leq d)$,

4. Use the COM_MIN algorithm [19] to each dimension table D_i of $D_{candidate}$. Completeness and minimality states that a relation is partitioned into at least two fragments which are accessed differently by at least one application [19]. This algorithm takes a set of simple predicates and then generates a set of complete and minimal predicates.

The fragmentation of each dimension table D_j in $D_{candidate}$ is based on partitioning domain of each selection attribute of D_j. To illustrate this domain partitioning, suppose that the domain values of attributes *Age* and *Gender* of dimension table *CUSTOMER* and *Season* of dimension table *TIME* are:
Dom(Age) =]0, 120], Dom(Gender) = {'M', 'F'}, and Dom(Season) = {"Summer", "Spring", "Autumn", "Winter"}. We assume that DBA splits domains of these attributes into sub domains as follows:
$Dom(Age) = d_{11} \cup d_{12} \cup d_{13}$, with $d_{11} =]0, 18]$, $d_{12} =]18, 60[$, $d_{13} = [60, 120]$.
$Dom(Gender) = d_{21} \cup d_{22}$, with $d_{21} = \{'M'\}$, $d_{22} = \{'F'\}$. $Dom(Season) = d_{31} \cup d_{32} \cup d_{33} \cup d_{34}$, where $d_{31} = \{"Summer"\}$, $d_{32} = \{"Spring"\}$, $d_{33} = \{"Autumn"\}$, and $d_{34} = \{"Winter"\}$.
Different sub domains of all three fragmentation attributes are represented in Figure 10.1.

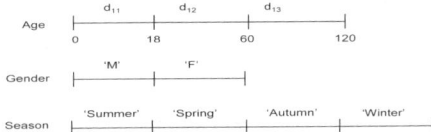

Fig. 10.1 An Example of Sub domains

10.2.3 Coding Fragmentation Schema

Domain partitioning of different fragmentation attributes may be represented by multidimensional arrays, where each array represents the domain partitioning of a fragmentation attribute. The value of each cell of a given array representing an attribute $A_i^{D_k}$ belongs to $[1..n_i]$, where n_i represents the number of sub domain of the attribute $A_i^{D_k}$. Based on this representation, fragmentation schema of each table is generated as follows: (1) If all cells of a given attribute have the different values this means that all sub domains will be considered in partitioning of corresponding dimension table. (2) If all cells for a given attribute have the same value this means that the attribute will not participate in the fragmentation process. (3) If some cells of a given attribute have the same value then their corresponding sub domains will be merged into one. The merged cells shrink their associated sub domains. The obtained sub domain is called a *merged sub domain*. Table 10.1 gives an example

Table 10.1 An example of Coding of Partitioning Schema

Gender	1	2		
Season	1	2	3	3
Age	1	1	2	

of coding of a fragmentation schema based on three attributes Gender, Season and Age.

Therefore, the dimension table CUSTOMER will be split using Age and Gender and TIME using Season. To materialize this fragmentation, DBA uses the following statements in order to create CUSTOMER and TIME tables.

```
CREATE TABLE CUSTOMER
(CID NUMBER,  Name Varchar2(20), Gender CHAR, Age Number)
PARTITION BY RANGE (Age)
SUBPARTITION BY LIST (Gender)
SUBPARTITION TEMPLATE (SUBPARTITION Female VALUES ('F'),
SUBPARTITION Male VALUES ('M'))
(PARTITION Cust_0_60 VALUES LESS THAN (60),
PARTITION Cust_60_120 VALUES LESS THAN (MAXVALUE));

CREATE TABLE TIME
(TID  NUMBER, Season VARCHAR2(10), Year    Number)
PARTITION BY LIST(Season)
(PARTITION Time_Summer VALUES('Summer'),
PARTITION Time_Spring VALUES ('Spring'),
PARTITION Time_Autumn_Winter VALUES('Automn', 'Winter'));
```

Since, the CUSTOMER and TIME have been partitioned into 4 and 3 fragments, respectively; fact table is then partitioned into 12 partitions.

10.2.4 Limitation of the Proposed Coding

The above coding suffers from multi-instantiation, where a fragmentation schema may be represented by multiple codings. In order to illustrate this problem, we consider the following example. Figure 10.2 shows two different codings, but in reality they refer to the same fragmentation schema. In Figure 10.2 (a), the fragmentation attributes Gender, Season and Age are decomposed as follows: Gender is decomposed into 2 sub domains, Season into 2 sub domains and 1 merge sub domain and Age into 1 one merged sub domain and 1 sub domain. The coding in Figure 10.2(b) has the same decomposition of the previous one, expect its coding has different numberings regarding the sub domains and the merged sub domains.

This problem can be solved using Restricted Growth Functions [26]. Let [n] be a set $\{1, \cdots, n\}$, a restricted growth function is a function $f : [n] \to [n]$ such that:
$$f(1) = 0$$

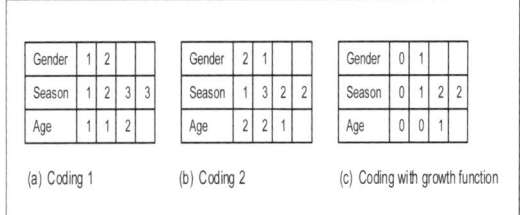

Gender	1	2		
Season	1	2	3	3
Age		1	1	2

(a) Coding 1

Gender	2	1		
Season	1	3	2	2
Age	2	2	1	

(b) Coding 2

Gender	0	1		
Season	0	1	2	2
Age	0	0	1	

(c) Coding with growth function

Fig. 10.2 Multi-instantiation of the coding

$$f(i+1) \leq max\{f(1), \cdots, f(i)\} + 1.$$

$f(i)$ defines the subset index where the item i belongs to.

This function is applied to domain partition of each fragmentation attribute. For instance, the application of the growth function to codings described in Figure 10.2(a,b) is given in Figure 10.2(c).

10.2.5 Effect of Horizontal Partitioning on Queries

After selecting horizontal partitioning schema of the data warehouse, each global query having conjunction of selection predicates G must be rewritten on horizontal fragments. Each one is defined by a conjunction of predicates P [8]. Three scenarios are possible to rewrite the query on the fragments [13]: (a) *no rewriting*: where $P \wedge G$ is *unsatisfiable*, implying that the fragment will not contribute to the answer to the query, (b) *perfect rewriting*: where $P \rightarrow G$, implying that the whole fragment will be in the answer to the query and (c) *partial rewriting*: neither P *contradicts* G nor P *implies* G, implying that there may exist tuples in the fragment that will contribute to the answer to the query. Queries having no rewriting and partial rewriting need other optimization techniques (BJIs or materialized views) to improve their performance.

10.3 Bitmap Join Indexes

Bitmap index is probably the most important result obtained in the data warehouse physical optimization field [10]. The bitmap index is more suitable for attributes having a reasonable cardinality, since its size strictly depends on the number of distinct values of the column on which it is built. Bitmap join indexes (BJIs) are proposed to speed up join operations. In its simplest form, it can be defined as a bitmap index on a table R *based on column(s) of another table S*, where S commonly joins with R in a specific way. A bitmap is a vector of bits whose value depends on predicate values. A bitmap B lists all rows with a given predicate P such that for

---

[8] This process is called, the localization of the fragments, in the context of the distributed databases [19].

each row r with ordinal number j that satisfies the predicate P, the jth bit in B is set to 1. Bitmaps represent efficiently low-cardinality data. However to make this indexing scheme practical for high-cardinality data, compression techniques must be used. Value-list indexes have been shown in [18] to outperform other access methods in queries involving MIN or MAX aggregate functions, as well as queries that compute percentile values of a given column. Bitmap indexes can substantially improve performance of queries with the following characteristics [7]:

- The WHERE clause contains multiple predicates on low-or-medium-cardinality columns (e.g., a predicate on Gender that has two possible values: female or male or a predicate on city with three possible values).
- Bitmap indexes have been created on some or all of these low-or-medium-cardinality columns.

Besides disk saving (due to the binary representation and possible compression [15]), bitmap indexes speed up queries having Boolean operations (such as AND, OR and NOT) and COUNT operations. They are supported by most of commercial DBMSs (Oracle, SQL Server, etc.).

As indicated earlier, a BJI is defined on one or several non key dimension attributes with low cardinality [9] (called indexable columns) for joining dimension tables with the fact table. An indexable attribute A_j of a given dimension table D_i for a BJI is a column $D_i.A_j$ such that there is a condition of the form $D_i.A_j \ \theta \ Expression$ in the WHERE clause. The operator θ must be among $\{=,<,>,\leq,\geq\}$.

10.3.1 Complexity Study of Selecting BJIs

Let $A = \{A_1, A_2, \cdots, A_K\}$ be the set of indexed candidate attributes for BJIs. Then, the possible number of BJIs with *only one* group of attributes, grows exponentially with K, and is given by:

$$\binom{K}{1} + \binom{K}{2} + ... + \binom{K}{K} = 2^K - 1 \qquad (10.1)$$

For $K = 4$, this number is 15. The possible number of BJIs with any combination of attribute groups is given by:

$$\binom{2^K - 1}{1} + \binom{2^K - 1}{2} + ... + \binom{2^K - 1}{2^K - 1} = 2^{2^K - 1} \qquad (10.2)$$

For $K = 4$, the number of possible cases is (2^{15}). Therefore, the problem of efficiently finding the set of BJIs that minimizes the total query processing cost while satisfying a storage constraint cannot be handled by first enumerating all possible BJIs and then computing the query cost for each candidate BJI.

---

[9] The domain of this attribute should be an enumerated domain like *gender*, *color*, etc.

10.3.2 Formulation of BJI Selection Problem

Due to the high complexity of BJI selection problem, we formalize it as an optimization problem with constraint as follows:

Given a data warehouse with a set of dimension tables $D = \{D_1, D_2, ..., D_d\}$ and a fact table F, a workload Q of queries $Q = \{Q_1, Q_2, ..., Q_n\}$, where each query Q_i $(1 \leq i \leq n)$ has an access frequency, and a storage constraint S, the aim of BJI selection problem is to find a set of BJIs among a pre-computed subset of all possible candidates, which minimizes the query processing cost and satisfies the storage requirements S.

To the best of our knowledge, only two algorithms were proposed to select BJIs [1, 5]. These algorithms were based on data mining techniques. The main idea behind these algorithms is to compute the set of frequent closed indexable attribute groups rather than all the possible combinations indicated above. The groups generated in the pruning step are then used in the second step to select the final configuration of indexes (for more details refer to [1, 5]). These algorithms consider all indexable attribute candidates and did not reduce the search space of the BJI selection problem as we do in this paper.

10.4 Identification of Similarity between Horizontal Partitioning and BJIs

To illustrate the similarity between horizontal partitioning and BJIs, we consider the following scenario that serves as a running example along this paper. Suppose we have a data warehouse represented by three dimension tables (TIME, CUSTOMER and PRODUCT) and one fact table (SALES). The population of this schema is given in Figure 10.3. The following query is executed on this schema.

```
SELECT Count(*)
FROM CUSTOMER C, PRODUCT P, TIME T, SALES S
WHEERE C.City='Poitiers'
AND P.Range='Beauty'
AND T.Month='June'
AND P.PID=S.PID AND C.CID=S.CID AND T.TID=S.TID
```

This query has three selection predicates defined on dimension table attributes *City*, *Range* and *Month* and three join operations. These selection attributes will be candidate for decomposing the data warehouse schema and defining BJIs. To optimize the above query, three main modes are available: (i) the use of horizontal partitioning (called HPFIRST), (ii) the use of BJIs (called, BJIFIRST) and (iii) mixed mode (called, HP+BJI) that combines both techniques.

HPFIRST: The database administrator (DBA) may derived partitioned the fact table SALES using fragmentation schemas of dimension tables: CUSTOMER, TIME and PRODUCT based on attributes *City*, *Month*, *Range*, respectively.

C_RID	CID	Name	City
6	616	Gilles	Poitiers
5	515	Yves	Paris
4	414	Patrick	Nantes
3	313	Didier	Nantes
2	212	Eric	Poitiers
1	111	Pascal	Poitiers

Customer

P_RID	PID	Name	Range
6	106	Sonoflore	Beauty
5	105	Clarins	Beauty
4	104	WebCam	Multimedia
3	103	Barbie	Toys
2	102	manure	Gardening
1	101	SlimForm	Fitness

Product

T_RID	TID	Month	Year
6	11	January	2003
5	22	February	2003
4	33	March	2003
3	44	April	2003
2	55	May	2003
1	66	June	2003

Time

S_RID	CID	PID	TID	Amount
1	616	106	11	25
2	616	106	66	28
3	616	104	33	50
4	545	104	11	10
5	414	105	66	14
6	212	106	55	14
7	111	101	44	20
8	111	101	33	27
9	212	101	11	100
10	313	102	11	200
11	414	102	11	102
12	414	102	55	203
13	515	102	66	100
14	515	103	55	17
15	212	103	44	45
16	111	105	66	44
17	212	104	66	40
18	515	104	22	20
19	616	104	22	20
20	616	104	55	20
21	212	105	11	10
22	212	105	44	10
23	212	105	55	18
24	212	106	11	18
25	313	105	66	19
26	313	105	22	17
27	313	106	11	15

Sales

Fig. 10.3 A sample of a data warehouse population

Consequently, the fact table is fragmented in 90 fragments [10], where each fact fragment $Sales_i$ $(1 \leq i \leq 90)$ is defined as follows:

$$Sales\_i = SALES \ltimes CUSTOMER_j \ltimes TIME_k \ltimes PRODUCT_m ,$$

$(1 \leq j \leq 3)$, $(1 \leq k \leq 6)$, $(1 \leq m \leq 5)$, where $\ltimes$ represents semi-join operation Figure 10.4(c) shows the fact fragment SALES_BJP corresponding to sales of *beauty products* realized by customers living at *Poitiers* city during month of *June*. The above query is then rewritten as follows:

*SELECT Count(*) FROM SALES **PARTITION**(SALES_BJP)* [11]

To execute it, the optimizer only loads the fact fragment SALES_BJP. This mode saves three join operations, which represents a real improvement.

BJIFIRST: The DBA selects an BJI defined on three dimension attributes: *City, Month* and *Range* as follows:

```
CREATE BITMAP INDEX sales_cust_city_prod_range_time_month_bjix
ON SALES(CUSTOMER.City, PRODUCT.Range, TIME.Month)
FROM SALES S, CUSTOMER C, TIME T, PRODUCT P
WHERE S.CID= C.CID AND S.PID=P.PID AND S.TID=T.TID
```

Figure 10.4a shows the generated BJI. To execute the above query, the optimizer just accesses the bitmaps corresponding to the columns representing *June, Beauty* and *Poitiers* and performs the AND operation (none join operation is performed).

HP+BJI: Instead of using the two optimization techniques in isolation, DBA may use them sequentially. He/she first partitions the data warehouse schema into 90 sub star schemas and then defines a BJI in each sub schema. To execute the above

---

[10] We suppose we have 3 cities, 6 months and 5 ranges of product.

[11] A Oracle Syntax is used.

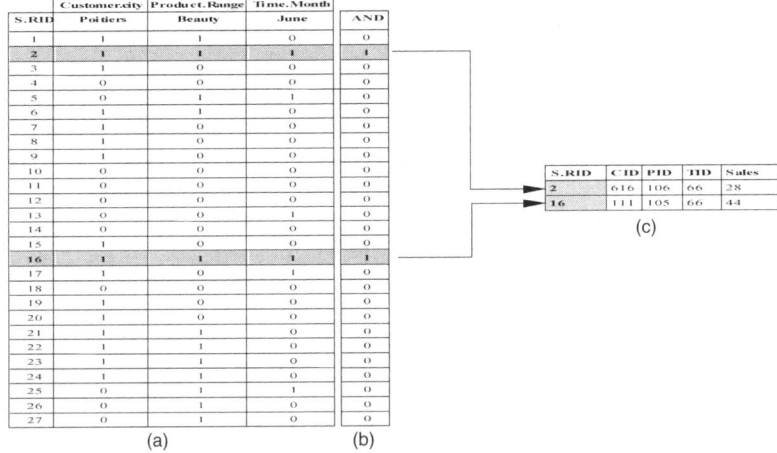

Fig. 10.4 (a) The bitmap join index (b) The result of AND operation, (c) The fact fragment

query, the optimizer accesses BJI that corresponds to the fact fragment SALES_BJP (marked by Grey rows in Figure 10.4 (a)).

Another interesting way, called HP&BJI, to combine these two optimization techniques is: partitioning the data warehouse schema and selecting BJIs only for queries that do not get benefit from partitioning. This strategy may guarantee a better performance of overall queries, reduces storage and maintenance costs required for indexes and prunes search spaces of BJI and horizontal selection problems [4].

Based on this discussion, we develop an new approach (HP&BJI) for combining horizontal partitioning and BJIs. To the best of our knowledge, our proposed work is the first article that addresses this issue.

10.5 Description of HP&BJI

Nowadays most commercial database systems support horizontal partitioning and BJIs. HP&BJI first horizontally partitions the data warehouse schema in several sub star schemas and then selects BJIs on these schemas. This method is more feasible, since horizontal partitioning preserves the schema of base tables [12]. Therefore, the obtained sub star schemas may further be indexed.

---

[12] A horizontal fragment has the same schema as its original base table.

10.5.1 Formalization of the Combined Selection

Given a data warehouse with a set of dimension tables $D = \{D_1, D_2, ..., D_d\}$ and a fact table F, a workload Q of queries $Q = \{Q_1, Q_2, ..., Q_n\}$, where each query Q_i $(1 \leq i \leq n)$ has an access frequency, a storage constraint S, threshold W representing the number of generated fragments. The aim of our problem is to partition the warehouse into N ($N \leq W$) sub schemas and to select BJIs such as the query processing cost is minimized and the storage requirement S is satisfied.

To deal with this problem, we propose the following methodology:

1. Enumeration of the set of all dimension attributes (*DA*) defined by selection predicates of queries: This set will be shared by horizontal partitioning and BJI algorithms.
2. Generation of complete and minimal set of dimension attributes *CMDA*: The predicates used for generating horizontal fragments shall be minimal and complete (see Section 2). The Completeness and minimality rule prunes the number of dimension attributes participating on the fragmentation process (*CMDA* $\subseteq$ *DA*).
3. Fragmentation of data warehouse schema: This partitioning is done using our genetic algorithm [3]. It starts with a set of queries $Q = \{Q_1, Q_2, \cdots, Q_n\}$, a maintenance bound W and *CMDA*. The obtained partitioning schema is defined on a subset of dimension attributes *CMDA*, denoted by *FASET* (*FASET* $\subseteq$ *CMDA*).
4. Identification of profitable queries: The generated fragments may not be benefit for all queries. In order to identify queries getting benefit from horizontal partitioning, we define the following metric for each query Q_j:

$$rate(Q_j) = \frac{C[Q_j, FS]}{C[Q_j, \phi]} \tag{10.3}$$

where $C[Q_j, FS]$ and $C[Q_j, \phi]$ represent the cost of executing the query Q_j on un-partitioned data warehouse and partitioned schema FS, respectively. The DBA has the right to set up this rate using a threshold λ as follows:

If $rate(Q_j) \leq \lambda$ then Q_j is a profitable query, otherwise no profitable query.

5. Identification of indexable attribute candidates: In order to ensure a high performance of overall queries, BJIs shall be selected. This selection is done by *considering only no profitable queries* $Q^{nobenefit} = \{Q'_1, Q'_2, \cdots, Q'_l\}$. Based on this set of queries, indexable attribute candidates are identified (*ABJI*). This set should be purified from fragmentation attributes. After this purification, we get a new set of real candidates for indexing, that we call *BJISET* (*BJISET* = *ABJI* − *FASET*).

The architecture of our approach is summarized in Figure 10.5.

Example 10.1. To understand our approach, let us consider the scenario based on our motivating example (section 4), where HPFIRST generates 90 fact fragments. Assume that DBA wants to fragment the database in only 18 fragments ($W = 18$).

In this case, we obtain a fragmentation schema defined on dimension attributes *City* and *Month* (*FASET* = {*Month,City*}). Consequently, the attribute *Range* of PROD-UCT is not taken in the fragmentation process (*BJISET* = {*Beauty*}). To speed up the whole queries, DBA may define a BJI on *Range*. This BJI is defined on each sub star schema.

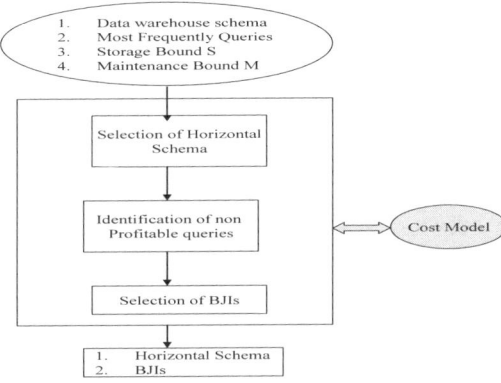

Fig. 10.5 Architecture of the proposed solution

10.5.2 Genetic Algorithm for Selecting Horizontal Schema

To select horizontal partitioning schema, we extend the genetic algorithm proposed in [2]. This extension concerns the use of restricted growth functions in order to reduce the time execution of this algorithm. An outline of this algorithm is as follows:

> Generate initial population ;
> Perform selection step;
> **while** stopping criterion not met **do**
> > Perform crossover step;
> > Perform mutation step;
> > Perform selection step ;
> end while.

For more details see [2, 3]. The quality of each generated solution is obtained using a cost model computing the number of inputs outputs required for executing the set of queries [2].

10.5.3 Greedy Algorithm for Generating BJIs

To select BJIs, we use a greedy algorithm. It is based on a mathematical cost models: one for estimating the number of inputs outputs required for executing queries using

BJIs and another one for estimating storage cost required for selected BJIs. These models adapted from those proposed by Aouiche et al. [1]. Our greedy algorithm starts with a configuration having a BJI defined on one attribute (of *BJISET*) having a smallest cardinality (let say, I_{min}), and iteratively improves the initial configuration, by adding other BJIs, until no further reduction in total query processing cost and no violation of the storage bound. Details of the algorithm are given in Algorithm 1.

Algorithm 5: Greedy Algorithm for BJIs Selection

---

1 **Inputs:** Set of non profitable queries: $Q^{noprofit} = \{Q'_1, Q'_2, \cdots, Q'_l\}$, *BJIASET*, *S*.
2 BJI_j: Bitmap join index defined on attribute A_j. $Size(BJI_j)$: storage cost of BJI_j
3 $C[Q', HPFIRST]$: cost of executing Q' using HPFIRST
4 **Output:** $Config_{finale}$: set of selected BJIs.
5 **begin**
6        $Config_{finale} = BJI_{min}$;
7        $S := S - Size(BJI_{min})$;
8        $BJISET := BJISET - A_{min}$; A_{min} is the attribute used to defined BJI_{min}
9   WHILE $(Size(Config_{finale}) \leq S)$ DO
10   FOR each $A_j \in BJISET$ DO
11   IF $(C[Q', (Config_{finale} \cup BJI_j))] < C[Q', HPFIRST])$
12   AND $((Size(Config_{finale} \cup BJI_j) \leq S))$ THEN
13                     $Config_{finale} := Config_{finale} \cup BJI_j$;
14                     $Size(Config_{finale}) := Size(Config_{finale}) + Size(BJI_j)$;
15                     $BJISET := BJISET - A_j$;
16 **end**

10.6 Experimental Studies

We have conducted an intensive experimental studies following two scenarios: (1) an evaluation of the four approaches (a) without optimization technique (called, NoneOP), (b) HPFIRST, (c) BJIFIRST and (d) HP&BJI. This evaluation is done using a mathematical cost model estimating the number of inputs outputs required for executing a set of queries and (2) a validation of the obtained solutions using APB benchmark dataset on ORACLE10g.

Dataset: We use the dataset from the APB1 benchmark[8]. Its star schema has one fact table Actvars and four dimension tables: Actvars(24 786 000 tuples), Prodlevel (9 000 tuples), Custlevel (900 tuples), Timelevel (24 tuples) and Chanlevel (9 tuples).

Workload: We have considered a workload of 55 single block queries (i.e., no nested subqueries) with 40 selection predicates defined on 9 different attributes: *ClassLevel, GroupLevel, FamilyLevel, LineLevel, DivisionLevel, YearLevel, MonthLevel, RetailerLevel, AllLevel*. The domains of these attributes are split into: 4, 2, 5, 2, 4, 2, 12, 4, 5 sub domains, respectively. Several classes of queries are considered:

15 queries with count operations (without aggregations), 16 with sum(), 11 with avg(), 6 with min() and 7 with max(). Each used selection predicate has a selectivity factor computed on the real data warehouse population. In our experimental studies, we did not consider update queries (update and delete operations).

Our algorithms have been implemented using Visual C++ performed under a Intel Centrino with a memory of 1 Gb and ORACLE 10g.

Set up of Genetic Algorithm : We have conducted many experimental studies to set up different parameters for the genetic algorithm (number of generations, mutation rate, cross over rate). Due to the stochastic nature of the genetic algorithm, we have executed several times each heuristic we consider the average. The values of these parameters are: *number of chromosomes = 40, number of generations = 400, crossover rate = 85, mutation rate = 5.*

10.6.1 Evaluation of four Optimization Approaches

In first experiments, we compare HPFIRST and BJIFIRST approaches. The maintenance constraint used by our horizontal partitioning algorithm is 100 ($W = 100$). Figure 10.6 shows performance in terms of cost of evaluating all queries (55), by varying storage capacity from 20 to 200 Mb. We observe that HPFIRST outperforms the BJIFIRST when the storage bound is between 20 Mb and 80 Mb. But, when we assign more storage, BJIs outperforms better, especially for *15 COUNT() queries.* This is because count() queries without aggregation do do access the fact table. This experiment is very interesting since it gives recommendations to DBA to well administrate his/her warehouse. If most of the queries have count operations without aggregations, it will better to use only BJIs.

Figure 10.7 shows the performance of horizontal partitioning when its maintenance constraint is relaxed. BJIs are selected according 200 Mb. Increasing the maintenance constraint means that a large number of dimension attributes will participate in the fragmentation process. Consequently, most queries will get benefit from the horizontal partitioning. In this case, the HPFIRST becomes interesting for the overall queries.

In order to evaluate our combined approach (HP&BJI), we consider the following scenario: We use genetic algorithm with a threshold $W = 100$ and $\lambda = 0.6$ in order to identify queries getting benefit from horizontal partitioning. As result, only 18 queries are no profitable among 55 queries (37 profitable). The attributes used in the obtained fragmentation schema five: ClassLevel, FamilyLevel, MonthLevel, AllLevel and RetailerLevel. These attributes will not be used by our greedy algorithm which uses the remaining 4 (GroupLevel, LineLevel, DivisionLevel, YearLevel). In this case, greedy algorithm is executed using 18 no profitable queries and 200 Mb as storage bound. As result, three BJIs are selected.

Figure 10.8 shows the performance of each approach. Our approach outperforms the two optimization approaches (NoneOP and HPFIRST), but it slightly outperforms BJIFIRST. This is due to the large number of count queries without aggrega-

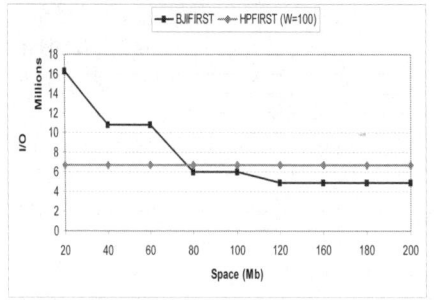

Fig. 10.6 HPFIRST vs. BJIFIRST(*S*)   **Fig. 10.7** BJIFIRST vs. HPFIRST(*W*)

tions, where BJIs are very efficient. Another interesting result is that HP&BJI saves storage cost, i.e., BJIFIRST needs 114 Mb for storing different BJIs and HP&BJI needs only 63 Mb which represents 50% of storage saving.

We conduct another experiment in order to study the effect of varying storage bound on performance of our approach. This storage is varied from 0 (where none BJI is selected) to 950 Mb (all BJIs candidates can be selected). We compare HP&BJI and HPFIRST (with $W = 100$). Figure 10.9 recapitulates the obtained results. HP&BJI outperforms HPFIRST since all candidate indexes are selected.

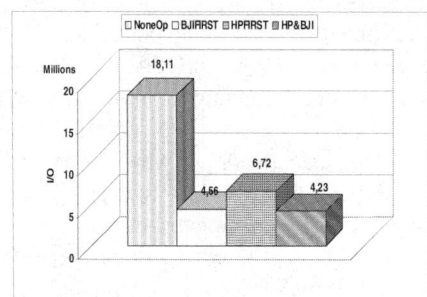

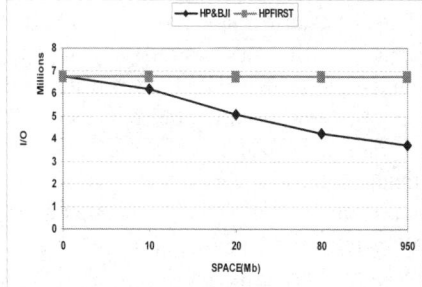

Fig. 10.8 Quality of HP&BJI   **Fig. 10.9** HP&BJI vs. storage

Performance of HP&BJI strongly depends on the choice of λ that determinates profitable and no profitable queries. To measure the impact of this parameter, we conduct an experiment by varying it from 0 (all queries are non profitable) to 1 (all queries are profitable). Figure 10.10 shows that: when λ is equal 0, HP&BJI reduces the cost obtained by HPFIRST by 25 % by assigning **950** Mb to selected BJIs. When it reaches 1, its performance is equal to HPFIRST (none index is created). This experiment shows the great importance of this parameter during the physical design. It is a real tool for well tuning the warehouse. To understand its real effect, some future experiments are required by having a fine variation of λ.

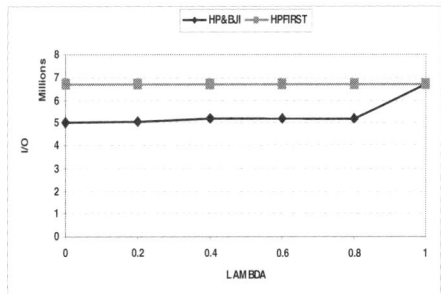

Fig. 10.10 Effect of lambda on performance

10.6.2 Validation on ORACLE10g

To validate our approach, we carried out an implementation under Oracle 10g using the DataSet from the benchmark Apb-1 release II. By using the generation files supplied by this benchmark, the data warehouse schema on ORACLE10g is created and populated. The architecture and details of our implementation are described in Figure 10.11.

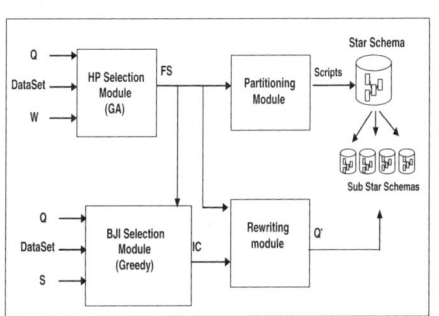

Fig. 10.11 Architecture of our Validation Tool

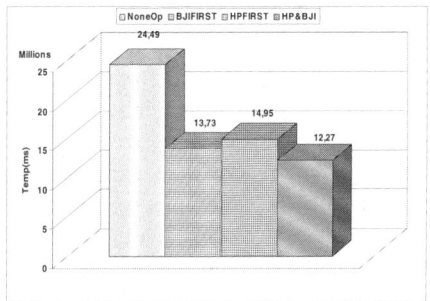

Fig. 10.12 Validation of the proposed approaches on Oracle10g

This architecture has four components: horizontal partitioning selection module, BJI selection module, partitioning module and rewriting module.

1. *Horizontal partitioning selection module (HPSM)*: this module receives a set of queries, a data warehouse schema and the maintenance constraint (*W*). It generates a partitioning schema using our genetic algorithm.

2. *BJI Selection Module (BJISM):* it receives a partitioned or non partitioned data warehouse schema, a set of queries and storage bound. It generates a configuration of BJIs (using greedy algorithm).

3. *Partitioning Module (PM):* PM receives a fragmentation schema *FS* generated by HPSM and then generates two types of scripts to partition the data ware-

house: the first ones for fragmenting dimension tables and the second for de-composing the fact table.

4. *Rewriting Module (RM):* this module receives a fragmentation schema FS and/or a configuration of BJI (IC) and a set of queries. It rewrites all queries on FS and IC. To rewrite a query Q_j on FS, an identification of valid sub star schemas is required. To rewrite Q_j on IC, Hints are used to force Oracle10g optimizer to use these indexes [13].

To make sure that query optimizer uses BJI, we check using *Explain Plan tool* of Oracle.

Implementation of Primary and Derived Partitioning : Recall that there are two types of tables to be fragmented: dimension and fact. Dimension tables may be partitioned using the primary fragmentation supported by main commercial database systems. But, it allows table to be partitioned only on one or two attributes using different partitioning modes: List, Range and Hash methods (for one attribute) and composite (for two attributes). Since our fragmentation algorithm may generate partitioning schema with more than two attributes per table, it is necessary to provide solution for generating this kind of partitioning. To do so, we have developed the following implementation: We add an additional column Col_i in each fragmented dimension table D_i. To fulfil this column, we generate a PLSQL script assigning a value of each instance of this table representing the number of fragment owning this instance. Finally, we partition the dimension table D_i using List method on that attribute.

Recently, Oracle11g proposes a new method for derived partitioning a table based on only one other table (see Section 2) which represents a real limitation for our case study. Therefore, we propose a new implementation to simulate this partitioning: We create a new column CF in the fact table. The value of each instance of this column is computed by concatenating different Col_i values of fragmented dimension tables. This solution may be implemented using a materialized view as shown in the following example:

```
CREATE MATERIALIZED VIEW alljoin
BUILD IMMEDIATE
AS
SELECT a.customer_level, a.product_level,a.channel_level,
a.time_level,a.unitssold, a.dollarsales, a.dollarcost,
prod_col||'-'||time_col||'-'||cust_col as   CF
FROM actvars a, prodlevel p, custlevel c, timelevel t
WHERE a.customer_level = c.store_level
AND a.product_level =   p.code_level
AND a.time_level = t.tid
```

In order to validate our approach on ORACLE10g, we use the same dataset and queries used by theoretical. To compute the real time required for executing each query, we use Aqua Data Studio (http://www.aquafold.com). This time is multiplied its access frequency. HPFIRST is executed with a maintenance constraint equal to

---

[13] The syntax of a hint using indexes is: SELECT /*+ INDEX (table [index], [index], ... [index]]) */...

100. The obtained fragmented schema has 96 sub star schemas using five attributes (see Section 6.1). The global schema is then partitioned using the resulting schema obtained by HPFIRST. All global queries are rewritten using RM. BJIFIRST using its greedy algorithm generates nine indexes, where each index is defined on one attribute. The theoretical storage cost required for these BJI is 3.5 Gb. All queries are executed using the selected BJIs using Hints. Finally, HP&BJI uses the fragmentation schema obtained by HPFIRST and generates indexes on no profitable queries (where λ is fixed to 0.6) with a storage capacity equal to 1 Gb. Four BJIs are selected (each BJI is defined on each indexable attribute). We execute all queries, where RM rewrites each query using its relevant optimization technique [14]. Buffer is emptying after each query execution.

Figure 10.12 shows the main results which are *quite similar* to those obtained by our theoretical studies. HP&BJI outperforms different approaches and saves 2.5 Gb of storage space. This space could be used for generating other redundant techniques like materialized views. BJIFIRST outperforms HPFIRST for the same reasons relied in Section 6.1 (presence of count queries without aggregations).

10.7 Conclusion

Data warehouses have grown very large in size and accessed with complex queries having several joins, selections and aggregations. To optimize these queries, several techniques were proposed and supported by most commercial database systems. A classification of these techniques into two main categories: redundant and non redundant techniques were proposed. In this paper, we focus on one redundant structure (bitmap join indexes) and a non redundant (horizontal partitioning). By an example, we showed the strong similarity between them since they optimize join operations between fact table and dimension tables and both defined on dimension attributes. But horizontal partitioning does not replicate data contrary to bitmap join indexes, thereby reducing storage requirement and minimizing maintenance overhead. We have proposed a new approach to select simultaneously a horizontal partitioning schema and bitmap join indexes to optimize a set of queries. It starts by selecting a horizontal schema using a genetic algorithm, and then selects bitmap join indexes by using greedy algorithm. Index selection algorithm considers only queries that do not get profit from horizontal partitioning and eliminating fragmentation attributes. This approach prunes the search space of bitmap join selection problem and horizontal selection problem. We have conducted several experimental studies that showed the cost savings with modest storage requirements. These experiments were conducted using a mathematical cost model and validated on Oracle10g. Since derived and primary partitioning are not well supported by commercial database systems, we proposed two techniques implementing these two types of fragmentation. Our approach can be easily incorporated in existing physical database design.

---

[14] Profitable queries are first rewritten on then executed on fragments. Non profitable queries are first rewritten on fragments and then executed using Hints with BJIs

It may also be used as a tool for well *administrating* and *tuning* the data warehouse, by setting up the value of λ in order to favourite horizontal partitioning, bitmap join index or combine them.

Currently, we are working on the problem of allocating generated fragments and bitmap join indexes in the parallel data warehouse machine.

References

1. K. Aouiche, O. Boussaid, and F. Bentayeb. Automatic Selection of Bitmap Join Indexes in Data Warehouses. *7th International Conference on Data Warehousing and Knowledge Discovery (DAWAK 05)*, August 2005.
2. L. Bellatreche and K. Boukhalfa. An evolutionary approach to schema partitioning selection in a data warehouse environment. *Proceeding of the International Conference on Data Warehousing and Knowledge Discovery (DAWAK'2005)*, pages 115–125, August 2005.
3. L. Bellatreche, K. Boukhalfa, and H. I. Abdalla. Saga: A combination of genetic and simulated annealing algorithms for physical data warehouse design. *in 23rd British National Conference on Databases*, pages 212–219, 2006.
4. L. Bellatreche, K. Boukhalfa, and M. K. Mohania. Pruning search space of physical database design. In *18 International Conference on Database and Expert Systems Applications (DEXA'07)*, pages 479–488, 2007.
5. L. Bellatreche, R. Missaoui, H. Necir, and H. Drias. A data mining approach for selecting bitmap join indices. *Journal of Computing Science and Engineering*, 2(1):206–223, January 2008.
6. S. Chaudhuri. Index selection for databases: A hardness study and a principled heuristic solution. *IEEE Transactions on Knowledge and Data Engineering*, 16(11):1313–1323, November 2004.
7. C. Chee-Yong. Indexing techniques in decision support systems. Phd. thesis, University of Wisconsin - Madison, 1999.
8. OLAP   Council.   Apb-1   olap   benchmark,   release   ii. *http://www.olapcouncil.org/research/resrchly.htm*, 1998.
9. Philipp J. Gill. Breaking the warehouse barrier. *Oracle Magazine*, 1(IX):38–44, January/February 2000.
10. M. Golfarelli, , and E. Rizzi, S. Saltarelli. Index selection for data warehousing. *Proceedings 4th International Workshop on Design and Management of Data Warehouses (DMDW'2002), Toronto, Canada*, pages 33–42, 2002.
11. Matteo Golfarelli, Vittorio Maniezzo, and Stefano Rizzi. Materialization of fragmented views in multidimensional databases. *Data & Knowledge Engineering*, 49(3):325–351, June 2004.
12. J. Gray and D. Slutz. Data mining the sdss skyserver database. Techreport Technical Report MSR-TR-2002-01, Microsoft Research, 2002.
13. S. Guo, S. Wei, and M. A. Weiss. On satisfiability, equivalence, and implication problems involving conjunctive queries in database systems. *IEEE Transactions on Knowledge and Data Engineering*, 8(4):604–612, August 1996.
14. H. Gupta. Selection and maintenance of views in a data warehouse. Ph.d. thesis, Stanford University, September 1999.
15. T. Johnson. Performance measurements of compressed bitmap indices. *Proceedings of the International Conference on Very Large Databases*, pages 278–289, 1999.
16. W. Labio, D. Quass, and B. Adelberg. Physical database design for data warehouses. *Proceedings of the International Conference on Data Engineering (ICDE)*, 1997.
17. H. Lei and K. A. Ross. Faster joins, self-joins and multi-way joins using join indices. *Data and Knowledge Engineering*, 28(3):277–298, November 1998.

18. P. O'Neil and D. Quass. Improved query performance with variant indexes. *Proceedings of the ACM SIGMOD International Conference on Management of Data*, pages 38–49, May 1997.
19. M. T. Özsu and P. Valduriez. *Principles of Distributed Database Systems : Second Edition*. Prentice Hall, 1999.
20. A. Sanjay, V. R. Narasayya, and B. Yang. Integrating vertical and horizontal partitioning into automated physical database design. *Proceedings of the ACM SIGMOD International Conference on Management of Data*, pages 359–370, June 2004.
21. A. Sanjay, C. Surajit, and V. R. Narasayya. Automated selection of materialized views and indexes in microsoft sql server. *Proceedings of the International Conference on Very Large Databases*, pages 496–505, September 2000.
22. Oracle Data Sheet. Oracle partitioning. *White Paper: http://www.oracle.com/technology/products/bi/db/11g/*, 2007.
23. T. Stöhr, H. Märtens, and E. Rahm. Multi-dimensional database allocation for parallel data warehouses. *Proceedings of the International Conference on Very Large Databases*, pages 273–284, 2000.
24. T. Stöhr and E. Rahm. Warlock: A data allocation tool for parallel warehouses. *Proceedings of the International Conference on Very Large Databases*, pages 721–722, 2001.
25. Zohreh Asgharzadeh Talebi, Rada Chirkova, Yahya Fathi, and Matthias Stallmann. Exact and inexact methods for selecting views and indexes for olap performance improvement. *To appear in 11th International Conference on Extending Database Technology (EDBT'08)*, Mars 2008.
26. Allan Tucker, Jason Crampton, and Stephen Swift. Rgfga: An efficient representation and crossover for grouping genetic algorithms. *Evol. Comput.*, 13(4):477–499, 2005.
27. D. C. Zilio, J. Rao, S. Lightstone, G. M Lohman, A. Storm, C. Garcia-Arellano, and S. Fadden. Db2 design advisor: Integrated automatic physical database design. *Proceedings of the International Conference on Very Large Databases*, pages 1087–1097, August 2004.

Chapter 11
Cost Model for X-BR-tree

Marcin Gorawski and Marcin Bugdol

Abstract The paper proposes an analytical cost model for a structure based on the x–BR-tree index. The model evaluates the cost, meant as a number of node accesses, for spatial selection queries. Additionally, experimental results are presented, to show the accuracy of analytical estimation compared with actual results.

11.1 Introduction

Current data warehouses development requires new methods of accessing spatial data [2, 5]. For the spatial queries cost optimizers, analytical models for prediction of data access cost are essential.

In papers [3, 4] the approximated cost estimators for indexes from R-tree family are presented. They give good results for uniformly and non-uniformly distributed data. These estimators turned out to be universal enough to be the base of analytical consideration in several crucial papers [1, 6].

In case of indexes based on the hierarchical space subdivision (quadtrees), these models reveal their imperfection. They assume that the size of the indexing structure nodes depends only on the objects distribution in the space according to the R-tree specification. The quadtrees and the indexes based on them divide the space in the regular way, for this reason the resulting structure is not tightly adjusted to the distribution of the spatial objects. Within the confines of the work in the field of spatial data warehousing, mathematical expressions estimating the cost of range queries using x-BR-tree [5] were presented.

Marcin Gorawski
Institute of Computer Science, Silesian University of Technology, Akademicka 16, 44-100 Gliwice, Poland, e-mail: m.gorawski@polsl.pl

Marcin Bugdol
Institute of Computer Science, Silesian University of Technology, Akademicka 16, 44-100 Gliwice, Poland, e-mail: marcin.bugdol@polsl.pl

11.2 X-BR-tree

The x-BR-tree (External Balanced Regular Tree) presented in [5], is a structure based on hierarchical, regular decomposition of the space. It derives from the idea of the quadtrees. It brings several modifications, which extend its capabilities, what makes it more efficient and more functional structure than the quadtrees. The x-BR-tree index is a balanced structure, all the leaf nodes appear at the same level and they correspond to disk pages. Thanks to the possibility of storing in internal nodes more then four entries (which situation occurs in quadtrees), the height of the tree is decreased and particular nodes can be used more effectively.

11.2.1 X-BR-tree structure

The x-BR-tree consists of two types of nodes. To the first type belong external nodes that are the tree leaves. They contain spatial objects, which number is determined by the node capacity C. In case of a leaf's overflow, its split is performed. It goes in the following way: the leaves are recursively divided into four quarters, each time the quarter containing the highest number of objects is selected, as long as resulting regions contain more then xC or less then $(1-x)C$ objects, where $x \in (0,5;1)$ is the split threshold [5]. The value of this parameter affects the number of required subdivisions, the closer to 0.5 the value is, the more subdivisions need to be performed.

The leaf's splitting algorithm is presented below:

```
leafSplit()
BEGIN
    DO
        subdivide the region containing the highest
        number of elements on four quarters;
        search for the quarter containing the highest
        number of objects;
    WHILE (number of elements in chosen quarter < x*C
            && number of elements in chosen
            quarter > (1-x)*C)
        move nodes to the new leaf;
        parent's entries update;
END
```

It was noticed, that the x parameter value cannot be selected randomly. The example below shows a situation, when the inappropriate selection of the split threshold may cause incorrect working of leaf split algorithm. It was assumed as follows: leaf capacity is 100, split threshold x equals 0.7 and objects are uniformly distributed. If 100 objects are inserted into the leaf, then in every region which is a quarter of the initial region, the number of entries is 25. Inserting another element results in the leaf's overflow and the need of its split. The new node should not contain more than 70 (0.7*100) or less than 30 ((1-0.7)*100) entries. It can be noticed, that the algorithm does not perform the leaf's split according to presented assumptions, because the number of objects in every new region will not exceed 26. Furthermore, execution of the algorithm will cause error due to infinite loop or stack overflow in recursive calls. Basing on above argumentation, the parameter x has to fulfill the following inequality:

$$\lfloor (1-x)*C \rfloor < \frac{1}{4}C + 1, \qquad (11.1)$$

where: C – node capacity, x – split threshold, $x \in (0,5;1)$.

The second type of nodes are internal nodes. They contain entries in the form of [address, pointer], where address contains directional symbol of the region encompassed by the child nodes, and the pointer field is a reference to the child. The address is a set of directional symbols which contains the following elements: NW, NE, SW, SE and *. These elements denote the consecutive quarters of a given region and symbol * denotes the remaining region.

The address allows inserting more data in the intermediate node, because the child node can now encompass not only one quarter of the parent space, but also smaller regions. Entries are considered according to their order in the intermediate node. The child's region depends not only on its address but also on the addresses of the entries located in front of it. This child's region is determined as the difference between the space encompassed by the region of the given child and the space encompassed by the entries' (children's) regions located before in front of the given child. In case of the intermediate node's overflow, its split is performed in the following steps:

- a quadtree is built, basing on the entries in the overflowed node,
- searching for the best split place,
- moving entries to the new created node,
- updating the entries in the parent node, in case of parent node missing, creating a new internal node.

Details of these steps were described with examples in [5].

The size and shape of nodes in the x-BR-tree index result from the way of division of the work space. Unfortunately, this division can not be predicted. It depends not only on the dataset, but also on the order of inserting elements. The example below illustrates the above mentioned problem.

Example 11.1. Several points were inserted into the index with following parameters:
leafs capacity – 3;
internal nodes capacity – 4;
split threshold – 0.7 (subdivision of the leaf will be continued until it contains no more than two points).

As can be seen on illustrations above (Fig. 11.1), the resulting structures in both cases are different. In (a) the number of leaves and intermediate nodes is higher then

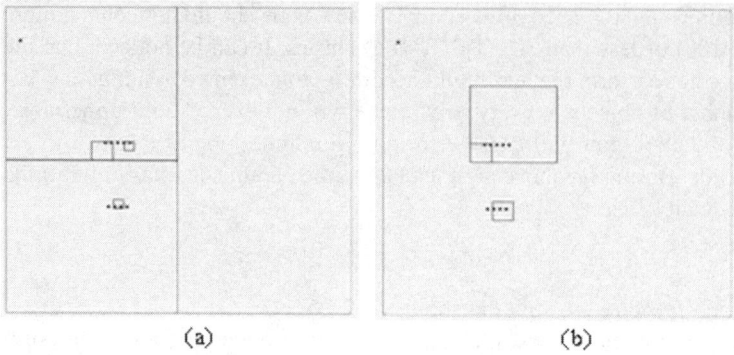

Fig. 11.1 The influence of the entries inserts order on the x-BR-tree structure

in case (b); moreover, the leaves are much smaller. Originally the index did not assume nodes join, so there is no possibility to make the node structure more effective. The example shows that the number of leaves and their shape do not depend only on the dataset, but, mostly on the elements insert order.

In section 11.3.1 experiment results are presented, showing the influence of the entries insertion order on the number of the x-BR-index leaves and directly on the efficiency of the response to spatial selection queries.

11.2.2 Cost Model

The cost model for spatial queries using the x-BR-tree index can be expressed as a probabilistic formula. Presented considerations aim to express the cost of a spatial query using information about the cardinality of the dataset. Now the model is limited to the leaves level in order to simplify the considerations. The data space, in which the model is discussed, is [0,1).

The selection query asks for all nodes that overlap the query window. The node is accessed when its region is included in the query region or when its region is intersected by the query region.

The probability that the query window q contains the data space s in the d–dimensional space is:

$$P_{cont} = \prod_{i=1}^{d} (q_i - s_i) \tag{11.2}$$

The illustration of the above equation is presented in Fig. 11.2. For simplicity, the two-dimensional space is assumed. The d–dimensional case is a simple extension of the two-dimensional case. The left upper corner of the data space is taken into consideration (it can be any point from this region). The shaded region in the picture represents places, in which this point can be located, so that the query region contains the whole data region.

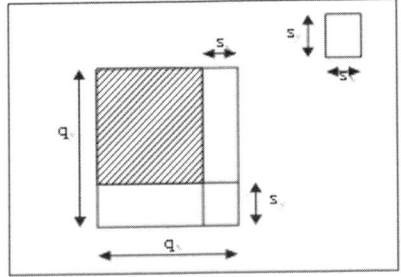

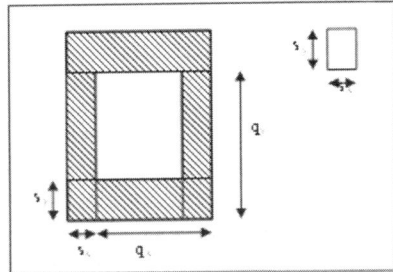

Fig. 11.2 Illustration of equation (11.2)

Fig. 11.3 Illustration of equation (11.3)

The probability that the data space s intersects the query window q in the d-dimensional space is:

$$P_{inter} = \prod_{k=1}^{d} (q_k + s_k) - \prod_{k=1}^{d} (q_k - s_k), \qquad (11.3)$$

The illustration of the above equation is presented in Fig. 11.3. Like in the previous equation, the work space was reduced to two dimensions. The location of the left upper corner of the data space is taken into consideration, so that the data space intersects the window query. In figure Fig. 11.3 this region is shaded.

The cost of execution of the selection query using x-BR-tree is the number of leaf accesses of x-BR-tree denoted as LA_ total, what corresponds to the number of reads from the external memory. This value depends on the size of a single leaf and on the size of the query window. The formula for the number of intersected leaves, depending on the query window size is:

$$LA\_total(q) = N_1 * (P_{cont} + P_{inter}) = N_1 * \prod_{k=1}^{d} (q_k + s_k), \qquad (11.4)$$

where: P_{cont} – probability that the query rectangle contains the data space, P_{inter} – probability that the data space intersects the query rectangle, d – number of dimensions, N_l – number of leaves, q_k – extent of a query rectangle q on dimension $k(k = 1, \ldots, d)$, s_k – average extent of a data rectangle on dimension k.

The simplest model is based on the equation (11.4). The number of leaves N_l in the index can be computed basing on the tree statistic. The size of an individual leaf can be calculated by dividing the size of one of the dimensions of data workspace by the d-th root of N_l:

$$s_k = \frac{1}{\sqrt[d]{N_1}}, \qquad (11.5)$$

where: s_k – extent of a data rectangle on dimension k, d – number of dimensions, N_l – number of leaves.

It is assumed, that the work space is two-dimensional and that every dimension of the space has the same length (square space). Combining equations (11.5) and (11.4) we obtain:

$$LA\_total(q) = N_1 * \left(q + \frac{1}{\sqrt{N_1}} \right)^2, \tag{11.6}$$

where: LA_total – total number of leaf accesses, N_l – number of leaves, q – extent of a query rectangle.

The above model does not take into consideration the tree creating algorithm, but basing on the number of leaves, it averages their size out and uses these value to predict the cost. An effort to obtain more precise estimation of the leaf number and their size was made. The following assumptions were made:

a) the work space is two-dimensional,
b) every dimension has the same size (a square),
c) he number of inserted points is 2^{2m},
d) the size of every dimension of the space is the power of 2, the space subdivision gives natural numbers as a result,
e) the nodes fanout is nearly maximal.

Having: leaf capacity C and the number of inserted elements n, it was considered, how the leaf number N_l depends on C and n.

$$
\begin{cases}
n \leq C & N_1 = 1 \\
\frac{3n}{4} \leq C < n & N_1 = 2 = 2^1 \\
\frac{2n}{4} \leq C < \frac{3n}{4} & N_1 = 3 = 3*2^0 \\
\frac{n}{4} \leq C < \frac{2n}{4} & N_1 = 4 = 2^2 \\
\frac{3n}{16} \leq C < \frac{n}{4} \Leftrightarrow \frac{3n}{4^2} \leq C < \frac{n}{4^1} & N_1 = 8 = 2^3 \\
\frac{2n}{16} \leq C < \frac{3n}{16} \Leftrightarrow \frac{2n}{4^2} \leq C < \frac{3n}{4^2} & N_1 = 12 = 3*2^2 \\
\frac{n}{16} \leq C < \frac{2n}{16} \Leftrightarrow \frac{n}{4^2} \leq C < \frac{2n}{4^2} & N_1 = 16 = 2^4 \\
\frac{3n}{64} \leq C < \frac{n}{16} \Leftrightarrow \frac{3n}{4^3} \leq C < \frac{n}{4^2} & N_1 = 32 = 2^5 \\
\frac{2n}{64} \leq C < \frac{3n}{64} \Leftrightarrow \frac{2n}{4^3} \leq C < \frac{3n}{4^3} & N_1 = 48 = 3*2^4 \\
\frac{n}{64} \leq C < \frac{2n}{64} \Leftrightarrow \frac{n}{4^3} \leq C < \frac{2n}{4^3} & N_1 = 62 = 2^6 \\
\vdots & \\
\vdots &
\end{cases}
$$

It can be seen, that the presented division on ranges can be written in a more general form, depending on parameter k, which is a natural number. The number of leaves also depends on this parameter and is presented as follows:

$$\begin{cases} n \leq C & N_1 = 1 \\ \frac{3n}{4^k} \leq C < \frac{n}{4^{k-1}} & N_1 = 2^{2k-1} \\ \frac{2n}{4^k} \leq C < \frac{3n}{4^k} & N_1 = 3 * 2^{2(k-1)} \\ \frac{n}{4^k} \leq C < \frac{2n}{4^k} & N_1 = 2^{2k} \end{cases} \qquad k = 1, 2, \dots \qquad (11.7)$$

It is known, that C belongs to exactly one of these ranges for exactly one k. To calculate the value of k, that is essential to estimate number of leaves, equation (11.7) has to be transformed in the following way:

$$\frac{3n}{4^k} \leq C < \frac{n}{4^{k-1}} \Leftrightarrow \qquad\qquad k = 1, 2, \dots$$

$$\Leftrightarrow \left(\frac{3n}{4^k} \leq C \quad \wedge \quad C < \frac{n}{4^{k-1}} \right) \Leftrightarrow$$

$$\Leftrightarrow \left(4^k \geq \frac{3n}{C} \quad \wedge \quad 4^{k-1} < \frac{n}{C} \right) \Leftrightarrow$$

$$\Leftrightarrow \left(log_4 4^k \geq log_4 \frac{3n}{C} \quad \wedge \quad log_4 4^{k-1} < log_4 \frac{n}{C} \right) \Leftrightarrow$$

$$\Leftrightarrow \left(k \geq log_4 \frac{3n}{C} \quad \wedge \quad k - 1 < log_4 \frac{n}{C} \right) \Leftrightarrow$$

$$\Leftrightarrow \left(k \geq log_4 \frac{3n}{C} \quad \wedge \quad k < log_4 \frac{n}{C} + 1 \right) \Leftrightarrow$$

$$\Leftrightarrow \left(k \geq log_4 \frac{3n}{C} \quad \wedge \quad k < log_4 \frac{n}{C} + log_4 4 \right) \Leftrightarrow$$

$$\Leftrightarrow \left(k \geq log_4 \frac{3n}{C} \quad \wedge \quad k < log_4 \frac{4n}{C} \right) \Leftrightarrow$$

$$\Leftrightarrow log_4 \frac{3n}{C} \leq k < log_4 \frac{4n}{C}$$

Similarly, other range can be transformed to get:

$$\begin{cases} n \leq C & N_1 = 1 \\ log_4 \frac{3n}{C} \leq k < log_4 \frac{4n}{C} & N_1 = 2^{2k-1} \\ log_4 \frac{2n}{C} \leq k < log_4 \frac{3n}{C} & N_1 = 3 * 2^{2(k-1)} \\ log_4 \frac{n}{C} \leq k < log_4 \frac{2n}{C} & N_1 = 2^{2k} \end{cases} \qquad (11.8)$$

Because, as mentioned above, there exists exactly one k, fulfilling exactly one of the above inequalities, therefore, in order to calculate k it has to be checked, if the ceiling of the expression lesser than or equal k is lesser than the expression greater than k. If yes, then this ceiling is the sought parameter k. If not, than in the same way the next inequality has to be checked. Next, by means of k, the number of leaves index is calculated. Even though the nodes fanout is assumed to be nearly maximal, basing on the experiments and literature it can affirmed, that the nodes' fanout reach about 70%. It means, that the predicted number of leaves store about 70% of all entries. It can be assumed, that adequately higher number of leaves store information about the whole data set. Finally, the total number of leaves is:

$$N_{1\_total} = \frac{1}{f}N_1, \tag{11.9}$$

where: N_{1_total} – number of leaves, f – node's fanout, N_1 – predicted number of leaves; according to equation (11.8).

Basing on N_{1_total} the leaf side's average size using equation (11.5) is calculated:

$$s_k = \frac{1}{\sqrt[d]{N_{1\_total}}}. \tag{11.10}$$

Finally, combining equations (11.4), (11.9), (11.10):

$$LA\_total(q) = \frac{1}{f}N_1 * \left(q + \frac{1}{\sqrt{\frac{1}{f}N_1}} \right)^2, \tag{11.11}$$

where: LA_total – total number of leaf accesses, f – node fanout, N_l – number of leaves; according to equation (11.8), q – extent of a query rectangle.

11.3 Tests

11.3.1 The Number of Leaves of X-BR-tree

The experiment was performed to show the differences in the leaves number depending on the elements inserting method. 4096, 16384 and 65536 points were inserted into the space of size 512x512. The leaf and internal node capacity was set to 4. The split threshold was set to 0.7 and 0.75, what means, that leaf splitting is continued as long as every region contains no more the two entries for 0.7 and no more the three entries for 0.75. The data set was uniformly distributed. The number of created leaves was compared, once for inserting points from "left" to "right" and from "top" to "bottom", the other time the same data set was inserted randomly. The results of the experiments are presented below:

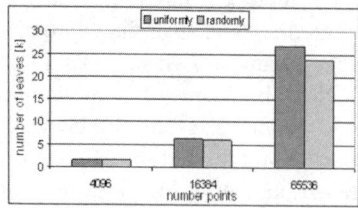   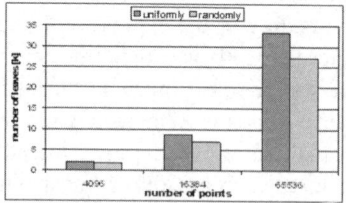

Fig. 11.4 Number of leaves depending on the number of inserted points for split threshold 0.75

Fig. 11.5 Number of leaves depending on the number of inserted points for split threshold 0.7

Basing on fig. 11.4 and fig. 11.5 it can be noticed, that the number of nodes in the x-BR-tree strongly depends on the insertion method.

For the split threshold 0.75, the differences for smaller data sets are not so significant. For the data set containing 65536 elements the number of leaves for the uniform insertion is more than 3000 higher (12%) than when the entries are inserted randomly. For the split threshold 0.7, the differences are even bigger. The number of nodes in every case differs not less than 20% .

As can be seen in the previous experiment, the number of nodes and particular leaves is very difficult to estimate. This number is used in the presented cost model, what makes designing a precise cost model problematic.

The above experiment leans towards the statement, that the random insertion of elements gives better results. It results from the properties of the x-BR-tree and its split algorithm. The algorithm divides the region in order to remain free space for next entries. During sequential inserting, created nodes are not completely utilized, because as the result of split smaller leaves are created and they are to small to encompass newly inserted elements. In case of random insertion, there is the possibility, that the free space in the nodes will be filled, because leaves have a bigger size.

11.3.2 Estimation of Cost Model

Two experiments were performed to estimate the accuracy of the model presented in section 2.2. Data sets of cardinality 20, 40 and 60 thousand points were used. The work space was 512x512 points wide. The x-BR-tree settings were:

- leaves and internal nodes' capacity – 4;
- split threshold – 0.7 and 0.75.

The points were inserted randomly in the work space. Their distribution was uniform in the first case and Gaussian in the second case.

11.3.2.1 Prediction Error

In this experiment a prediction relative error for both presented cost estimating models for given queries was tested. The average prediction relative error is defined as:

$$\delta = \frac{1}{k} \sum_{i=1}^{k} \frac{|x_i - v_i|}{v_i}, \tag{11.12}$$

where: δ – prediction average relative error, k – number of queries, x_i – predicted number of leaf accesses for i-th query, v_i – real number of leaf accesses for i-th query.

For every size of the queries (from 10% to 90% of region of the work space, a step of 10%) 200 random queries were generated. The error was measured for ever query, and the result were averaged out. The symbols on all plots are as follows:

N – cardinality of data set,

"unif", "Gauss" – data set distribution (uniform and Gaussian),

ST – split threshold.

The chart denoted as "simple" shows the results obtained using equation (11.6), and the chart "log4" presents the results obtained basing on formula (11.11).

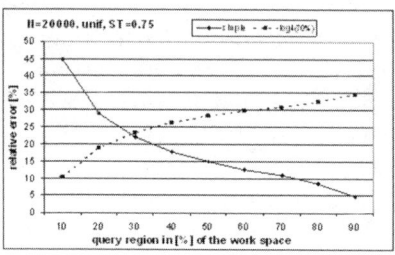

Fig. 11.6 Relative error of the cost model depending on the query size for data set 20k, split threshold 0.75 and uniform data set distribution

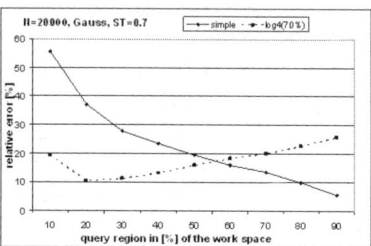

Fig. 11.7 Relative error of the cost model depending on the query size for data set 20k, split threshold 0.7 and Gaussian data set distribution

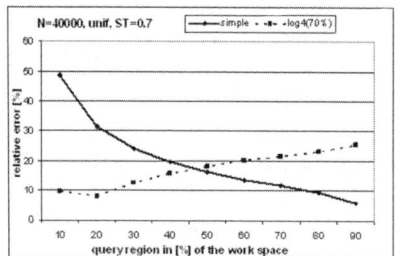

Fig. 11.8 Relative error of the cost model depending on the query size for data set 40k, split threshold 0.7 and uniform data set distribution

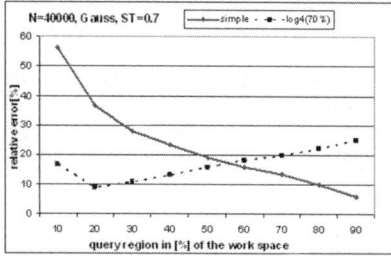

Fig. 11.9 Relative error of the cost model depending on the query size for data set 40k, split threshold 0.7 and Gaussian data set distribution

Basing on results of the above experiments (fig. 11.6–11.11) it can be affirmed, that for small query size the model "log4" gives results with a smaller error (about 10-20%). It can be seen, that along with the increase of the query size, the error also grows and reaches the level about 30-40% for large regions of the queries. This is because this model bases on the analytically estimated number of leaves. The assumptions made for equation (11.11) are difficult to fulfill, because the "ideal" x-BR-tree is very rare in real world. If the query size is small, then the selected

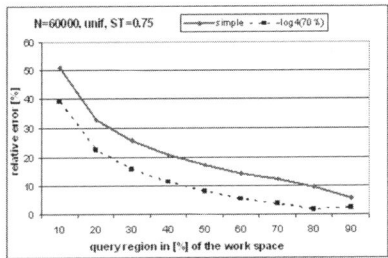

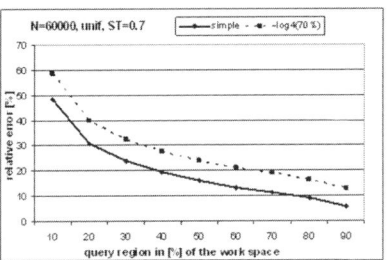

Fig. 11.10 Relative error of the cost model depending on the query size for data set 60k, split threshold 0.75 and uniform data set distribution

Fig. 11.11 Relative error of the cost model depending on the query size for data set 60k, split threshold 0.7 and uniform data set distribution

region of index differs from the ideal in a smaller degree. When the query size is growing, then the difference between the predicted and the actual number of node accesses is higher. For data set of cardinality 60000 points it can be seen (fig. 11.10 and 11.11), that for split threshold equal 0.75 the error is smaller than for value 0.7 of these parameter. It results from better leafs "packing", and one of the cost models assumption was complete utilization of the leaves.

The "simple" model is less accurate for small queries (error up to 50%), but this error decreases when the query region increases. It results from the fact, that it relies on the average leaf size, calculated basing on the number of leaves, which is read from the gathered tree statistic. The smaller query size, the more leaf size differs from the average. The increase of the query size causes, that more leaves with larger size are intersected, so the average size of accessed leaves closes to the one calculated analytically.

As can be seen, on most of the plots error charts for both models cross each other for queries of size 30-40% of work space. Both models can be combined in order to give a constant, low error. For queries smaller than 35% of the workspace equation (11.11) should be used, and for larger query region the estimation will be more precise when using formula (11.6). In this way the error of "combined" model should not exceed 30%, what seems to be a good result in the first approach to this issue.

11.3.2.2 Estimated Number of Leaves

The next experiment compares the number of leaves accesses with the estimated values during the processing of a query. The number of leaves accesses was tested depending on the query size. The query region was changing from 10% to 90% of workspaces region, a step of 10% . For every region size 200 random queries were generated. The estimation was made individually for every query, and the result were averaged. The estimation of leaves accesses was based on the model that is a combination of both approaches presented in section 11.2.2. According to the conclusion described in the previous section (11.3.2.1), for queries smaller than 35% of workspace, the equation (11.6) was used and for larger queries the equation (11.11) was applied. The symbols on all plots are as follows:

N – cardinality of data set,

"unif", "Gauss" – data set distribution (uniform and Gaussian),

ST – split threshold.

The charts denoted as "actual" presents the actual number of leaves accesses, and the chart "estim." presents the estimated value.

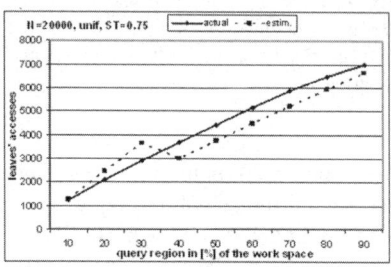

Fig. 11.12 Actual and estimated number of leaves accesses depending on the query size for data set 20k, split threshold 0.75 and uniform data set distribution

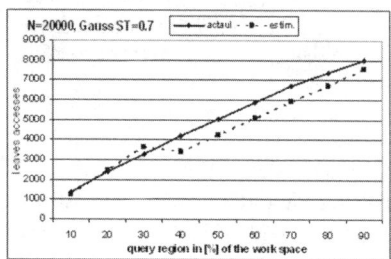

Fig. 11.13 Actual and estimated number of leaves accesses depending on the query size for data set 20k, split threshold 0.7 and Gaussian data set distribution

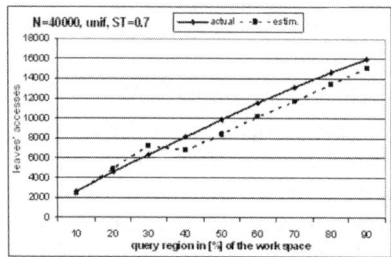

Fig. 11.14 Actual and estimated number of leaves accesses depending on the query size for data set 40k, split threshold 0.7 and uniform data set distribution

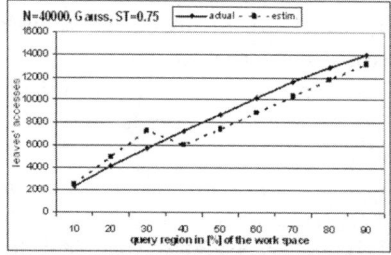

Fig. 11.15 Actual and estimated number of leaves accesses depending on the query size for data set 40k, split threshold 0.75 and Gaussian data set distribution

Basing on the result of the above experiment, it can be noticed that the estimated value of the number of leaves accesses when processing spatial queries does not differ from the actual one. In fig. 11.12, 11.13, 11.14 and 11.15 for data sets containing 20k and 40k elements exists a point, where charts of actual and estimated value cross each other. This point corresponds to the border value for equation (11.6) and (11.11). For the 60k data set (fig. 11.16 and 11.17), the charts are not crossing, and the difference between the estimated and the actual value is almost constant. This

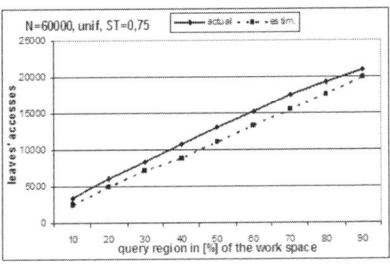

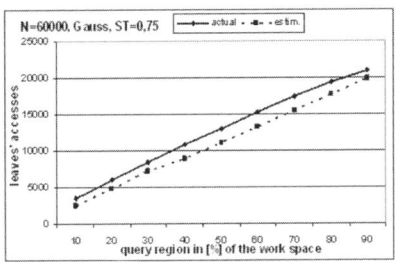

Fig. 11.16 Actual and estimated number of leaves accesses depending on the query size for data set 60k, split threshold 0.75 and uniform data set distribution

Fig. 11.17 Actual and estimated number of leaves accesses depending on the query size for data set 60k, split threshold 0.75 and Gaussian data set distribution

corresponds to the decreasing average relative error when the query size increases, what could have been observed in the previous experiment.

11.4 Conclusion

A cost model for spatial selection queries using the x-BR-tree index was proposed. Two solutions were constructed, which mostly base on probabilistic and estimation. The tests show, that every solution has its range of query size, in which it gives the most precise results. Moreover, these ranges are disjoint. The combination of both models results in more precise estimation for every query size. Such a solution is quite accurate, the average relative error rarely rises above 30% . The difficulties with getting accurate estimation result from the characteristic of the x-BR-tree and its split algorithm.

Further works should be focused on developing the presented model in a way it considers the cost of the access to the higher levels of the indexing structure.

References

1. Dellis E., Seeger B., Vlachou A. (2005) Nearest Neighbor Search on Vertically Partitioned High-Dimensional Data. Proceedings of the 7th International Conference Data Warehousing and Knowledge Discovery (DaWaK 2005): 243-253.
2. Gorawski M., Malczok R. (2005) On Efficient Storing and Processing of Long Aggregate Lists. DaWak2005 (LNCS 3589), Copenhagen, Denmark.
3. Faloutsos C., Kamel I.(1994) Beyond Uniformity and Independence: Analysis of R-trees Using the Concept of Fractal Dimension, In Proceedings of the 13th ACM Symposium on Principles of Database Systems (PODS).
4. Theodoridis Y., Sellis T. (1996) A model for the Prediction of R-tree Performance. Proc. Symp. Principles of Database Systems.

5. Vassilakopoulos M., Manolopoulos M. (1999) External Balanced Regular (x-BR) Trees: New Structure for Very Large Spatial Databases. Technical Report TR99-13.
6. Yu S., Atluri V., Adam N. (2005) Selective View Materialization in a Spatial Data Warehouse. DaWaK 2005: 157-167.

Chapter 12
Querying and Mining Trajectory Databases Using Places of Interest

Leticia Gómez, Bart Kuijpers and Alejandro Vaisman

Abstract The study of moving objects has been capturing the attention of Geographic Information System (GIS) researchers. Moving objects, carrying location-aware devices, produce trajectory data in the form of a sample of (O_{id}, t, x, y)-tuples, that contain object identifier and time-space information. Recently, the notion of stops and moves was introduced. Intuitively, if a moving object spends a sufficient amount of time in a certain geographic place (which we denote a *place of interest of an application*), this place is considered a *stop* of the object's trajectory. In-between stops, a trajectory has *moves*. In this paper we study how moving object data analysis can benefit from replacing raw trajectory data by a sequence of *stops and moves*. We first propose a formal model and query language (denoted $\mathscr{L}_{mo}$) to express complex queries involving spatial data stored in a GIS, non-spatial data (stored in a data warehouse) and moving object data. This query language also supports different forms of aggregation. We then study the compression of trajectory data produced by moving objects, using the concepts of stops and moves. We show that stops and moves are expressible in $\mathscr{L}_{mo}$ and that there exists a fragment of this language (that can be expressed by means of regular expressions) allowing to talk about temporally ordered sequences of stops and moves. We use this fragment to perform data mining over trajectory data. We present an implementation and a case study, and discuss different applications of our approach.

Leticia Gómez
Instituto Tecnológico de Buenos Aires, Av. Madero 399, Buenos Aires, Argentina, e-mail: lgomez@itba.edu.ar

Bart Kuijpers
Hasselt University and Transnational University of Limburg, Gebouw D, B-3590, Diepenbeek, Belgium, e-mail: bart.kuijpers@uhasselt.be

Alejandro Vaisman
Universidad de Buenos Aires, Ciudad Universitaria, Pabellon I, Buenos Aires, Argentina (1428), e-mail: avaisman@dc.uba.ar

12.1 Introduction

Geographic Information Systems (GIS) have been extensively used in various application domains, ranging from economical, ecological and demographic analysis, to city and route planning [23, 26]. In recent years, *time* is playing an increasingly important role in GIS and spatial data management [19]. One particular line of research in this direction, concerns *moving object data*. Moving objects, carrying location-aware devices, produce trajectory data in the form of a sample of (O_{id},t,x,y)-tuples, that contain object identifier and time-space information. Recently, the notions of *stops* and *moves* were introduced [1, 3, 18]. These concepts serve to compress the trajectory data that is produced by moving objects using application-dependent places of interest. A designer may want to select a set of places of interest that are relevant to her application. For instance, in a tourist application, such places can be hotels, museums and churches. In a traffic control application, they may be road segments, traffic lights and junctions, stored in GIS layers. If a moving object spends a sufficient amount of time in a place of interest, this place is considered a stop of the object's trajectory. In between stops, the trajectory has moves. Thus, we can replace a raw trajectory by a sequence of application-relevant stops and moves, which also add semantic information to the model.

We motivate our work with the following example. Figure 12.1 (left) shows a simplified map of Paris, containing two hotels, denoted Hotel 1 and Hotel 2 (H1 and H2 from here on), the Louvre and the Eiffel tower. We consider three moving objects, O1, O2 and O3. Object O1 goes from H1 to the Louvre, the Eiffel tower, spends just a few minutes there, and returns to the hotel. Object O2 goes from H2 to the Louvre, the Eiffel tower, (spending a couple of hours visiting each place), and returns to the hotel. Object O3 leaves H2 to the Eiffel tower, visits the place, and returns to H2. Figure 12.1 (center) shows part of these trajectory samples. All points of the same trajectory are temporally ordered and stored together (i.e., the raw trajectories table is sorted by O_{id} and t). In what follows, we will use the object identifier as the trajectory identifier, unless specified.

Many useful applications open in this scenario. For instance, a GIS user may be interested in finding out trajectory information, like "number of persons going from H1 to the Louvre and then to the Eiffel tower (stopping to visit both places) in the same day". An analyst may want to discover hidden information using data mining techniques. For example, she would like to identify interesting patterns in the trajectory data using association rule mining. She may also want to verify a certain pattern, like "people do not visit two museums in the same day". Complex queries that aggregate non-spatial information, and also involve GIS and moving object data, must also be addressed. For instance, "total sales in museums located on the left bank of the Seine, such that people visit them before going to the Eiffel Tower in the same day".

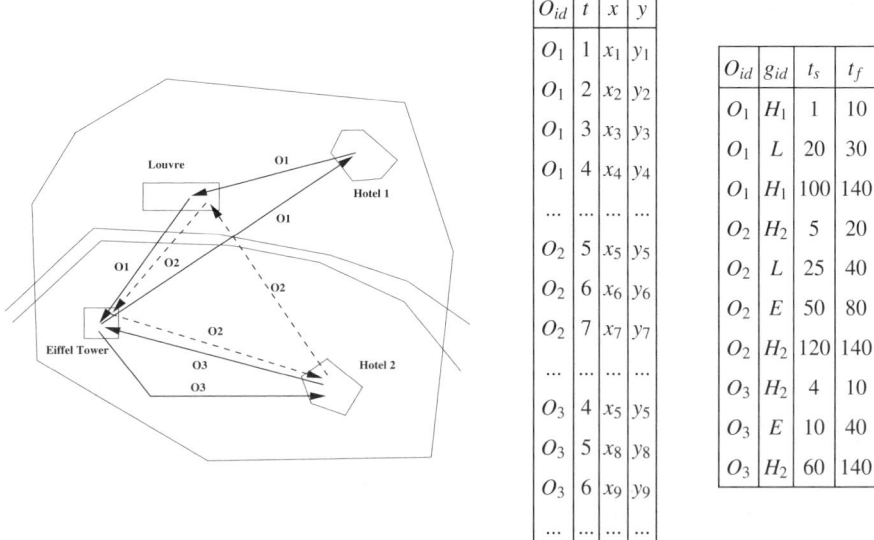

O_{id}	t	x	y
O_1	1	x_1	y_1
O_1	2	x_2	y_2
O_1	3	x_3	y_3
O_1	4	x_4	y_4
...	...	...	...
O_2	5	x_5	y_5
O_2	6	x_6	y_6
O_2	7	x_7	y_7
...	...	...	...
O_3	4	x_5	y_5
O_3	5	x_8	y_8
O_3	6	x_9	y_9
...	...	...	...

O_{id}	g_{id}	t_s	t_f
O_1	H_1	1	10
O_1	L	20	30
O_1	H_1	100	140
O_2	H_2	5	20
O_2	L	25	40
O_2	E	50	80
O_2	H_2	120	140
O_3	H_2	4	10
O_3	E	10	40
O_3	H_2	60	140

Fig. 12.1 Running example (left), its moving object fact table (center), and its compressed fact table (right)

12.1.1 Contributions and Paper Organization

A common framework integrating moving object, spatial and non-spatial data can be a powerful tool for the tasks mentioned above. We first present an overview of the conceptual model and query language (supporting aggregation) that integrates GIS and non-spatial data (stored in a data warehouse) in a unified framework (Section 12.2). Full details of this model are given in [8] and [7]. We also give a geometric definition of stops and moves, and show that they are computable from the raw trajectory data. At the basis of the query language is a multi-sorted first-order language $\mathcal{L}_{mo}$ for moving object and GIS data in which one can specify properties of moving objects, geometric elements of GIS layers and non-spatial GIS data stored in a data warehouse (Section 12.3). This language was first introduced by the authors in an extended abstract [9][1]. Here we provide a more detailed presentation. We then discuss the advantages of computing a concise table from the raw trajectory data, using stops and moves (Section 12.4). Section 12.5 introduces *smRE*, a sub-language of $\mathcal{L}_{mo}$ that allows us to talk about temporally ordered sequences of stops and moves. The syntax of this language is given in the form of regular expressions. We show that this language considerably extends the language proposed by Mouza and Rigaux [18], and can be used to efficiently express data mining and pattern matching tasks over trajectory data. Section 12.6 presents a preliminary im-

---

[1] A technical report is available [10]

plementation, and the use of *smRE* for data mining, through a case study based on real-world data.

12.1.2 Related Work

The field of moving objects databases has been extensively studied in the last ten years, especially regarding data modeling an indexing. Güting and Schneider [12] provide a good reference to this large corpus of work. Wolfson *et al* stated a set of capabilities that a moving object database must have, and introduced the DOMINO system, that develops those features on top of existing database management systems (DBMS) [25]. Hornsby and Egenhofer [13] introduced a framework for modeling moving objects, that supports viewing objects at different granularities, depending on the sampling time interval. For mining trajectories in road networks, Brakatsoulas *et al.* [2] proposed to enrich trajectories of moving objects with information about the relationships between trajectories (e.g., *intersect*, *meets*), and between a trajectory and the GIS environment (*stay within*, *bypass*, *leave*). They also propose a mining language denoted SML (for Spatial Mining Language). This language is oriented to traffic networks, and it is not clear how it could be extended to other scenarios. Moreover, all information on moving objects must be processed (on the contrary, we use semantic information to reduce, if possible, the amount of data to be considered). Also in the framework of road traffic mining, Gonzalez *et al.* [11] use a partitioning approach for obtaining interesting driving and speed patterns from large sets of traffic data. They compute frequent path-segments at the area level with a support relative to the traffic in the area (i.e., a kind of adaptive support), and propose an algorithm to automatically partition a road network and build a hierarchy of areas. The work of Lee *et al.* [16] is aimed at discovering common sub-trajectories, using a partitioning strategy which divides a trajectory into a set of line segments, and then groups similar line segments together into a cluster.

Techniques that add semantic information to trajectory data have been recently proposed. Giannotti *et al.* [6] study trajectory pattern mining, based on so-called Temporally Annotated Sequences ($\mathscr{TAS}$), an extension of sequential patterns, where there is a temporal annotation between two nodes. In this way, $s_1, 2, s_2$ defines a pattern that starts at s_1 and after 2 seconds arrives at s_2. In other words, a trajectory pattern is a set of trajectories that visit the same sequence of places with similar travel times between each of them. They also propose three different mining methods. They also introduce the concept of Region of Interest (RoI). Although with similar goals, our work clearly differs from [6] in several ways. We work with stops and moves instead of pre-defined regions of interest. This allows to identify which of the RoIs are really relevant to a trajectory. We also use these stops and moves to "encode" or compress a trajectory, which, in many practical situations is enough to identify interesting sequences very efficiently. A basic difference is also that, in, [6], the authors focus on computing the RoIs dynamically from the trajectories. On the contrary, in our approach, the user defines the places of interest of an application in advance, and from them we compute the stops and moves to perform trajectory mining. Finally, our approach allows integration between trajectories and background geographic data, an issue mentioned albeit not addressed in [6].

Mouza and Rigaux [18] presented a model where trajectories are represented by a sequence of moves. They propose a query language based on regular expressions, aimed at obtaining so-called mobility patterns. Note that this language, as well as the proposals commented above, *does not relate trajectories with the GIS environment*, which limits the types of queries that can be addressed. With a similar idea, Damiani *et al.* [3] introduced the concept of stops and moves, in order to enrich trajectories with semantically annotated data. Alvares *et al.* [1] presented a framework for trajectory analysis based on stops and moves. In this paper we will show how these ideas can be effectively implemented and used.

The problem of trajectory similarity in moving object databases is a new topic in the spatio-temporal database literature. Existing work focuses on the spatial notion of similarity, sometimes borrowing from the time-series analysis field. This is the approach followed by Pelekis *et al.* [22] introduced a framework consisting of a set of distance operators based on parameters of trajectories like speed and direction, and propose distance operators based on this. Frentzos *et al.* [5] proposed an approximation method for supporting the k-most-similar-trajectory search using R-tree structures. We will present a different approach, based on association rule mining, in Section 12.6.

Data aggregation is still quite an open field, either in GIS or in a moving objects scenario. Meratnia and de By [17] study trajectory aggregation by identifying similar trajectories and merging them in a single one, and dividing the area under study into homogeneous *spatial units*. Papadias *et al* [20] index historical aggregate information about moving objects. Our approach for spatial aggregation is described in [8] and its implementation discussed in [4][2]. Kuijpers and Vaisman [15] presented a taxonomy of aggregate queries on moving object data. The model and query language we present here covers the different types of aggregation queries in this taxonomy.

12.2 Preliminaries and Background

Spatial data in a GIS are organized in thematic layers, containing information on geometric objects. For instance, one layer may contain rivers, another one road networks, etc. Although these geometric objects could be annotated with numerical and/or textual data, given the size of the data involved, and that aggregation will be relevant in our discussion, we will assume (although this is not a limitation of our model) that non-spatial data is stored in a *data warehouse*. Typically, in a data warehouse, numerical data are stored in *fact tables* built along several *dimensions*. For instance, if we are interested in the sales of certain products in stores in a given

---

[2] An implementation of the system (called Piet) can be found at http://piet.exp.dc.uba.ar/piet

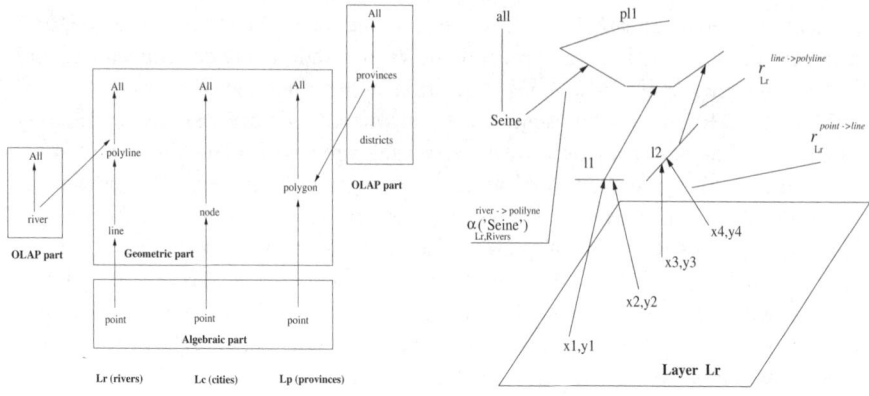

Fig. 12.2 A GIS dimension schema (left) and A GIS dimension instance (right)

region, we may consider the sales amounts in a fact table over the three dimensions store, time and product. In general dimensions are organized into *aggregation hierarchies*. Thus, stores can aggregate over cities which in turn can aggregate into regions and countries. Each of these aggregation levels can also hold descriptive attributes like city population, the area of a region, etc. On-line Analytical Processing (OLAP) provides tools for exploiting the data warehouse, for instance, through roll-up and drill-down operations [14].

A *GIS dimension* [4] consists of a set of graphs, each one describing geometries (polygons, polylines, points) in a thematic layer. Figure 12.2 (left) depicts the *schema* of a GIS dimension: the bottom level of each hierarchy, denoted the *Algebraic part*, contains the infinite points in a layer, and could be described by means of linear algebraic equalities and inequalities [21]. Above this part there is the *Geometric part,* that stores the identifiers of the geometric elements of GIS and is used to solve the geometric part of a query (i.e., find the polylines in a river representation). Each point in the Algebraic part may correspond to one or more elements in the Geometric part. Thus, at the *GIS dimension instance* level we will have rollup *relations* (denoted $r_L^{geom_1 \rightarrow geom_2}$). These relations map, for example, points in the Algebraic part, to geometry identifiers in the Geometric part in the layer L. For example, $r_{L_{province}}^{point \rightarrow Pg}(x, y, pg_1)$ means that point (x, y) corresponds to a polygon identified by pg_1 in the Geometric part, in the layer representing provinces (note that a point may correspond to more than one polygon, or to polylines that intersect with each other). Finally, there is the *OLAP part* of the GIS dimension. This part contains the conventional OLAP structures. The levels in the geometric part are associated to the OLAP part via a function, denoted $\alpha_{L,D}^{dimLevel \rightarrow geom}$. For instance, $\alpha_{L_r,Rivers}^{riverId \rightarrow g_r}$ associates information about a river in the OLAP part (*riverId*), to the identifier of a polyline (g_r) in a layer containing rivers (L_r) in the Geometric part.

Example 12.1. Figure 12.2 (left) shows the schema of a GIS dimension, where we have defined three layers, for rivers, cities, and provinces, respectively. The schema is composed of three graphs; the graph for rivers contains edges saying that a point

(x,y) in the algebraic part relates to a line identifier in the geometric part, and that in the same portion of the dimension, this line corresponds to a polyline identifier.

In the OLAP part we have information given by two dimensions, representing districts and rivers, associated to the corresponding graphs, as the figure shows. For example, a river identifier at the bottom level of the *Rivers* dimension representing rivers in the OLAP part, is mapped to the polyline level in the geometric part in the graph of the rivers layer L_r.

Figure 12.2 (right) shows a portion of a GIS dimension instance of the rivers layer L_r in the dimension schema on the left. Here, an instance of a GIS dimension in the OLAP part is associated to the polyline pl_1, which corresponds to the Seine river. For simplicity we only show four different points at the *point* level $\{(x_1,y_1),\ldots,(x_4,y_4)\}$. There is a relation $r_{L_r}^{point \rightarrow line}$ containing the association of points to lines in the *line* level, and a relation $r_{L_r}^{line \rightarrow polyline}$, between the line and polyline levels, in the same layer.   □

Elements in the geometric part can be associated with *facts*, each fact being quantified by one or more *measures*, not necessarily a numeric value. The OLAP part may contain not only fact tables quantifying geometric dimensions, but also classical OLAP fact tables defined in terms of the OLAP dimension schemas.

Moving objects are integrated in the framework above, using a distinguished fact table denoted *Moving Object Fact Table* (MOFT).

Let us first say what a trajectory is. In practice, trajectories are available by a finite sample of (t_i,x_i,y_i) points, obtained by observation.

Definition 12.1 (Trajectory). A *trajectory* is a list of time-space points $\langle (t_0,x_0,y_0), (t_1,x_1,y_1),\ldots,(t_N,x_N,y_N) \rangle$,
where $t_i,x_i,y_i \in \mathbb{R}$ for $i = 0,\ldots,N$ and $t_0 < t_1 < \cdots < t_N$. We call the interval $[t_0,t_N]$ the *time domain* of the trajectory.   □

For the sake of finite representability, we may assume that the time-space points (t_i,x_i,y_i), have rational coordinates.

A moving object fact table (MOFT for short, see the table in the right hand side of Figure 12.1), contains a finite number of identified trajectories.

Definition 12.2 (Moving Object Fact Table). Given a finite set $\mathscr{T}$ of trajectories, a *Moving Object Fact Table* (MOFT) for $\mathscr{T}$ is a relation with schema $< O_{id}, T, X, Y >$, where O_{id} is the identifier of the moving object, T represents time instants, and X and Y represent the spatial coordinates of the objects. An instance $\mathscr{M}$ of the above schema contains a finite number of tuples of the form (O_{id},t,x,y), that represent the position (x,y) of the object O_{id} at instant t, for the trajectories in $\mathscr{T}$.   □

We now define what the stops and moves of a trajectory are. In a GIS scenario, this definition is dependent on the particular places of interest in a particular application. For instance, in a tourist application, places of interest may be hotels, museums and churches. In a traffic application, places of interest may be road segments, road junctions and traffic lights. First, we define the notion of "places of interest of an application".

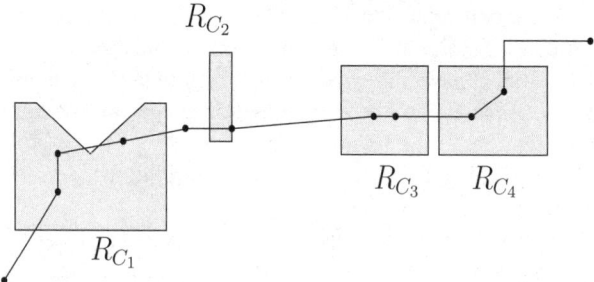

Fig. 12.3 An example of a trajectory with two stops and three moves.

Definition 12.3. [Places of Interest] A *place of interest (PoI)* C is a tuple (R_C, Δ_C), where R_C is a (topologically closed) polygon, polyline or point in $\mathbb{R}^2$ and Δ_C is a strictly positive real number. The set R_C is called the *geometry* of C and Δ_C is called its *minimum duration*. The *places of interest of an application* $\mathscr{P}_{\mathscr{A}}$ is a finite collection of PoIs with mutually disjoint geometries. □

Definition 12.4. [Stops and moves of a trajectory] Let $T = \langle (t_0, x_0, y_0), (t_1, x_1, y_1), ..., (t_n, x_n, y_n) \rangle$ be a trajectory. Also, $\mathscr{P}_{\mathscr{A}} = \{ C_1 = (R_{C_1}, \Delta_{C_1}), ..., C_N = (R_{C_N}, \Delta_{C_N}) \}$.

A *stop of T with respect to $\mathscr{P}_{\mathscr{A}}$* is a maximal contiguous subtrajectory $\langle (t_i, x_i, y_i), (t_{i+1}, x_{i+1}, y_{i+1}), ..., (t_{i+\ell}, x_{i+\ell}, y_{i+\ell}) \rangle$ of T such that for some $k \in \{1, ..., N\}$ the following holds: (a) $(x_{i+j}, y_{i+j}) \in R_{C_k}$ for $j = 0, 1, ..., \ell$; (b) $t_{i+\ell} - t_i > \Delta_{C_k}$.

A *move of T with respect to $\mathscr{P}$* is: (a) a maximal contiguous subtrajectory of T in between two temporally consecutive stops of T; (b) a maximal contiguous subtrajectory of T in between the starting point of T and the first stop of T; (c) a maximal contiguous subtrajectory of T in between the last stop of T and ending point of T; (d) the trajectory T itself, if T has no stops. □

Figure 12.3 illustrates these concepts. In this example, there are four places of interest with geometries $R_{C_1}, R_{C_2}, R_{C_3}$ and R_{C_4}. The trajectory T is depicted here by linearly interpolating between its sample points, to indicate their order. Let us imagine that T is run through from left to right. If the three sample points in R_{C_1} are temporally far enough apart (longer than Δ_{C_1}), they form a stop. Imagine that further on, only the two sample points in R_{C_4} are temporally far enough apart to form a stop. Then we have two stops in this example and three moves.

We remark that our definition of stops and moves of a trajectory is arbitrary and can be modified in many ways. For example, if we would work with linear interpolation of trajectory samples, rather than with samples, we see in Figure 12.3, that the trajectory briefly leaves R_{C_1} (not in a sample point, but in the interpolation). We could incorporate a tolerance for this kind of small exits from PoIs in the definition, if we define stops and moves in terms of continuous trajectories, rather than on terms of samples. Finally, in what follows we will assume that samples are taken at regular and relatively short intervals. The following property is straightforward.

Proposition 12.1. *There is an algorithm that returns, for any input* $(\mathscr{P}_{\mathscr{A}}, T)$ *with* $\mathscr{P}_{\mathscr{A}}$ *the places of interest of an application, and* T *a trajectory* $\langle (t_0, x_0, y_0), (t_1, x_1, y_1), ..., (t_n, x_n, y_n) \rangle$, *the stops of* T *with respect to* $\mathscr{P}_{\mathscr{A}}$. *This algorithm works in time* $\mathscr{O}(n \cdot p)$, *where* p *is the complexity of answering the point-query [23].* □

12.3 Querying Moving Object Data

The model introduced in Section 12.2 supports a language (in fact, a multi-sorted first-order logic), that we denote $\mathscr{L}_{mo}$. We now define $\mathscr{L}_{mo}$ formally.

Definition 12.5. The first-order query language $\mathscr{L}_{mo}$ has four types of variables: *real variables* $x, y, t, ...$; *name variables* $O_{id}, ...$; *geometric identifier variables* $g_{id}, ...$ and *dimension level variables* $a, b, c, ...$, (which are also used for dimension level attributes). Besides (existential and universal) quantification over all these variables, and the usual logical connectives $\wedge, \vee, \neg, ...$, we consider the following functions and relations to build atomic formulas in $\mathscr{L}_{mo}$:

- for every rollup function in the OLAP part, we have a function symbol $f_{D_k}^{A_i \to A_j}$, where A_i and A_j are levels in the dimension D_k in the OLAP part;
- analogously, for every rollup relation in the GIS part, we have a relation symbol $r_{L_k}^{G_i \to G_j}$, where G_i and G_j are geometries and L_k is a layer;
- for every α relation associating the OLAP and GIS parts in some layer L_i, we have a function symbol $\alpha_{L_k, D_\ell}^{A_i \to G_j}$, where A_i is an OLAP dimension level and G_j is a geometry, L_k is a layer and D_ℓ is a dimension;
- for every dimension level A, and every attribute B of A, there is a function $\beta_{D_k}^{A \to B}$ that maps elements of A to elements of B in dimension D_k;
- we have functions, relations and constants that can be applied to the alphanumeric data in the OLAP part (e.g., we have the $\in$ relation to say that an element belongs to a dimension level, we may have $<$ on income values and the function *concat* on string values);
- for every MOFT, we have a 4-ary relation $\mathscr{M}_i$;
- we have arithmetic operations $+$ and $\times$, the constants 0 and 1, and the relation $<$ for real numbers.
- finally, we assume the equality relation for all types of variables.

If needed, we may also assume other constants. □

Different types of aggregation can be added to the language. The list below, although not complete, covers the most interesting and usual cases (see [15] for an extensive list of examples of moving object aggregation queries).

- The COUNT operator applied to sets of the form $\{O_{id} \mid \phi(O_{id})\}$, where moving objects identifiers satisfying some $\mathscr{L}_{mo}$-definable property ϕ are collected;

- the COUNT operator applied to sets of the form $\{(O_{id}, t) \mid \phi(O_{id}, t)\}$, where moving objects identifiers combined with time moments, satisfying some $\mathscr{L}_{mo}$-definable property ϕ, are collected (assuming that this set is finite; otherwise the count is undefined);
- the COUNT operator applied to sets of the form $\{(O_{id}, t, x, y) \mid \phi(O_{id}, t, x, y)\}$, where moving objects id's combined with time and space coordinates, satisfying some $\mathscr{L}_{mo}$-definable property ϕ, are collected (assuming that this set is finite);
- the AREA operator applied to sets of the form $\{(x,y) \in \mathbb{R}^2 \mid \phi(x,y)\}$, which define some $\mathscr{L}_{mo}$-definable part of the plane $\mathbb{R}^2$ (assuming that this set is linear and bounded);
- the COUNT, MAX and MIN operators applied to sets of the form $\{t \in \mathbb{R} \mid \phi(t)\}$, when the $\mathscr{L}_{mo}$-definable condition ϕ defines a finite set of time instants and the TIMESPAN operator when ϕ defines an infinite, but bounded set of time instants (the semantics of COUNT, MAX and MIN is clear and TIMESPAN returns the difference between the maximal and minimal moments in the set);
- the MAX-L, MIN-L, AVG-L and TIMESPAN-L operators applied to sets of the form $\{(t_s, t_f) \in \mathbb{R}^2 \mid \phi(t_s, t_f)\}$, which represents an $\mathscr{L}_{mo}$-definable set of time intervals. The meaning of these operators is respectively the maximum, minimum and average lengths of the intervals if there is a finite number of intervals and the timespan of the union of these intervals in the last case;
- the AREA operator applied to sets of the form $\{g_{id} \mid \phi(g_{id})\}$, where identifiers of elements of some geometry (in the geometric part of our data model), satisfying an $\mathscr{L}_{mo}$-definable ϕ are collected. The meaning of this operator is the total area covered by the geometric elements corresponding to the identifiers.

Definition 12.5 describes the syntax of $\mathscr{L}_{mo}$. The interpretation of all variables, functions, relation, and constants is standard, as well as that of the logical connectives and quantifiers. We do not define the semantics formally but illustrate it through an elaborated example.

Example 12.2. Let us consider the query *"Total number of buses running in the morning in the Paris districts with a monthly income of less than €1500,00."* We use the MOFT $\mathscr{M}$ (Figure 12.1, center), that contains the moving objects samples. For clarity, we will denote the geometry polygons Pg, polylines Pl and point Pt. We use *distr* to denote the level district in the OLAP part of the dimension schema. The GIS layer which contains district information is called L_d. We assume that the layers to which a function refers are implicit by the function's name. For instance, in $\alpha_{L_d,Distr}^{distr \to Pg}(n) = p_g$, the district variable n is mapped to the polygon with variable name p_g in the layer L_d. The query returning the *region* with the required income is expressed:

$$\{(x,y) \mid \exists n \exists g_1 (r_{L_d}^{Pt \to Pg}(x,y,g_1) \wedge \alpha_{L_d,Distr}^{distr \to Pg}(n) = g_1 \wedge$$
$$\beta_{Distr}^{distr \to income}(n) < 1.500)\}$$

Here, $r_{L_d}^{Pt \to Pg}(x, y, g_1)$ relates (x,y)-points to polygons in the district layer; the function $\alpha_{L_d, Distr}^{distr \to Pg}(n) = g_1$ maps the district identifier n in the OLAP part to the geometry identifier g_1; and $\beta_{Distr}^{distr \to income}(n)$ maps the district identifier n to the value of the *income* attribute which is then compared through the OLAP relation $<$ with an OLAP constant $1,500$.

The instants corresponding to the morning hours mentioned in the fact table are obtained through the rollup functions in the Time dimension. We assume there is a category denoted *timeOfDay* in the Time dimension, and a roll up to that level from the category *hour* (i.e., *hour* $\to$ *timeOfDay*). The aggregation of the values in the fact table corresponding only to morning hours is computed with the following expression: $\mathscr{M}_{morning} = \{(O_{id}, t, x, y) \mid f_{Time}^{hour \to timeOfDay}(t) =$ "Morning" $\wedge \mathscr{M}(O_{id}, t, x, y)\}$. In this formula "Morning" appears as a constant in the OLAP part. Finally, the query we discuss reads:

$$\text{COUNT}\{(Oid) \mid (\exists x)\, (\exists y)\, (\exists g_1)\, (\exists n)\, (\mathscr{M}_{morning}(O_{id}, t, x, y) \wedge$$
$$r_{L_d}^{Pt \to Pg}(x, y, g_1) \wedge \alpha_{L_d, Distr}^{distr \to Pg}(n) = g_1 \wedge \beta_{Distr}^{distr \to income}(n) < 1,500)\}.$$

□

Proposition 12.2. *Moving object queries expressible in $\mathscr{L}_{mo}$ are computable. The proposed aggregation operators are also computable.* □

Proof. (Sketch) The semantics of $\mathscr{L}_{mo}$ is straightforward apart from the subexpressions that involve $+$, $\times$ and $<$ on real numbers and quantification over real numbers. These subexpressions belong to the formalism of constraint databases and they can be evaluated by quantifier elimination techniques [21]. The restrictions we imposed on the applicability of the aggregation operators make sure that they can be effectively evaluated. In particular, the area of a set $\{(x, y) \in \mathbb{R}^2 \mid \phi(x, y)\}$ is computable when this set is semi-linear and bounded, and can be obtained by triangulating such linear sets and adding the areas of the triangles. □

12.4 The Stops and Moves Fact Table

Let the places of interest of an application be given. In this section, we describe how we go from MOFTs to application-dependent compressed MOFTs, where (O_{id}, t_i, x_i, y_i) tuples are replaced by $(O_{id}, g_{id}, t_s, t_f)$ tuples. In the latter, O_{id} is a moving object identifier, g_{id} is the identifier of the geometry of a place of interest and t_s and t_f are two time moments that encode the time interval $[t_s, t_f]$ of a stop. The idea is to replace the MOFT (containing the raw trajectories), by a *stops MOFT* that represents the same trajectory more concisely by listing its stops and the time intervals spent in them.

In practice, the MOFTs can contain huge amounts of data. For instance, suppose a GPS takes observations of daily movements of one thousand people, every ten seconds, during one month. This gives a MOFT of $1000 \times 360 \times 24 \times 30 = 259,200,000$ records. In this scenario, querying trajectory data may become extremely expensive. Note that a MOFT only provides the position of objects at a given instant. Sometimes we are not interested in such level of detail, but we look for more aggregated information instead. For example, we may want to know how many people go from a hotel to a museum on weekdays. Or, we can even want to perform data mining tasks like inferring trajectory patterns that are hidden in the MOFT. These tasks require semantic information, not present in the MOFT. In the best case, obtaining this information from that table will be expensive, because it would imply a join between this table and the spatial data. As a solution, we propose to use the notion of *stops and moves* in order to obtain a more concise MOFT, that can represent the trajectory in terms of places of interest, characterized as *stops*. This table cannot replace the whole information provided by the MOFT, but allows to quickly obtain information of interest without accessing the complete data set. In this sense, this concise MOFT, which we will denote SM-MOFT behaves like a summarized materialized view of the MOFT. The SM-MOFT will contain the object identifier, the identifier of the geometries representing the Stops, and the interval $[t_s, t_f]$ of the stop duration. Notice that we do not need to store the information about the moves, which remains implicit, because we know that between two stops there could only be a move. Also, if a trajectory passes through a PoI, but remains there an insufficient amount of time for considering the place a trajectory stop, the stop is not recorded in the SM-MOFT. The case study we will present in Section 12.6 will show the practical implications of these issues.

Definition 12.6 (SM-MOFT). Let $\mathscr{P}_{\mathscr{A}} = \{C_1 = (R_{C_1}, \Delta_{C_1}), ..., C_N = (R_{C_N}, \Delta_{C_N})\}$ be the PoIs of an application, and let $\mathscr{M}$ be a MOFT. The *SM-MOFT* $\mathscr{M}^{sm}$ of $\mathscr{M}$ *with respect to* $\mathscr{P}_{\mathscr{A}}$ consists of the tuples $(O_{id}, g_{id}, t_s, t_f)$ such that (a) O_{id} is the identifier of a trajectory in $\mathscr{M}$ [3]; (b) g_{id} is the identifier of the geometry of a PoI $C_k = (R_{C_k}, \Delta_{C_k})$ of $\mathscr{P}_{\mathscr{A}}$ such that the trajectory with identifier O_{id} in $\mathscr{M}$ has a stop in this PoI during the time interval $[t_s, t_f]$. This interval is called the *stop interval* of this stop. □

The table in Figure 12.1 (right) shows the SM-MOFT for our running example. Proposition 12.3 below, states that SM-MOFTs can be defined in $\mathscr{L}_{mo}$.

Proposition 12.3. *There is an* $\mathscr{L}_{mo}$ *formula* $\phi_{sm}(O_{id}, g_{id}, t_s, t_f)$ *that defines the SM-MOFT* $\mathscr{M}^{sm}$ *of* $\mathscr{M}$ *with respect to* $\mathscr{P}_{\mathscr{A}}$. □

We omit the proof of this property but remark that the use of the formula $\phi_{sm}(O_{id}, g_{id}, t_s, t_f)$ allows us to speak about stops and moves of trajectories in $\mathscr{L}_{mo}$. We can therefore add predicates to define stops and moves of trajectories as syntactic sugar to $\mathscr{L}_{mo}$.

---

[3] We could also use a trajectory identifier other than the object's id, if we want to analyze several trajectories of an object in different days. We use this approach in Section 12.6.

12.5 A Query Language for Stops and Moves

We will sketch a query language based on path regular expressions, along the lines proposed by Mouza and Rigaux [18]. However, our language (denoted *smRE*) goes far beyond, taking advantage of the integration between GIS, OLAP and moving objects provided by our model. Moreover, queries that do not require access to the MOFT can be evaluated very efficiently, making use of the SM-MOFT. In this section we show through examples, that *smRE* can be used to query for trajectory patterns, and that *smRE* turns out to be a subset of $\mathscr{L}_{mo}$.

We will assume that there is a different dimension for each type of (application-dependant) place of interest in the OLAP part of the model. For instance, there will be a dimension for hotels, with bottom level *hotelId*, or a dimension for restaurants, with bottom level *restaurantId*. Aggregation levels can be defined as required. There will also be a layer in the *Geometric part* of the GIS dimension, that could be designed in different ways. For simplicity, we consider that all places of interest with the same geometry will be stored together, meaning that, for example, there will be a layer (i.e., a hierarchy graph) for polygons representing hotels, and/or one hierarchy for lines representing street segments. There are also the functions introduced in Section 12.2. For example, $\alpha_{L_p,Hotel}^{hotelId \rightarrow Pg}$ maps a hotel identifier to a polygon representing it, in a layer for polygonal PoIs (L_p). All identifiers of PoIs in $\mathscr{M}^{sm}$ are members of some dimension level in the OLAP part, and are mapped to a geometry through the function α. We will also need some operators on time intervals. We say that an interval $I_1 = [t_1, t_2]$ strictly precedes $I_2 = [t_3, t_4]$, denoted $I_1 \lessdot I_2$, if $t_1 < t_2 < t_3 < t_4$. Note that all stop intervals I_1, I_2 of the same trajectory are such that either $I_1 \lessdot I_2$ or $I_2 \lessdot I_1$.

The idea is based on the construction (described in Definition 12.7), of a graph representing the stops and moves of a *single trajectory*.

Definition 12.7 ($\mathscr{SM}$-Graph). Let us consider a trajectory sample T of moving objects, the PoIs of an application $\mathscr{P}_A = \{C_1 = (R_{C_1}, \Delta_{C_1}), ..., C_N = (R_{C_N}, \Delta_{C_N})\}$, a MOFT $\mathscr{M}$, and its SM-MOFT $\mathscr{M}^{sm}$ with respect to A. Also, for clarity but w.l.o.g., consider that all the tuples in $\mathscr{M}^{sm}$ are *ordered* according to their stop interval attributes, that is, if t_1 and t_2 are two consecutive tuples in $\mathscr{M}^{sm}$, $t_1.I \lessdot t_2.I$, where *I* represents the time interval in the tuple (i.e., $[t_s, t_f]$). An $\mathscr{SM}$-Graph for $\mathscr{M}^{sm}$, denoted $\mathscr{G}(\mathscr{M}^{sm})$, is a graph constructed as follows:

a) For each $g_{id} \in \prod_{G_{id}}(\mathscr{M}^{sm})$ there is a node v in $\mathscr{G}$, denoted $v(g_{id})$, with a *node number* $n \in \mathbb{N}$, different for each node.
b) There is an edge m in $\mathscr{G}$ between two nodes v_1 and v_2, for every pair t_1, t_2 of consecutive tuples in $\mathscr{M}^{sm}$ with the same O_{id}.
c) For each node $v \in \mathscr{G}$ the *extension* of v, denoted $ext(v)$ is given by the identifier of the PoI that represents the node in the OLAP part of the model.
d) For each node $v \in \mathscr{G}$ the *label* of v, denoted $label(v)$ is the name of the dimension of the PoI in the OLAP Part (i.e., the name of the dimension D mentioned above).

O_{id}	G_{id}	t_s	t_f
O_1	H_1	0	10
O_1	M_1	15	30
O_1	M_2	40	50
O_1	M_2	60	70
O_1	M_3	80	100
O_1	T_1	120	150
O_1	T_2	180	200
O_1	H_1	220	240
O_1	T_2	280	340
O_1	M_3	410	Now

Fig. 12.4 An SM-MOFT (left), and its $\mathscr{SM}$-Graph (right)

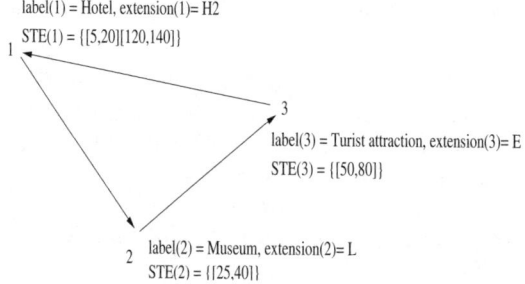

label(1) = Hotel, extension(1)= H2
STE(1) = {[5,20][120,140]}

label(3) = Turist attraction, extension(3)= E
STE(3) = {[50,80]}

label(2) = Museum, extension(2)= L
STE(2) = {[25,40]}

Fig. 12.5 The $\mathscr{SM}$-Graph for our running example

e) For each node $v \in \mathscr{G}$ the *stop temporal elements* of v, denoted $STE(v)$ is a set of stop intervals $\{I_1, ..., I_k\}$ (technically, a temporal element), such that there is an interval $I_i \in STE(v)$ for each edge incoming to v in $\mathscr{G}$. □

Note that an object may be at a PoI (long enough for considering this place a stop in the trajectory) more than once within a trajectory.

Example 12.3. Figure 12.4 (left) shows an SM-MOFT for one moving object's trajectory. The distinguished term "Now" indicates, as usual in temporal databases, the *current* time. We denote H_i, M_i, and T_i, hotels, museums and tourist attractions, respectively. Figure 12.4 (right) shows the corresponding $\mathscr{SM}$-Graph for object O_1. As an example, the extension of node 3 is $ext(3) = M2$, its label is $label(3) = Museums$, and $STE(3) = \{[80, 100], [410, Now]\}$.

Figure 12.5 shows the $\mathscr{SM}$-Graph for the trajectory of object O_2 in the running example of Figure 12.1. □

Now we are ready to define our query language based on Stops and Moves. The language combines the notions of regular expressions and first order constraints.

The $\mathscr{SM}$-Graph $\mathscr{G}$ can be seen as an automaton accepting regular expressions over the places of interest.

Definition 12.8 (R.E. for Stops and Moves). A *regular expression on stops and moves*, denoted *smRE* is an expression generated by the grammar

$$E \longleftarrow dim \mid dim[cond] \mid (E)^* \mid (E)^+ \mid E.E \mid \varepsilon \mid ?$$

where $dim \in D$ (a set of dimension names in the OLAP part), ε is the symbol representing the empty expression, "." means concatenation, and *cond* represents a condition that can be expressed in $\mathscr{L}_{mo}$. The term "?" is a wildcard meaning "any sequence of any number of *dim*". □

Aggregation is built on top of *smRE*: for each trajectory T in an SM-MOFT such that there is a sub-trajectory of T that matches the *smRE*, the query returns the O_{id} of T. Aggregate functions can be applied over this result. The following examples provide an overview of the language. We begin with the query "*Total number of trajectories from a Hilton hotel to a tourist attraction, stopping at a museum,*" which reads in *smRE*:

$\text{COUNT}(H[name = "Hilton"].?.M.?.T)$

As another example, the query "*Total number of trajectories that went from a Hilton hotel to the Louvre, in the morning*" is expressed in *smRE*:

$$\text{COUNT}(H[name = "Hilton"].?.M[name = "Louvre" \wedge$$
$$f_{Time}^{timeId \rightarrow TimeOfDay}(t_s) = "morning"])$$

In these queries, the conditions are evaluated over the *current* nodes (the node the parser is currently evaluating). For instance, in the latter, if the parser is at node 1 in Figure 12.4, the condition $name = "Hilton"$ returns "true" if $ext(1).name = "Hilton"$ and $label(1) = "Hotel"$. Also, t_s is a special variable representing the starting point of the time interval of the node that is being visited when evaluating the expression. The next query illustrates the full power of the language. Note that here, the SM-MOFT is not enough, and we need to go to the geometry. However, for many useful queries and patterns, much simpler expressions will suffice. The query is: "*Total number of trajectories going from a tourist attraction to a museum in the 19th district of Paris in the morning,*" and in *smRE* reads:

$$\text{COUNT}(T.?.M[f_{Time}^{timeId \rightarrow TimeOfDay}(I.t_s) = "morning" \wedge$$
$$(\exists\, g_{id})\,(\exists\, x)\,(\exists\, y)\,(\exists\, O_{id})\, \exists\, (t_1)\,(\exists\, p)\,(\exists\, pg)\,(\exists\, d)\,(M(O_{id}, t_1, x, y)\, \wedge$$
$$\alpha_{L_p, Museum}^{m_{id} \rightarrow Pg}(p) = g_{id}\, \wedge r_{L_p}^{point \rightarrow Pg}(x, y, g_{id})\, \wedge \alpha_{L_d, Distr}^{distr \rightarrow Pg}(d) = p_g\, \wedge$$
$$pg.number = 19\, \wedge\, f_{L_{dist}}^{point \rightarrow Pg}(x, y) = pg])$$

The function $\alpha_{L_p,Museum}^{mid \rightarrow Pg}(p) = g_{id}$, maps the id of the PoI (i.e., a museum) in the extension of the *current* node (p), to the polygon representing it in the geographic part (g_{id}). The rollup $r_{L_p}^{point \rightarrow Pg}(x, y, g_{id})$ identifies the x, y coordinates corresponding to g_{id}. The function $\alpha_{L_d,Distr}^{distr \rightarrow Pg}(d) = p_g$ has the meaning already explained, i.e., it maps a district identifier d in the *Distr* dimension to a polygon identifier in layer L_d. The equality $f_{L_{dist}}^{point,Pg}(x, y) = pg$ checks that the point of the trajectory belongs to the 19th district. M is the MOFT containing the trajectory samples.

Proposition 12.4. *The* smRE *language is a subset of* $\mathscr{L}_{mo}$. $\square$

Proof. (Sketch) The proof is built on the property that, for each trajectory in an SM-MOFT the SM-Graph can be unfolded, and transformed into a sequence of nodes, given that for all nodes v in the graph, all intervals in $STE(v)$ are disjoint. This sequence can then be queried using any FO language with time variables, like $\mathscr{L}_{mo}$ $\square$

12.6 Implementation and Case Study

In this section we present a description of the implementation of our proposal, including the construction of the SM-MOFT, and the details of the language implementation (based on the formal language explained in Section 12.5). Finally, we discuss the use of the *smRE* language for data mining tasks. Each description is presented along with experimental results using a case study based on data obtained from the INFATI Project[4]. Our intention was to experiment with real-world data, and at the same time, to work with a large database. The original data set contained a total of 1.9 million records of the form (O_{id}, x, y, t), collected by GPS devices, at intervals of one second. Since we needed a larger database, we modified and expanded the original one, until we obtained a MOFT with 30,808,296 tuples, corresponding to trajectories of 6.276 moving objects. Therefore, we worked with a MOFT containing a mixture of real-world and synthetic data.

Since the original data set did not include places of interest, we created them in order to complete the experimental evaluation. We worked with the following kinds of PoIs: restaurants, coffee shops, hotels and two tourist attractions: an aquarium and a zoo. For the *minimum duration* (see Definition 12.3), we adopted the following criteria: 15 minutes for coffee shops, 40 minutes for restaurants and zoos, 45 minutes for hotels and 20 minutes for the aquarium. These PoIs are shown in Figure 12.6, using the GIS tool we developed[5]. We created a total of seventeen PoIs.

We ran our tests on a dedicated IBM 3400x server equipped with a dual-core Intel-Xeon processor, at a clock speed of 1.66 GHz. The total free RAM memory was 4.0 Gb, and there was a 250Gb disk drive.

---

[4] http://www.cs.aau.dk/ stardas/infati

[5] http://piet.exp.dc.uba.ar/piet/index.jsp

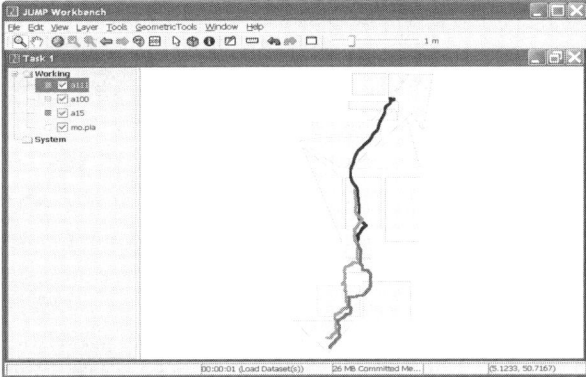

Fig. 12.6 PoIs and two trajectories

12.6.1 Computing the SM-MOFT

We first give details of the computation of the SM-MOFT from the MOFT containing the raw trajectories. We process the MOFT one trajectory at a time. A cursor is placed at the first tuple of the trajectory, and only two points need to be in main memory at the same time. We used the automaton shown in Figure 12.7 to detect the sequence of PoIs that can become a *stop* in the trajectory. The transitions in this automaton can be either a *readPoint()* action, or the empty string λ. There are four states in the automaton: *StartTrajectory*, *EndTrajectory*, *InsidePOI*, and *OutsidePOI*.

StartTrajectory: This is the initial state. If the first point in the trajectory belongs to a PoI, the transition is to the *InsidePOI* state (we have recognized the beginning of a POI). If not, the transition is to the *OutsidePOI* state.

InsidePOI: This state can be reached from any state, except *EndTrajectory*. Different situations must be analyzed:

- The previous states were *OutsidePOI* or *StartTrajectory*. In the first case, the *previous* point must belong to a move. In the latter, we are at the start of the trajectory. The *current* point corresponds to a POI, which is a candidate to become a stop (we call this a *candidate stop*). The time instant of the PoI becomes the initial time of the interval of this potential stop.
- The previous state was *InsidePOI*: if two consecutive points (the *previous* and the *current* ones) are both *inside the same POI*, then the action will be: read the next input (i.e., move to the next point). Otherwise, we have reached the boundary of the PoI, and we are entering another one; thus, before reading the next input, we need to compute the *duration* of the interval in order to check if the sub-trajectory inside the PoI was actually a stop. If we are using *trajectory sampling*, the timestamp of the *previous* point is the ending time of the stop interval.

The timestamp of the *current* point is used as the starting time of the interval of the new PoI the object is entering. If we are using *linear interpolation*, we build a line between both points and calculate the intersection between this line and the PoI (and, of course, the corresponding time instant).

OutsidePOI: this intermediate state can be reached from any state, except *EndTrajectory*. Again, different situations must be analyzed:

- The previous states were *OutsidePOI* or *StartTrajectory*. In the first case, the *previous* point must belong to a move. In the latter we are at the start of the trajectory. The algorithm reads the next input point.
- The previous state was *InsidePOI*: the automaton has detected that the object has left a candidate stop, and proceeds as explained above, computing the duration of the candidate stop to define if the object is still within a move, or if it has found a *stop*.

EndTrajectory: The last state, when the cursor has consumed all the tuples in the MOFT.

To give an idea of practical results, in our case study, starting from a MOFT containing 30,808,296 tuples, we obtained an SM-MOFT with 105,684 tuples (i.e., 0.343% of the original size). The process of generating the SM-MOFT took 1 hour and 6 minutes.

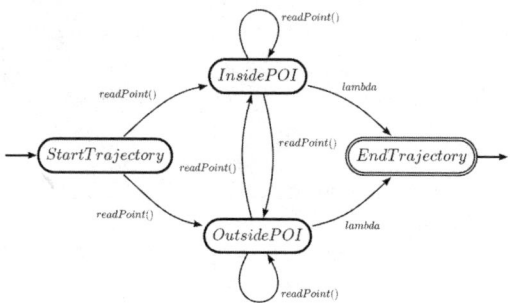

Fig. 12.7 Automata for Stops & Moves calculation

12.6.2 Implementing the smRE Language

We describe now the implementation of the *smRE* language, which is based on the formal language of Section 12.5[6].

---

[6] A demo can be found at http://piet.exp.dc.uba.ar/moving

The PoIs are stored as OLAP dimensions. Thus, we can place conditions over attributes in such dimensions. For example, if we have defined a dimension for restaurants and characterized them by prices and types of food, we can ask for an specific restaurant (e.g., name or ID) or for Italian restaurants, i.e., we can work at different aggregation levels. We may also place conditions over the instants when a stop in a trajectory is reached. An XML document stores all the attributes that characterize a dimension. We have defined a set of reserved words to be used in the conditions over a stop. These words are: (a) *ts*: represents the beginning of the time interval associated to a stop; (b) *ts_date*: represents the *date* part of *ts*; (c) *ts_time*: represents the *time* part of *ts*; (d) *tf, tf_date, tf_time* are analogous to the previous ones, but for the end of the interval associated to a stop; (e) *t, t_date, t_time* are analogous to the previous ones, but for an instant within the interval associated to a stop.

For the data warehouse representing PoIs we have adopted the well-known *star schema*. The MOFT and the SM-MOFT are factless fact tables [14] containing a time dimension. We worked with two separated dimensions for *time*: *date* and *time*, which is usual in practice. This decision was taken because populating a time dimension with members spanning one year and granularity up to the second would require 604,800 tuples. Splitting this dimension into date and time (the latter storing each second of a day), we only need 366 tuples for the *date* dimension and 86.400 for the *time* dimension. The hierarchy of levels for the *date* dimension is: date → day → month → quarter → year. For the *time* dimension we have: time →second → minute → hour → range. The *range* level will have the members: "Midnight", "Early Morning", "Morning", "Afternoon", "Evening" and "Night". Finally, the schemas of the tables are: $\mathcal{M}(O_{id}$, t_date, t_time, x, y) and $\mathcal{M}^{sm}(O_{id}$, Gid, ts_date, ts_time, tf_date, tf_time). The language works, by default, with the SM-MOFT table (see below). For the function f (the rollup functions in the OLAP part of the model) we use the term $rup(x)$, where x is the member whose rollup r computes. We do not need to specify the dimension, which is implicit since all conditions are applied locally at the node being visited.

We will illustrate the implemented language through examples. We will use a different font to indicate that we are referring to the actual implementation. We will work with the PoIs H (hotel), R (restaurant), C (coffee shop), and Z(zoo). The corresponding dimensions have the attributes: *ID* (in all dimensions); *type of food* and *price* for restaurants; and *price* for coffee shops.

Q1: *Trajectories that begin at the "Hilton" hotel, stop at an Italian restaurant and finish at a cheap coffee shop.*

```
H[name="Hilton"].R[food="Italian"].C[price="cheap"]
```

Q2: *Trajectories that begin at the "Sheraton", stop at an Italian restaurant (during the first quarter of 2002), and finish at a cheap coffee shop, leaving the latter in the afternoon.*

```
H[name="Sheraton"].
R[food="Italian" and rup(ts_date)="2002.Q2"].
C[price="cheap" and rup(tf_time)="Afternoon"]
```

Q3: *Trajectories of the following form: (a) there is a stop at the "Hilton", and then at an Italian restaurant; this sequence occurs at least one time, and may be repeated any number of consecutive times; (b) after this sequence, the trajectories may include visits to other places, and finish at the Zoo.*

```
(H[name="Hilton"].R[food="Italian"])+.?.Z[ ]
```

Q4:*Trajectories that visited the "Hilton" and stayed in it during the afternoon.*

```
H[name="Hilton" and rup(t_time)="Afternoon"]
```

All queries, except Q4 use the $\mathcal{M}^{sm}$ table. While Q1 uses only attributes associated to dimensions, Q2 includes rollup functions for ts_date and tf_time (using the *date* and *time* dimensions, respectively). Q3 shows the use of a repetitive group. Q4 needs to access the original MOFT, instead the SM-MOFT, because it asks for an instant t between ts_time and tf_time. Notice that the query could not be solved just using ts_time and tf_time, because both of them may rollup to mornings of different days, and time instants in between may rollup to "Midnight", "Early Morning", or any other possible range. Our implementation detects this need, and proceeds in the best possible way, accessing the original MOFT only when needed.

For solving path expressions we implemented the $\mathcal{SM}$-Graph, explained in Section 12.5. First, we build the automaton for the regular expression. The algorithm takes advantage of the order in the temporal elements associated to the nodes, and unfolds the graph, reproducing the sequences of stops in the trajectory. This unfolded graph is the input to be processed by the automaton. A query is solved at most in two steps.

Step 1. If the query does not include a rollup function, we can solve it in just one step. We match the regular expression to the $\mathcal{SM}$-Graph. Thus, for each O_{id} we obtain the sub-trajectories that match the query. Consider the query:

```
R[price="cheap"].?.Zoo[ts_date="20/09/200?"]
```

We obtain the following matches for $O_{id}= 100$:

```
R[ID="Paris" and price="cheap" and
ts_date="18/09/2000" and ts_time="12:00:05" and
tf_date="18/09/2000" and tf_time="14:04:20"].
Zoo[ID="Central" and ts_date="20/09/2000" and ts_time="12:30:00" and
tf_date="20/09/2000" and tf_time="13:45:04"]

R[ID="Paris" and price="cheap" and
ts_date="16/08/2001" and ts_time="23:15:05" and
tf_date="17/08/2001" and tf_time="01:00:10"].
C[ID="Best" and ts_date="17/08/2001" and ts_time="01:10:00" and
tf_date="17/08/2001" and tf_time="02:00:03"].
Zoo[ID="Central" and ts_date="20/09/2001" and ts_time="11:20:00" and
tf_date="20/09/2001" and tf_time="13:00:00"]
```

The first sub-trajectory shows that there exists a direct path between a cheap restaurant and the zoo:

```
Cheap Paris Restaurant[18/09/2000 12:00:05,18/09/2000 14:04:20]
Central Zoo[20/09/2000 12:30:00,20/09/2000 13:45:04]
```

In the second sub-trajectory there is a path between a cheap restaurant and the zoo with a coffee shop as intermediate stop.

```
Cheap Paris Restaurant [16/08/2001 23:15:05,17/08/2001 01:00:10]
Best coffee [17/08/2001 01:10:00,17/08/2001 02:00:03]
Central Zoo [20/09/2001 11:20:00,20/09/2001 13:00:00]
```

If the query includes the reserved word "t" (instead of "ts" or "tf"), the algorithm must perform an extra verification. For example, if in the query above we replace the term Zoo[ts_date="20/09/200?"] by Zoo[t_date="20/09/200?"], once the interval [ts_date ts_time, tf_date tf_time] was computed, the algorithm will check if this interval includes t_date.

Step 2.
Step 2.1. If the query includes a rollup function, once the sub-trajectories in *Step 1* are obtained, an MDX[7] query is performed to solve the rollup part. Our implementation uses Mondrian[8] as the OLAP server. Let us consider the query:

```
R[price="cheap"].?.Zoo[rup(ts_time)="Morning"]
```

Here, before the rollup function could be computed, step 2.1. must obtain the candidate values for ts_date matching the regular expression (for the dimension Zoo). Then, the algorithm executes the MDX query to find which of the following expressions are true: rup("12:30:00") = "Morning", and rup("11:20:00") = "Morning" (note that in our example, only the latter verifies the rollup).

Step 2.2. If the query involves a rollup of the reserved word "t", we have already explained that the algorithm uses $\mathcal{M}$ (instead of $\mathcal{M}^{sm}$). Let us say, for example, that we replace Zoo[rup(ts_time) = "Morning"] in the query shown in *Step 2.1*, by Zoo[rup(t_time)="Morning"]. We need to find out if there exists a sample point that rolls up to "Morning", because it may happen that even though ts_time rolls up to "Afternoon" and tf_time rolls up to "Night", these situations may occur in different days, and in this case, there exists an instant in the interval rolling up to "Morning".

Finally, we remark that our implementation also supports aggregation, as explained in Section 12.5. For example:

```
COUNT(R[price="cheap"].?.Zoo[t_date="20/09/2001"] )
```

---

[7] MDX is a standard language adopted by most OLAP tools
[8] http://mondrian.sourceforge.net/

12.6.3 Using smRE for Data Mining

There are many practical situations in which we are interested in finding which are the trajectories in the database that verify the same sequence of stops. In these cases, we do not need to check if these trajectories are similar in the usual time-series sense, but in a more semantically-oriented way. Further, we may be interested in different kinds of similarity, with respect to certain patterns. For example, two trajectories that would not be similar under any usual metric, may contain the pattern H.R.?.C (see above). For certain kinds of analysis, this may suffice for considering both trajectories similar.

We propose a two-step method for discovering trajectory patterns. The first one consists in finding association rules using places of interest, with a certain support and confidence, in order to reduce the number of combinations of places of interest that must be checked. Then, we use smRE to analyze the sequences followed by the moving objects and analyze trajectory patterns. Then, we can either calculate the support of a certain pattern (using the aggregate function COUNT, or check which are the trajectories that follow the pattern.

Association Rules for Stops and Moves. We use the *Apriori* algorithm [24] for finding association rules involving stops in trajectories, taking advantage of the information stored in the SM-MOFT. We first need to define what a transaction means in this scenario. In the case of a Market Basket Analysis, for instance, a transaction is clearly determined by the items bought together at the same moment by the consumer. On the contrary, moving objects have a semi-infinite trajectory and there is no clear notion of what a transaction is. In our case study we have considered that a transaction is a sequence of trajectory stops occurred *during the same day*. Other criteria could be used, for example, a transaction could be defined as all stops occurred between 6:00 AM on one day and 5:59 AM of the following day. Then, each trajectory of a moving object could be thought as a sequence of sub-trajectories (transactions, in the association rule sense), each one corresponding to a different day. Figure 12.8 shows a fragment of the SM-MOFT produced from the raw trajectory database. We used an implementation of the *Apriori* algorithm included in the Weka framework[9]. The input to this algorithm is a record containing the whole trajectory of an object in each observed day. Figure 12.9 depicts the form of this table, specifically prepared for discovering association rules at the finest granularity level. The names of the attributes reflect PoI identifiers instead of dimension names. For example, "H_G", "R_C", "C_A", denote particular hotels, restaurants and coffee shops, respectively, while "A" denotes the aquarium. Since we are also interested in multilevel association rules, i.e., rules with itemsets of different granularity, we also need a table where the attributes (items) are the dimension levels instead of the identifiers of the PoIs. We used the following classification attributes: *price* for coffee shops, *number of stars* for hotels, and *type of food* for restaurants. For the experiments with the Apriori algorithm we

---

[9] http://www.cs.waikato.ac.nz/ml/weka/

ID	POI	ts	tf
101	3	26/10/2001 11:00:03	26/10/2001 12:00:03
101	9	26/10/2001 14:10:00	26/10/2001 15:02:05
101	3	26/10/2001 23:30:00	27/10/2001 02:00:01
101	2	27/10/2001 09:22:00	...

Fig. 12.8 The SM-MOFT table for the case study

ID	Date	Z	H_G	R_C	C_A	A	...
101	26/10/2001	?	TRUE	?	?	TRUE	...
101	27/10/2001	?	TRUE	?	?	?	...
101	31/10/2001	TRUE	?	?	?	TRUE	...
...	...	...	...	...	...	...	...

Fig. 12.9 Input transactions for *Apriori* algorithm

generated the *daily transactions of the 6,276 moving objects.* The execution time for this process was 10 seconds and *29,268 transactions* were produced. We required a *minimal support and confidence of 25% and 70%,* respectively. Finally, the only rule produced, working at the finest granularity level, was:

C_L, H_F $\Rightarrow$ Z

Using higher levels of aggregation (i.e., rules where items are of coarser granularity), new rules may be discovered. Applying the *Apriori* algorithm we obtained the following rules (the last two columns on the right indicate support and confidence, respectively):

Hotel_5st, Zoo	$\Rightarrow$ Exp_Cof	29.54	99.79
Zoo	$\Rightarrow$ Exp_Cof	33.03	99.63
Hotel_5st	$\Rightarrow$ Exp_Cof	35.80	99.57
Exp_Cof, Zoo	$\Rightarrow$ Hotel_5st	29.54	89.75
Zoo	$\Rightarrow$ Hotel_5st	29.60	89.30
Zoo	$\Rightarrow$ Exp_Cof, Hotel_5st	29.54	89.12
Exp_Cof, Hotel_5st	$\Rightarrow$ Zoo	29.54	82.51
Hotel_5st	$\Rightarrow$ Zoo	29.60	82.33
Hotel_5st	$\Rightarrow$ Exp_Cof, Zoo	29.54	82.16
Aquarium	$\Rightarrow$ Cheap_Cof	26.23	71.28

Note that these rules do not account for the temporal order in which these sequences of stops occurred. For that, we need sequential pattern analysis, as we explain next. As a final comment, the rules we showed above were produced in a total time of 5 seconds. This fact remarks the need of computing the SM-MOFT before the mining process.

Sequential Patterns for Trajectories. We now show how the *smRE* language introduced in this paper can be used to find trajectory patterns that also account for the temporal order in which the PoIs are visited in a trajectory. For this analysis, we will use the rules discovered in the previous section. Let us begin with the rule:

Aquarium $\Rightarrow$ Cheap_Coffee

Two possible orders exist, expressed by the *smRE* queries:

Q1= COUNT (aquarium[ ].?.coffee[price="cheap"])
Q2= COUNT(coffee[price="cheap"].?.aquarium[ ])

From a total of 29,268 transactions, the expression Q1 was verified by 6,966 trajectories. This gives a support of 23.80%. Q2 was verified by 4,287 trajectories, with a support of 14.65%. This suggests that the pattern "people stop at coffee shops after visiting the aquarium" is the strongest of the two. Let us now analyze the rule:

Coffee_Exp, Hotel_5star $\Rightarrow$ Zoo

The possible combinations, expressed by the following *smRE* queries, are:

Q1=COUNT(coffee[price="expensive"].?.hotel[star="5"].?.zoo[])
Q2=COUNT(coffee[price="expensive"].?.zoo[].?.hotel[star="5"])
Q3=COUNT(hotel[star="5"].?.coffee[price="expensive"].?.zoo[])
Q4=COUNT(hotel[star="5"].?.zoo[].?.coffee[price="expensive"])
Q5=COUNT(zoo[].?.coffee[price="expensive"].?.hotel[star="5"])
Q6=COUNT(zoo[].?.hotel[star="5"].?.coffee[price="expensive"])

The following table summarizes the results, which shows that strongest pattern here the one expressed by query Q1.

Query	# of trajectories	support (%)
Q1	8088	27.63
Q2	5427	18.54
Q3	6	0.02
Q4	7662	26.18
Q5	9	0.03
Q6	5391	18.42

For query evaluation we used the $\mathcal{SM}$-Graph explained in Section 12.5, with a slight variation: instead of producing a graph for each moving object, we generated a graph for each transaction. Thus, we generated 29,268 graphs, each one corresponding to a transaction (i.e., a daily trajectory of a moving object). The six *smRE* queries were run 5 times. We report the minimum, average and maximum execution times for each query.

Query	Min (sec)	Max (sec)	Avg (sec)
Q1	151.76	154.91	153.48
Q2	152.09	156.05	153.78
Q3	152.87	154.19	153.48
Q4	151.48	154.64	153.19
Q5	151.97	154.39	153.47
Q6	151.19	154.33	152.74

12.7 Future Work

The framework we presented in this paper supports a seamless integration of spatial, non-spatial, and moving object data. We are currently in the process of including the implementation described in Section 12.6 into the Piet framework [4]. The *smRE* language is a promising tool for mining trajectory data, specifically in the context of sequential patterns mining with constraints, and we will continue working in this direction.

We believe that many research directions open from the work presented here. For example, along the same research line presented in the paper, we are now working on extending well-known sequential patterns algorithms, in order to compare these algorithms against the two-step process presented in this paper. Further, efficient automatic extraction of patterns using the *smRE* language could be explored. This means that, instead of writing the query expression, we would like to generate the ones with a given minimum support. Relationships between objects (like the distance changes between them during a certain period of time) can also be studied, as well as situations where the positions of the PoIs are not fixed. Updates to the MOFT and the SM-MOFTs must be studied, not only for the changes in trajectory data (i.e., new objects or trajectories), but also under changes in the PoIs.

12.8 Acknowledgments

This work has been partially funded by the European Union under the FP6-IST-FET programme, Project n. FP6-14915, GeoPKDD: Geographic Privacy-Aware Knowledge Discovery and Delivery, the Research Foundation Flanders (FWO Vlaanderen), Project G.0344.05., and the Scientific Agency of Argentina, Project PICT n. 21350.

References

1. L. O. Alvares, V. Bogorny, B. Kuijpers, J. A. F. de Macedo, B. Moelans, and A. Vaisman. A model for enriching trajectories with semantic geographical information. In *ACM-GIS*, 2007.
2. S. Brakatsoulas, D. Pfoser, and N. Tryfona. Modeling, storing and mining moving object databases. In *Proceedings of IDEAS'04*, pages 68–77, Washington D.C, USA, 2004.
3. M. L. Damiani, J. A. F. de Macedo, C. Parent, F. Porto, and S. Spaccapietra. A conceptual view of trajectories. *Technical Report, Ecole Polythecnique Federal de Lausanne, April 2007*, 2007.
4. A. Escribano, L. Gomez, B. Kuijpers, and A. A. Vaisman. Piet: a gis-olap implementation. In *DOLAP*, pages 73–80, Lisbon, Portugal, 2007.
5. E. Frentzos, K. Gratsias, and Y. Theodoridis. Index-based most similar trajectory search. In *ICDE*, pages 816–825, 2007.
6. F. Giannotti, M. Nanni, F. Pinelli, and D. Pedreschi. Trajectory pattern mining. In *KDD*, pages 330–339, San Jose, California, USA, 2007.
7. L. Gomez, S. Haesevoets, B. Kuijpers, and A. Vaisman. Spatial aggregation: Data model and implementation. In *Submitted for review*, 2008.
8. L. Gomez, S. Haesevoets, B. Kuijpers, and A. A. Vaisman. Spatial aggregation: Data model and implementation. *CoRR*, abs/0707.4304, 2007.
9. L. Gomez, B. Kuijpers, and A. A. Vaisman. Aggregation languages for moving object and places of interest. In *To appear in Proceedings of SAC 2008 - ASIIS track*.
10. L. Gomez, B. Kuijpers, and A. A. Vaisman. Aggregation languages for moving object and places of interest data. *CoRR*, abs/0708.2717, 2007.
11. H. Gonzalez, J. Han, X. Li, M. Myslinska, and J. P. Sondag. Adaptive fastest path computation on a road network: A traffic mining approach. In *VLDB*, pages 794–805, 2007.
12. R. H. Güting and M. Schneider. *Moving Objects Databases*. Morgan Kaufman, 2005.
13. K. Hornsby and M. Egenhofer. Modeling moving objects over multiple granularities. *Special issue on Spatial and Temporal Granularity, Annals of Mathematics and Artificial Intelligence*, 2002.
14. R. Kimball and M. Ross. *The Data Warehouse Toolkit: The Complete Guide to Dimensional Modeling, 2nd. Ed.* J.Wiley and Sons, Inc, 2002.
15. B. Kuijpers and A. A. Vaisman. A data model for moving objects supporting aggregation. In *ICDE Workshops*, pages 546–554, Istambul, Turkey, 2007.
16. J.-G. Lee, J. Han, and K.-Y. Whang. Trajectory clustering: a partition-and-group framework. In *SIGMOD Conference*, pages 593–604, 2007.
17. N. Meratnia and R. de By. Aggregation and comparison of trajectories. In *Proceedings of the 26th VLDB Conference*, Virginia, USA, 2002.
18. C. Mouza and P. Rigaux. Mobility patterns. *Geoinformatica*, 9(23):297–319, 2005.
19. T. Ott and F. Swiaczny. *Time-integrative Geographic Information Systems–Management and Analysis of Spatio-Temporal Data*. Springer, 2001.
20. D. Papadias, Y. Tao, J. Zhang, N. Mamoulis, Q. Shen, and J. Sun. Indexing and retrieval of historical aggregate information about moving objects. *IEEE Data Eng. Bull.*, 25(2):10–17, 2002.
21. J. Paredaens, G. Kuper, and L. Libkin, editors. *Constraint databases*. Springer-Verlag, 2000.
22. N. Pelekis, I. Kopanakis, G. Marketos, I. Ntoutsi, G. L. Andrienko, and Y. Theodoridis. Similarity search in trajectory databases. In *TIME*, pages 129–140, 2007.
23. P. Rigaux, M. Scholl, and A. Voisard. *Spatial Databases*. Morgan Kaufmann, 2002.
24. R. Srikant and R. Agrawal. Mining generalized association rules. In *VLDB*, pages 407–419, 1995.
25. O. Wolfson, P. Sistla, B. Xu, and S. Chamberlain. Domino: Databases fOr MovINg Objects tracking. In *Proceedings of SIGMOD'99*, pages 547 – 549, 1999.
26. M. F. Worboys. *GIS: A Computing Perspective*. Taylor&Francis, 1995.

Chapter 13
OLAP-Sequential Mining: Summarizing Trends from Historical Multidimensional Data using Closed Multidimensional Sequential Patterns

Marc Plantevit, Anne Laurent, and Maguelonne Teisseire

Abstract Data warehouses are now well recognized as the way to store historical data that will then be available for future queries and analysis. In this context, some challenges are still open, among which the problem of mining such data. OLAP mining, introduced by J. Han in 1997, aims at coupling data mining techniques and data warehousing. These techniques have to take the specificities of such data into account. One of the specificities that is often not addressed by classical methods for data mining is the fact that data warehouses describe data through several dimensions. Moreover, the data are stored through time, and we thus argue that sequential patterns are one of the best ways to summarize the trends from such databases. Sequential pattern mining aims at discovering correlations among events through time. However, the number of patterns can become very important when taking several analysis dimensions into account, as it is the case in the framework of multidimensional databases. This is why we propose here to define a condensed representation without loss of information: closed multidimensional sequential patterns. This representation introduces properties that allow to deeply prune the search space. In this paper, we also define algorithms that do not require candidate set maintenance. Experiments on synthetic and real data are reported and emphasize the interest of our proposal.

13.1 Introduction

Data warehouses are now well spread over companies. They contain valuable information that can easily be queried and visualized with the OLAP tools, provided the fact that the user is able to design on-line his own queries. However, it is still challenging to provide the user with tools that can automatically extract relevant knowledge from such huge amounts of data. Data warehouses are indeed different

LIRMM, Université Montpellier 2, CNRS, 161 Rue Ada 34392 Montpellier, France, e-mail: {plantevi,laurent,teisseire}@lirmm.fr

from usually mined databases as they contain aggregated data, described by means of several dimensions that can possibly be organized through hierarchies. In this paper, we thus try and extend existing methods that are now recognized for mining classical databases to this framework. As data are historized, we argue that sequential patterns are well-suited to this task. Sequential patterns have been studied for more than ten years [1], with a lot of research and industrial applications (*e.g.* user behavior, web log analysis, discovery of patterns from proteins' sequences, security and music). Algorithms have been proposed, based on the APriori-based framework [23, 9, 2], or on other approaches [13, 8]. Sequential patterns have recently been extended to multidimensional sequential patterns by [14, 15, 22]. They aim at discovering patterns that take time into account and that involve several dimensions. For instance in [15], rules like *A customer who bought a surfboard together with a bag in NY later bought a wetsuit in SF* are discovered. Note that such sequences can also contain a wild-card item ∗ instead of a dimension value. For instance, considering the previous example, if there is no frequent pattern in the database describing the fact that wetsuits were later bought in SF, or NY etc, but there are numerous wetsuits bought whatever the city, then the rule *A customer who bought a surfboard together with a bag in NY later bought a wetsuit* will be mined, represented as $\langle(surfboard, NY)(wetsuit, *)\rangle$.

Sequential patterns are usually extracted from the simple schema: (*e.g. products, customer_id* and *date*) but the number of mined patterns can be very huge. This is why condensed representations were proposed for the itemset framework ([10, 12, 24, 5]) and for sequential patterns ([21, 18]). In both cases, the approaches allow a condensed representation and a pruning strategy in the search space.

However, these works are not suitable for multidimensional sequential patterns because they only consider a particular case for candidate generation. In our context, a super-sequence may indeed result from several cases (1) a longer sequence (more items) or (2) a more general sequence based on the relation between dimension values and the wild-card value ∗ (more general items).

The main contributions of this paper are a theoretical framework for mining closed multidimensional sequential patterns and some algorithms called *CMSP* (Closed Multidimensional Sequential Pattern mining) to mine such patterns. When considering multidimensional data, the number of possible patterns is combinatorially explosive and the generate-and-prune methods are no more scalable for long sequences, as highlighted in [11, 16]. This is why we adopt the pattern growth paradigm ([13]) to propose a greedy approach for mining frequent sequences without candidate generation.

The paper is organized as follows. First we recall the related work in Section 13.2 and we detail why existing works are not suitable for mining data warehouse. Then we present the core of our proposition: the definitions are introduced in Section 13.3 while the *CMSP* algorithms are detailed in Section 13.4. Experiments on synthetic and real data, reported in Section 13.5, show that our method performs well both on runtime and number of extracted closed sequences. Finally, we provide some concluding remarks and suggestions for future work in Section 13.6.

13.2 Related Work

In this Section, we first recall from [15] the seminal definitions of multidimensional sequential patterns. Then we present existing works from the literature on closed patterns.

13.2.1 Multidimensional Sequential Patterns

To the best of our knowledge, three proposals exist for mining sequential patterns when considering several dimensions.

The approach proposed by [14] mines sequences over one single dimension (*e.g.* product) labeled by multidimensional patterns. However, no combination of dimensions is possible through time (within the sequence).

[22] is very particular since the dimensions are embedded one within the other one (web *pages* are visited within one *session* during one *day*).

In [15], rules not only combine several dimensions but they also combine these dimensions over time. For instance in the rule *A customer who bought a surfboard together with a bag in NY later bought a wetsuit in SF, NY* appears before *SF*, and *surfboard* appears before *wetsuit*.

As the last approach is more general than the other two ones, we focus here on the concepts of multidimensional sequential patterns introduced in [15].

More formally, let us consider a database *DB* where data are described with respect to n dimensions. We consider a 3-bin partitioning of the dimensions:

- the set of those dimensions that will be contained within the rules (*analysis dimensions*) is denoted by D_A;
- the set of those dimensions on which the counting will be based (*reference dimensions*) is denoted by D_R;
- the set of those dimensions that are meant to introduce an order between events (*e.g. time*) is denoted by D_T.

The database can then be partitioned into *blocks* defined by their positions on the reference dimensions.

A *multidimensional item* e is a m-tuple defined over the set of the m D_A dimensions. We consider $e = (d_1, d_2, \ldots, d_m)$ where $d_i \in Dom(D_i) \cup \{*\}, \forall D_i \in D_A$ and where $*$ stands for the *wild-card* value. For instance, $(1,2)$ is a multidimensional item defined with respect to two dimensions.

A *multidimensional itemset* $i = \{e_1, \ldots, e_k\}$ is a non-empty set of multidimensional items. All items of the itemset have to be "incomparable" to preserve the notion of set. For instance, $\{(1,1),(1,2)\}$ is a multidimensional itemset whereas $\{(1,1)(1,*)\}$ is not an itemset because $(1,1) \subseteq (1,*)$.

A *multidimensional sequence* $\varsigma = \langle i_1, \ldots, i_l \rangle$ is a non-empty ordered list of multidimensional itemsets. For instance, $\varsigma_1 = \langle \{(1,1),(1,2)\}\{(1,*),(*,4)\}\{(1,3)\} \rangle$ is a multidimensional sequence.

Sequences that contain k items and g itemsets are called g-k-sequences:

Definition 13.1 (g-k-Sequence). A g-k-sequence S is a sequence that is composed of g itemsets and k items as following:

$$S = \langle \{e_1^1, e_2^1, \ldots, e_{k_1}^1\}, \{e_1^2, e_2^2, \ldots, e_{k_2}^2\}, \ldots, \{e_1^g, e_2^g, \ldots, e_{k_g}^g\} \rangle \text{ where } \Sigma_1^g(k_i) = k.$$

A multidimensional sequence can be included into another one:

Definition 13.2 (Sequence inclusion). A multidimensional sequence $\varsigma = \langle a_1, \ldots, a_l \rangle$ is said to be a subsequence of $\varsigma' = \langle b_1, \ldots, b_{l'} \rangle$ if there exist integers $1 \leq j_1 \leq j_2 \leq \ldots \leq j_l \leq l'$ such that $a_1 \subseteq b_{j_1}, a_2 \subseteq b_{j_2}, \ldots, a_l \subseteq b_{j_l}$.

For instance, the sequence $\langle \{(1,2), (*,3)\}\{(2,2)\} \rangle$ is a subsequence of the sequence $\langle \{(1,*), (*,3)\}\{(*,2)(*,3)\} \rangle$.

We consider that each block defined over D_R contains one multidimensional data sequence, which is thus identified by that block. A block *supports* a sequence ς if all items of ς can be matched (each value on each analysis dimension has to be matched except with wild-card value *) with an item of the data sequence with respect to time order.

Thus, the *support* of a multidimensional sequence is the number of those blocks defined over D_R which contain this sequence.

When considering the *classical* case of sequential patterns, the sets of analysis, reference, and order dimensions consist of only one dimension (usually the *product*, *customer_id* and *time* dimensions). Note that even in this classical case, the number of frequent sequential patterns discovered from a database can be huge. And this problem becomes worse in the case of multidimensional patterns since multidimensional framework produces more patterns than classical framework.

For this reason, it is necessary to study condensed representations. We aim at representing the sequential patterns *and* their support. Thus, we do not consider the solution of representing *only* maximal sequential patterns, since this would result in the loss of the information about the support of subsequences.

In this paper, we consider *closed patterns*. They indeed allow to represent the patterns in a compressed manner without any loss of information.

13.2.2 Closed Patterns

A major challenge in mining frequent patterns is the fact that such mining often generates a huge number of patterns satisfying the minimum support threshold. This is because if a pattern is frequent, each of its subpatterns is also frequent. A pattern will contain an exponential number of smaller subpatterns. To overcome this problem, closed frequent pattern mining were proposed by [10]. Frequent closed patterns algorithms, which heavily draw on Formal Concept Analysis (FCA) mathematical settings [6, 20], present a novel alternative with a clear promise to dramatically reduce, without information loss, the size of the frequent pattern set. From the frequent closed patterns, the support of frequent non-closed patterns can be inferred.

Based on the previous approaches [5, 10, 12, 24], a closed pattern is defined as follows:

Definition 13.3 (Closed Pattern). A (sequential) pattern α is *closed* if there does not exist any pattern β such that $\alpha \subseteq \beta$ and $support(\alpha) = support(\beta)$.

For instance, let us suppose that the sequences $\langle a \rangle_3$ and $\langle a,b,c \rangle_2$ are closed, where $\langle a \rangle_3$ stands for the sequence $\langle a \rangle$ having support 3. Then it can be deduced that the sequences $\langle a,c \rangle$ and $\langle b,c \rangle$, which are included in the previous ones, have support 2. If their support was 3 then the sequence $\langle a \rangle$ would not be closed. Thus, their frequency is directly correlated to the frequency of $\langle a,b,c \rangle$. All the sequences are shown in Figure 13.1 where the closed sequences are circled.

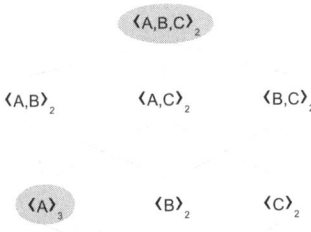

Fig. 13.1 Searching all the frequent sequences from the closed ones

It should be noticed that many works have been done on the extraction of closed itemsets [5, 12, 24, 19] but only two approaches have been proposed for sequential closed patterns: BIDE and CloSpan.

CloSpan [21] first extracts a set of closed sequence candidates, which contains the set of frequent sequences. In this first set, some sequences are not closed. Thus, CloSpan prunes the non-closed sequences in a second step. CloSpan uses the pattern-growth approach, which is different from the APriori-like candidate-generation-and-test approaches. CloSpan decomposes the database in order to discard non-needed computations [11]. In order to reduce the space search, the database is projected by the current mined sequence also called prefix sequence. The projected database according to the sequence α is denoted $DB|\alpha$. For instance, given the data sequence $S = \langle (abcd)ea(bc)(ac) \rangle$ and $\alpha = \langle (ab)a \rangle$, $S|\alpha = \langle (bc)(ac) \rangle$. As soon as a sub-pattern or a super-pattern of the current sequence shares the same projected database as the current one, we do not need to explore this database in order to grow this sequence. Indeed, their subtrees can be merged into one without having to mine a subtree in the search space already mined.

BIDE [18] enhances the previous approach (CloSpan). The authors propose an approach without any candidate maintenance-and-test paradigm. This approach prunes the search space more deeply. It checks a pattern closure in a more efficient way while consuming less memory than CloSpan. Indeed, BIDE does not maintain the set of historic closed patterns.

It should be noted that these two approaches not only reduce the number of sequences to be considered, but also result in better performances (both in time and memory).

We can also cite the work of [17] which considers closed sequential patterns in multidimensional framework. However, this approach uses a condensed representation of [14]. So this approach mines sequences over one single dimension (*e.g.* product) labeled by multidimensional patterns. Thus, no combination of dimensions is possible through time (within the sequence).

OLAP Mining has been studied since 1997 [7], aiming at designing methods to automatically extract relevant knowledge from multidimensional databases. In this framework, the challenges are numerous, as this kind of data is different from classical databases that are usually mined. First, multidimensional databases contain aggregated data. Moreover, this data is described using dimensions, which can be organized through hierarchies. Finally, the data is historized so as to report the evolution through time. Discovering trends from such data can thus be seen as the task of extracting the relevant frequent sequences that occur. This is the reason why we choose here to study sequential patterns, as efficient methods have been designed to extract such trends, while remaining scalable (typically by using algorithms that do not have to manage sets of candidates) and concise (typically by using closed sequential patterns). However to the best of our knowledge, multidimensional sequential patterns have not been considered in the existing work. So, we propose a theoretical framework for mining closed multidimensional sequential patterns.

13.2.3 Particularity of the Multidimensional Framework

In this section, we explain why it is quite difficult to apply existing work on sequential pattern to the multidimensional framework. These reasons are essentially due to the inclusion of wild-carded -sequences.

Unfortunately, the classical framework (one analysis dimension) is no longer suitable when considering wild-carded multidimensional sequential patterns. For instance, if we assume that $\langle \{(a_1,b_1),(*,b_2)\}\rangle_2$ is closed, then by calculating the other sequences, it could be calculated that the sequences $\langle \{(a_1,b_1),(a_1,b_2)\}\rangle$ and $\langle \{(a_1,b_1),(a_2,b_2)\}\rangle$ are in the same case as previously (support should be 2). However, it may happen that the sequences $\langle \{(a_1,b_1),(a_1,b_2)\}\rangle$ and $\langle \{(a_1,b_1),(a_2,b_2)\}\rangle$ have a support of 1. This may occur because a super-sequence may result from several cases: a longer sequence (more items) or a more general sequence based on the relation between dimension values and the wild-card (more general items). More precisely, it is due to the fact that all values of domain dimensions are contained in wild-card.

13.3 CMSP - Closed Multidimensional Sequential Patterns

In order to define Closed Multidimensional Sequential Patterns, we introduce a specialization relation between patterns to catch the specific context of the multidimensional data.

Definition 13.4 (Specialization/Generalization). A multidimensional sequential pattern $\alpha = \langle a_1, \ldots, a_l \rangle$ is more general than $\beta = \langle b_1, \ldots, b_{l'} \rangle$ $(l \le l')$ (and β is more specific than α) if there exist integers $1 \le j_1 \le j_2 \le \ldots \le j_l \le l'$ such that $b_{j_1} \subseteq a_1, b_{j_2} \subseteq a_2, \ldots, b_{j_l} \subseteq a_l$.

If β is more specific than α, we write $\alpha \subset_S \beta$ where $\subset_S$ denotes a *specialization relation*.

Example 13.1. The sequence $\beta = \langle \{(a_1,b_1),(a_2,b_2)\}\{(*,b_1)\} \rangle$ is more specific than the sequence $\alpha = \langle \{(a_1,*),(a_2,b_2)\} \rangle$. We denote $\alpha \subset_S \beta$. We can note that this definition is different from the inclusion definition (definition 13.2). Here, the main idea is that a sequence is more specific than another one if it is at least longer than the other one and its items should be more specific. For instance, $\langle (1,*) \rangle \subset_S \langle (1,1),(1,1) \rangle$ and $\langle (1,*) \rangle \not\subset_S \langle (1,1),(1,1) \rangle$.

We can now define closed multidimensional sequence and closed multidimensional sequential patterns as follows:

Definition 13.5. (Closed Multidimensional Sequence) A multidimensional sequence α is closed if there does not exist β such that $\alpha \subset_S \beta$ and $support(\alpha) = support(\beta)$

Definition 13.6. (Closed Multidimensional Sequential Pattern) Let *minsup* be a minimal support threshold, a sequence s is a closed multidimensional sequential pattern if s is closed and $support(s) \ge minsup$.

Example 13.2 (Closed Multidimensional Sequential Patterns and Inference).
With a minimal support threshold equal to 3 and the database shown in Table 13.1, the set of closed patterns is given by the first part of Table 13.2.

With a minimal support threshold equal to 2, the set of closed sequential patterns is given by Table 13.2. Unclosed sequences can be inferred from the closed ones. For instance, the support of the sequences $\langle (*,b_2) \rangle$ and $\langle (a_2,*) \rangle$ can then be computed as being equal to 3.

Thus, two levels of knowledge can be inferred from closed patterns:

a) for subsequences containing fewer items;
b) for subsequences containing more general items (more wildcards).

These two levels can be mixed in order to infer even more general knowledge.

1	$\langle\{(a_1,b_1),(a_1,b_2)\}\{(a_2,b_2)\}\{(a_1,b_3)\}\{(a_1,b_2)(a_2,b_2)\}\rangle$
2	$\langle\{(a_1,b_2),(a_2,b_1)\}\{(a_3,b_2)\}\{(a_2,b_1)\}\{(a_2,b_1)\}\rangle$
3	$\langle\{(a_4,b_4)\}\{(a_2,b_1)\}\{(a_1,b_1)(a_2,b_2))\}\rangle$

Table 13.1 Running Example

$\langle(a_1,*)\rangle_3$
$\langle(a_2,*),(a_2,*)\rangle_3$
$\langle(a_2,*),(*,b_2)\rangle_3$
$\langle(*,b_1),(a_2,*)\rangle_3$
$\langle(*,b_2),(*,b_2)\rangle_3$

$\langle\{(a_1,b_1),(*,b_2)\}\rangle_2$
$\langle\{(a_1,b_2),(*,b_1)\},(a_2,*),(a_2,*)\rangle_2$
$\langle\{(a_1,b_2),(*,b_1)\}(*,b_2),(a_2,*)\rangle_2$
$\langle(a_2,b_1),(a_2,*)\rangle_2$
$\langle(a_2,b_1),(*,b_1)\rangle_2$
$\langle(a_2,b_1),(*,b_2)\rangle_2$
$\langle(a_2,*),(2,2)\rangle_2$
$\langle(a_2,*),(1,*)\rangle_2$
$\langle(*,b_1),(a_2,b_2)\rangle_2$
$\langle(*,b_1),(a_1,*)\rangle_2$

Table 13.2 Closed multidimensional sequences with support 2 and 3

13.4 *CMSP*: Mining Closed Multidimensional Sequential Patterns

As mentioned in the introduction, generate-and-prune methods cannot be scalable for long sequences. This non-scalability problem is worse in a multidimensional framework since the number of possible patterns is combinatorially explosive.Thus, we adopt the pattern-growth paradigm in order to define complete and scalable algorithms for mining multidimensional closed sequential patterns. The definitions we consider here are taken from the approaches that are recognized as being efficient for mining for sequential patterns. The first approach is described in Section 13.4.2. It considers the methods defined in CloSpan [21]. The second approach we consider here is based on Bide [18] described in Section 13.4.3. In this approach, no candidate set is maintained.

We define below the definitions that are common to these two approaches, and we then detail on each of them the implementation we propose. Experimental results are reported in Section 13.5.

13.4.1 Order Within The Itemset of a Sequence

Ordering items within the itemsets is one of the main basis to improve the implementation and to discard already examined cases. The existing methods presented in [21, 18] for ordering sequences are not directly applicable to the multidimensional framework. Indeed wild-carded items are not explicitly present in databases. Such items are retrieved by inference since there is no associated tuple in the database.

| 1 | $\langle\{(a_1,b_1),(a_1,b_2)\}\rangle$ |
| 2 | $\langle\{(a_1,b_2),(a_2,b_1)\}\rangle$ |

Table 13.3 Where is the sequence $\langle\{(a_1,b_2),(*,b_1)\}\rangle$?

Table 13.3 shows an example of a database that cannot be treated by these two methods, since wild-carded items are not explicitly present in the database. Thus, no total lexicographic order can be defined between the elements of the itemsets. So these methods cannot mine the sequence $\langle\{(a_1,b_2),(*,b_1)\}\rangle$. As an example, CloSpan finds the frequent item (a_1,b_2) with a support of 2 and then, it constructs the projected database prefixed by the sequence $\langle\{(a_1,b_2)\}\rangle$. This projected database contains the sequences $\langle\{\}\rangle$ and $\langle\{(a_2,b_1)\}\rangle$. Thus the item $(*,b_1)$ does not appear to be frequent in this projected database whereas it is frequent in the initial database.

This trivial example highlights the need to introduce a lexical order taking wild-carded items into account.

It should be noted that it is not possible to extend the whole database with all the possible wild-carded items before the mining process. For example, if we consider a database containing m analysis dimensions and n_i items in an itemset i, this transformation would produce $(2^m - 1) \times n_i$ items instead of n_i leading to a database of size $(2^m - 1)\sum_{t_i \in DB} n_{t_i}$.

It is then necessary to take all wild-carded items into account *during* the process of closed multidimensional sequential patterns and not *before* as a pre-treatment.

We will then introduce an lexical order and functions to locally materialize the wild-carded items.

It is necessary to have a lexicographic order when mining frequent patterns since it is the basis foundation of the non-duplication of items during the computation. We now define the concept of *extended itemset*.

Definition 13.7 (Extended Itemset). A frequent itemset is said to be *extended* if it is equal to its downward closure according to the specialization relation $(\subset_S)$.

The extended itemsets enable to mine wild-carded items which can be deduced from data sequences.

In order to optimize the computation of closed multidimensional sequential patterns, we introduce a *lexico-graphico-specific* (LGS) order. This order results from an alpha-numerical order according to the precision of the items (number of * in the item). Thus the priority is given to the most specific items during the mining process. For instance, itemset $i_1 = \{(a_1,b_1),(a_2,b_1),(a_1,*),(a_2,*),(*,b_1)\}$ is sorted w.r.t LGS order.

We define a function which transforms an itemset (transaction) into its extended itemset.

Definition 13.8 (Function LGS-Closure). *LGS-Closure* is an application from an itemset i to the closure of i w.r.t. the LGS order $<_{lgs}$.

Example 13.3 (LGS-Closure). $LGS\text{-}Closure(\{(a_1,b_1),(a_2,b_1)\}) = \{(a_1,b_1),$-
$(a_2,b_1),(a_1,*),(a_2,*),(*,b_1)\}$

This closure is illustrated in the Figure 5. Note that we do not return the most general item (*,*) of the lattice . This item does not need to be mined since it is a tautology.

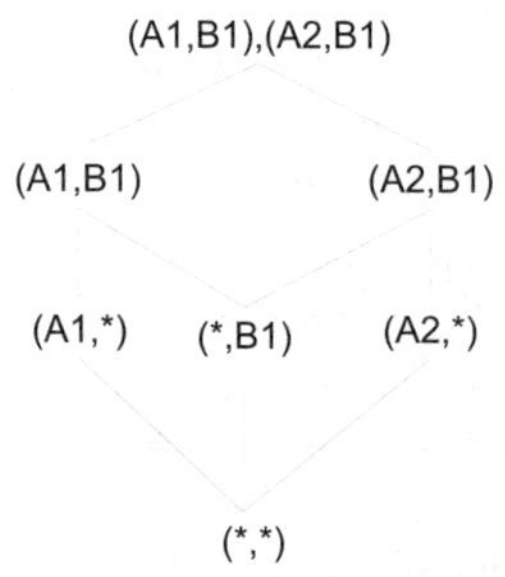

```
              (A1,B1),(A2,B1)


        (A1,B1)              (A2,B1)


       (A1,*)    (*,B1)    (A2,*)



                (*,*)
```

Fig. 13.2 LGS-Closure

The extraction of frequent items is then performed on each extended itemset. In the pattern-growth approach, the sequences are greedily extracted by adding a frequent item to a frequent *prefix sequence*. The prefix sequence can be extended by adding a frequent item in a new itemset or by adding a frequent item in the last itemset of the prefix sequence. It is thus necessary to define an efficient way to extend a prefix sequence according to its last itemset. Furthermore, we have to preserve the notion of set of an itemset (two comparable items cannot appear together within an itemset). For that purpose, we define a restriction as follows.

Definition 13.9 (Function LGS-Closure$_X$). The function $LGS\text{-}Closure_X(i)$ in an application from an itemset i to the closure of i taking filtering of the itemset $X = \{x_1 \leq_{lgs} \ldots \leq_{lgs} x_{k'}\}$ into account such that:

$$LGS\text{-}Closure_X(i) = \{e \in LGS\text{-}Closure(i) \ s.t. \ e \geq_{lgs} x_{k'} \ and \ \nexists x_j \in X \mid x_j \subseteq e\}$$

Example 13.4 (LGS-Closure$_X$). $LGS\text{-}Closure_{\{(a_1,b_1)\}}(\{(a_1,b_1),(a_1,b_2),(a_1,b_3)\}) = \{(*,b_2),(*,b_3)\}$

13.4.2 CMSP_Cand

In this section, we define an algorithm adapted from CloSpan.

Closed sequential patterns are extracted using algorithms 6 (*CMSP_Cand*) and 14 (SequenceGrowing) following a depth-first strategy.

Instead of scanning the whole database level by level in the same way as APriori-like methods, the database is projected according to the current examined prefix sequence. This projection is quite different from [13]. Since we should take into account wild-carded items, the database projection should take into account the transaction (itemset of the block data sequence) where item was found, and not only the item itself like in [13]. To take into account this transaction, we use the *LGS-Closure* function by filtering the already found items.

For instance, if we consider the following data sequence $S = \langle (1,1), \{(1,2),(1,3)\}, (2,2) \rangle$ and the current prefix sequence $\alpha = \langle (1,2) \rangle$. According to [13], the projected database $S|\alpha = \{\_(1,3)\}, (2,2) \rangle$ where $\_(1,3)$ indicates that the item $(1,3)$ and the last itemset of α shares the same itemset in the data sequence. With our algorithm, the projected database is quite different since we take into account wild-card values. The projected database is built as follows: $S|\alpha = \_LGS\text{-}Closure_{\{(1,2)\}}(\{(1,2)(1,3)\}), \{(2,2)\}$, thus we have: $S|\alpha = \{\_(1,3)\_(1,*)\_(*,3)\}, \{(2,2)\}$.

The use of projected database prevents from scanning already seen data. Indeed, if we consider a frequent sequence α and the current examined prefix sequence β such that $\beta \subseteq_S \alpha$ or $\alpha \subseteq_S \beta$ and such that the projected database is the same for β and α, then it is not necessary to expand this last sequence. We just need to copy the subtree (already mined) of the sequence α to the sequence β.

We can note that:

- if $\alpha \subseteq_S \beta$ then α cannot be closed;
- if $\beta \subseteq_S \alpha$ then the sequences prefixed by β are already known, thus allowing us to discard the frequent suffixes of β.

In the latter case, it should be noted that β cannot be closed. However, it is necessary to keep this sequence as it can be included in some other ones, thus avoiding database scans.

Algorithm 17 considers locally frequent items from projected fragments of the database. It is based on the *LGS-Closure* function (definition 13.9). The projected database is scanned only once in order to extract all frequent items. Two types of items can be mined:

a) The items which cannot be included in the last itemset of the prefix sequence ς. These items should be included in a new itemset of ς. In order to mine such items and to take into account wild-carded item, we need to extend all transactions of the projected database (step by step) thanks to the function *LGS-Closure*.

b) The items which can be included in the last itemset of the prefix sequence ς. In that case, we use the function *LGS-Closure* parametrized with the last itemset of ς.

The last task of Algorithm 6 is to eliminate non-closed multidimensional sequences from the set of closed sequence candidates. The problem is to check out for each multidimensional sequence ς, whether there exists a multidimensional sequence ς' such that $\varsigma \subset_S \varsigma'$ and $support(\varsigma) = support(\varsigma')$. A naive algorithm, which compares each multidimensional sequence with other ones in the set, cannot work because of its quadratic complexity in the number of closed sequence candidates. We adopt the fast subsumption checking algorithm introduced by Zaki [24]. The value of support is very dense. Thus $support$ cannot be a relevant hash key which enables a sparse distribution of keys. [24] proposes using the sum of sequences' identifiers (denoted $\tau(D_S)$)as its hash key instead of using support. However, in sequence framework, the equivalence of $\tau(D_S)$ does not imply the equivalence of support. Thus, for the multidimensional sequences that share the same $\tau(D_S)$, we need to check their support in order to eliminate the invalid candidates. This hash key, also used in CloSpan, is easy to compute. Furthermore, it enhances the space search reduction. Thus, the complexity of this operation is $\Theta(\sum n_{\tau_i}^2)$ where n_{τ_i} is the number of closed sequence candidates that share the same τ_i. The n_{τ_i} are significantly less than the total number of closed sequence candidates ($\sum n_{\tau_i}$).

Algorithm 6: *CMSP_Cand*

Data: Database *DB*, minimal support *minsup*
Result: The set of closed *C*

1 **begin**
2   /* Initialization */
3   *Set* $L \leftarrow \{\}$
4   *Set* $C \leftarrow \{\}$
5   *Sequence* $\alpha \leftarrow \langle\rangle$
6   /*Frequent sequence mining (depthfirst)*/
7   *SequenceGrowing*$(\alpha, DB, L, minsup)$
8   /*Pruning of non-closed in *L*/
9   **foreach** $s_1 \in L$ **do**
10   **foreach** $s_2 \in L$ **do**
11   **if** $s_1 \subseteq_S s_2$ *et* $support(s_1) = support(s_2)$ **then**
12                 $delete(s_1, L)$
13   **endif**
14   **endfch**
15   **endfch**
16     $C \leftarrow L$
17   **return** C
18 **end**

Example

Let us consider the multidimensional sequence database from Tab. 13.4 . We want to discover all closed multidimensional sequential patterns with *minsup* equal to 2.

Algorithm 7: SequenceGrowing: Mining algorithm

Data: Sequence α,projected database $DB|\alpha$, closed sequence candidate set L, minimal
　　　　support *minsup*

Result: The set of sequences prefixed by α

1 **begin**
2　　　　/*α may be closed*/
3　　　　$insert(\alpha, L)$
4　　　　/*Check if the sequence was already checked out */
5　　　　**if** $\exists \beta \mid (\alpha \subseteq_S \beta$ or $\beta \subseteq \alpha)$ *and they both share the same projected database* **then**
6　　　　　　*Copy the descendants of β in α*
7　　　　　　**return**
8　　　　**endif**
9　　　　Set $F_l \leftarrow getFrequentItems(DB|\alpha, minsup)$
10　　　　**foreach** $\alpha' \leftarrow \alpha.b$ **do**
11　　　　　　*Build $DB|\alpha'$*
12　　　　　　$SequenceGrowing(\alpha', DB|\alpha', L, minsup)$
13　　　　**endfch**
14 **end**

Algorithm 8: getFrequentItems: Localy frequent item mining

Data: Projected database $DB|\alpha$, *minsup*

Result: localy frequent item set F_l

1 **begin**
2　　　　/*We assume that for each data sequence S_i of $DB|\alpha$ we have:
　　　　$S_i = LGS\text{-}Closure_{lastItemset(\alpha)}(same).otherTrans$ We should examine all the data
　　　　sequences of DB*/
3　　　　**foreach** $S_i \in DB|\alpha$ **do**
4　　　　　　**foreach** *item _e in same* **do**
5　　　　　　　　*handle _e*
6　　　　　　**endfch**
7　　　　　　**foreach** *itemset is in other* **do**
8　　　　　　　　/*Search all items which could be inserted inyo a further itemset of α*/
9　　　　　　　　SearchOtherTransFrequentItem e in $LGS\text{-}Closure(is)$
10　　　　　　　　/*Search all items which could be inserted into the last itemset of α*/
11　　　　　　　　**if** *is supports lastItemset(α)* **then**
12　　　　　　　　　　SearchSameTransFrequentItem $\_e$ in $LGS\text{-}Closure_{lastItemset(\alpha)}(is)$
13　　　　　　　　**endif**
14　　　　　　**endfch**
15　　　　**endfch**
16　　　　**return** $(F_l = \{e|support(e) \geq suppmin\})$
17 **end**

The main algorithm **CMSP_Cand** calls routine **SequenceGrowing** with the empty sequence $\langle\rangle$, DB and $minsup = 2$ as parameters.

The first step aims at discovering all the frequent items on DB thanks to routine **getFrequentItems**:

$\{(a_1,b_1,c_1)_2, \ (a_1,b_2,c_3)_2, \ (a_1,b_1,*)_2, \ (a_1,b_2,*)_2, \ (a_1,b_3,*)_2, \ (a_1,*,c_1)_2,$
$(a_1,*,c_2)_2, (a_1,*,c_3)_2, (*,b_1,c_1)_2,$

B_1	$\langle\{(a_1,b_2,c_3)\}\{(a_1,b_1,c_1),(a_1,b_3,c_2)\}\rangle$
B_2	$\langle\{(a_1,b_2,c_2)(a_1,b_2,c_3)\}\{(a_1,b_1,c_1),(a_1,b_3,c_4)\}\{(a_1,b_1,c_1)\}\rangle$

Table 13.4 Multidimensional Sequence Database DB

$(*,b_2,c_3)_2,\ (a_1,*,*)_2,\ (*,b_1,*)_2,\ (*,b_2,*)_2,\ (*,b_3,*)_2,\ (*,*,c_1)_2,\ (*,*,c_2)_2,$
$(*,*,c_3)_2\}$

The sequences are mined with a depth-first strategy according to the order LGS.

The prefix sequence $\langle(a_1,b_1,c_1)\rangle$ is examined. All sequences with prefix $\langle(a_1,b_1,c_1)\rangle$ are searched on $DB|\langle(a_1,b_1,c_1)\rangle$.

Sequences $\langle\{(a_1,b_1,c_1),(a_1,b_3,*)\}\rangle$ and $\langle\{(a_1,b_1,c_1),(*,b_3,*)\}\rangle$ are discovered. There is no frequent item on the projected database according to $\langle\{(a_1,b_1,c_1),(a_1,b_3,*)\}\rangle$ et $\langle\{(a_1,b_1,c_1),(*,b_3,*)\}\rangle$.

The discovery of frequent sequences continue with the examination of the prefix sequence $\langle(a_1,b_2,c_3)\rangle$.

When prefix sequence $\langle\{(a_1,b_2,c_3)\}\{(a_1,b_1,c_1)\}\rangle$ is considered. Algorithm SequenceGrowing detects that $\langle\{(a_1,b_2,c_3)\}\{(a_1,b_1,c_1)\}\rangle$ and $\langle(a_1,b_1,c_1)\rangle$ share the same projected database. Thus, the exploration of the prefix sequence $\langle\{(a_1,b_2,c_3)\}\{(a_1,b_1,c_1)\}\rangle$ can be stopped. Indeed, sequences $\langle\{(a_1,b_2,c_3)\},\{(a_1,b_1,c_1),(a_1,b_3,*)\}\rangle$ and $\langle\{(a_1,b_2,c_3)\}\{(a_1,b_1,c_1),(*,b_3,*)\}\rangle$ are discovered without scanning the projected database $DB_{\langle(a_1,b_1,c_1)\rangle}$.

The discovery of frequent sequences goes on with the examination of the prefix sequence $\langle(a_1,b_1,*)\rangle$.

The process is iterated untill the extraction of all the sequences with prefix equal to $\langle(*,*,c_3)\rangle$.

Finally, closed sequences are retrieved from the closed candidates set. Only sequences $\langle\{(a_1,b_2,c_3)\}\{(a_1,b_1,c_1),(a_1,b_3,*)\}\rangle$ and $\langle\{(a_1,*,b_2)\}\rangle$ are closed.

13.4.3 CMSP_Free: Mining Closed Multidimensional Sequential Patterns Without Candidate Set Maintenance

The previous algorithm, *CMSP_Cand* Algorithm 6, needs to maintain a set of potentially closed sequences (set L). In post-processing, it has to compute closed sequences among candidate sequences of this set. This maintenance is expensive (quadratic in the size of the set) even if optimization techniques allow to reduce this cost. In this section, we propose an algorithm without candidate-set-maintenance. This approach is based on Bide [18]. We first detail some preliminar definitions (Sequence extensions) then we present the associated algorithm.

13.4.3.1 Sequence Extensions

According to the definition of closed multidimensional sequential pattern, if a g-k-sequence $S = s_1, \ldots, s_g$ is not closed then there exists a sequence S' with the same support of S such that $S \subset_S S'$. Definition 13.10 enumerates the five possible ways to have a more specific sequence from a g-k-sequence.

Definition 13.10. A more specific sequence can be built in five different ways from a g-k-sequence $\langle s_1, s_2, \ldots, s_g \rangle$:

- *inter itemset* forward extension $S' = \langle s_1, s_2, \ldots, s_g, \{e'\} \rangle$;
- *intra itemset* forward extension $S' = \langle s_1, s_2, \ldots s_g \cup \{e'\} \rangle$;
- *inter itemset* backward extension $S' = \langle s_1, s_2, \ldots, s_i, \{e'\}, s_{i+1}, \ldots, s_g \rangle$;
- *intra itemset* backward extension $S' = \langle s_1, s_2, \ldots s_i \cup \{e'\}, s_{i+1}, \ldots, s_g \rangle$;
- *specialization* of an item $\exists i \in \{1, \ldots, g\}, \exists e, \exists e'$ s.t. $e \subset_S e'$: $S' = \langle s_1, s_2, \ldots, s_{i-1}, s_i[e'/e], s_{i+1}, \ldots, s_g \rangle$ where $s_i[e'/e]$ is the substitution of e by e' in s_i.

We will notice that the last point can easily be detected thanks to the order of sequence we consider as soon as the four ones (extensions) are detected.

Theorem 13.1 (Bi-Directional Extension). *A sequence S is closed if and only if there does not exist neither any backward or forward extension nor any specialization that preserves the support of S.*
The proof trivially comes from the definition of closed multidimensional sequential patterns.

In order to check if a sequence is closed, we have to check if there exists some backward or forward extension or specialization of an item, thanks to theorem 13.1.

It is easy to find the forward extensions of a sequence:

Lemma 13.1 (Forward Extension). *Let S be a sequence, the complete set of forward extensions of S is equivalent to the set of locally frequent items on the projected database according to S such that their support is equal to $support(S)$.*

Proof. Locally frequent items are discovered by scanning the projected database according to prefix sequence S_p. Since each event occurs during or after the prefix sequence S_p, if an item e occurs in all data sequence from the projected database, then e is a forward extension.

All events (items) that occur after the first instance of the sequence S_p is included in the projected database $DB|_{S_p}$, which means that the complete set of forward extensions can be extracted by scanning the projected database DB_{S_p}.

It is harder to detect the backward extensions of a sequence than forward extensions. There are two types of backward extension:

- $S' = s_1, s_2, \ldots, s_i, \{e'\}, s_{i+1}, \ldots, s_g$
- $S' = s_1, s_2, \ldots s_i \cup \{e'\}, s_{i+1}, \ldots, s_g$

An item can be inserted in a new itemset between two itemsets s_i and s_{i+1} (inter itemset backward extension). An item can also be inserted in an already defined itemset.

As a sequence can appear several times within a block data sequence, we can identify g intervals to localize the potential backward extension of a g-k sequence.

Figure Fig. 13.3 describes the g intervals of a multidimensional prefix sequence in a multidimensional data sequence.

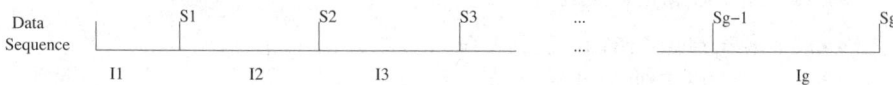

Fig. 13.3 The g intervals that may contained backward extensions of prefix g-k-sequence $S_p = \langle s_1, s_2, \ldots, s_g \rangle$ in a block data sequence

We have to maximize these intervals in order to detect all backward extension items.

Definition 13.11 (i^{th} Maximal Interval). Let $S_p = \langle s_1, s_2, \ldots, s_g \rangle$ be a g-k prefix sequence and S be a block data sequence, the ith maximal interval of S according to S_p is defined as follow:

- if $i = 1$: the subsequence from the beginning of S to $la(s_1)$ excluded where $la(s_1)$ is the last appearance of the itemset s_1 in S such that $la(s_1) < la(s_2) < \ldots < la(g)$.
- if $1 < i \leq g$: the subsequence between the first appearance of the sequence $\langle s_1, s_2, \ldots, s_{i-1} \rangle$ (denoted by $fa(\langle s_1, s_2, \ldots, s_{i-1} \rangle)$) and $la(s_i)$ excluded such that $la(s_i) < la(s_{i+1}) < \ldots < la(g)$.

As an example, the first maximal interval of the sequence $s = \langle \{(1,1)\}\{(1,2)\} \rangle$ in the data sequence $S = \langle \{(1,1)\}\{(1,2)\}\{(1,1)\}\{(1,2)\}\{(1,1)\}\{(1,2)\} \rangle$ is the subsequence $\langle \{(1,1)\}\{(1,2)\}\{(1,1)\}\{(1,2)\} \rangle$. The second maximal interval of s in S is $\langle \{(1,2)\}\{(1,1)\}\{(1,2)\}\{(1,1)\} \rangle$.

Lemma 13.2 (Backward Extension Checking). *Let $S_p = \langle s_1, s_2, \ldots, s_g \rangle$ be a g-k prefix sequence, if there exists an item e that appears in each ith maximal intervals of S_p in DB, then e is a backward extension.*

Otherwise, if there is no item e that appears in each ith maximal interval of S_p in DB, then S_p cannot have a backward extension.

Proof. Let $S_p = \langle s_1, s_2, \ldots, s_g \rangle$ be a g-k-prefix sequence, if there exists an item e that appears in each ith maximal interval of S_p in DB (each ith maximal interval of S_p in each data sequence of DB), then we can build the sequence $S'_p = \langle s_1, s_2, \ldots, s_{i-1} \cup \{e\}, s_i, \ldots, s_g \rangle$ or $S' = \langle s_1, s_2, \ldots, s_{i-1}, \{e\}, s_i, \ldots, s_g \rangle$ such that $S_p \subset_S S'_p$ and $support(S'_p) = support(S_p)$. Thus, e is a backward extension of S_p in DB.

Suppose that there exists a sequence $S'_p = \langle s_1, s_2, \ldots, s_{i-1} \cup \{e\}, s_i, \ldots, s_g \rangle$ or $S'_p = \langle s_1, s_2, \ldots, s_{i-1}, \{e\}, s_i, \ldots, s_g \rangle$ such that $S_p \subset_S S'_p$ and $support(S'_p) = support(S_p)$. In each data sequence of DB that contain S_p, item e must appear after the first appearance of $\langle s_1, \ldots, s_{i-1} \rangle$ and before the last appearance of the subsequence $\langle s_i, \ldots, s_g \rangle$. That means that e must appear in each ith maximal interval of S_p in DB. Thus, if we cannot find an item that appears in each ith maximal interval of S_p then there is no backward extension of the sequence S_p in DB.

A prefix sequence cannot be closed if there exists a specialization of an item of the sequence; LGS order allows us to extract closed sequences by considering sequences that contain the most specific items (no or few $*$). Thus, if there exists a specialization of an item of a sequence, then the specialized sequence that contains at least one more specific items is already extracted and added in the set of closed multidimensional sequential patterns. As a consequence, if a sequence is potentially closed (no backward and forward extension), it is sufficient to check if there is no more specific sequence in the set of already mined closed sequence. It should be noted that this set is significantly smaller than the set of frequent sequences. In the worst case, it is necessary to consider all already mined closed sequences that have the same support of the current examined prefix sequence.

13.4.3.2 Pruning The Search Space

While seeking new sequences with frequent sequence enumeration algorithm , we can use the bidirectional closure property (theorem 13.1) to check if the current prefix sequence is closed in order to generate a set of non-redundant knowledge. Although this property allows to return a more compact set, it does not allow to retrieve sequences more efficiently. For instance, there is no closed sequence prefixed by a sequence s, therefore it is useless to continue to search such sequences in this case. We define a pruning method to reduce space search by not considering unpromising sequence.

As noticed previously, a sequence may appear several times in a data sequence. In Definition 13.11, we introduced the notion of maximal interval to detect all the backward extensions. Now, we want to minimize these intervals in order to detect the unpromising sequences. We thus define the notion of ith minimal interval.

Definition 13.12 (i^{th} Minimal Interval). Let S be a data sequence that supports a g-k-sequence prefix sequence $S_p = \langle s_1, s_2, \ldots, s_g \rangle$, the ith minimal interval of S_p in S is defined as follow:

- if $i = 1$: it is the subsequence before the $fa(s_1)$.
- if $1 < i \leq g$: it is the subsequence from $fa(\langle s_1, \ldots, s_{i-1} \rangle)$ to $fa(s_i)$ excluded such that $fa(s_i) < fa(s_{i+1}) \leq \ldots \leq fa(s_g)$.

Theorem 13.2 (Pruning). *Let $S_p = \langle s_1, s_2, \ldots, s_g \rangle$ be a g-k prefix sequence, if there exists an integer i such that there is an item e that appears in each ith minimal interval of S_p in DB, then there does not exist closed sequence with prefix S_p.*

Proof. If an item e appears in each ith minimal interval of S_p, then we can use the new prefix sequence S'_p that contains e. Indeed, $S_p \subset_S S'_p$ and $support(S'_p) = support(S_p)$. Thus, all locally frequent items on $DB|_{S_p}$ are also frequent on $DB|_{S'_p}$. Therefore, S_p is an unpromising sequence. There is no closed sequence with prefix S_p. The examination of S_p can thus be interrupted.

Let us consider the multidimensional sequence database from Tab. 13.4. We can stop the exploration of the prefix sequence $\langle(a_1,b_1,c_1)\rangle$ because item (a_1,b_2,c_3) appears in each first interval of $\langle(a_1,b_1,c_1)\rangle$ in DB. Thus, there is no hope to discover frequent closed sequence from prefix $\langle(a_1,b_1,c_1)\rangle$.

Thanks to theorems and definitions, we can now define the algorithm for mining closed multidimensional sequential patterns without candidate set maintenance.

13.4.3.3 Algorithm *CMSP_Free*

Algorithms 9 and 10 describe the extraction of closed sequential patterns without candidate set maintenance. These algorithms follow the same structure for mining frequent multidimensional sequences in depth first. Indeed, in the worst case (each frequent sequence is closed), the search spaces are the same. However, we introduce a pruning condition to efficiently reduce the search space. Algorithm 10 describes the key part of the extraction. First, if the number of backward and forward extensions of the current prefix sequence S_p is 0, then S_p is potentially closed and we have to check if there is no more specific sequence in set *FCS* that contains the already discovered closed multidimensional sequential patterns. If there is no such sequence with same support, then S_p is added to *FCS*. Set *FCS* is partitioned into subsets according to the support of the closed sequences. Thus, the search of more specific closed sequence than S_p is carried out on a subset of *FCS*. In the worst case, the complexity of this verification is $O(l_\sigma)$ where l_σ is the number of already mined closed sequences which support is equal to σ. Finally, each locally frequent item e on projected database is taking into account. The algorithm checks if it is possible to prune the search space according to the prefix sequence $S_p.e$ (e is added in the last itemset of S_p or in a new one). If it is not possible, the algorithm computes the number of backward extensions of $S_p.e$ and continue the discovery of closed sequences with this new prefix sequence $S_p.e$.

13.5 Experiments

In this section, we report experiments performed on synthetic data and real data.

Algorithm 9: *CMSP_Free*

Data: Database *DB*, minimal support threshold *minsup*
Result: The set of closed multidimensional sequential patterns *FCS*

1 **begin**
2     $FCS = \phi$
3     $F1 = getFrequentItems(DB, minsup)$
4   **foreach** *1-sequence $f1 \in F1$* **do**
5   **if** *Pruning of f1 is not possible)* **then**
6   /*Counting the backward extensions.*/
7             $BEI = $ #backward extensions of sequence $f1$ in DB
8   Call subroutine $CMSP\_F(DB|_{f1}, f1, minsup, BEI, FCS)$
9   **endif**
10   **endfch**
11   **return** *FCS*
12 **end**

Algorithm 10: routine *CMSP_F*

Data: Projected Database $DB|_{S_p}$, prefix sequence S_p, minimal support threshold *minsup*,
      number of backward extensions *BEI*
Result: The current set of closed multidimensional sequential patterns *FCS*

1 **begin**
2   /*Search for frequent items and forward extensions*/
3     $LFI = getFrequentItems(DB|_{S_p}, minsup)$
4     $FEI = |\{z \in LFI \, / \, support(z) = support(S_P)\}|$
5   **if** $(BEI + FEI) = 0$ **then**
6   /*Checking for specialization*/
7   **if** $(\nexists \alpha \in FCS \mid S_p \subset_S \alpha \wedge support(\alpha) = support(S_p))$ **then**
8            $FCS = FCS \cup \{S_P\}$
9   **endif**
10   **endif**
11   **foreach** $i \in LFI$ **do**
12   /*Adding frequent item to the prefix sequence (intra or inter itemset) and compute
        the projected database*/
13         $S'_p = \langle S_p.i \rangle$
14         $DB|_{S'_p} = DB|_{S'_p}$
15   **endfch**
16   **foreach** $i \in LFI$ **do**
17   /*Checking for pruning */
18   **if** *Pruning of S'_p is not possible* **then**
19             $BEI = $ #backward extensions of sequence S'_p in DB
20   call subroutine $CMSP\_F(DB|_{S_p}i, S'_p, minsup, BEI, FCS)$
21   **endif**
22   **endfch**
23 **end**

13.5.1 Synthetic Data

We generated a database thanks to *IBM Quest Market-Basket Synthetic Data Generator* (100,000 tuples). Items (1 dimension) were then transformed into multidi-

mensional items (5 dimensions). Since approach without candidate maintenance has
to compute backward and forward extension to determine if a sequence is closed,
we suppose that an approach with candidate set maintenance is more efficient in
sparse data (number of frequent sequences similar to number of closed ones). Experiments reported here confirm it. As soon as the minimal support threshold is
low, the approach with candidate set maintenance is adapted. Indeed, the runtime of
such approach is very sensitive to the number of frequent sequences since frequent
sequences are potentially closed and retrieving all closed sequences is quadratic in
the size of the set of candidate sequences. An approach without candidate set maintenance is more robust since it does not consider any set of candidates. Furthermore,
an approach without candidate set maintenance provides efficient search space pruning properties. Figure 13.4(c) reports the behavior of *CMSP* according to the size of
de database (number of data sequences). The runtime increases with the size of the
database. Thus we can consider that *CMSP* is scalable according to this parameter.

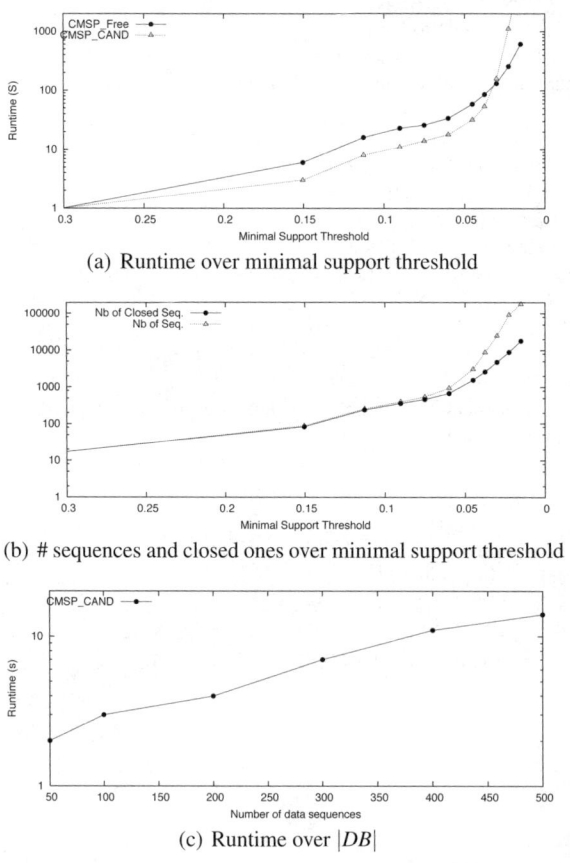

(a) Runtime over minimal support threshold

(b) # sequences and closed ones over minimal support threshold

(c) Runtime over $|DB|$

Fig. 13.4 Experiments carried out on synthetic data

13.5.2 Real Data Cube

We report experiments performed on real data. They aim at showing the representative power of closed multidimensional patterns. They were performed on data cube issued from EDF (Electricité De France, the main French energy supplier and electricity producer) marketing context. This data cube describes the marketing activity on a very large EDF customer database (about 30 million of residential customers). We consider five analysis dimensions. As soon as the number of frequent sequences becomes too important, an approach with candidate set maintenance is not adapted whereas *CMSP* allows the knowledge discovery with low support. We also notice the representative power of closed multidimensional sequential patterns. Indeed, a small number of closed sequences provides the representation of all frequent sequences without any loss of information on the support. As an example, $100,000$ sequences can be retrieved thanks to only about 100 closed sequences.

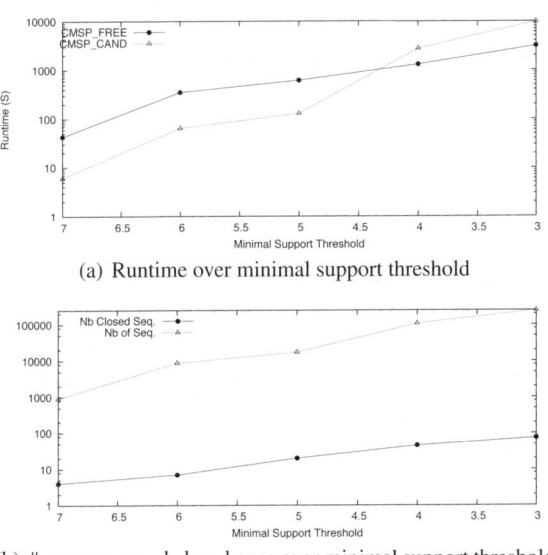

(a) Runtime over minimal support threshold

(b) # sequences and closed ones over minimal support threshold

Fig. 13.5 Experiments carried out on real data

13.6 Conclusion

In this paper, we propose a novel framework (definitions and algorithms) for mining closed multidimensional sequential patterns. Mining closed patterns leads to a condensed representation of the patterns without any loss of information. This advantage allows the computation of several measures (*e.g.* confidence for sequential rules) without any extra-scan of the database as all support values are known. Some works had been done on closed patterns and on closed sequential patterns. But we show in this paper that they cannot be directly applied to the multidimensional framework because of the *wild-carded* items we consider, leading to a non-easy lexical order. This paper introduces a new challenge with the inference of wild-carded items which are not directly materialized in the data sequences. Two approaches have been investigated, extending the *pattern growth* framework, with or without candidate maintenance and they are compared. Experiments on synthetic data and real data show the interest of our proposition.

In future work, we plan to consider time constraints and hierarchies which could be easily considered according to the definitions in this framework. It would be interesting to compare *CMSP* algorithms against an adaptation of work on closed itemset generation using FCA. However, it is necessary to provide an closure operator on multidimensional sequence. The use of more condensed representations could allow a more efficient multidimensional sequential pattern mining. These representations (non-derivable [4], k-free [3]) exist in itemset framework but they do not exist yet for sequential or multidimensional patterns. This work presents thus a great challenge for future work.

Acknowledgements

This work was partially funded by the EDF R&D Corporation in the framework of a collaboration aiming at studying OLAP Mining for discovering atypical temporal evolutions in data cubes. Thus the authors would like to thank Françoise Guisnel, Sabine Goutier and Marie-Luce Picard, for providing real data to assess our approach.

References

1. R. Agrawal and R. Srikant. Mining sequential patterns. In *Proc. 1995 Int. Conf. Data Engineering (ICDE'95)*, pages 3–14, 1995.
2. J. Ayres, J. Flannick, J. Gehrke, and T. Yiu. Sequential pattern mining using a bitmap representation. In *KDD*, pages 429–435. ACM, 2002.
3. J.-F. Boulicaut, A. Bykowski, and C. Rigotti. Free-sets: A condensed representation of boolean data for the approximation of frequency queries. *Data Min. Knowl. Discov.*, 7(1):5–22, 2003.
4. T. Calders and B. Goethals. Mining all non-derivable frequent itemsets. In T. Elomaa, H. Mannila, and H. Toivonen, editors, *PKDD*, volume 2431 of *Lecture Notes in Computer Science*, pages 74–85. Springer, 2002.
5. M. El-Hajj and O. R. Zaïane. Finding all frequent patterns starting from the closure. In X. Li, S. Wang, and Z. Y. Dong, editors, *ADMA*, volume 3584 of *Lecture Notes in Computer Science*, pages 67–74. Springer, 2005.
6. B. Ganter and R. Wille. Applied lattice theory: Formal concept analysis, 1997.

7. J. Han. OLAP mining: Integration of OLAP with data mining. In *IFIP Conference on Data Semantics*, pages 1–11, 1997.
8. J. Han, J. Pei, and Y. Yin. Mining frequent patterns without candidate generation. In W. Chen, J. F. Naughton, and P. A. Bernstein, editors, *SIGMOD Conference*, pages 1–12. ACM, 2000.
9. F. Masseglia, F. Cathala, and P. Poncelet. The PSP Approach for Mining Sequential Patterns. In *Proc. of PKDD*, volume 1510 of *LNCS*, pages 176–184, 1998.
10. N. Pasquier, Y. Bastide, R. Taouil, and L. Lakhal. Discovering frequent closed itemsets for association rules. In C. Beeri and P. Buneman, editors, *ICDT*, volume 1540 of *Lecture Notes in Computer Science*, pages 398–416. Springer, 1999.
11. J. Pei. *Pattern-growth Methods for Frequent Pattern Mining*. PhD thesis, School of Computing Science, Simon Fraser University, Canada, 2002.
12. J. Pei, J. Han, and R. Mao. Closet: An efficient algorithm for mining frequent closed itemsets. In *ACM SIGMOD Workshop on Research Issues in Data Mining and Knowledge Discovery*, pages 21–30, 2000.
13. J. Pei, J. Han, B. Mortazavi-Asl, J. Wang, H. Pinto, Q. Chen, U. Dayal, and M.-C. Hsu. Mining sequential patterns by pattern-growth: The prefixspan approach. *IEEE Transactions on Knowledge and Data Engineering*, 16(10), 2004.
14. H. Pinto, J. Han, J. Pei, K. Wang, Q. Chen, and U. Dayal. Multi-dimensional sequential pattern mining. In *CIKM*, pages 81–88. ACM, 2001.
15. M. Plantevit, Y. W. Choong, A. Laurent, D. Laurent, and M. Teisseire. M^2sp: Mining sequential patterns among several dimensions. In A. Jorge, L. Torgo, P. Brazdil, R. Camacho, and J. Gama, editors, *PKDD*, volume 3721 of *Lecture Notes in Computer Science*, pages 205–216. Springer, 2005.
16. C. Raïssi and P. Poncelet. Deducing bounds on the support of sequential patterns. Technical Report RR08015, LIRMM, Montpellier, France, 2008.
17. P. Songram, V. Boonjing, and S. Intakosum. Closed multidimensional sequential pattern mining. In *ITNG*, pages 512–517. IEEE Computer Society, 2006.
18. J. Wang, J. Han, and C. Li. Frequent closed sequence mining without candidate maintenance. *IEEE Trans. Knowl. Data Eng.*, 19(8):1042–1056, 2007.
19. J. Wang, J. Han, and J. Pei. Closet+: searching for the best strategies for mining frequent closed itemsets. In *KDD '03: Proceedings of the ninth ACM SIGKDD international conference on Knowledge discovery and data mining*, pages 236–245, New York, NY, USA, 2003. ACM.
20. S. B. Yahia, T. Hamrouni, and E. M. Nguifo. Frequent closed itemset based algorithms: a thorough structural and analytical survey. *SIGKDD Explorations*, 8(1):93–104, 2006.
21. X. Yan, J. Han, and R. Afshar. Clospan: Mining closed sequential patterns in large databases. In D. Barbará and C. Kamath, editors, *SDM*. SIAM, 2003.
22. C.-C. Yu and Y.-L. Chen. Mining sequential patterns from multidimensional sequence data. *IEEE Transactions on Knowledge and Data Engineering*, 17(1):136–140, 2005.
23. M. J. Zaki. Spade: An efficient algorithm for mining frequent sequences. *Machine Learning*, 42(1/2):31–60, 2001.
24. M. J. Zaki and C.-J. Hsiao. Charm: An efficient algorithm for closed itemset mining. In R. L. Grossman, J. Han, V. Kumar, H. Mannila, and R. Motwani, editors, *SDM*. SIAM, 2002.

Chapter 14
Modeling and Querying Temporal Semistructured Data Warehouses

Carlo Combi, Barbara Oliboni, and Giuseppe Pozzi

Abstract The amount of data stored in repositories is growing and growing in size. When joining information from different repositories we may obtain semistructured data warehouses, featuring an irregular or an incomplete structure for data. As any other aspect in human life, these data also feature temporal information, whose relevance is not negligible. Some modeling and querying techniques are needed in extracting knowledge from these data warehouses.

This paper deals with temporal semistructured data warehouses, their modeling and querying. We propose here a graph-based data model to represent semistructured temporal data warehouses, and a query language to suitably retrieve the considered information.

14.1 Introduction

In the last years, the amount of data stored in repositories, such as databases and data warehouses, increased. The main differences between data managed by Data warehouse Systems and Database Management Systems are that in the data warehouse context (i) very few updates are needed, (ii) historical data are required, and (iii) queries are used to perform data analysis. Moreover, information to be maintained can be semistructured in nature: i.e., data may have an irregular or incomplete structure, and a rapidly evolving or missing schema [1]. Semistructured data are becoming more and more relevant in any application domain [14], and can be considered as a general description of XML information [31]. Data warehouses

---

Carlo Combi, Barbara Oliboni

Università degli Studi di Verona, Dipartimento di Informatica, Strada le Grazie 15, 37134 Verona, Italy, e-mail: `carlo.combi,barbara.oliboni@univr.it`

Giuseppe Pozzi

Politecnico di Milano, Dipartimento di Elettronica e Informazione, P.za Leonardo da Vinci 32, 20133 Milano, Italy, e-mail: `giuseppe.pozzi@polimi.it`

storing semistructured data [2, 12] need for suitable data models that are able (i) to manage typical aspects of semistructured information, (ii) to represent and use classical notions of the data warehouse context such as facts and dimensions, and (iii) to support the usual OLAP (on-line analytical processing) functions on semistructured data, as drill-down and roll-up. Furthermore, a fundamental aspect to consider when dealing with historical data is time: when storing and analyzing information, we have to consider temporal aspects and dimensions of data.

According to these requirements, we propose here a data model to describe data warehouses of semistructured data, where temporal dimensions (i.e., temporal aspects of stored information) are suitably managed. The data model, namely Graphical sEmistructured teMporal Data Warehouse model (GEMDW), is a graph-based data model allowing one to have labeled nodes and edges. To the best of our knowledge our proposal is the only one dealing with concepts related to data warehouses (i.e., facts and dimensions), in the semistructured data context. Moreover, we defined a suitable query language, namely Data Warehouse Query Language (DW-QL), which is a temporal query language based on path expressions. GEMDW and DW-QL allow one to model and to query a data warehouse with temporal semistructured data.

The paper is structured as follows. Section 14.2 introduces related work concerning (i) the graphical representation and querying of semistructured data, and (ii) XML warehouses. Section 14.3 introduces the GEMDW data model to represent semistructured temporal data warehouses. Section 14.4 defines a suitable query language, whose structure is SQL-like, to query over a warehouse of temporal semistructured data. Section 14.5 summarizes the obtained results and sketches out some future research directions.

14.2 Related work

In this section, we briefly recall some related work on temporal semistructured data models and languages, and on XML warehouses.

14.2.1 Temporal Semistructured Data Models and Languages

In the last decade, research issues related to semistructured data were considered and tackled into account. Semistructured data may have an irregular or incomplete structure, and a rapidly evolving or missing schema [1]. Several proposals for representing and querying semistructured information were proposed in the literature. The common approach for modeling semistructured data is based on labeled graphs where nodes denote objects or values, and edges represent relationships between them [20, 27].

Semistructured data can be considered as a general description of XML informa-tion [31]. XML documents can be easily represented as trees or graphs: for example the XPath data model [30] allows the representation of an XML document as a tree. This means that general graph-based data models, as the one we propose in this work, can be used to graphically represent XML information. In [27], the au-thors propose the Object Exchange Model (OEM), which is a graph-structured data model where the basic idea is that each object has a label that describes its meaning. A graph based data model similar to the one proposed in [27] is presented in [20]. In this proposal all data sources are uniformly modeled: data are stored in the model own graph data repository or in external sources which are also viewed as graphs.

Due to the fact that in the semistructured data context both the (possible) schema and information may change with respect to the time, temporal aspects are strictly related to this context. Thus, issues related to representing and querying changes in semistructured data have been considered in the literature, with the proposal of some graph based temporal data models [4, 9, 13, 15, 16, 26], and of the related query languages [9, 10, 25]. In [4], the authors define a logical data model for XML doc-uments, enriching them by the concept of valid time. Next, Wang and Zaniolo [29] introduce the concept of transaction time for XML, too.

In [9], the authors propose the Delta Object Exchange Model (DOEM), which is based on the Object Exchange Model (OEM), and takes into account the trans-action time dimension. The graph based data model proposed in [16] is very gen-eral and extensible: it represents semistructured data by using graphs with edge la-bels composed by a set of descriptive properties (e.g. name, transaction time, valid time, security properties of relationships). A given property can be present in one edge and missing in another one. The model allows one to represent temporal as-pects and to consider only a temporal dimension or multiple temporal dimensions. In [26], the authors propose the Temporal Graphical Model (TGM), which is based on directed labeled graph composed by two kinds of nodes (complex and simple nodes), and two kinds of edges (relational and temporal edges). Complex and sim-ple nodes represent objects and their properties respectively. This model represents the valid time dimension. In [15] the authors propose a data model based on la-beled graphs: the model is general enough to uniformly capture different temporal aspects of semistructured data, such as valid and transaction times. The Graphical sEmistructured teMporal data model (GEM) sketched in [15] is the starting point for the work proposed in [13], which is based on labeled graphs and allows one to represent in a uniform way semistructured data and their temporal aspects focus-ing on transaction time. Moreover, in [13], the authors define the set of constraints needed to manage in a correct way the transaction time dimension, and describe the operations used to modify a GEM graph.

Since semistructured data models are often based on labeled graphs, semistruc-tured query languages usually use *Path Expressions*. A path expression represents a path on the graph, and thus it identifies the objects composing the path itself. Among the proposals presented in the literature, we recall here Lorel [2, 24], UnQL [8], and StruQL [20]. StruQL [20] is a declarative language for querying and construct-ing graph-structured data and is the central component of STRUDEL, a Web-site management system. STRUDEL addresses the problems of creating and maintaining "data-intensive" Web sites, i.e., sites that integrate information from multiple and diverse sources. STRUDEL is based on a semistructured data model using labeled directed graphs. STRUDEL's graph model is similar to that of OEM [27]: a data graph contains objects connected by means of directed edges labeled with string-valued attribute names. Objects are either nodes (with object identifier) or atomic values. STRUDEL also provides named collections of objects. StruQL is a high-level declarative language for managing site's structure. A StruQL query is a function from a set of input graphs to an output graph.

A query language for semistructured temporal data is the one proposed in [9], which is an extension of the Lorel query language, based on the DOEM (Delta-OEM) [9] data model, and taking (implicitly) into account the transaction time dimension. In [10], the authors propose a SQL-like query language, which is able to extract information from semistructured temporal databases represented according to the graphical data model proposed in [13]. In the XML data context, in [25], the authors also consider some performance issues, by providing indexing techniques which help in performing queries over temporal XML documents.

14.2.2 *XML Warehouses*

A data warehouse is a repository of data coming from different and heterogeneous data sources. This means that data stored in a data warehouse are semistructured in nature, because in different documents the same information can be represented in different ways, and moreover, the document schemata can be available or not. In the last years, the amount of semistructured information stored in data repositories has grown up, thus topics related to their representation and management are very relevant both in the industrial and academic contexts.

Data warehouses can be used to store XML documents and Web data. XML data can be stored in XML data warehouses [23], information from the Web can be stored in Web data warehouses [7], and XML data from the Web can be stored in XML Web data warehouses [32].

Information stored into a data warehouse is often time-varying, thus it could be useful to consider and represent time to allow the comparison of data stored in different periods, i.e., to consider the data evolution. In this context, the time dimension to consider can be related either to the validity of information (valid time), or to the presence of information in the warehouse (transaction time).

Different approaches were proposed to consider and represent temporal information in a data warehouse [17, 18, 19, 21]. In [17], the authors propose a model for representing changes in data dimensions of multi-dimensional data warehouses. The proposed approach is an extension of the multi-dimensional data model [22], introduces temporal extensions, structure versioning, and transformation functions, and allows one to represent the valid time dimension by means of the time stamping of data. Moreover, this proposal considers the structure version, which is a view on a temporal data warehouse valid for a given time interval. Thus, the proposed system is able to represent successive versions of structures, and provides transformation functions to map data from a structure version to a different one. In [19], the authors propose an architecture for temporal data warehouse systems which allows one to register different temporal versions of dimension data, and the transfer of data between different versions. The authors extend the model of [17] to represent also modifications at the schema level, such as the insertion of a new dimension level. An extension of the model proposed in [19], tacking into account both valid and transaction times of structural modifications, is presented in [21]. This bi-temporal model supports valid and transaction times on both the schema and the instance levels. In [5], the authors propose a multiversion data warehouse by considering two different kinds of versions: real versions, which handle changes in the schema structure, and alternative versions, which handle changes made by a user for simulating alternative business scenarios useful to predict trends by means of the what-if analysis. The time dimension considered in this proposal is the valid time.

Time dimensions are considered also when information stored in data warehouses are XML (Web) information. In [23], the authors propose a method based on ordered trees and on changes (deltas) for managing versions in XML data warehouses. In this proposal, the time of a document version is the time at which the system acquired this version, thus this proposal considers the transaction time dimension. In [28], the authors propose XML-based techniques for managing a multiversion document as a unit, and representing successive versions by means of delta changes. The versions have a valid version interval that can be represented by means of either version numbers or timestamps. In the case of timestamps, the considered time dimension is the valid time.

14.3 A Data Warehouse for Temporal Semistructured Data - GEMDW

In this section we propose the GEMDW model (Graphical sEmistructured teMporal Data Warehouse model), which is based on the GEM data model [13], to properly represent temporal semistructured data warehouses. GEMDW describes temporal semistructured data which are managed, stored, and queried in a data warehouse. GEMDW is based on labeled graphs: labels describe properties as in [16], but unlike the model proposed in [16] they may be defined both on nodes and edges. Thus, GEMDW enables one to make nodes and edges self-descriptive, increasing the compactness in representing data.

A data warehouse is modeled by a rooted, connected, directed, and labeled graph, and is identified by a quadruple $\langle N, E, \Gamma, r \rangle$, where:

- N: is the finite set of labeled nodes of the graphs;
- E: is the finite set of labeled and directed edges;

- Γ: is the finite set of properties that can be represented by a label. Every property p_i is related to a $domain(p_i)$;
- r: is the unique root node, where $r \in N$.

A node stores information, representing both entities and attributes. Nodes can be *Complex* or *Simple* ones. A *complex* node describes the structure of the object and is graphically depicted by a rectangle. A *simple* node describes the attributes of a complex node, and is graphically depicted by an ellipse. A child node of a complex node can be either a simple node or a complex node. A complex node is empty if it has no outgoing edge. A simple node can have no child, and simply describes the value of an attribute. A simple node is empty if it contains no value.

The root r of a GEMDW graph is a node belonging to the set N and representing the *entry point* of the graph. The root node is a complex node. Any child of the root must be a complex node. If the root node has no outgoing edge, the data warehouse is empty. Edges describe the relationships among the several objects of the graph that represents the data warehouse. We shall next consider the criteria for a graph to correctly represent a data warehouse.

A label is a set of couples $\{(p_1 : x_1), ..., (p_m : x_m)\}$ where:

a) every p_i is the name of the i-th property;
b) $x_i \in domain(p_i)$ is the value of the i-th property;
c) $\forall i, j(p_i = p_j \Rightarrow i = j)$, i.e., every *name* of a property is unique;
d) a mandatory property is expressed as $(p_i!x_i)$.

Both nodes and edges are labeled, thus properties can be defined both for nodes and edges.

A label contains two mandatory properties: *Name* and *Type*. Given a node, the *Name* property represents the name of the considered data, and the *Type* property represents the type of the node that can be either *Complex* or *Simple*. *Complex* and *Simple* nodes represent entities and attributes, respectively. The value of a *Simple* node is described by the *Value* property. The root node must be labeled by the *Name* property: we always assume the *name* of the root node as the name of the data warehouse. Graphically speaking, the *Type* property is represented by using ellipses and rectangles, and not reported in the label.

Given an edge, the *Name* property represents the name of the relationship between the connected nodes, and the *Type* property represents the nature of a relationship between two nodes, and assumes a key role when we have to use OLAP operators, as *Type* enables one to browse the graphs. The classic notation to describe an edge from node v to node w by a label l is $v \xrightarrow{l} w$.

Labels of edges are explicitly used in GEMDW to manage the constructs for specifying data warehouses through the usual modeling concepts of facts and dimensions. Edge labels may be of any of the following types:

- *Fact*: type of an edge that links r (root of the data warehouse graph), with the root of a subgraph related to a fact (i.e., a subgraph *Fact*);
- *Dimension*: type of an edge that links r with the root of a dimension subgraph;

- *Time Dimension*: type of an edge that links *r* to the root of a subgraph that represents the temporal hierarchy;
- *Instance*: type of an edge that links *r* to an instance (i.e., a record in the E/R terminology) both of a fact and of a dimension;
- *Attribute*: type of an edge that links an instance node to a node that represents an attribute of the object;
- *Measure*: type of an edge that links an instance node of a fact to an instance node that represents a measure;
- *Dimension Link*: type of an edge that links a node of a subgraph *Fact* to an instance of one of the dimensions of the data cube;
- *Time Dimension Link*: type of an edge that links a node of a subgraph *Fact* to an instance of the dimension *Time*;
- *Hierarchy*: type of an edge that links the root of the dimension to the subgraph that represents the hierarchy of that dimension;
- *View*: type of an edge that links the root *r* to a subgraph that represents the application of a query, particularly of an OLAP query over a fact stored by the data warehouse;
- *Next*: type of edges that are used in the graphs of temporal dimensions to define partial orders among nodes representing different time units;
- *User Defined Types*: types that enable users to defined "ad-hoc" edges for specific requirements of the data warehouse.

In the previous edge labels, two specific kinds of labels, i.e., *Time Dimension* and *Time Dimension Link*, deal with temporal aspects of data. To warrantee consistency and correctness of data represented by GEMDW, some constraints hold. The root node *r* must have:

- *n* outgoing edges of type *Dimension*; every edge points to the root of a subgraph of one dimension under analysis;
- one outgoing edge of type *Fact* pointing to the root of the subgraph of the fact under analysis;
- one outgoing edge of type *Time Dimension*, if the temporal dimension is considered, pointing to the root of the subgraph representing the temporal hierarchy.

Every dimension must have one complex node as the root node, where the *Name* of the node is the name of the dimension. Every temporal dimension must have a root node whose *Name* is *Time*. The subgraphs *Fact* have a root node, of complex type, whose *Name* is the name of the fact. Figure 14.1 represents an example of the above mentioned constraints.

In the example of Figure 14.1 we represent few nodes of a data warehouse containing information on patient admissions. In particular, in this figure we depict only the data warehouse root and the related roots of subgraphs representing facts and dimensions. The name of the data warehouse is *DWAdmission* as reported by the value of property *Name* of the root node. The considered fact is the *Admission*, while the dimensions are *Patient* and *Physician*. The node with name *Time* is the root of the subgraph representing the temporal hierarchy.

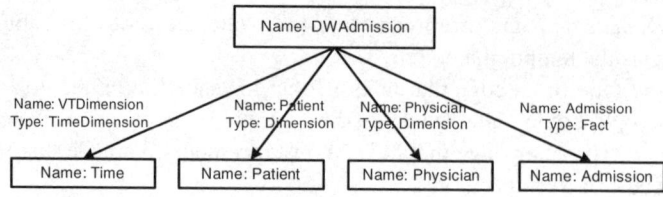

Fig. 14.1 An example of a simple GEMDWgraph

14.3.1 Hierarchy of Dimensions

In GEMDW a hierarchy is specified within the dimension: the subgraph is linked to the root node by an edge labeled *Hierarchy*. Instances of the dimension are linked by an edge *Instance* to the element of the hierarchy, internally to that dimension, they refer to. According to the nature of semistructured data, an element can exist without a link to the hierarchy, as that information could lack or be not relevant.

Figure 14.2 depicts a part of a graph of a data warehouse related to a hierarchy of the dimension *Patient*. The edge labeled *Name: HomeAddress, Type: Attribute* links the node *Patient2* to the node labeled *Name: Chelsea*. This edge asserts that the fact *Patient2* resides in the city of Chelsea, county of Suffolk, state of Mass. The edge labeled *Name: Birthplace, Type: Attribute*, linking the node *Patient2* to the node labeled *Name: Middlesex*, asserts the birth place.

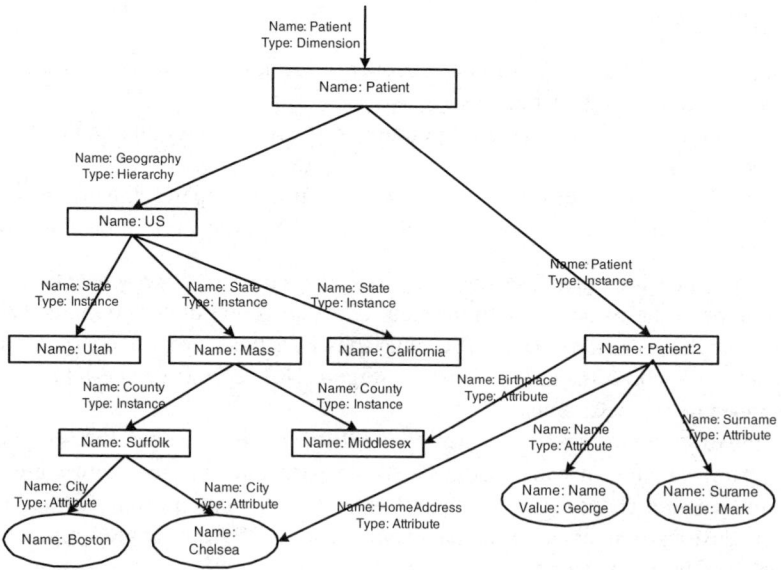

Fig. 14.2 Hierarchy of a dimension

To browse the hierarchy in both directions, since edges are directed, we have to add new edges with new directions. If $v \xrightarrow{l} w$ and $w \xrightarrow{m} k$, then:

a) we add the *Level: down* property to m;
b) we define a new edge m' such that $m' = l \setminus (Level : down) \cup (Level : up)$ and $(Level : up) \in m'$ and $k \xrightarrow{m'} w$.

We depict hierarchies by one single edge, for readability reasons.

The proposed approach enables one to represent more than one hierarchy, without having to replicate all the instances, and produces a less complex graph.

14.3.2 Multi-Fact Schema

GEMDW must store data from several facts, providing a multi-fact (or fact-constellation or galaxy) schema, and sharing those dimensions common to several facts (with no redundancy or replication). However, such a requirement increases both the number of constraints inside the graph and the workload to check for consistency.

In this way, the root node for every dimension of the fact has one outgoing edge of type *DimensionLink* to the root node of the dimension related to that fact. Similarly, every instance of a fact must be linked to one dimension, at least. Figure 14.3 depicts a multi-fact schema: the fact *Admission* has dimensions *Patient*, *Physician* and *Time*. The fact *Surgery* has dimensions *Physician* and *Time*.

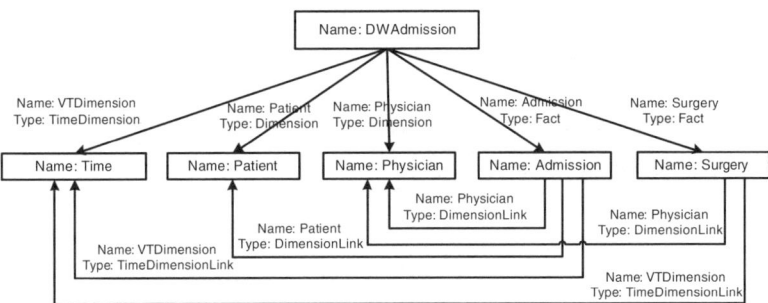

Fig. 14.3 An example of a graph for a fact-constellation schema

14.3.3 Attributes with Multiple Cardinality

GEMDW must also enable one to define multi-cardinality attributes. As an example, during a patient's admission, several physicians can be involved in taking care of that patient. Multi-cardinality attributes are managed by using several edges inside the graph, where one edge links the instance of one fact to one dimension. As in Figure 14.4 *Admission1* has two outgoing edges to the two instances of the dimension *Physician*. Such a double edge asserts that *Admission1* references two physicians. We observe that this graph aims at drawing the attention on the concept of multiple attribute: in fact, the graph does not show the edges that link the root of the fact *Admission* to the dimensions (see Section 14.3.2). Moreover, data of the other dimensions and the related edges linking instances of the fact to the dimensions are not represented for readability reasons.

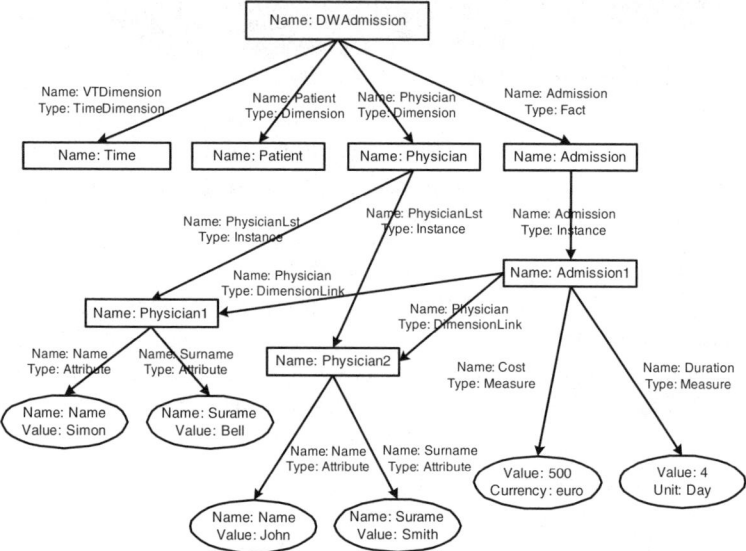

Fig. 14.4 Example: the attribute *Physician* of *Admission1* is a multi-cardinality attribute

14.3.4 Atemporal Aggregations

OLAP operators are used very often in querying a data warehouse. The most common aggregation operators are *Count, Sum, Avg, Max, Min*. In this section, we focus on the classical aggregation operators *roll-up* and *drill-down* for data warehouses.

As an example, we want to display data, grouping patients by their origin. When we group data inside a data warehouse, we must select:

a) the fact we want to aggregate some measure of;
b) the operator by which we shall aggregate the measures of the fact;
c) the dimension(s) according to which we shall aggregate data;

d) the aggregation level of every dimension, on the basis of the available levels of
every aggregation.

Measures can be classified as *flow measure* (a cumulative analysis over a given
temporal period: e.g., the total number of items sold in one day), *level measure* (a
punctual analysis at a given timestamp: e.g., the number of inhabitants of a city),
unit measure (an analysis of relative data performed at a given timestamp: e.g., the
currency exchange rate). This classification enables one to define how the measures
of a fact can be aggregated.

We can also define a default operator, chosen among the available ones, for the
aggregation over a graph. The *Operator* property is specified for the edge that links
the node with the value of the measure to the node of the instance of the fact. As
an example, Figure 14.5 describes the property *Operator: SUM* over the label that
links *Admission1* to the measure of *Cost*.

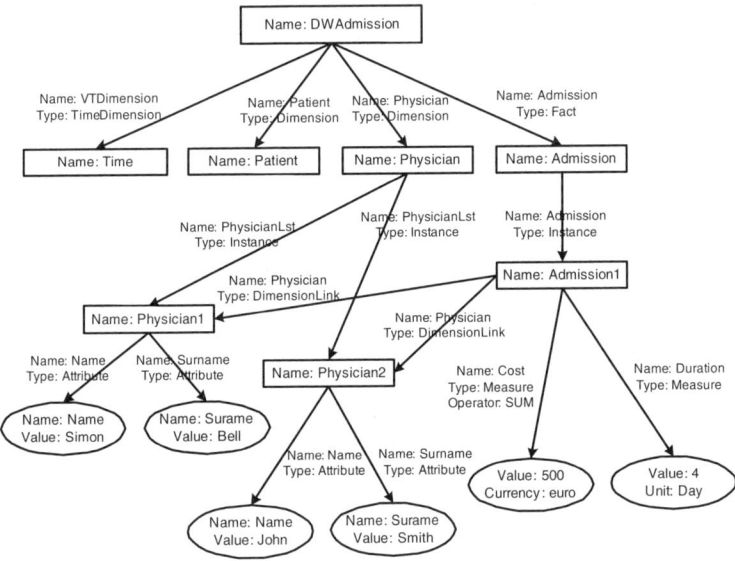

Fig. 14.5 Part of a GEMDW graph: adding the *Operator* property

In order to successfully perform aggregations, an element must be linked to the
hierarchy that is included in the dimension. Moreover, an element can also be not
linked to a leaf of the subgraph that represents the hierarchy. As an example, in Figure 14.6 *Patient1* points to the node *California*, showing that a node can point to
an intermediate node of a hierarchy. Again in Figure 14.6, if we aggregate data on
County, we can find no group for *Patient1*. Thus, the aggregation is possible only according to the hierarchy specified in the dimension we consider for the aggregation
itself.

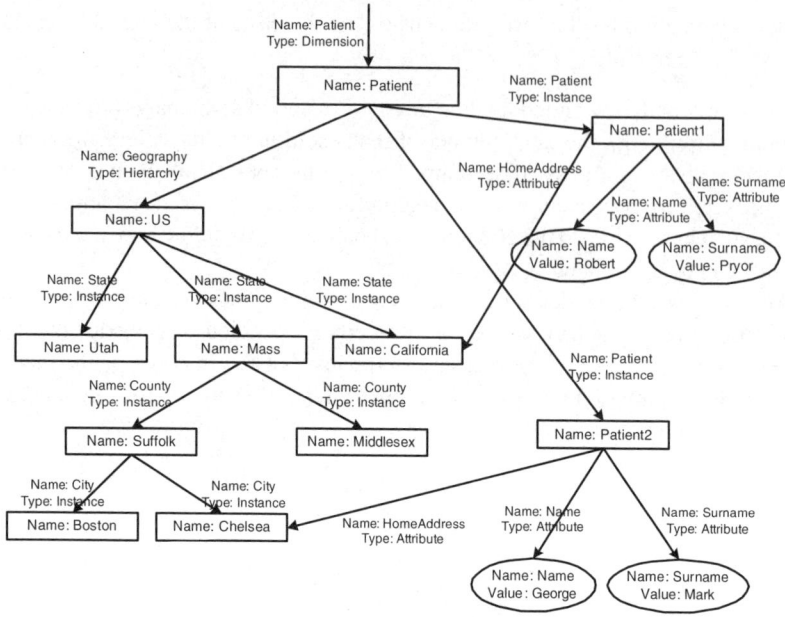

Fig. 14.6 Part of a graph: the *Patient* dimension with a hierarchy

14.3.5 Temporal Aspects

In considering temporal aspects of a data warehouse, we focus on versioning mechanism and on temporal aggregation, and provide some details about their management in **GEMDW**. As temporal data model of reference, we consider here [11]. The *valid time* (**VT**) of a fact is the time when the fact is true in the modeled reality: **VT** is generally provided by the user. The *transaction time* (**TT**) of a fact is the time when the fact is current in the database and may be retrieved: **TT** is generally system generated. The *event time* (**ET**) of a fact is the occurrence time of a real-world event that either initiates or terminates the validity interval of the fact. The *availability time* (**AT**) of a fact is the time when the fact is known and believed correct by the information system. We shall next define the data warehouse time (**DWT**), to describe the **VT** of data inside the data warehouse.

14.3.5.1 Versioning

Version management concerns both schema evolution and data evolution. Schema evolution occurs when the schema changes, e.g. when we add a new dimension for the analysis of data. Data evolution occurs when data must be updated, for instance because of an error which has been detected. For instance, we may have to update the attribute *Name* of the patient referenced by *Admission1*. The data model must provide suitable techniques to manage these evolutions.

Since we are dealing with semistructured data as a general representation of (well formed) XML data, there is no strict distinction between schema and data: the schema is implicitly defined by the data. Thus, we may want to deal with the two evolutions (of the schema and of the data) by an overall solution. We propose to exploit properties of labels to represent the temporal aspect that describe the different versions. We call this property DWT, or data warehouse time.

The value stored by the label does not refer to any temporal dimension related to the source of the data and it is independent from that source. Semantically, the DWT defines the temporal interval during which the data is valid and believed as correct by the data warehouse. DWT is stored as the semi-open interval $[DWT_s, DWT_e)$, where DWT_s is the beginning timestamp of the time of the data warehouse, and DWT_e is the terminating timestamp of *VT*. We use *now* to assert that DWT_e is the current timestamp. If a label has no DWT specified, that label is always valid within the data warehouse.

Changes to the DWT are logical changes. When we insert new nodes or new edges, the interval of DWT includes the current timestamp. When we delete nodes or edges, we perform a logical deletion by "closing" the DWT time of the corresponding data. When we update nodes or edges, we combine insert and delete operations. Figure 14.7 depicts the update of the attribute *Name* of the patient referenced by *Admission1*.

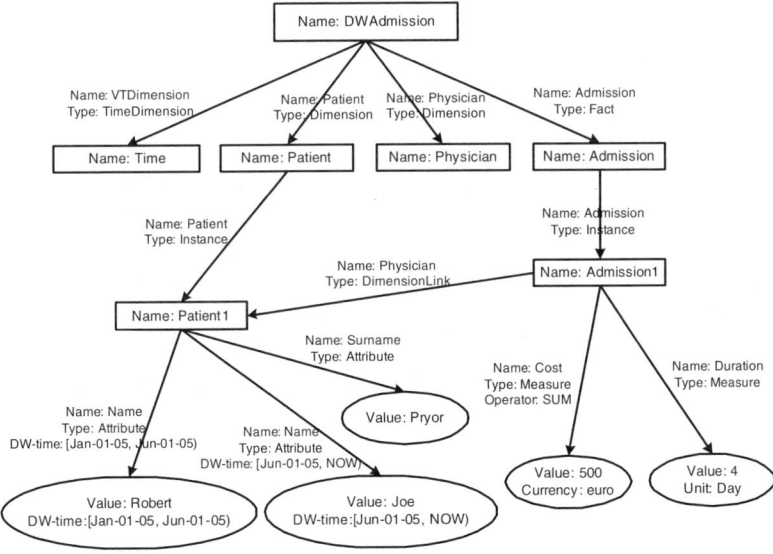

Fig. 14.7 Data evolution: update of the name of the patient referenced by *Admission1*

Figure 14.8 depicts an update of data over time. If we update the physician referenced by *Admission1*, this update does not remove the edge linking the two nodes, but rather modifies the **DWT** of the edge by "closing" the interval and creating a new edge pointing to the new physician: this new edge has the proper **DWT**.

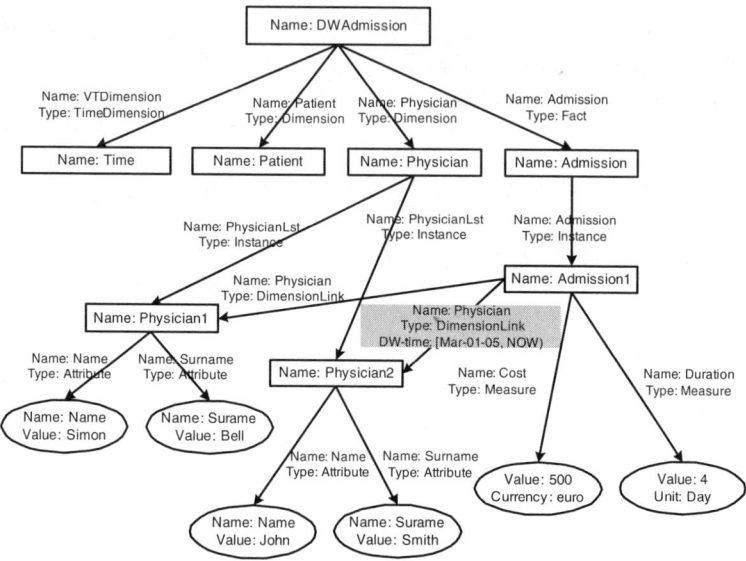

Fig. 14.8 Data evolution: on March 1st, 2005 the new physician of *Admission1* is entered

One more example of versioning concerns changes to dimensions. In Figure 14.9 we may want to add a new dimension with **DWT** valid from January 1st, 2005, asserting that the analysis of facts *Admission* will be performed over the dimensions *Patient, Physician, Time* and on the new dimension *Diagnosis*. This new requirement obviously has to preserve the consistency of represented data: there will be no edge linking an instance of *Admission* to an instance of *Diagnosis* whose data warehouse time does not belong to the interval expressed by the label **DWT** of the edge linking the root node of *Admission* to the root node of *Diagnosis*. Finally, in **GEMDW** we keep the possibility of updating **DWT** to cope with possible errors when inserting data.

14.3.5.2 Temporal Constraints

Some constraints can be defined over temporal information in **GEMDW**. These constraints can be summarized as follows:

- every label must have one single **DWT**;

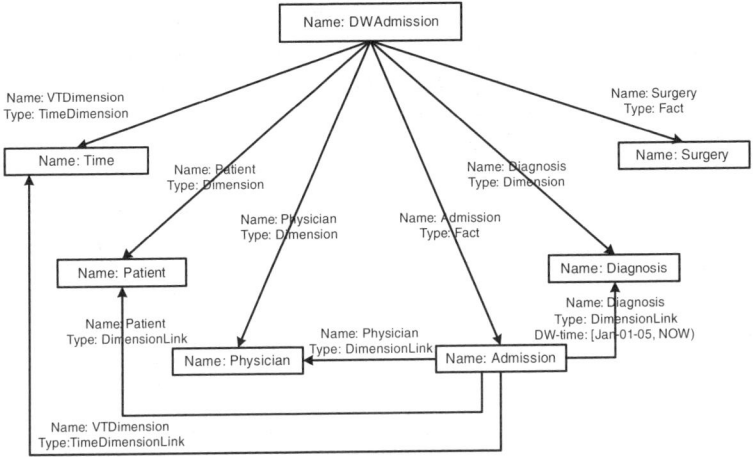

Fig. 14.9 Schema evolution: adding a new dimension

- the data warehouse time of an edge, expressed by the property DWT, must be included within the temporal interval expressed by the DWT of the node the edge starts from;
- let us suppose that at time t the set of dimensions to which the root of a fact is bound is D. Thus, every instance of the fact must be linked by edges of type *DimensionLink* (*TimeDimensionLink*, for the temporal dimension) to all the dimensions in D with at least one edge valid at time t;
- let f and d be a node instance of a fact and a node instance of a dimension, respectively. Let E_1 and E_2 be two edges with a label such that $E_1 : f \xrightarrow{L_1} d$ and $E_2 : f \xrightarrow{L_2} d$.
  If $(DW - time : DWT_1) \in L_1$ and $(DW - time : DWT_2) \in L_2$, then $DWT_1 \cap DWT_2 = \phi$.

14.3.5.3 Temporal Aggregation of Data

Granularities, i.e., suitable partitions of the time domain, have been widely discussed in the literature [6]. GEMDW provides constructs to define temporal granularities and to define links between a fact and its related temporal dimension.

The approach proposed by GEMDW is quite intuitive, even if it is not very efficient in terms of required amount of memory. In fact, in GEMDW we add a second graph (namely, granularity graph) to represent the entire granularity. This granularity graph is linked to the root node by an edge of type *Temporal Dimension*: this edge refers to a complex node, which is the root of the graph of granularities and whose name is chosen by the user. The granularity graph has a hierarchical structure, to enable one to define aggregations on the temporal dimension.

In the granularity graph, a set of nodes can be aggregated in the value "A" only if all the nodes have the same parent node. The result "A" of the aggregation of the temporal axis is the parent node. The granularity graph may have versions, too: thus, edges and nodes may have labels containing the property DWT. The system enables one to define granularities valid over one time interval, only.

Figure 14.10 depicts a data warehouse where information has been collected according to different granularities in different periods. The year 2004 is described at the granularity of months. For March 2004, some days are specified too. The first part of year 2005 is described at the granularity of 4-monthly period (year → 4-monthly period → month); the second part of year 2005 is described at the granularity of week.

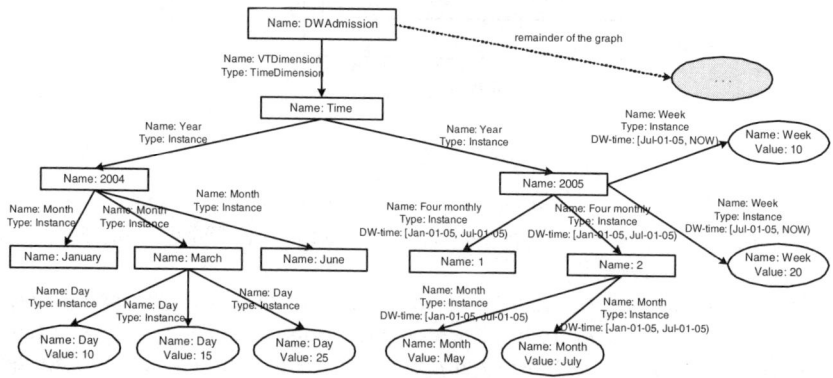

Fig. 14.10 Graph with temporal granularities of the data warehouse

Finally, GEMDW provides a way for specifying the (partial) order between granules. This is achieved by inserting edges between the nodes of the granularity graph. These edges have one compulsory property *Type*, whose value is *Next*. An edge of type *Next* links a node to its successor at the same granularity[1]. The only exception is the last node, which - obviously - has no successor: thus we add a label to the node with the *End-granule* property. This property assumes the value *End-granule: Yes* to assert that there is no successor. When changing the graph of granularity, the property *End-granule* can switch to *No*, after having inserted a successor. We recall that the temporal hierarchy can be browsed in both directions (as in Section 14.3.1).

To specify the time linked to a fact we use labeled edges: a labeled edge links a node instance of a fact to a node instance in the granularity graph. The property *Type* will assume the value *TimeDimensionLink*. Figure 14.11 depicts an example of a link to a temporal subgraph: the name of the edge is *ValidTime* (i.e., the valid time of the fact), and the label has the property DWT (i.e., the data warehouse time).

---

[1] It is worth noting that in the graphs depicted in this paper, the edges *Next* are not represented for sake of clarity

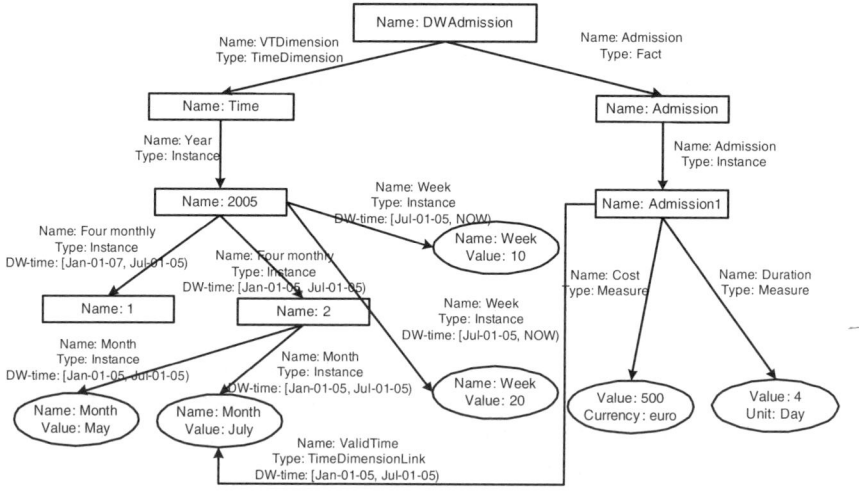

Fig. 14.11 Graph of the data warehouse: temporal links

GEMDW enables one to define the time of a fact as an interval rather than one single granule. To obtain the interval of the node *Fact*, we use two nodes like those defined for the single granule, and add the property *Interval* (Figure 14.12). *Interval* is set to *Start* in the edge that links the beginning granule of the interval; the property (*Interval*) is set to *End* in the edge the links the ending granule of the interval.

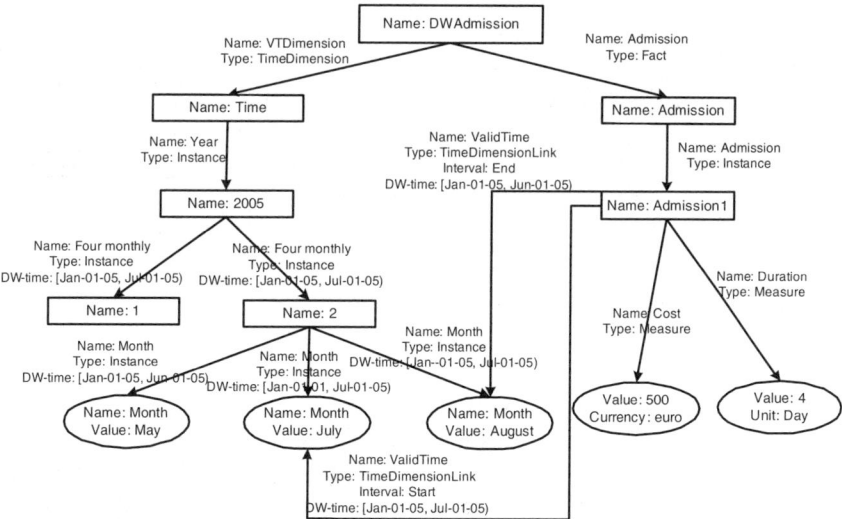

Fig. 14.12 Graph of the data warehouse: time of the fact as an interval

The used model enables one to (i) define a virtually unlimited number of temporal dimensions (*Valid time, Transaction time, Event time, Availability time, ...*), and (ii) to specify that at a given time *t* one instance of a fact can be linked to more granularitires, enabling a temporal aggregation at different granularity levels.

14.3.6 Views

When dealing with data warehouses, very complex queries or queries involving huge quantities of data may require high workloads. In these cases, use of materialized views could benefit, despite that they may require a huge amount of storage memory. GEMDW enables one to save the graph resulting from a query (thus introducing the concept of view), to use it as a starting point for a newer query. The saved graph (i.e., the view) has a root node, which, in turn, is linked to the root node of the graph of the data warehouse by an edge of type *View* labeled with the user-defined name.

When generating a new view starting from a previously defined one, the root nodes of the two views are connected by an edge which stores the invariant of the second view with respect to the first one.

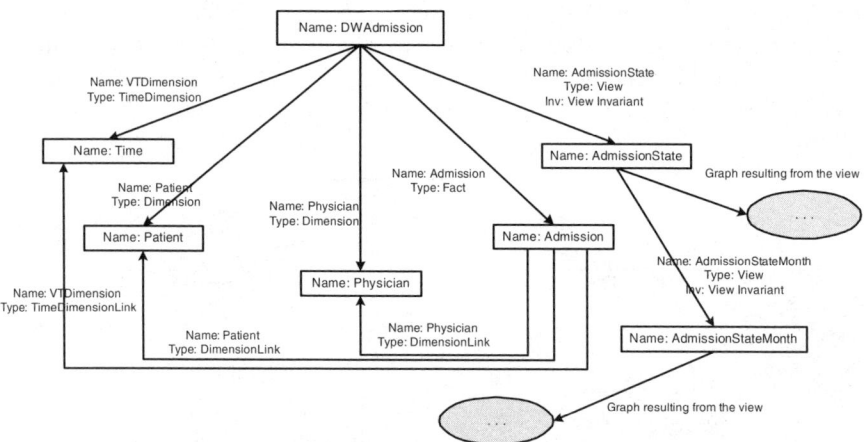

Fig. 14.13 Part of a graph in GEMDW: query materialization

As an example, we move from the data warehouse of Figure 14.1, and we plan to perform a query to extract admissions for every State where the admission occurred. We may want to save the result as a view, labeling it as *AdmissionState*: in Figure 14.13 the *AdmissionState* view is directly linked to the root *DWAdmission*. Next we may want to consider the admissions of every State for every month, i.e., by splitting data also according to the month during which the admission occurred. We may now move from the previously stored view (*AdmissionState*) to obtain the derived view *AdmissionStateMonth*, which splits the results of the previous view according to the month when the facts happened, and accordingly aggregates data. Figure 14.13 depicts both views.

Edges of type *View* come with the following properties:

a) *Name*: the name of the query;
b) *Type*: View;
c) *Inv*: a string storing the invariant of the query with respect to the starting view;
d) *Description* (optional): a string providing a description in natural language of the semantics of the query. This helps to avoid two different users to define the same view, saving the required storing space.

Figure 14.14 depicts a drill-down operation applied to the graph of Figure 14.13. Let us assume to have a new view *AdmissionMonth* aggregating data over the temporal dimension *Month*. Moreover, let us assume that we want to perform a drill-down operation over the *AdmissionStateMonth* view reducing the aggregation of the dimension *Person* to the basic level. If we consider the data warehouse, we can observe that the view *AdmissionState* is already included. Thus, in this case, we only need to link the root of *AdmissionStateMonth* to the root of *AdmissionState*: we do not need to materialize the view, which is already included in the data warehouse.

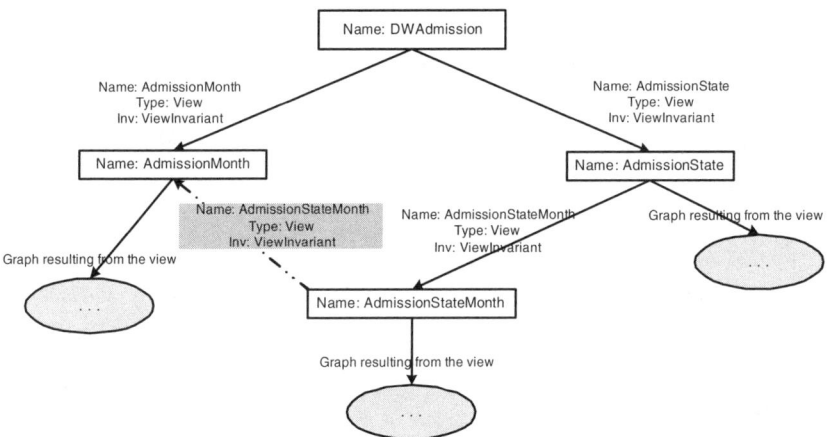

Fig. 14.14 Part of a graph in GEMDW: drill-down

After having materialized a view, the resulting graph must be generated: if we performed a *roll-up* operation, the nodes of the fact over which we performed the *roll-up* will now point to the (temporal) dimension node over which they were grouped.

14.4 DW-QL: a Query Language for GEMDW

In this section we define DW-QL, a query language to retrieve information represented by GEMDW. DW-QL semantics have been defined by using an extension of the well known StruQL [20], one of the main languages for semistructured data, to manage both labeled edges and nodes. DW-QL could benefit from XPath technology [30], should GEMDW have been implemented through XML.

We shall consider the typical queries roll-up, drill-down, slicing, and selection.

14.4.1 Roll-Up in DW-QL

The roll-up operation aims at aggregating data by removing a level of detail inside a hierarchy: this helps to consider data in a decision process. The roll-up requires one to define the fact over which the operation is performed, the dimension(s) to be aggregated, the measure(s) and the operator(s) needed for the aggregation. The general syntax for the roll-up operation is the following:

```
CREATE [Materialized] RollUp
    INPUT datagraph
    FACT factName
    MEASURE measureName
    [WITH operator] ([, measureName [WITH operator]])*
    [DIMENSION dimensionName
        ON dimensionAttribute TO level
        ([, dimensionName ON dimensionAttribute TO level])*]
    [TIMEDIMENSION dimensionName TO level]
    [TIME time]
    OUTPUT resultgraph
```

The `Materialized` token specifies if the aggregation is to be materialized, and thus the resulting graphs is stored inside the data warehouse, or virtual. The `INPUT` clause relates to the data structure to be used for the roll-up operation. The `FACT` clause relates to the name of the fact over which we are going to perform the roll-up operation. The `MEASURE` clause relates to the name of the measure to be aggregated, while the `operator` token is used to aggregate the measure.

The `DIMENSION` clause relates to the timeless dimensions for the roll-up operations, while the `TIMEDIMENSION` clause relates to the temporal dimensions of aggregations. `dimensionName` defines the name of the dimension over which we want to aggregate data. `dimensionAttribute` defines the attribute of the dimension connected to the hierarchy. `level` defines the level within the hierarchy to which we want to elevate the aggregation.

The `TIME` clause defines the data warehouse time DWT according to which we aggregate: by default, we assume TIME="now". TIME can also be defined as an interval, in the form of $TIME[DW_s, DW_e]$, where DW_s is the beginning timestamp and DW_e is the ending timestamp of the considered interval, or as a timestamp, in the form of TIMEDW_e.

As an example, if we want to perform a roll-up of the graph of Figure 14.13, aggregating the measures Cost and Duration of the fact Admission at the level State of the dimension Patient, we obtain the following DW-QL query:

```
CREATE Materialized RollUp
    INPUT DWAdmission
    FACT Admission
    MEASURE Cost, Duration WITH AVG
    DIMENSION Patient ON HomeAddress TO State
    OUTPUT AdmissionState
```

14.4.2 Drill-Down in DW-QL

The drill-down operation aims at reducing the aggregation over data which was previously performed by a roll-up operation. Thus, the drill-down operation can be performed over a view whose data were previously processed by a roll-up operation.

As an example, we want to perform a drill-down over the view AdmissionState-Month we obtained by the above roll-up operation, removing the aggregation over the dimension Patient. We can proceed in two different ways. We can look for a materialized view (if any) representing the aggregation at the level of Month for the dimension Time as in Figure 14.14. Alternatively, or if no suitable materialized view is defined, we can transform a drill-down operation in a set of OLAP operations which move from the original data warehouse and lead us to the wanted result. Thus, the resulting query can be written as follows:

```
CREATE Materialized DrillDown
    INPUT AdmissionStateMonth
    FACT Admission
    MEASURE Cost, Duration WITH AVG
    TIMEDIMENSION Time TO Month
    OUTPUT AdmissionMonth
```

14.4.3 Slicing in DW-QL

The slicing operation aims at reducing the dimensions of the data cube by fixing a value for one dimension. The general syntax for slicing is:

```
CREATE [Materialized] Slicing
    INPUT datagraph
    FACT factName
    [DIMENSION dimensionName ON dimensionAttribute R value
```

```
        ([, dimensionAttribute R value])*
        ([, dimensionName ON dimensionAttribute R value
        ([, dimensionAttribute R value])*])*
    [TIMEDIMENSION dimensionName TR timeExpression]
    [TIME time]
    OUTPUT resultgraph
```

With respect to the syntax introduced in Section 14.4.1, this new syntax extends the concepts of DIMENSION (used to slice on a timeless dimension) and of TIMEDIMENSION (used to slice on a temporal dimension).

dimensionName defines the dimension over which we want to complete the slice operation. dimensionAttribute defines the attribute of the dimension to be used for the condition part. R is the relationship to be considered: allowed operators are $=, >, \geq, <, \leq, \neq$. TR defines a temporal relationship based on the operators $=, >, \geq, <, \leq, \neq, IN, NOT IN$. timeExpression, in turn, features the following syntax:

```
timeExpression ::= SGranule | Interval | NOW
SGranule ::= GranuleName:value | GranuleName:value, SGranule
Interval ::= <LBRACE> Granule <SEMICOLON> Granule <RPAREN>
```

SGranule defines the name of the granule we want to refer to: e.g., the date March 10*th*, 2004 is translated as Year:2004, Month:March, Day:10. The operators IN and NOT IN can be used with an Interval, only: e.g. the interval [Mar-10-04; now) is translated as [year:2004, Month:March, Day:10th; now).

As an example, if we want to execute a slicing of the dimension Physician, by imposing Physician="Simon Bell", we obtain the following query:

```
CREATE Materialized Slicing
    INPUT DWAdmission
    FACT Admission
    DIMENSION Physician ON Name="Simon", Surname="Bell"
    OUTPUT AdmissionSimonBell
```

If we want to perform a slicing of the time dimension over the admissions from May, 2005 to July, 2005, we execute the following query:

```
CREATE Materialized Slicing
    INPUT DWAdmission
    FACT Admission
    TIMEDIMENSION Time IN
            [Year:2005, Month:May; Year:2005, Month:July)
    OUTPUT AdmissionMay2005July2005
```

14.4.4 Selection in DW-QL

The selection operation aims at reducing the set of data considered, by formulating a selection criterium over one (or more) measure(s) of a fact. The full syntax is:

```
CREATE [Materialized] Selection
    INPUT datagraph
    FACT factName
    MEASURE measureName R value ([, measureName R value])*
    [TIME time]
OUTPUT resultgraph
```

With respect to the syntax introduced in Section 14.4.1, this new syntax extends the concepts of MEASURE, where MeasureName is the name of the measure, R is the relationship and value is the required value.

As an example, if we want to select all the admissions whose cost did not exceed the amount of € 500,00, we perform the following query:

```
CREATE Materialized Selection
    INPUT DWAdmission
    FACT Admission
    MEASURE Cost ≤ 500,00
OUTPUT LowCostAdmissions
```

14.5 Conclusions

In this paper, we proposed a data model to represent temporal semistructured data warehouses, and its related query language. The data model is a graph-based model capable of managing both the typical aspects of semistructured information and the temporal facets of data. Moreover, our approach allows one to represent and use the classical notions of the data warehouse context, such as facts and dimensions. The proposed query language supports the usual OLAP functions, such as drill-down, roll-up, slicing, and selection on temporal semistructured data.

As future work, we plan (i) to introduce some more flexibility in our query language in order to aggregate data representing the same information, but having different structures; (ii) to enrich our query language to retrieve information across different versions of data and considering all the different temporal dimensions such as valid time, transaction time, event time, and availability time; (iii) to design and realize a first prototype based on the proposed model and language for the management of XML warehouses; and (iv) to provide suitable drivers to port the query language on some of the commercially available data warehouse systems.

Acknowledgements This research was partially funded by several grants from the Università di Verona, Dipartimento di Informatica, and from the Politecnico di Milano, Dipartimento di Elettronica e Informazione. We thank the master student Roberto Pietrangeli, from the Università di Verona, who helped in developing the proposed model during his master thesis work.

References

1. S. Abiteboul. Querying semi-structured data. In Afrati and Kolaitis [3], pages 1–18.
2. S. Abiteboul, D. Quass, J. McHugh, J. Widom, and J. L. Wiener. The Lorel query language for semistructured data. *Int. J. on Digital Libraries*, 1(1):68–88, 1997.
3. F. N. Afrati and P. G. Kolaitis, editors. *Database Theory - ICDT '97, 6th International Conference, Proceedings*, volume 1186 of *Lecture Notes in Computer Science*. Springer, 1997.
4. T. Amagasa, M. Yoshikawa, and S. Uemura. A data model for temporal XML documents. In M. T. Ibrahim, J. Küng, and N. Revell, editors, *DEXA*, volume 1873 of *Lecture Notes in Computer Science*, pages 334–344. Springer, 2000.
5. B. Bebel, J. Eder, C. Koncilia, T. Morzy, and R. Wrembel. Creation and management of versions in multiversion data warehouse. In H. Haddad, A. Omicini, R. L. Wainwright, and L. M. Liebrock, editors, *SAC*, pages 717–723. ACM, 2004.
6. C. Bettini, S. Jajodia, and S. Wang. *Time Granularities in Databases, Data Mining, and Temporal Reasoning*. Springer, 2000.
7. S. S. Bhowmick, S. K. Madria, W. K. Ng, and E.-P. Lim. Web warehousing: Design and issues. In Y. Kambayashi, D. L. Lee, E.-P. Lim, M. K. Mohania, and Y. Masunaga, editors, *ER Workshops*, volume 1552 of *Lecture Notes in Computer Science*, pages 93–104. Springer, 1998.
8. P. Buneman, S. B. Davidson, M. F. Fernandez, and D. Suciu. Adding structure to unstructured data. In Afrati and Kolaitis [3], pages 336–350.
9. S. S. Chawathe, S. Abiteboul, and J. Widom. Managing historical semistructured data. *Theory and Practice of Object Systems*, 5(3):143–162, 1999.
10. C. Combi, N. Lavarini, and B. Oliboni. Querying semistructured temporal data. In T. Grust, H. Höpfner, A. Illarramendi, S. Jablonski, M. Mesiti, S. Müller, P.-L. Patranjan, K.-U. Sattler, M. Spiliopoulou, and J. Wijsen, editors, *International Conference on Extending Database Technology Workshops*, volume 4254 of *Lecture Notes in Computer Science*, pages 625–636. Springer, 2006.
11. C. Combi, A. Montanari, and G. Pozzi. The T4SQL temporal query language. In M. J. Silva, A. H. F. Laender, R. A. Baeza-Yates, D. L. McGuinness, B. Olstad, Ø. H. Olsen, and A. O. Falcão, editors, *CIKM*, pages 193–202. ACM, 2007.
12. C. Combi and B. Oliboni. Temporal semistructured data models and data warehouses. In R. Wrembel and C. Koncilia, editors, *Data Warehouses and OLAP: Concepts, Architectures and Solutions*, pages 277–297. Idea Group Inc., Hershey, PA, 2006.
13. C. Combi, B. Oliboni, and E. Quintarelli. A graph-based data model to represent transaction time in semistructured data. In F. Galindo, M. Takizawa, and R. Traunmüller, editors, *DEXA*, volume 3180 of *Lecture Notes in Computer Science*, pages 559–568. Springer, 2004.
14. C. Cunningham, I.-Y. Song, and P. P. Chen. Data warehouse design to support customer relationship management analyses. In I.-Y. Song and K. C. Davis, editors, *International Workshop on Data Warehousing and OLAP (DOLAP)*, pages 14–22. ACM, 2004.
15. E. Damiani, B. Oliboni, E. Quintarelli, and L. Tanca. Modeling semistructured data by using graph-based constraints. In R. Meersman and Z. Tari, editors, *OTMOnTheMove (OTM) Workshops*, volume 2889 of *Lecture Notes in Computer Science*, pages 20–21. Springer, 2003.
16. C. E. Dyreson, M. H. Böhlen, and C. S. Jensen. Capturing and querying multiple aspects of semistructured data. In M. P. Atkinson, M. E. Orlowska, P. Valduriez, S. B. Zdonik, and M. L. Brodie, editors, *International Conference on Very Large Data Bases*, pages 290–301. Morgan Kaufmann, 1999.
17. J. Eder and C. Koncilia. Changes of dimension data in temporal data warehouses. In Y. Kambayashi, W. Winiwarter, and M. Arikawa, editors, *DaWaKInternational Conference on Data Warehousing and Knowledge Discovery*, volume 2114 of *Lecture Notes in Computer Science*, pages 284–293. Springer, 2001.
18. J. Eder, C. Koncilia, and D. Mitsche. Automatic detection of structural changes in data warehouses. In Y. Kambayashi, M. K. Mohania, and W. Wöß, editors, *DaWaKInternational Conference on Data Warehousing and Knowledge Discovery*, volume 2737 of *Lecture Notes in Computer Science*, pages 119–128. Springer, 2003.

19. J. Eder, C. Koncilia, and T. Morzy. The COMET metamodel for temporal data warehouses. In A. B. Pidduck, J. Mylopoulos, C. C. Woo, and M. T. Özsu, editors, *CAiSE*, volume 2348 of *Lecture Notes in Computer Science*, pages 83–99. Springer, 2002.

20. M. F. Fernández, D. Florescu, J. Kang, A. Y. Levy, and D. Suciu. STRUDEL: A Web-site management system. In J. Peckham, editor, *SIGMOD Conference*, pages 549–552. ACM Press, 1997.

21. C. Koncilia. A bi-temporal data warehouse model. In J. Eder and T. Welzer, editors, *CAiSE Short Paper Proceedings*, volume 74 of *CEUR Workshop Proceedings*. CEUR-WS.org, 2003.

22. C. Li and X. S. Wang. A data model for supporting on-line analytical processing. In *CIKM*, pages 81–88. ACM, 1996.

23. A. Marian, S. Abiteboul, G. Cobena, and L. Mignet. Change-centric management of versions in an XML warehouse. In P. M. G. Apers, P. Atzeni, S. Ceri, S. Paraboschi, K. Ramamohanarao, and R. T. Snodgrass, editors, *Proceedings of 27th International Conference on Very Large Data Bases*, pages 581–590. Morgan Kaufmann, 2001.

24. J. McHugh, S. Abiteboul, R. Goldman, D. Quass, and J. Widom. Lore: A database management system for semistructured data. *SIGMOD Record*, 26(3):54–66, 1997.

25. A. O. Mendelzon, F. Rizzolo, and A. A. Vaisman. Indexing temporal XML documents. In M. A. Nascimento, M. T. Özsu, D. Kossmann, R. J. Miller, J. A. Blakeley, and K. B. Schiefer, editors, *International Conference on Very Large Data Bases*, pages 216–227. Morgan Kaufmann, 2004.

26. B. Oliboni, E. Quintarelli, and L. Tanca. Temporal aspects of semistructured data. In *TIME - International Symposium on Temporal Representation and Reasoning*, pages 119–127, 2001.

27. Y. Papakonstantinou, H. Garcia-Molina, and J. Widom. Object exchange across heterogeneous information sources. In P. S. Yu and A. L. P. Chen, editors, *ICDE*, pages 251–260. IEEE Computer Society, 1995.

28. F. Wang and C. Zaniolo. Temporal queries in XML document archives and Web warehouses. In *TIME*, pages 47–55. IEEE Computer Society, 2003.

29. F. Wang and C. Zaniolo. XBiT: An XML-based bitemporal data model. In P. Atzeni, W. W. Chu, H. Lu, S. Zhou, and T. W. Ling, editors, *ER*, volume 3288 of *Lecture Notes in Computer Science*, pages 810–824. Springer, 2004.

30. World Wide Web Consortium. XML Path Language (XPath) Version 1.0, 1999. http://www.w3.org/TR/xpath.

31. World Wide Web Consortium. W3C eXtensible Markup Language (XML) 1.0 specifications (third edition), 2004. http://www.w3.org/TR/2004/REC-xml-20040204/.

32. L. Xyleme. Xyleme: A dynamic warehouse for XML data of the Web. In M. E. Adiba, C. Collet, and B. C. Desai, editors, *IDEAS*, pages 3–7. IEEE Computer Society, 2001.

Chapter 15
Designing and Implementing OLAP Systems from XML Documents

Franck Ravat, Olivier Teste, Ronan Tournier, and Gilles Zurfluh

Abstract There has been a lot of research on OLAP (On-Line Analytical Processing) systems during the past decade. These systems allow decision makers to improve their decisions. Despite numerous multidimensional conceptual models, none tackle the problem of analysing data extracted from text-rich XML documents. These documents represent a lot of unavailable information for actual OLAP systems. Moreover, the implementation of such a system requires an adapted design process. In this paper, we present an adapted "galaxy" model for the analysis of text-rich XML documents. This model is associated to an adapted design process and a tool that takes in charge all automated tasks of the process.

15.1 Introduction

OLAP (On-Line Analytical Processing) systems allow decision makers to gain insight within enterprise performance by consulting and analysing aggregated historical business data [8]. These systems are based on well mastered techniques that allow numeric centric information analysis [35] within specially designed multidimensional databases (MDB). Nevertheless, according to a recent study [36], only 20% of corporate information system data is transactional, i.e. numeric data. The remaining 80% (mainly text-rich documents) stays out of reach of OLAP technology. This is due to the lack of adapted OLAP systems and methods in order to be able to take into account non numerical indicators such as textual indicators. Not taking into account these data sources may lead to erroneous decisions [36]. Recently XML [39] technology has provided a large framework for sharing documents within corporate networks of over the Web. Textual data in XML format is now a conceivable data source for OLAP systems.

Franck Ravat, Olivier Teste, Ronan Tournier, Gilles Zurfluh
IRIT (UMR5505), Université de Toulouse, 118 rte de Narbonne, F-31062 Toulouse Cedex 9, FRANCE, e-mail: {ravat,teste,tournier,zurfluh}@irit.fr

Our goal is to integrate these text-rich data sources within an OLAP system. More precisely, we intend to offer a complete design method for OLAP systems built on documents. This method must rest on: a multidimensional model sufficiently rich for integrating textual data; a design approach taking into account both user requirements and available data sources (documents); and a CASE[1] tool. From this goal, several issues arise: 1) to offer a global solution that includes a model, an approach and a tool; 2) to ensure the integration of all the information that is in documents (content, structure and metadata); and 3) the necessity not to restrain the user by the analysis of document data with only numeric indicators (document contents being mainly composed of textual data).

Definition 15.1. We define *XML Document Warehousing* as a storage stage (e.g. a data warehouse) adapted to handle text-rich XML document data and associated to an analysis stage allowing OLAP style processing on non-numeric analysis indicators.

15.1.1 Related works

According to the authors of [10] two types of XML documents may be encountered: 1) *Data-centric XML documents* that are raw data documents close to database content, where XML tags are used to separated data as lines and columns would in a database (e.g. logs, invoices, dumps of databases ...); and 2) *Document-centric XML documents* also known as text-rich XML documents which are the digital equivalent of our traditional paperwork (e.g. scientific articles, e-books ...).

We divide related works in two categories: multidimensional modelling and design processes.

15.1.1.1 Multidimensional Modelling

We consider four subcategories for modelling. The first one is related to *traditional multidimensional modelling* [18]. A recent survey may be found in [33] and current issues are highlighted in [34]. Multidimensional modelling is based on the concepts of facts (analysis subjects) and dimensions (analysis axes). All these models, conceptually or logically oriented, have been conceived for traditional numeric data analysis and do not deal with documents.

The second subcategory concerns *multidimensional modelling for the analysis of data-centric XML documents*. The analysis of documents like logs or outputs of Web services has been introduced in several articles such as [16]. See [24, 38, 40] for a more complete list of works. Although these articles consider textual data through the use of XML documents, these propositions limit themselves to numeric indicators do not take into consideration more complex data.

---

[1] CASE : Computer Aided Software Engineering.

The third subcategory concerns *multidimensional modelling allowing complex data analysis*. In [24] the authors define an xFACT, a complex hierarchical structure containing structured and unstructured data (such as documents). Measures, called contexts, may be seen as complex objects. In [3], a complete XML approach for modelling complex data analysis is presented. These works do not take into account more complex text-rich XML documents and are limited to numeric indicators.

Nevertheless some works focussed on text-rich documents and the fourth subcategory concerns *multidimensional modelling for the analysis of document-centric documents*. In [27] the authors combine traditional numeric analysis and information retrieval techniques to assist analyses by providing documents relevant to the ongoing analysis context. In [17, 22, 23, 36], the authors present applications of document-centric document analysis using a star schema [18] but still with numeric analysis indicators. Recently, in [26], the concept of multidimensional document analysis was introduced using an xFACT [24] and specific aggregation functions inspired by text mining techniques but these are not detailed. These articles do not take into account complex document-centric document properties (e.g. structure and complete content). Moreover, they are no detailed adapted formal conceptual model.

So far, and to our knowledge, there is no proposal for designing and implementing an OLAP system that allows document-centric document content analysis. Up to now, apart from [26], research has been based on quantitative analyses, e.g. the number of publications that contain a specific keyword. Textual data is provided for the analysis through dimensions which model analysis axes and not subjects of analysis, moreover analysis indicators (measures) are always numeric.

15.1.1.2 Design Processes

To our knowledge, design processes have only be specified for traditional multidimensional models. Their goal is to implement a multidimensional database and they may be classified in three approaches:

Firstly, *bottom-up approaches* are data driven approaches. Multidimensional schemas are derived from the analysis of available data sources without considering user needs. In [11] and [5], a multidimensional schema is built from E/R schemas of the data sources, taking full advantage of the data sources' semantics. But, as the domain represented may be broad, this may require a great deal of resources and time. To get round this problem, in [14], the authors provide a method for the user to designate relevant sources; but, users have to consult the data source schemas and they might not master them. In [21], Architecture Driven Modernization (ADM) is used to derive semi-automatically a multidimensional conceptual schema from sources. However, in this approach, user requirements are not much considered.

Secondly, *top-down approaches* are demand driven approaches. Multidimensional schemas are derived from the analysis of user requirements. In this approach data sources are not taken into account. In [18], the author presents a general methodology for managing decisional projects but with no detailed process for the specification of multidimensional schemas. In [29], the authors present a design process that rests on UML notations. With this design process, the designer translates user requirements in a UML class diagram. This diagram is then enriched and transformed into a multidimensional conceptual schema. But, without taking into account data sources, it is possible to design inconsistent schemas that will lack data in the sources.

Thirdly, *mixed approaches* combine both previous design processes, taking into account both user requirements and data sources. Within this approach, user requirements are translated into one (possibly more) "ideal" multidimensional schema and the analysis of the data sources also produces "candidate" multidimensional schemas. A confrontation phase allows the comparison between the different multidimensional schemas and allows the designer to come up with a final schema. In [6], the authors present a method that designs several ideal schemas. In [2, 7, 28], the authors present a method that generates several candidate schemas. But within these works, the confrontation phase may be tedious. In [20], one ideal schema is confronted to one candidate schema. All these approaches are not formally described.

Some approaches, such as [37], settle for ETL processes (Extract, Transform, Load) and focus on data integration but with XML documents, the handled data structures are different. All these approaches have been conceived for models based on the duality of the fact and dimension concepts and these models are not adapted to represent analyses based on text-rich XML documents [31]. As a consequence, to our knowledge, there is a need for adapting an approach and a complete design process with different levels of abstraction (conceptual, logical and physical) is still an open issue.

15.1.2 *Objectives and contributions*

The objectives of this paper are: 1) to allow the analysis of the contents of text-rich documents and their metadata with the use of numeric and textual indicators; 2) to allow multidimensional analysis of data extracted from text-rich XML documents; and 3) to offer a complete solution for the design and the implementation of such a multidimensional database.

The contributions are: 1) a model that allows an easy representation of the multidimensional elements available for expressing analyses; 2) an approach that enables the integration of XML documents within the decisional system; and 3) a tool to ease the design and implementation process.

This paper is organised as follows: Section 2 defines a multidimensional model adapted for expressing analysis on document-centric documents; section 3 specifies an approach for designing and implementing a multidimensional database from XML documents; and section 4 presents an adapted design tool.

15.2 Multidimensional Model for XML Document Data Analysis

In order to allow the analysis of document-centric XML documents, several characteristics have to be taken into account: 1) the hierarchical structure of the textual data of the documents; 2) the content mainly composed of textual data; and 3) the metadata associated to the document. Moreover, the model should not restrain the decision maker by offering limited or pre-specified analysis solutions based on numerical analyses. In the past decade, numerous multidimensional models have been proposed, but none handle these issues (see section 1.1).

15.2.1 Conceptual Model

To answer to these issues, we defined a multidimensional model nicknamed "galaxy" model [31]. The galaxy allows flexibility in the specification of multidimensional analyses by not restraining the decision maker with predefined analysis subjects.

A dimension is composed of hierarchically organised *attributes*. These attributes allow the representation of the multidimensional aspect of the data, each attribute being a graduation of the analysis axis, i.e. detail levels or granularity levels.

Definition 15.2. A *dimension* $D = (A^D, H^D, I^D, I^{StarD})$ where:

- $A^D = \{a^{D_1}, \ldots, a^{D_r}\}$ is a set of *attributes*,
- $H^D = \{H^{D_1}, \ldots, H^{D_s}\}$ is a set of *hierarchies*,
- $I^D = \{i^{D_1}, \ldots, i^{D_t}\}$ is a set of *dimension instances*. Each attribute has a value for each instance $a^D_u(i^D_x)$, called an *attribute instance*.
- $IStar^D = \{IStar^D_1, IStar^D_2 \ldots\}$ is set of functions $IStar^D_i : I^D \rightarrow (I^D_1)^* \times \ldots \times (I^D_n)^*$ each associating the instances of the D dimension to the instances of other linked dimensions through $Star^G$ ($\forall k \in [1..n]$, $D_k \in D^G$, $D_k \neq D$ and $D_k \in Star^G(D)$, i.e. D_k is associated/linked to D).[2]

Within the hierarchies that organise the dimension attributes, there exist two types of attributes: *parameters* which represent a particular level of detail and *weak attributes* which represent complementary data of a parameter.

Definition 15.3. A *hierarchy* noted H^D_i or $H = (Param^H, Weak^H)$ where:

- $Param^H = \langle p^H_1, \ldots, p^H_{n_p} \rangle$ is an ordered set of attributes, called *parameters*, which represent the levels of granularity of the dimension, $k \in [1..n_p]$, $p^H_k \in A^D$ and $p^H_1 = a^D_1$;
- $Weak^H : Param^H \rightarrow 2^{A^D - Param^H}$ is an application possibly associating *weak attributes* to parameters, completing the parameter semantic.

---

[2] The notation $(I)^*$ represents a finite set of elements of I.

The galaxy is based on: 1) a unique concept of dimension that represents not only an analysis axis but also a possible subject of analysis (namely a fact); 2) a gathering of dimensions into specific groups indicating compatibility for the specification of analyses with the use of these dimensions.

Definition 15.4. A *Galaxy* $G = (D^G, Star^G, Lk^G)$ where:

- $D^G = \{D_1, \ldots, D_n\}$ is a set of *dimensions*,
- $Star^G : D_i \rightarrow 2_j^D$ is a function that associates each dimension D_i to its linked dimensions $D_j \in D^G$ $(D_j \neq D_i)$. This expression models nodes c_z that may be expressed through: $\{D_{c_1}, \ldots, D_{c_n}\} \subseteq D^G | \forall i, j \in [c_1..c_n], i \neq j, \exists D_i \rightarrow 2^{D_j} \in Star^G$. This represents dimensions compatible within a same analysis.[3]
- $Lk^G = \{g_1, g_2, \ldots\}$ is a set of functions that associate attributes together. Due to space restriction, these will not be detailed (consult [31] for more details).

Note that each attribute of a dimension is a possible analysis indicator.

15.2.2 Case Study

This application aims at analysing the performance of research institutes. More precisely, we wish to analyse scientific articles and research project reports produced by researchers. There is a need for two analyses: firstly, the analysis of research articles published at a certain date, in conferences and by authors; and secondly, the analysis of reports published by authors at a certain date. The result is a galaxy composed of 5 dimensions grouped into 2 groups (nodes).

Let $G_1 = (D^{G_1}, Star^{G_1}, Lk^{G_1})$, where:

$D^{G_1} = \{CONFERENCES, ARTICLES, TIME, AUTHORS, REPORTS\}$;

$Star^{G_1} = \{CONFERENCES \rightarrow (ARTICLES, TIME, AUTHORS), ARTICLES \rightarrow (CONFERENCES, TIME, AUTHORS), TIME \rightarrow (CONFERENCES, ARTICLES, AUTHORS, REPORTS), AUTHORS \rightarrow (CONFERENCES, ARTICLES, TIME, REPORTS), REPORTS \rightarrow (TIME, AUTHORS)\}$;

In these research institutes, authors are described by their name, status (professor,...), research team and institute (or company). Let the *AUTHORS* dimension (noted D_A for short) with two hierarchies be: $D_A = (A^{D_A}, H^{D_A}, I^{D_A}, IStar^{D_A})$, where:

$A^{D_A} = \{Author, Name, Status, Team, Institute\}$,

$H^{D_A} = \{HA, HSt\}$,

$I^{D_A} = \{author_1, author_2, \ldots\}$,

$IStar_1^{D_A} = \{author_1 \rightarrow (conference_1, paragraph_{125}, date_{10}), \ldots\}$.

$IStar_2^{D_A} = \{author_1 \rightarrow (date_{23}, report_2), \ldots\}$.

Associated to this definition we propose a graphical formalism in order to easily represent a galaxy (see Fig. 15.1). Each dimension is represented by a rectangle

---

[3] The notation 2^E represents the *powerset* of E.

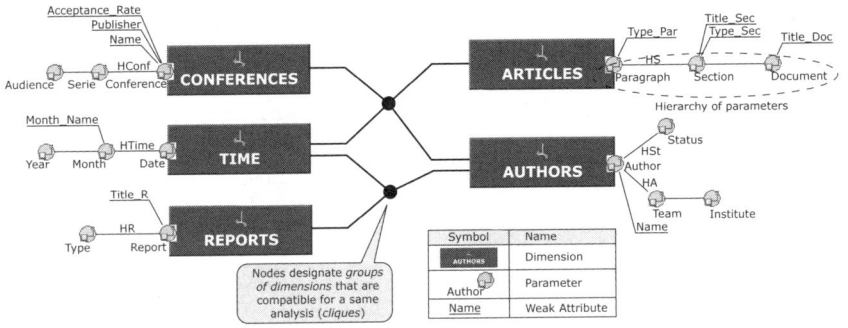

Fig. 15.1 Analysis of scientific publications and research reports.

whose hierarchies are represented by a graph. Dimensions are grouped into one or more sets (nodes on the graphic representation) in order to represent the different dimensions compatible for an analysis within a galaxy. The galaxy being represented by a graph, these groups or nodes are called cliques[4]. Note that in this example, some dimensions are similar to traditional OLAP dimensions (*CONFERENCES*, *TIME*, *REPORTS* and *AUTHORS*) except that their attributes may be designated as analysis subjects. The other dimension (*ARTICLES*) holds the complete content of the scientific article, i.e. text-rich documents. Its parameters are composed of large quantity of textual data.

The galaxy model has the advantage of being able to easily represent the textual content of XML text-rich documents as well as their structure in order to facilitate the specification of multidimensional analyses [31].

15.2.3 OLAP analysis with a galaxy

Within this subsection, we provide an analysis example using the galaxy. This is to show that how the galaxy supports analysis specifications. These are expressed with the use of adapted aggregation functions for textual data [26, 30], as well as adapted multidimensional operations. In [31] we have proposed a set of algebraic operations for specifying analyses by manipulating the concepts modelled by the galaxy. Through a FOCUS operation an analysis subject is designated and data is extracted from the galaxy into a multidimensional table (mTable), i.e. a bi-dimensional table [12]. mTables display a subject of analysis in its centre cells according to two analysis axes (one in columns and the other in lines). They act as inputs for a closed set of manipulation operations for modifying analyses (SELECT, DRILLDOWN, ROLLUP and ROTATE).

---

[4] In a graph, a *clique* is a complete subgraph, i.e. every vertex is connected every other vertex in the subgraph.

Table 15.1 Left, the number of published articles per author and per conference; right, the same analysis but with the top keywords of the corresponding publications.

COUNT(ARTICLES.Document)		AUTHORS		
	Institute Author	Inst1		
		A1	A2	A3
CONFERENCES	Name			
	ER	3	2	1
	SSDBM	2	-	-
	DaWaK	1	1	2

TOP_KEYWORD(ARTICLES.Document)		AUTHORS		
	Institute Author	Inst1		
		A1	A2	A3
CONFERENCES	Name			
	ER	XML, Docments	XML, Data Warehouse	Data Mining, Clustering
	SSDBM	XML, Temporal DB	-	-
	DaWaK	Data mining	Data mining	Data Mining, Clustering

For example, in order to analyse the production of articles, a decision maker could make a simple analysis and count the number of articles by author and by conference as in any existing OLAP frameworks (table 15.1, left). But with the use of the galaxy and associated operations, the decision maker can go further and analyse the subjects that concern these publications (table 15.1, right). The subject of the publications is obtained with the use of an adapted aggregation function (TOP_KEY-WORD) on the *Document* attribute of the *ARTICLES* dimension (i.e. the complete textual content of the articles) and that returns here the two major keywords for each set of article [26].

The following sections detail our approach that allows a user to create a galaxy schema and then to load it with data extracted from XML documents.

15.3 Design Process

The objective of the design process is to allow the design and the implementation of a multidimensional database modelled with a galaxy. But, several issues have to be solved: How are user requirements (analysis requirements) translated into a galaxy? How may available XML documents within the data sources be taken into account? Up to now and to our knowledge, there is no design process that considers text-rich (i.e. document-centric) XML documents as data sources for OLAP systems.

Due to the assets stated previously, our design process rests upon a mixed approach, taking into account user requirements as well as XML documents that are in the data sources. This mixed approach uses an iterative process in order to refine the galaxy schema. We defined three phases for our approach:

- Concurrent analysis of user requirements and document sources (steps 1 and 2);
- Confrontation of the outputs of the two previous analysis phases in order to detect and to solve incompatibilities (step 3, 4a and 4b);
- Implementation of a multidimensional database described with a galaxy schema and loaded with data extracted from XML documents (step 5).

All three phases are summarized in Fig. 15.2 (steps are numbers in brackets). The designer starts by analysing concurrently the user requirements, producing a galaxy schema (step 1), and the data sources, producing their description (step 2). This first phase allows the creation of a dictionary. With the use of this dictionary, within a

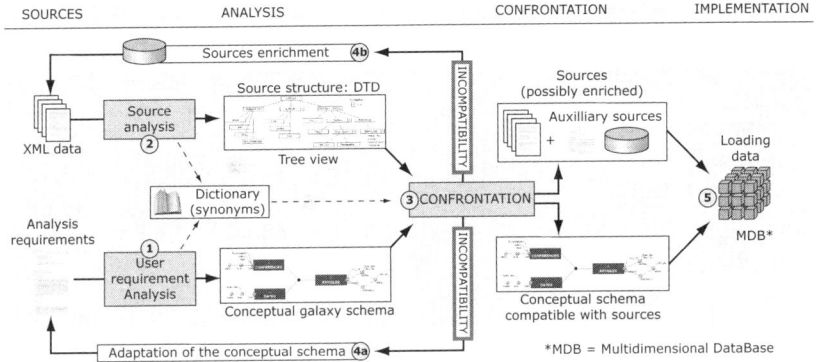

SOURCES   ANALYSIS   CONFRONTATION   IMPLEMENTATION

Fig. 15.2 Left, the number of published articles per author and per conference; right, the same analysis but with the top keywords of the corresponding publications.

confrontation phase (step 3), the designer then makes certain that compatibility is ensured between both results of the analysis phase by comparing the galaxy and the sources. In case of incompatibility, the designer modifies either the galaxy (step 4a) or the sources (step 4b) or even both and the process is iterated until no more incompatibilities arise. After a successful confrontation, the process continues by loading data within the multidimensional database (step 5). These phases are described in the following subsections.

15.3.1 Analysis Phase

The analysis phase is composed of two concurrent steps: on the one hand, the analysis of the user requirements (or analysis requirements) in order to specify a galaxy schema and on the other hand the analysis of the available data sources (text-rich XML documents).

15.3.1.1 User requirements analysis

The objective of this step is to produce a conceptual schema (a galaxy) as close as possible to the user requirements. This schema represents the multidimensional structures of the database that are used for expressing OLAP analyses. Questionnaires and typical analytical queries are used as input.

Typical queries represent the multidimensional analyses that a decision maker wants to specify. They are expressed with the use of a pseudo query language. In such queries, some elements (subjects) are analysed according to other elements (axes) with possible restrictions: *"Analyse what subject according to which analysis axes for what data"* (see example displayed in Fig. 15.3). The elementary informa-

Q1: **Analyse** the number of references **according to** the name of the author of these references and their institute **and according to** the name of conferences where the articles contain these references for authors of the institute inst1.	Q3: **Analyse** the number of articles **according to** the name of the author **and according to** the years of publication **for** publications in a conference of interna-tional audience.
Q2: **Analyse** the content of articles **according to** the author's name **and according to** the year of publication of the article **for** article contents limited to section of the type introduction.	Q4: **Analyse** the number of project reports **according to** the authors (name, status and institute) **and according to** the year of publication of the report **for** reports of scientific type.

Fig. 15.3 Examples of typical queries.

tion of each clause of these queries is converted into dimension attributes of the future galaxy schema. For example, in Q3, the following attributes are identified: *number of articles, authors' name, publication year, conference audience.*

Questionnaires are the result of user interviews that will provide valuable information on the domain of expertise. More precisely, this information is used to regroup attributes within dimensions and to organize them hierarchically. For example, in the four previous queries, it is possible to detect several attributes that concern authors and that may be regrouped together into an *AUTHORS* dimension: *authors, name, team, institute, status.* Complementary domain information, extracted from the questionnaires, allows the organisation of these attributes into 2 hierarchies (see Fig. 15.1). This information will also allow regrouping dimensions into one or more cliques (e.g. two cliques in the galaxy presented in Fig. 15.1).

The user requirement analysis step is summarised in Fig. 15.4. For the rest of the paper, we shall use a galaxy schema composed of a unique clique and three dimensions: *CONFERENCES, ARTICLES* and *TIME.*

Once the galaxy is created, all the attributes' (parameters and weak attributes) semantics are integrated within the dictionary for synonymy differentiation. For example, there are two attributes *Name*: one for a conference, the other of an author. The dictionary can be completed with words similar to those used to designate attributes in order to fulfil its task of distinguishing synonyms.

15.3.1.2 Document source analysis

Concurrently to the user requirement analysis, the available data sources are analysed. The goal is identifying the different available XML tags, thus the elements

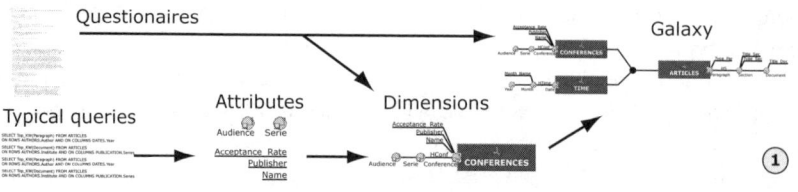

Fig. 15.4 Examples of typical queries.

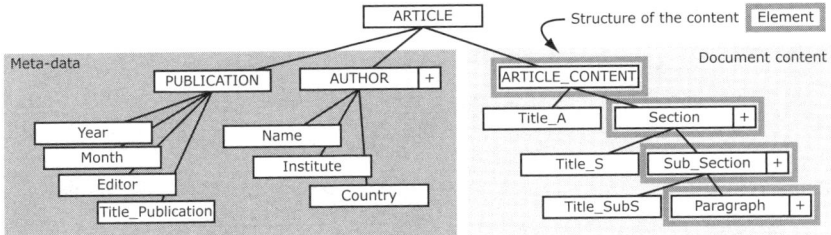

Fig. 15.5 Example of a document structure ("+" represents a cardinality of [1..*]).

of interest within the source XML documents (content, structure of the content and metadata) and updating the synonymy dictionary.

To do this, the documents structure is used as input: the DTD[5] , viewed as a tree. The DTD is either available within the data sources or it is built from well formed XML document sources. If only XSchema is available, it is converted into a DTD with some information loss (e.g. data types). From this tree view, with the use of the XML tags, the designer identifies: 1) the textual content of the documents (e.g. the textual data that constitutes the paragraphs of scientific papers); 2) the structure associated to this content (e.g. the elements that group paragraphs into subsections, themselves grouped into sections...); and 3) the metadata of the document (authors, date of publication...). The following rules are used to guide the analysis [32]:

- *Content* is held within elements usually far from the root of the document, i.e. leaves farthest from the root;
- The *structure of the content* is the hierarchy of elements allows one to reach the elements that hold the content data previously identified;
- Contrarily to content, *metadata* is held within elements that are close to the root.

This identification should be done in this order as once the elements that hold the content are identified; the associated structure may be easily deduced. As to metadata, it is in within some of the remaining elements. For example, in scientific articles, the DTD is extracted and displayed as a tree (see Fig. 15.5), notations are inspired by [4]. The content of the document (the textual data) may be found within the element farthest from the root: *Paragraph* (4 elements away from the root). The structure associated to this content is the hierarchy of elements below *ARTICLE_-CONTENT*. It is composed of the elements: *ARTICLE_CONTENT, Section, Sub_-Section* and *Paragraph*. The elements below *AUTHOR* and *PUBLICATION* (only 2 elements away from the root) represent the metadata associated to the document (here these elements correspond to information on the authors and the publication). The document source analysis phase is summarised in Fig. 15.6.

Tags from the elements of interest are inserted within the dictionary with synonyms that will ease understanding. For example, paragraphs of a document may be

---

[5] DTD : Document Type Definition, a grammar for expressing the structure of XML documents from http://www.w3.org/XML

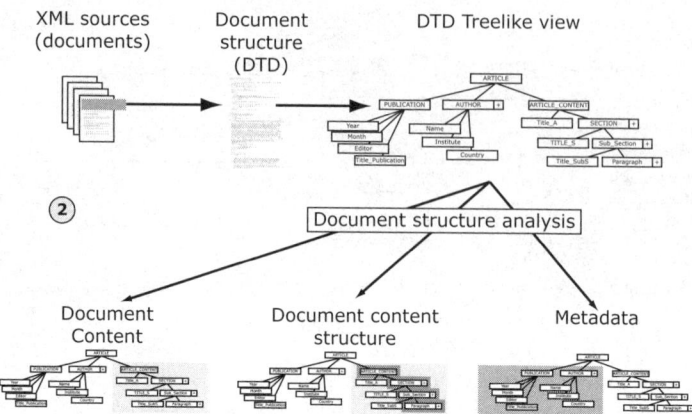

Fig. 15.6 Analysis of the data sources.

represented by a tag *<p>*, authors by *<au>*. As a consequence, these tags will be associated with the term *paragraph* for *p* and *author* for *au*.

The next step is to ensure the compatibility between the output of the user requirement analysis and the document source analysis phases.

15.3.2 Confrontation Phase

The goal of the confrontation phase is to ensure the compatibility between the outputs of the concurrent analysis phases: the galaxy schema (translation of the user requirements) and the document sources. Through a first step of comparison and association, the galaxy and sources are compared and incompatibilities detected. These later are dealt in afterwards. In the end, the user produces an association index that will allow data to be loaded within the multidimensional database structures.

15.3.2.1 Comparison and Association

The confrontation phase starts with a direct association process that links together elements of the data sources to elements (attributes) of the galaxy schema, see Fig. 15.7. This phase uses as input the galaxy schema previously produced and a tree-like view of the DTD structure of the XML data sources.

This is done by associating an element of the data sources' DTD to an attribute of the galaxy schema. To ease this process, the galaxy schema is converted into a DTD representation. In this representation, each clique is converted into an XML tree of elements and each element represents an attribute of the galaxy (due to lack of space, this conversion is not detailed here). Both structures are compared and attributes of the galaxy are associated with elements from the data sources. The association is

③ Association

Data source structure (DTD)

Incompatibilities
detected

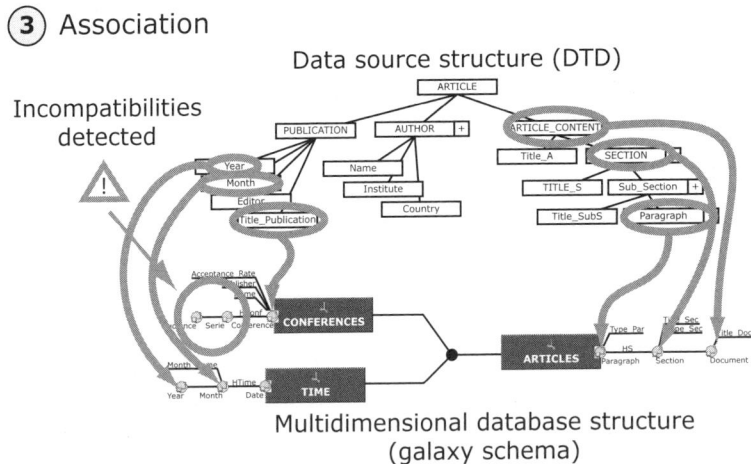

Multidimensional database structure
(galaxy schema)

Fig. 15.7 Comparison: association (for simplicity weak attributes are not linked).

done in a semi-automatic way as associations are suggested with the help of the synonym dictionary. The user is requested to intervene if synonymy problem occur or if elements of the DTD do not correspond to attributes of the galaxy.

For each association between an element of the source DTD and an attribute of the galaxy schema, an index is updated with a line that summarises the association, i.e. an XPath [39] expression expressed from the root element to the linked element from the source and the corresponding attribute:

[*XPath expression to the element*]/[*Element*] : [*Dimension name*].[*Attribute name*]

For example, the elements *Year* (respectively *Month*) below the element *PUBLICATION* of the DTD will be associated to the attributes *Year* (resp. *Month*) of the galaxy. The corresponding association in the index is an XPath expression for the element from the source associated to the corresponding attribute in the galaxy:

/ARTICLE/PUBLICATION/Year : TIME.Year

The association process continues until all possible associations between the source elements and the attributes of the galaxy are done.

15.3.2.2 Dealing with Incompatibilities

Incompatibilities arise when an attribute of the galaxy may not be associated to an element in DTD of the data source. Note that the data sources have been through ETL processing and are already cleansed with no errors. As a consequence, the handled incompatibilities are here are not very complex. We consider only two incompatibility types in our environment (although other more detailed types exist [37]):

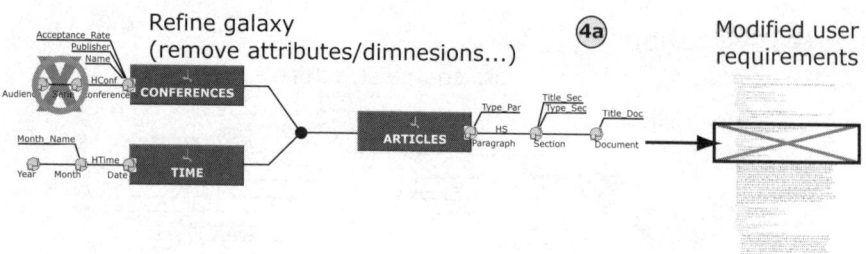

Fig. 15.8 Adapting the galaxy.

- *No data*: the data within the source does not exist or the data is only partially available (e.g. authors have their affiliations but not their);
- *Incompatible data*: the data exists in the source but it is incompatible. Incompatible cardinality, buried within other data, incompatible format... (e.g. first and last names of authors are together whereas only the last name would be required);

The last issue is less critical than the first as usually a conversion will help a lot. In our environment, as long as the conversion may be specified with an XQuery expression, the incompatible data issue may be solved. We thus concentrate on the more critical issue: lack of data. There are two possible solutions to this issue: to handle this incompatibility either within the galaxy or within the data sources. The first approach consists in adapting the galaxy in order to make it compatible with the data sources consists in removing incompatible elements, thus changing the analysis objectives (see Fig. 15.8).

The second approach consists in modifying the sources to render them compatible or, if possible, adding the missing data to the documents using auxiliary sources such as additional documents or domain documents. In order to do this, the new data must be compatible and there is a necessity for having a way of linking both data sources together (a compatible key or at least semantic join without any synonymy problems). The steps of the process are summarized in Fig. 15.9.

Two technical solutions may be considered for processing the data sources enrichment. If modifying the data sources is conceivable, the new data is added to the documents within the data sources. Otherwise, the new data is added separately and a linking index is used between the source data and the newly added data (using Ids for the links between two XPath expressions–one for the source data, one for the corresponding linked data). In both cases a unified DTD view is presented to the user, so that he will manipulate a unique DTD and not several.

For example, if the data sources do not have detailed information about conferences, such as the audience, the series, the publisher (...). It would be possible to use complementary information such as those from the DBLP XML database [9] and use this data as complementary sources.

The process is iterated until no more incompatibilities arise. The designer may then proceed to the loading phase.

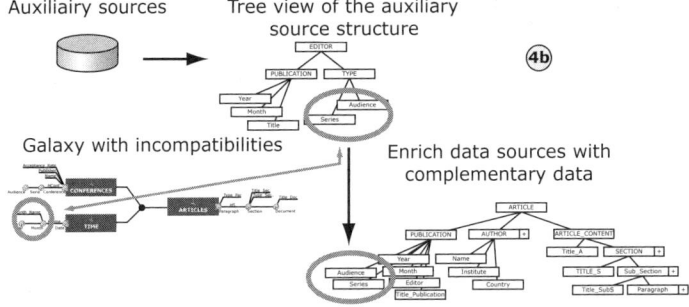

Fig. 15.9 Adding missing data to the XML documents sources.

15.3.3 Implementation: Creation of Multidimensional Structures and Loading

The objective of this phase is to create the multidimensional database that will be used by decision makers. First, the specification of the galaxy schema is used to generate the structures of the multidimensional database. Second, the association index generated at the end of a successful confrontation phase is used to load data extracted from sources into the empty structures of the multidimensional database. The phase is fully automatic and will be detailed in the section that describes our tool. The implementation phase is summarised in Fig. 15.10.

Once data is loaded within the MDB, the user may start analyses. Our design process allows a realistic implementation of the multidimensional schema, i.e. an OLAP systems that complies not only with the user requirements (the analysis requirements) but also with the XML document sources. In order to validate this approach we have implemented a data integration tool.

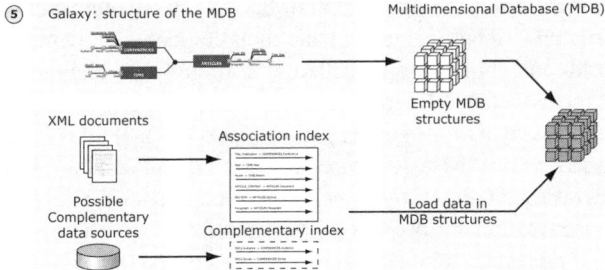

Fig. 15.10 Step 5: Loading source data within the multidimensional database.

15.4 Data Integration Tool

The objective of our tool is to help the user in the process of designing and implementing an OLAP system by automating some of the steps of the design process:

- The design of the galaxy schema (within step 1);
- The association of elements from the source document DTD to the attributes of the galaxy schema (within step 3);
- The modification / refining of the MDB (step 4a);
- The automatic generation of the structures of the MDB (within step 5);
- The loading of data extracted from the document sources within the structures of the multidimensional database (within step 5).

As a consequence, the tool focuses on assisting the user during certain steps 1, 3 (association only), 4a and 5 (see Fig. 15.2). The next part describes the architecture of the tool followed by the description of its interfaces.

15.4.1 Tool Architecture

The tool is used to create the structures of the multidimensional database through a galaxy schema and then loading data within these structures. The architecture of the tool rests on six components: two user interfaces each with an associated process, and two storage space (a document warehouse and a multidimensional database). The two interfaces will be described later (see section 4.2).

The *document warehouse* and the multidimensional database are stored within a ROLAP architecture in an Oracle 10g2 DBMS. The system uses part of Oracle XMLDB to handle the XML data within the ROLAP environment. The document warehouse is used to render the source XML documents available.

The *multidimensional database* (MDB) is composed of a meta-base and a database. The meta-base holds the description of the galaxy structures and the database holds these structures (relational tables) and their content data. Dimensions are de-normalised tables and cliques are modelled by foreign keys. The multidimensional structures and the associated descriptive data (meta-base) are generated by the user with the use of a galaxy editor (see left part of Fig. 15.11).

Data is loaded within these structures from the document warehouse with the use a data integrator that allows the generation of the association index by the user. This index is used within scripts that will extract data from the documents to the empty relational tables that represent the structures of the galaxy (see right part of Fig. 15.11).

Two interfaces, described hereinafter, assist the designer in the design and implementation process.

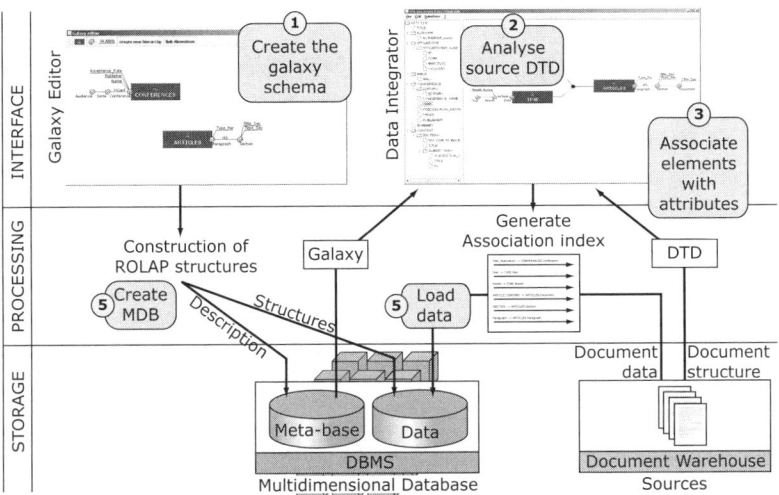

Fig. 15.11 Architecture of the tool (numbers correspond to the steps in section 15.3).

15.4.2 Tool Interfaces

The tool is manipulated with two interfaces: the first is a graphic editor that allows the designer to create a galaxy schema and the second is used to express associations between DTD elements of the sources and galaxy attributes (see Fig. 15.12).

The galaxy editor is a graphic editor for creating a galaxy schema. The user selects the elements he wishes to create (dimension, parameter or weak attribute) and associates them together in order to first build hierarchically organised dimensions. The user then links dimensions together in order to create the galaxy. Once a galaxy schema has been specified, the corresponding multidimensional structures and descriptive metadata may be automatically created within the multidimensional database (see Fig. 15.12). Each dimension of the galaxy schema is translated into a denormalised relation as in a star schema [18] and associated to some descriptive data (stored in the meta-base). Note that this generation should only be done once all incompatibilities between the galaxy and the sources have been solved. These are solved by comparing the galaxy and the DTD of the source with an available graphic viewer (XML Spy, or XML Doctor)[6], or directly with the use of the second interface. In case of incompatibilities, the user either enriches the data sources with XQuery scripts and/or modifies the galaxy schema using the galaxy editor interface.

When the source schema and the galaxy schema have no more incompatibilities, the XML *data integrator* interface is used. With this interface a designer associates elements from the DTD of the XML documents with attributes of the galaxy. (see

---

[6] ALTOVA XMLSpy from `http://www.altova.com/products/xmlspy/xml\`
`_editor.html` and XML Doctor from `http://sourceforge.net/projects/`
`xmldoctor`

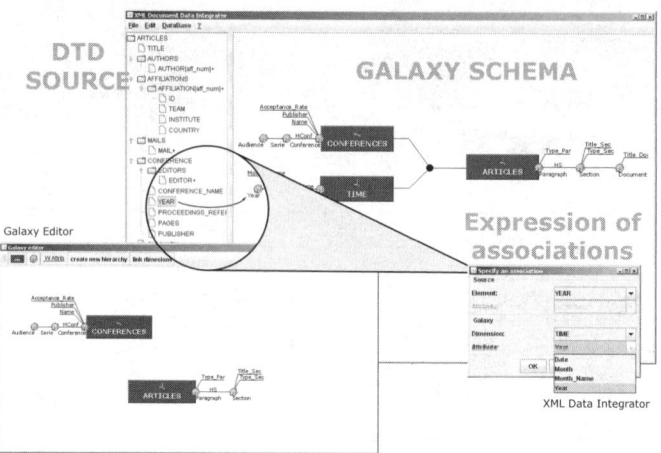

Fig. 15.12 Screenshots of galaxy editor (left) and the XML data integrator (right).

Fig. 15.12). Note that for each attribute of the galaxy, the tool suggest elements whose semantics seem close to the attribute (this is done with the dictionary). Associations specified are translated into links that will be used in order to extract data from XML documents and load it within the empty structures of the multidimensional database (see Fig. 15.11). We recall that the index is composed of XPath expressions associated to attribute names from the galaxy. A script combining SQL and XQuery queries is used to populate the dimension data. The XQuery part uses the XPath expressions to get the source data and returns the data that is then inserted, with the use of SQL, into the different relations of the multidimensional database (data types must be compatible).

We are currently using XML documents from the INEX IEEE XML document collection [15]. This collection of documents is composed of journal articles from the IEEE published between 1995 and 2002, transcribed into XML and represents over 12,000 documents.

15.5 Conclusion and Future Works

This paper aims at allowing OLAP analyses of documents. In order to do so, we have proposed a design and implementation method of OLAP schemas from text-rich (document-centric) XML documents. We have proposed a multidimensional model that has the advantage of resting on a unique concept (a galaxy) and that does not restrain the decision maker with limited predefined analyses with only numeric indicators [31]. The dimensions, which are multi hierarchical, allow the representation of document structures, content and metadata as well as their links. Associated to this model we have defined a design process that rests on a mixed approach, allowing the design and the implementation of a galaxy. The approach analyses jointly decision makers' requirements and the data sources (documents) in order to provide valid OLAP schemas. A confrontation phase ensures the compatibility between the multidimensional schema and the available data sources. The schema is possibly refined through an iterative process. In order to validate our proposition, we have implemented a CASE tool allowing the design and implementation of galaxy schemas. The tool rests on graphic interfaces that provide an easy representation of the multidimensional schema and its associated loading process.

We consider three future directions. So far we have used a collection of XML documents that is uniform regarding a single DTD. We consider taking into account more heterogeneous sources such as XML documents with different structures (DTD or XSchema). As a solution, one could employ schema relaxation [1] as well as dictionaries for finding synonymy within the different xml elements. Throughout the paper, we based our approach on an existing XML document collection: the INEX IEEE XML document collection [15]. Had such a collection been unavailable, more complex ETL processes [37] would have been taken into consideration in order to build a uniform collection of XML documents. Another important direction would be to help the designer with semi-automatic generation of optimisations that are required by the slow processing of textual data. These optimisations, (e.g. materialised views [13]), would be generated as the galaxy is created and the data loaded.

References

1. Amer-Yahia, S., Cho, S., Srivastava, D.: Tree pattern relaxation. In: EDBT '02: Proceedings of the 8th International Conference on Extending Database Technology, pp. 496–513. Springer-Verlag, London, UK (2002)
2. Bonifati, A., Cattaneo, F., Ceri, S., Fuggetta, A., Paraboschi, S.: Designing data marts for data warehouses. ACM Trans. Softw. Eng. Methodol. **10**(4), 452–483 (2001)
3. Boussaïd, O., BenMessaoud, R., Choquet, R., Anthoard, S.: X-warehousing: an xml-based approach for warehousing complex data. In: 10th East-European Conference on Advances in Databases and Information Systems (ADBIS 06), Thessaloniki, Greece, *LNCS*, vol. 4152, pp. 39–54. Springer, Heidelberg, Germany (2006)
4. Braga, D., Campi, A., Ceri, S.: XQBE (XQuery By Example): A visual interface to the standard XML query language. ACM Trans. Database Syst. **30**(2), 398–443 (2005)
5. Cabibbo, L., Torlone, R.: A logical approach to multidimensional databases. In: EDBT '98: Proceedings of the 6th International Conference on Extending Database Technology, pp. 183–197. Springer-Verlag, London, UK (1998)
6. Carneiro, L., Brayner, A.: X-META: A methodology for data warehouse design with metadata management. In: Lakshmanan [19], pp. 13–22
7. Cavero, J.M., Piattini, M., Marcos, E.: MIDEA: A multidimensional data warehouse methodology. In: ICEIS (1), pp. 138–144 (2001)
8. Colliat, G.: OLAP, relational, and multidimensional database systems. SIGMOD Rec. **25**(3), 64–69 (1996)
9. DBLP: Computer science bibliography. XML available from: http://dblp.uni-trier.de/xml
10. Fuhr, N., Grosjohann, K.: XIRQL: A query language for information retrieval in XML documents. In: Research and Development in Information Retrieval, pp. 172–180 (2001)

11. Golfarelli, M., Rizzi, S.: Methodological framework for data warehouse design. In: DOLAP'98, ACM First International Workshop on Data Warehousing and OLAP, pp. 3–9 (1998)
12. Gyssens, M., Lakshmanan, L.V.S.: A foundation for multi-dimensional databases. In: VLDB '97: Proceedings of the 23rd International Conference on Very Large Data Bases, pp. 106–115. Morgan Kaufmann Publishers Inc., San Francisco, CA, USA (1997)
13. Harinarayan, V., Rajaraman, A., Ullman, J.D.: Implementing data cubes efficiently. SIGMOD Rec. 25(2), 205–216 (1996)
14. Hüsemann, B., Lechtenbörger, J., Vossen, G.: Conceptual data warehouse modeling. In: M.A. Jeusfeld, H. Shu, M. Staudt, G. Vossen (eds.) DMDW, CEUR Workshop Proceedings, vol. 28, p. 6. CEUR-WS.org (2000)
15. INEX: INitiative for the Evaluation of XML retrieval (INEX). XML document collection used until 2005, from http://inex.is.informatik.uni-duisburg.de/
16. Jensen, M.R., Møller, T.H., Pedersen, T.B.: Specifying OLAP cubes on XML data. J. Intell. Inf. Syst. 17(2-3), 255–280 (2001)
17. Keith, S., Kaser, O., Lemire, D.: Analyzing large collections of electronic text using OLAP. In: APICS 2005, 29th Conf. in Mathematics, Statistics and Computer Science (2005)
18. Kimball, R., Ross, M.: The Data Warehouse Toolkit: The Complete Guide to Dimensional Modeling. John Wiley & Sons, Inc., New York, NY, USA (2002)
19. Lakshmanan, L.V.S. (ed.): Design and Management of Data Warehouses 2002, Proceedings of the 4th Intl. Workshop DMDW'2002, Toronto, Canada, May 27, 2002, CEUR Workshop Proceedings, vol. 58. CEUR-WS.org (2002)
20. Luján-Mora, S., Trujillo, J.: A comprehensive method for data warehouse design. In: 5th Intl. Workshop on Design and Management of Data Warehouses (DMDW'03), vol. 77. CEUR Workshop Proceedings, CEUR-WS.org (2003)
21. Mazón, J.N., Trujillo, J.: A model driven modernization approach for automatically deriving multidimensional models in data warehouses. In: Parent et al. [25], pp. 56–71
22. McCabe, M.C., Lee, J., Chowdhury, A., Grossman, D., Frieder, O.: On the design and evaluation of a multi-dimensional approach to information retrieval (poster session). In: SIGIR '00: Proceedings of the 23rd annual international ACM SIGIR conference on Research and development in information retrieval, pp. 363–365. ACM, New York, NY, USA (2000)
23. Mothe, J., Chrisment, C., Dousset, B., Alaux, J.: DocCube: multi-dimensional visualisation and exploration of large document sets. J. Am. Soc. Inf. Sci. Technol. 54(7), 650–659 (2003)
24. Nassis, V., Rajugan, R., Dillon, T.S., Rahayu, J.W.: Conceptual design of XML document warehouses. In: Y. Kambayashi, M.K. Mohania, W. Wöß (eds.) DaWaK, Lecture Notes in Computer Science, vol. 3181, pp. 1–14. Springer (2004)
25. Parent, C., Schewe, K.D., Storey, V.C., Thalheim, B. (eds.): Conceptual Modeling - ER 2007, 26th International Conference on Conceptual Modeling, Auckland, New Zealand, November 5-9, 2007, Proceedings, Lecture Notes in Computer Science, vol. 4801. Springer (2007)
26. Park, B.K., Han, H., Song, I.Y.: XML-OLAP: A multidimensional analysis framework for XML warehouses. In: A.M. Tjoa, J. Trujillo (eds.) DaWaK, Lecture Notes in Computer Science, vol. 3589, pp. 32–42. Springer (2005)
27. Pérez-Martínez, J.M., Berlanga-Llavori, R., Aramburu-Cabo, M.J., Pedersen, T.B.: Contextualizing data warehouses with documents. Decis. Support Syst. 45(1), 77–94 (2008)
28. Phipps, C., Davis, K.C.: Automating data warehouse conceptual schema design and evaluation. In: Lakshmanan [19], pp. 23–32
29. Prat, N., Akoka, J., Comyn-Wattiau, I.: A UML-based data warehouse design method. Decis. Support Syst. 42(3), 1449–1473 (2006)
30. Ravat, F., Teste, O., Tournier, R.: OLAP aggregation function for textual data warehouse. In: J. Cardoso, J. Cordeiro, J. Filipe (eds.) ICEIS (1), pp. 151–156 (2007)
31. Ravat, F., Teste, O., Tournier, R., Zurfluh, G.: A conceptual model for multidimensional analysis of documents. In: Parent et al. [25], pp. 550–565
32. Ravat, F., Teste, O., Tournier, R., Zurfluh, G.: Integrating complex data into a data warehouse. In: SEKE, pp. 483–. Knowledge Systems Institute Graduate School (2007)

33. Ravat, F., Teste, O., Tournier, R., Zurfluh, G.: Algebraic and graphic languages for OLAP manipulations. International Journal of Data Warehousing and Mining **4**(1), 17–46 (2008)
34. Rizzi, S., Abelló, A., Lechtenbörger, J., Trujillo, J.: Research in data warehouse modeling and design: dead or alive? In: DOLAP '06: Proceedings of the 9th ACM international workshop on Data warehousing and OLAP, pp. 3–10. ACM, New York, NY, USA (2006)
35. Sullivan, D.: Document Warehousing and Text Mining: Techniques for Improving Business Operations, Marketing, and Sales. John Wiley & Sons, Inc., New York, NY, USA (2001)
36. Tseng, F.S.C., Chou, A.Y.H.: The concept of document warehousing for multi-dimensional modeling of textual-based business intelligence. Decis. Support Syst. **42**(2), 727–744 (2006)
37. Vassiliadis, P., Simitsis, A., Georgantas, P., Terrovitis, M., Skiadopoulos, S.: A generic and customizable framework for the design of etl scenarios. Inf. Syst. **30**(7), 492–525 (2005)
38. Vrdoljak, B., Banek, M., Skocir, Z.: Integrating XML sources into a data warehouse. In: J. Lee, J. Shim, S. goo Lee, C. Bussler, S.S.Y. Shim (eds.) DEECS, *Lecture Notes in Computer Science*, vol. 4055, pp. 133–142. Springer (2006)
39. W3C: eXtensible Markup Language (XML) 1.0. W3C Recommendation (29/09/2006), from http://www.w3.org/TR/2006/REC-xml-20060816
40. Yin, X., Pedersen, T.B.: Evaluating XML-extended OLAP queries based on a physical algebra. In: DOLAP '04: Proceedings of the 7th ACM international workshop on Data warehousing and OLAP, pp. 73–82. ACM, New York, NY, USA (2004)

Printed in the United States